THE MANAGEMENT OF EGYPT'S CULTURAL HERITAGE VOLUME 2

Egypt is rich in a cultural heritage that can be traced from the remote prehistoric past through the various stages of world civilisation. Ancient Egypt's monuments link us to the past and make us aware of past human achievements. It is our duty to protect and preserve this heritage so that we, and future generations, can share in this historical legacy of our predecessors.

The Lower Nile Valley is the birthplace of one of the first and most resilient great civilizations. In the course of its long and distinguished history, Egypt has bequeathed to us a legacy of spectacular monuments and a dazzling array of artefacts. However, unimposing sites and objects of everyday life also provide an invaluable insight to the various aspects of ancient Egyptian society and are just as important as the more spectacular sites and 'treasures'. Today, such archaeological sites and monuments all over Egypt are threatened by urban sprawl, development projects, agricultural expansion, pollution and looting. ECHO has been founded to help in securing the protection and conservation of Egypt's threatened heritage.

The archaeological record is a finite resource, which is easily destroyed without proper protection. There are an incredible number of sites and monuments everywhere in Egypt, as well as the countless artefacts in museums and storerooms, requiring constant monitoring, protection and maintenance.

The Management of Egypt's Cultural Heritage is the second volume in a series of Cultural Heritage Management (CHM) discourses; this ground-breaking series is the first academic collection of papers dedicated to the practice of CHM in Egypt. The papers in this volume are written by specialists in their fields whose expertise cover many areas of cultural heritage management, from the theoretical to the practical, tangible to intangible heritage, from cutting edge technology to simple conservation measures. The periods covered range from the Predynastic to the Coptic and Islamic periods. This volume is an invaluable addition to the library of heritage managers, conservators, archaeologists, and lecturers, anyone interested in preserving Egypt's cultural and natural heritage.

Fekri A. Hassan is emeritus Petrie Professor of Archaeology, Institute of Archaeology, University College London and Honorary President of the Egyptian Cultural Heritage Organisation.

Geoffrey J. Tassie is a Research Fellow in the TOPOI Excellence Cluster at the Freie Universität, Berlin and the Managing Director of the Egyptian Cultural Heritage Organisation.

Lawrence S. Owens is a lecturer in bioarchaeology, Birkbeck College, University of London.

Aloisia De Trafford was the Assistant Editor of the African Archaeological Review.

Joris van Wetering is Editor of ECHO Publications.

Okasha El Daly is Head of Projects at the Qatar Museums Authority.

I0869035

ECHO

Actively making archaeology work to protect Egypt's heritage

The Egyptian Cultural Heritage Organisation

E C H O

The Management of Egypt's Cultural Heritage

Executive Series Editor F. A. Hassan
Institute of Archaeology, University College London, UK

Edited by L. S. Owens & A. De Trafford
Birkbeck College, University of London, UK, and Egyptian Cultural Heritage Organisation, UK & Egypt

Commissioning Editors G. J. Tassie & J. van Wetering
TOPOI Excellence Cluster at the Freie Universität, and Egyptian Cultural Heritage Organisation, UK & Egypt

Arabic Translations by Okasha El Daly
Qatar Museums Authority

Golden House Publications
First edition – 2015

Egyptian Cultural Heritage Organisation Discourses on Heritage Management Series No. 2

This title is published by

Golden House Publications

Volume Two 2015

For more information on how to become a member of ECHO and other ECHO projects and promotions visit our website on: www.e-c-h-o.org. The production of this book has been done in collaboration with the Egyptian Heritage Institute (**EHI**) and Heritage Egypt (**HE**) society.

A catalogue record of this publication is available from the British Library

ISBN 978-1-906137-40-3

Printed in the United Kingdom

London 2015

Images Front Cover: Luxor Temple ca. 1930 (John H. Hamer). Back Cover Top Row: Egyptian Museum being protected by protestors (AFP), the Sphinx with scaffolding (G. J. Tassie), encroachments at Dahshur (Monica Hanna); Bottom Row: a bulldozer on the site of Tell Atrib, scaffolding around the statue of Ramesses II before its removal to the GEM, a row of Belle Époque houses in a street in Alexandria (G. J. Tassie).

Photographs of Philae (top) and the Pyramids at Giza (bottom), taken during the 1920s to 1930s by John H. Hamer. Although Philae has now been moved above the level of the waters of the inundation and the pyramids are no longer in the midst of an armed conflict, it amply illustrates some of the threats that Egypt's cultural heritage has faced in the past. However, the monuments of Egypt are still at risk from extremists, looters, pollution and environmental threats.

List of Contributors

Nathalie Cohen
Museum of London Archaeology
Mortimer Wheeler House
46 Eagle Wharf Road
London N1 7ED
enquiries@mola.org.uk

Aloisia De Trafford
Egyptian Cultural Heritage Organisation
14, Vincent Road
Kingston-upon-Thames
Surrey KT1 3HJ
United Kingdom
adetrafford@yahoo.com

Mo'men Ghanem
Cultural Heritage Program
French University in Egypt
Cairo
Egypt
www.ufe.edu.egy

David W. J. Gill
University Campus Suffolk
St Edmund House
Ipswich, Suffolk IP4 1LZ
United Kingdom
david.gill @ucs.ac.uk

Fekri A. Hassan
Cultural Heritage Program
French University in Egypt
Cairo
Egypt
fekrihassan@hotmail.com

Nigel J. Hetherington
Past Preservers,
Apartment 32
49, El-Falakay Street
Cairo
Egypt
nigel@pastpreservers.com

Mohamed Hussein Hosny
Cultural Heritage Program
French University in Egypt
Cairo
Egypt
mohosny47@yahoo.com

Dirk Huyge
Royal Museums of Art and History (RMAH), Brussels (Belgium)
d.huyge@kmkg.be

Janet Johnstone
Egyptian Cultural Heritage Organisation
14, Vincent Road
Kingston-upon-Thames
Surrey KT1 3HJ
United Kingdom
jjohnstoneecho@hotmail.com

Emad el-Khalil
Alexandria Centre for Maritime Archaeology
and Underwater Cultural Heritage (CMA)
Alexandria University,
Egypt
emadkhalil@foa.edu.eg

Kelly Krause
Heritage in Action
LLC
San Francisco
USA
info@heritageinaction.com

Lawrence Stewart Owens
Birkbeck College
University of London
Malet Street,
London, WC1E 7HX
United Kingdom
lawrence_owens@yahoo.co.uk

Geoffrey John Tassie
Egyptian Cultural Heritage Organisation
14, Vincent Road
Kingston-upon-Thames
Surrey KT1 3HJ
United Kingdom
egyptianheritage@yahoo.co.uk

Gemma Tully
Institute of Archaeology,
Egyptology and Northeast African Archaeology
Humboldt Universität zu Berlin
Germany
gemmatully@hotmail.com

Joris van Wetering
Egyptian Cultural Heritage Organisation
Groningsestraat 19
2587, RJ Scheveningen – Den Haag
The Netherlands
jflvwetering@gmail.com

PREFACE

Although preserving monuments and artefacts is not a new concept, the term cultural heritage management (CHM) is relatively recent, first starting to be used in the early 1980s. The management of cultural heritage encompasses all aspects of culture and management: legal protection, physical safeguarding, conservation, survey, excavation, documentation, education, and display. However, before cultural heritage can be managed, the term 'cultural heritage' requires definition. Cultural heritage can be considered to include elements of material culture, music, dance, and oral tradition that have meaning and value placed upon them by past and present populations. Egypt's legacy of cultural remains stretches back over 300,000 years of human occupation, including Palaeolithic cultures, early state, the growth of the Persian, Greek, Roman and Arab empires and, of course, Egypt's Pharaonic past. The publication of this book represents another step in the management of Egypt's cultural heritage, raising awareness of the various issues and difficulties involved.

For lecturers there have been scarce scholarly articles and even fewer books dedicated to the management of Egypt's cultural heritage. The instigation of the Egyptian Cultural Heritage Organisation's Discourses on Heritage Management Series gives the coterie of heritage managers, archaeologists, conservators and others involved a forum for discussing and disseminating their views. The subjects covered include technological advancement, changes in theoretical viewpoint, and methodology. The issues raised are not only of importance to a select few, but for the whole of humanity.

Monuments link us to the past and make us aware of past human achievements. They affirm our identity, exhibiting all the ingenuity of past human endeavour. The cultural heritage of Egypt is the affirmation of our common human legacy, documenting many of humanity's major developments and achievements. In the course of its long and distinguished history, Egypt has bequeathed to us a legacy of spectacular monuments and a dazzling array of treasures. However, there is much more to the legacy of Egypt than what thrills us at first. Many unimposing sites and objects of everyday life provide an invaluable insight into the various aspects of ancient Egyptian society.

The archaeological record is a finite resource, which is easily destroyed without proper protection. Today, Egypt's cultural heritage faces more pressure than at any time in its long and illustrious history; archaeological sites and monuments all over Egypt are threatened by urban sprawl, development projects, agricultural expansion, pollution, mindless wilful destruction, and looting. The destruction and looting of sites has increased substantially since the revolution of 25th January 2011, with more human induced damage being done to Egypt's cultural heritage in the past four years than in the previous 45. The incredible number of sites and monuments everywhere in Egypt, those that have been excavated and those yet to be discovered, as well as the countless artefacts in museums and storerooms, requiring constant monitoring, protection and maintenance, is much more than any one nation can bear. Much of the intangible heritage is being eroded by globalisation and dependence on modern technology, turning people away from many of the traditional folk arts, resulting in the likelihood that these will be lost when the present aging practitioners leave this world. Action is needed now, we must work together to save this world legacy, we have got to try to minimise any further damage and destruction. Action can take numerous forms, from direct intervention to education. It is our duty to protect and preserve this heritage so that we, and future generations, can partake in this historical legacy and realise our human potential in the great creative achievements of our predecessors.

F. A. Hassan & G. J. Tassie
(December 2014)

TABLE OF CONTENTS

List of Contributors vi

Preface viii

List of Figures xi

List of Plates xiv

Map of Egypt xv

Chronology xvi

ECHO xvii

Acknowledgements xvii

1 Introduction: Brave New Worlds. A New Era in Egyptian Heritage Management 1

Lawrence S. Owens

2 Egyptian Cultural Heritage at the Dawn of the Arab Spring – a Future for the Past 6

Kelly Krause

3 Egypt's Heritage in Times of Conflict and Crisis 14

G. J. Tassie, A. De Trafford and J. van Wetering

4 Creating Egyptian Archives and the Production of Perfect Paperwork? 48

Nathalie Cohen

5 Contemporary Egyptian Dialogues: Collaborative Approaches to Museum Displays of Ancient Egypt 57

Gemma Tully

6 Egyptian Antiquities on the Market 67

David W. J. Gill

7 "Battered Bulls" Again: Destruction and First Attempts at Conservation of Rock Art in Egypt 78

Dirk Huyge

8 Purity, Power and Nudity: Social Dynamics of Hammams in History 86

Fekri A. Hassan

9 The Nile Delta in Peril: Cultural Heritage Management in the Delta 100

G. J. Tassie, J. van Wetering and A. De Trafford

10 The Great Festival of Luxor: A Brief Study of the Mawlid of Aboul Haggag and its Cultural Significances 131

Mohamed Hussein Hosny and Mo'men Ghanem

11 Where Did the Nile Harbours Go? 163

Emad el-Khalil

12 Single-Context Recording in the Context of Archaeological Fieldwork in Egypt, Part One 175

G. J. Tassie

13 Is the Writing on the Wall for the Writing on the Wall? Opposition to - and Defence of - Egyptian Graffiti and Street Art 185

Lawrence S. Owens

Addendum 198

Abbreviations and Glossary of Terms 198

Arabic Abstracts 201

International and Egyptian Heritage Institutes 208

UNESCO World Heritage Conventions 211

Egypt and the World Heritage List 213

Evolution of National Legal Instruments 220

A Short History of the Egyptian Antiquities Service 226

Ministry of Antiquities Regulations 228

The Faiyum Declaration 232

Codes of Ethics 234

List of Figures

Figure No.	Title	Page No.
2.1	The Nahdet Misr (Renaissance of Egypt) Monument by Mukhtar now located in front of Cairo University	7
2.2	The tomb of Auguste Mariette in the grounds of the Museum of Egyptian Antiquities, Cairo	9
3.1	Illicit digging versus archaeological excavation	17
3.2	The illegal cemetery/looting at Dahshur	22
3.3	The partially restored house of Gamal al-Din al Dhahbi in Old Cairo	24
3.4	Bab el-Nasr, the northern gate of the old city walls of Cairo being restore in 2003	25
3.5	The Barquq Complex located in Al-Muizz Street being restored in 2003	26
3.6	The restored wakala of Bazabah in Old Cairo	27
3.7	Modern encroachment on the Pyramid of Amenemhat I at Lisht	28
3.8	The extent of the looting activities at Gurob	29
3.9	The inspection of one of the looter's pits over one of the poorer shaft tombs at Gurob	30
3.10	A modern cemetery being built over the ancient cemetery at Gerzeh	30
3.11	Extent of looting activities at Tell el-Hibeh	31
3.12	The aftermath of the looting activities at Tell el-Hibeh	32
3.13	The empty cases in the Mallawi National Museum after the theft and ransacking	33
3.14	The wall around the Giza archaeological area	37
5.1	The Nebamun exhibition at the British Museum	59
6.1	Value of Egyptian antiquities sold at Sotheby's, New York	68
6.2	One of the photos of the stores in the Ma'adi Museum supplied by ECHO	69
6.3	Blocks from the Temple of Isis, Behbeit el-Hagar	71
7.1	Almost half of the site of Abu Tanqura Qibli at el-Hosh has been quarried away using explosives in the 1960s and/or 1970s.	79
7.2	A view of the Abu Tanqura Qibli quarry towards the south. Along the edge is broken-up rock art.	80
7.3	A broken-up rock art panel at Abu Tanqura Qibli with Predynastic depictions of an antelope and an elephant	80
7.4	A view of Wadi Abu Subeira with localisation of the Late Palaeolithic rock art site CAS-6 and a modern clay mine in operation	81
7.5	Detail of a rock art panel with Predynastic and later imagery at Wadi Barramiya in the Eastern Desert.	82
7.6	Complex Epipalaeolithic geometric design (height: 35 cm) in situ at Abu Tanqura Bahari 14 at el-Hosh.	83
7.7	The Late Palaeolithic rock art site CAS-6 in Wadi Abu Subeira has been	83

	recently fenced off with barbed wire to keep mining companies out	
8.1	Delacroix, Eugene, *Women of Algiers in their apartments*, oil on canvass, 1834	89
8.2	*Gerome Jean-Leon*, Moorish Bath, oil on canvass, 1880	90
8.3	Jean-August-Dominique. *Turkish Bath*, oil on canvass fixed to panel, 1863	91
9.1	Sunset over a delta village	101
9.2	Panoramic view of the Rosetta Branch of the Nile in the Minufiyeh Province	102
9.3	The village of Kom el-Ahmer in the Minufiyeh Province	102
9.4	Daily life in the city of Samanud	103
9.5	The site of Tell Basta (Bubastis) surrounded by the modern city of Zagazig	103
9.6	The site of Tell Basta (Bubastis) surrounded by the modern city of Zagazig	104
9.7	The monumental remains at Tanis (San el-Hagar)	105
9.8	Monumental elements and huge mud-brick walls and tell at Tanis (San el-Hagar)	106
9.9	The site of Tell el-Timai (Mendes) surrounded by the modern village	108
9.10	The DAI excavations at Tell el-Fara'in (Buto)	108
9.11	Waterlogged graves at the Predynastic to Early Dynastic site of Minshat Ezzat	113
9.12	The site of Ezbet el-Tell (Kufur Nigm) showing the low *kom*	114
9.13	The site of Ezbet el-Tell (Kufur Nigm) showing the low *kom*	115
9.14	The Graeco-Roman remains at Tell el-Muqdam (ancient Leontopolis) showing modern building activities in the background	117
9.15	The remains of the *kom* of Awalad Dawood where there is an Early Dynastic administrative building	118
9.16	The large *kom* of Tell el-Dab'a/Qanan	119
9.17	Modern development in the centre of Alexandria	119
9.18	The Graeco-Roman remains at Kom el-Dikka in the centre of Alexandria	120
9.19	Belle Époque buildings in Minufiyeh and Alexandria	121
9.20	The site of Tura with a railway line built through the middle of the cemetery	122
10.1	The Dorah Procession	154
10.2	Ordinal values attributed to the participants' responses (from 1 to 5)	155
10.3	Comparison of the different significances among the interviewees	155
10.4	The open museum district on the Eastern Bank of Luxor	156
10.5	Aerial view of the project site location	157
10.6	Land use analysis of the project	158
10.7	Urban analysis of the project	159
10.8	Traffic analysis for the project	160
10.9	Traffic strategy for the project	161
10.10	Urban analysis of the Mahattah Street	162
11.1	The harbour before the temple of Amun-Ra at Karnak. One of many representations of T-shaped harbours in Ancient Egypt	165

11.2	A river harbour and waterfront activities, depicted in the Tomb of May (c. 1365 BC) at Tell El-Amarna	166
11.3	A depiction of constructed river port and quays from the Palestrina Mosaic, late second century BC	167
11.4	An early 20th century riverboat moored at a temporary quay made from Nile clay, while offloading its cargo of carts	167
11.5	The esplanade in front of Karnak	168
11.6	The tribune in the foreground and avenue of sphinxes and first pylon in the background	169
11.7	The ramp of King Taharqo	170
11.8	The ramp of King Taharqo	170
11.9	The steps of the northern quay at Karnak	171
12.1	Single Context Recording Form, left: obverse and right: reverse	178
12.2	Open area excavation at the Giza Plateau Mapping Project's excavations of the workers village Giza	179
13.1	Graphic protests to the whitewashing of street art	189
13.2	Detail of El Zeft and Mira Shihadeh's 'Circle of Hell'	190
13.3	Stencil of a woman in a hijab	191
13.4	Anubis with a machine gun	193

List of Plates

Table No.	Title	Page No.
10.1	Aboul Hagag's Mosque on top of the church, in the middle of Luxor Temple	141
10.2	The Zikr performance	141
10.3	Al Mermah	142
10.4	Al Mermah	142
10.5	Al tahteeb performance	143
10.6	The kettle drums following the simulacra of the tomb of Aboul Haggag	143
10.7	The Barque in the Aboul Haggag Festival	144
10.8	The Barque in the Opet (depicted on the wall of the Luxor Temple) Festival	144
10.9	The Dorah procession, 2009	145
10.10	Women preparing food for the festival	145
10.11	The minaret with the obelisk as the most popular symbolic features of the place	146
10.12	Political events appear to be a new function in the Plaza after Jan 25th revolution in Egypt	146
10.13	Night panoramic view of the Plaza	147
10.14	The entrance to the Mosque of Aboul Haggag	147
10.15	The minaret of Mosque of Aboul Haggag integrated into Luxor Temple	148
10.16	The integration of the Mosque of Aboul Haggag with the Luxor Temple	148

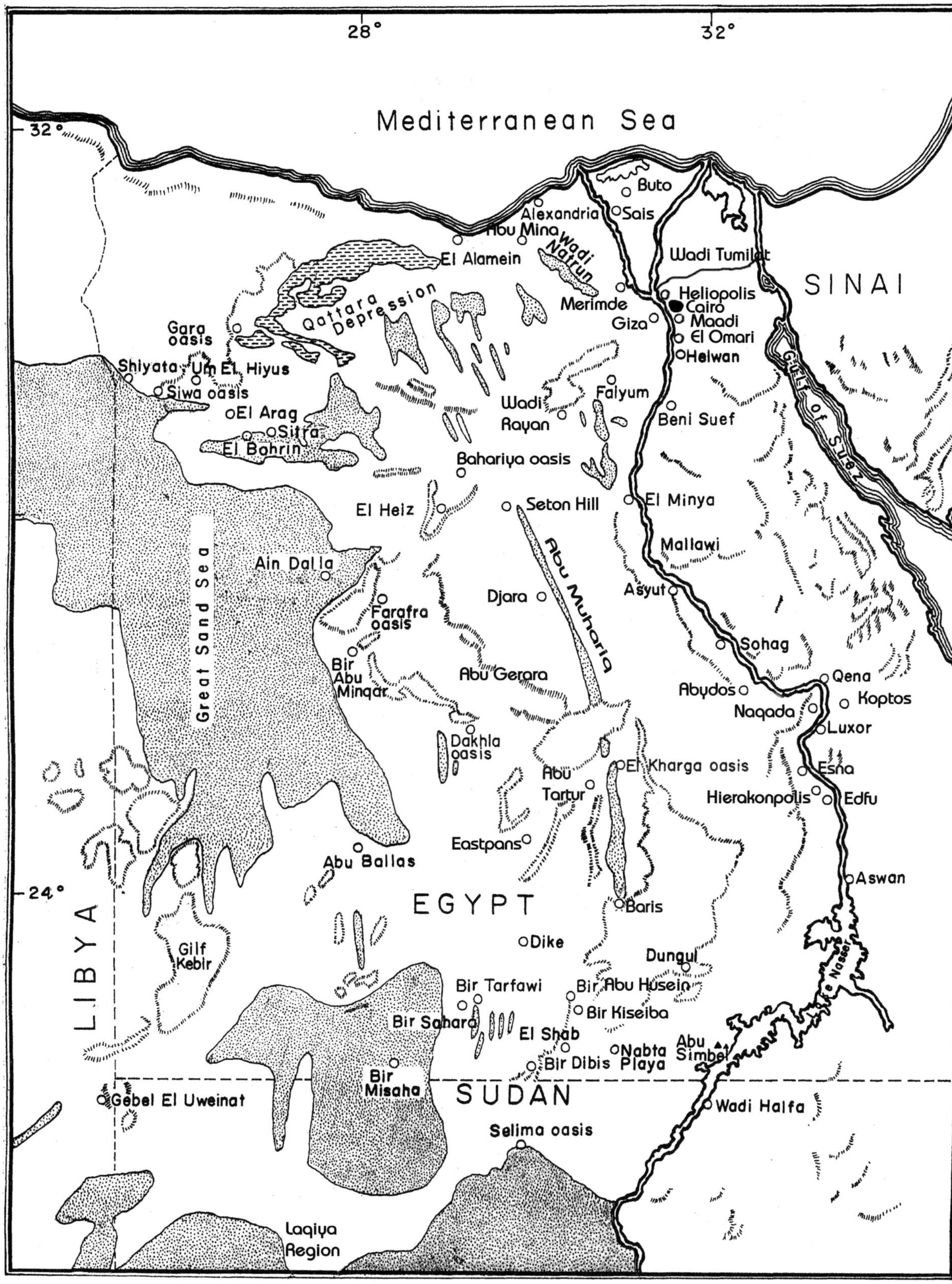

Map of Egypt showing sites mentioned in text and other key sites.

Date	Egypt	Nubia
5,500 BC	Neolithic (5300-4000) Merimdian (5000-3900 BC) Bashendi B (5300-4000 BC) Faiyum Neolithic (5200 - 3800 BC) Badarian (4400 – 3900 BC) Predynastic (4000 – 3300 BC)	Neolithic Abkan (5300-3500 BC) Khartoum Neolithic(5000-3780 BC)
4,000 BC	Naqada I (3900 – 3700 BC) Maadian (3900-3350 BC) Naqada II (3700 – 3300 BC) Protodynastic (3300 – 3060 BC) Naqada III (3300 – 2700 BC)	A-Group (3650 – 2950 BC) Pre-Kerma (3350-2500 BC)
3,000 BC	Early Dynastic (3060 – 2613 BC) (Dyn. I – Dyn. III) Old Kingdom (2613 – 2181 BC) (Dyn. IV – Dyn. VI) First Intermediate (2181-2055 BC) (Dyn. VII – Dyn. XI)	Hiatus (Egyptians drive A-Group out?) C-Group (2500 – 1500 BC) Early Kerma (2500-2050 BC)
2,000 BC	Middle Kingdom (2055 – 1650 BC) (Dyn. XI – Dyn. XIII) Second Intermediate (1650 – 1550 BC) (Dyn. XIV – Dyn. XVII) New Kingdom (1550 – 1069 BC) (Dyn. XVIII – Dyn. XX)	Middle Kerma (2050-1750 BC) Classic Kerma (1750-1500 BC) Late Kerma (1500-1100 BC) Egyptian dominance of Nubia (Kerma and Kush) from 1500 BC
1,000 BC	Third Intermediate (1069 – 747 BC) (Dyn. XXI – Dyn. XXIV) Late Period (747 – 332 BC) (Dyn. XXV – Dyn. XXX)	Napatan (1000 – 300 BC)
500 BC	Ptolemaic (332 – 30 BC)	Meroitic (300 BC – AD 350)
0	Roman (30 BC – AD 306) Coptic (AD 100 -) Byzantine (AD 306 - 641)	Post-Meroitic (AD 350 - 550) Blemmyes (AD 250-500)
AD 500	Islamic Conquest (AD 641) Umayyads (AD 661 - 750) Abbasids (AD 750 - 870) Tulnids (AD 870 - 905) Ikhshidids (AD 905 - 969)	Noubadian Kingdom (AD 350-550) Medieval Period (AD 550 - 1500)
AD 1000	Fatimids (AD 969 - 1171) Ayyubids (AD 1171 - 1250) Mamluks (AD 1250 - 1571)	Christian Era (AD 550-1400) Islamic Era (AD 1400-present)
AD 1500	Ottomans (AD 1517 - 1798) Napoleon's Expedition (AD 1798 - 1801) Mohammed Ali's Dynasty (AD 1805 - 1952) British Mandate (AD 1882 - 1953)	Post-Medieval (AD 1500 - 1900) Funj Kingdom (AD 1504-1820) Turkiyya (AD 1820-1883) Mahdist Era (AD 1883-1898)
AD 2000	Arab Republic of Egypt (AD1953-present)	

Chronology of Egypt and Nubia.

ECHO

The Egyptian Cultural Heritage Organisation (ECHO) was founded to highlight the various issues involved in cultural heritage studies, including visitor management, excavation, surveying, protection, conservation, restoration, legislation, looting, ownership, public archaeology, site and monument records, interpretation and education. Although cultural heritage management has been practiced in Egypt for over 150 years and debates on cultural heritage issues raged even longer, it is only in the last few decades that it has been formulated into a discipline in its own right. The ECHO Board of Trustees would like to take this opportunity to welcome all ECHO's members to being part of the first company to devote itself to not only debating matters of cultural heritage, but that actively works to protect it. Together we can help secure protection for Egypt's cultural heritage, so that future generations can enjoy and learn from it.

Titles Already Published by ECHO

Hassan, F. A., Tassie, G. J., De Trafford, A., Owens, L. S. & van Wetering, J. (eds.) 2009. *Managing Egypt's Cultural Heritage: Proceedings of the First Egyptian Cultural Heritage Organisation Conference on Egyptian Cultural Heritage Management.* London: Golden House Publications.

Tassie, G. J. & Owens, L. S. 2010. *Standards of Archaeological Excavation: A Fieldguide to Methodology, Recording Techniques, and Conventions,* first edition. London: Golden House Publications.

Forthcoming ECHO Titles

Tassie, G. J. & Owens, L. S. Forthcoming. *Standards of Archaeological Excavation: A Fieldguide to Methodology, Recording Techniques, and Conventions,* second edition. London: Golden House Publications.

Acknowledgements

The editors and board of ECHO Trustees would like to acknowledge the work, time and knowledge of all contributors to this volume. ECHO would also like to thank Dr Monica Hanna, Dr Carol Redmount and Dr Ian Shaw for allowing use of their photographs. Thanks are also due to Wolfram Grajetzki from Golden House Publications for his hard work and patience in producing this work. This volume would not have been possible without the support of the ECHO members and other supporters, to whom we are very grateful for their continued support and enthusiasm.

Chapter 1

Brave New Worlds:
A New Era in Egyptian Heritage Management

Lawrence S. Owens

In 2009, ECHO published the first volume of proceedings on Egyptian cultural heritage management[1], and while this volume follows on the themes raised in its predecessor, it is born unto an Egypt that is almost unrecognisable by pre-2011 eyes. The social changes that have occurred since 2011 have been monumental, even for a nation whose history is imbued with the constant cut and thrust of revolution, change and transformation. The previous volume contained numerous concerns about Egyptian heritage that were essentially long-standing fixtures on heritage management lists: the dangers of encroachment, the necessity for storage and registration, the need for conservation, the inherent value of heritage, and the vital necessity for a full sites and monuments record so that we could have a handle on what was happening and where. Yet one might reasonably assume from reading the volume that these were essentially long-term issues, and that while the needs and desires of archaeologists, tourists and local populations were imbalanced enough to displease almost everyone, emendations and change would come about as a slow, continual process.

◆

Egyptian Cultural Ground Zero was reached on 11th February 2011, when Mubarak departed office after thirty years in power. The collapse of the old guard presaged free elections, a new constitution, an end to military courts for civilians, a free media and the formation of new political parties and syndicates. However, the army's solidarity with protesters vanished alacritously, with Tahrir Square being repeatedly cleared of demonstrations, which were then banned under new laws. A news blackout was imposed, with extensive attacks on journalists, followed by disruption of mobile phone and Internet services as the government attempted to limit coverage of events and communication between protesters.[2]

Public protests gathered force throughout that year. Key areas included the destruction of secret files, a weak constitutional referendum (failing to limit presidential power), the continuation of military trials for civilians, the failure of SCAF[3] to remove ex-NDP[4] members from official posts, lack of a minimum wage, amnesty for political prisoners, the slow rate of socio-political change, the seemingly overly-generous treatment of Mubarak and his family and demands for the removal of Field Marshal Tantawi[5] and the ceding of power to a democratically-elected government.[6] Million-strong gatherings in Tahrir Square were heavily targeted by security forces throughout 2011, dispersing demonstrators with a level of force that sparked international condemnation. By November 2011 it was apparent that the military government intended to retain power when it published the Selmy Document.[7] The resulting backlash led to the resignation of the interim government. The military's attempts to retain power by disqualifying ten presidential candidates[8] and crippling the power of the presidency when it became apparent that their candidate could not win were unsuccessful, and Mohamed Morsi became the first civilian president of Egypt on the 30th of June, 2012.

---

[1] www.e-c-h-o.org/chm1.htm
[2] CPJ. January 28, 2011 3:50 PM ET. http://cpj.org/x/40f9
[3] Supreme Council of the Armed Forces
[4] National Democratic Party – presided over by Hosni Mubarak (1981-2011)
[5] Commander-in-chief of the Egyptian Armed Forces and chairman of the SCAF
[6] http://muftah.org/scaf-above-the-constitution-below-the-revolution/
[7] A bill that forbade civilians from auditing the army's budget (El-Shami 2011)
[8] www.theguardian.com/world/2012/apr/15/egypt-bars-10-presidential-election-candidates

Morsi's presidency reflected the long-suppressed factionalism of a nation under change. Immediate changes included the introduction of a new cabinet under Hesham Kandil, and the appointment of Fatah al-Sisi as Minister of Defence. Public dissent broke out immediately. Morsi's tolerance of religious extremism – Salafist reactions to "The Innocence of Muslims", the resulting declaration of fatwahs, calls to destroy non-Islamic monuments (including the pyramids of Giza[9,10]), public attacks on Christian, Bahá'í and Shia minorities, and the public torture and lynching of four Shiites by a Salafist mob[11] – led to the widespread conclusion that he favoured strict Islamic practice. Early drafts of the heavily delayed constitution confirmed these fears, enshrining hard-line Islamic (Sharia) law[12,13], favouring the military and the police, and failing to consolidate rights for women or social/religious minorities.

Protest broke when Morsi granted himself the power to create unassailable and irreversible laws, and granted immunity (i.e. no retrial) to police officers accused of killings under the previous regime. The resulting demonstrations, attacks on official buildings, stock market collapses, widespread sex crimes, clashes between Morsi supporters and detractors, the deployment of tanks, numerous deaths, thousands injured and widespread condemnation of SCAF/police reprisals were fuelled by allegations that pro-Morsi supporters had been paid to assault protestors and rape women; further allegations that the Muslim Brotherhood had been engaged in the torture of protestors alienated Morsi from his moderate support. His attempts to stifle televised/printed dissent attracted international condemnation, as did his decision to appoint hard-line Islamist Adel el-Khayat[14] as governor of Luxor.

With a revolution planned for the 30th of June, Morsi refused to stand down, deflecting blame for unrest on Mubarak supporters; this plaint failed to win over military forces that published an agenda swearing to defend the Egyptian people from 'terrorists and fools'.[15] Morsi was removed from power on the 2nd/3rd of July 2013, Adly Mansour being appointed as interim president. The presidency passed to Abdel Fattah el-Sisi[16] following his victory over Hamdeen Sabahi in May 2014. The Muslim Brotherhood was declared to be a terror organisation and outlawed; over 500 officials were sentenced to death[17] or life imprisonment[18], and between 16-40,000 members and supporters imprisoned. The recriminations continue up to the present day.[19]

◆

It seems somewhat disorienting, or perhaps inappropriate – in the midst of such a violent and tragic time – to consider damage to Egypt's historical and archaeological heritage. Detractors would have ample ammunition to decry what could reasonably be described as heartless prioritisation of materials over people, or trivialising the suffering that has been wrought on Egypt's population since 2011 (and in the thirty years prior) by focusing upon tangible and intangible aspects of culture rather than the plight of the people who are its inheritors. And yet, as with all aspects of history in the making, this is very much a debatable point, and there are no simple answers.

Egyptians' relationships with their own history are immensely complicated, as befits the multifactorial nature of modern populations' own background, and the fluctuating tempo of (recent) socio-political changes as summarised above. In general terms, it is a resource that is both finite and endlessly under threat. Looting has characterised Egyptian culture since at least the Predynastic period, and is both deplorable yet understandable. It is primarily driven by the economics of desperation, and can otherwise be largely attributed to lack of education as much as cupidity. The 2011 revolution and the power and authority vacuum that existed thereafter is a very different issue, however.[20] Casual looting has been replaced by organised and systematic plundering on an appalling scale, carried out by gun-toting gangs

[9] www.frontpagemag.com/2012/raymond-ibrahim/muslim-brotherhood-destroy-the-pyramids/
[10] http://english.alarabiya.net/articles/2012/11/12/249092.html
[11] www.hrw.org/news/2013/06/27/egypt-lynching-shia-follows-months-hate-speech
[12] http://www.wsj.com/articles/SB10001424052702304579404579234034147153224
[13] http://rt.com/op-edge/morsi-sharia-constitution-egypt-409/
[14] A prominent member of Al-Gama'a al-Islamiyya, widely suspected of engineering the 1994 Luxor massacre
[15] www.reuters.com/article/2013/07/03/us-egypt-protests-finalhours-idUSBRE96202920130703
[16] Minister of Defence and First Deputy Prime Minister
[17] www.newrepublic.com/article/117180/egypt-imprisons-muslim-brotherhood-members-sentences-500-die
[18] http://edition.cnn.com/2014/04/28/world/africa/egypt-politics/
[19] http://www.reuters.com/article/2015/02/02/us-egypt-brotherhood-court-idUSKBN0L60VK20150202
[20] Ikram, S. 2014. www.theepochtimes.com/n3/648156-the-loss-and-looting-of-egyptian-antiquities/

using industrial digging equipment, cratering the landscape in such a devastating manner that the damage can be seen from space (see **Tassie *et al.*** Chapters 3 and 9). Damage has taken many forms, and while intentional looting of both sites and museums has been particularly preeminent, accelerated urban sprawl and the resultant destruction of sites, historic buildings (see **Tassie *et al.*** Chapter 3) and unexcavated archaeological areas has also condemned countless thousands of vitally important – and irreplaceable – heritage monuments to oblivion.

This would perhaps beg the question: does it matter? Can we really stand as judge to heritage's disappearance while the aftermath of 2011 is still being felt among Egyptian people? Is this the time and place? It is an obvious truism that heritage matters. Of course it does. But to whom does it matter? Over what should it be prioritised? And do heritage professionals have the nerve – or even the right – to intercede at such a time? At its most positive, one might disavow concerns about heritage in favour of more direct and constructive social intervention that had a more specific positive effect on the brutalised population of Egypt in the aftermath of all the changes summarised above. At its most negative, a cynic might argue that Egypt's indifference to its past is so long-standing that this is merely an acceleration of an extant and unremarkable tendency. The enthusiasm with which developers have exploited official lethargy and legal loopholes to demolish historic buildings and sites (see **Tassie *et al.*** Chapters 3 and 9) is certainly disheartening, as is the constant and unrelenting national and international demand for Egyptian antiquities (see **Gill** Chapter 6) that prompts amateur diggers and professional looters alike to take to the fields and destroy the fruit of millennia in a matter of months. The same cynic would probably also point at the radicalised sector of recent Egyptian society, who have taken a more Salafist attitude towards Egypt's ancient past: Mohammed Mahdi Akef's[21] memorable statement "the hell with Egypt" may be an extreme view, but it found considerable support among those for whom Egypt and its heritage were of secondary importance to Islamic ideology, and who have proposed programmes of destruction that have tragic antecedents in Mali, Tunisia, Iraq, Syria, Afghanistan, Saudi Arabia, Morocco, Pakistan, India, the Balkans and elsewhere.[22, 23, 24]

However, the author is more than happy to report that this view has not reflected reality in the large majority of cases. The roll call of cultural heritage damage is certainly considerable (see **Tassie *et al.*** Chapters 3 and 9; **Gill** Chapter 6; and **Huyge** Chapter 7), and the victims have included some truly shocking casualties – perhaps even Tutankhamun himself[25] – but perhaps the most enduring image to come out of the recent conflicts was the human cordon that encircled the Cairo Museum to prevent its being looted in the aftermath of the revolution. The indignant responses of ordinary citizens to the destruction of both their archaeology and urbanscapes (see **Tassie *et al.*** Chapter 3), and the lengths they have gone to protect them, would necessarily give detractors pause for thought.

The fact of the matter is that a very significant portion of Egyptian society do feel a genuine connection to their past (**Krause** Chapter 2; **Tully** Chapter 5; **Hosny and Ghanem** Chapter 11). The brave, new, post-dictatorship world is an uncertain one, and while recent decades have left much of the population disenfranchised from all manner of social developments and constructs (including, to an extent, their past – see **Tully** Chapter 5), the unique heritage of Egypt has had an instrumental role in producing a similarly unique set of people with which it is inextricably intertwined (see **Owens** Chapter 13). It is heartening, when talking about 'heritage' and how it matters, to realise that this is not a purely selfish exercise on the part of archaeologists and heritage managers, for even in the darkest hours of the Egyptian transition from revolution to bloody struggle to revolution, there were those who put their lives on the line – and even lost their lives – in defending, saving and producing (see **Krause** Chapter 2 and **Owens** Chapter 13) the cultural heritage to which we must now return with our sleeves rolled up in order to protect.

The perspicacious reader will have noticed that the vast majority of the references I have cited here are electronic in origin, which is in itself a significant point, given that the battle for Egyptian democracy, independence and self-determination has been fought with digital weapons, in the digital eye of the world. Successive governments' repeated attempts to crush the flow of publically available information highlight

---

[21] Head of the Muslim Brotherhood from 2004 to 2010

[22] www.frontpagemag.com/2012/raymond-ibrahim/muslim-brotherhood-destroy-the-pyramids/2/

[23] MacEoin, D. 2014. www.gatestoneinstitute.org/4973/destruction-middle-east-antiquities

[24] www.independent.co.uk/news/world/middle-east/the-photos-saudi-arabia-doesnt-want-seen--and-proof-islams-most-holy-relics-are-being-demolished-in-mecca-8536968.html

[25] www.theguardian.com/culture/2015/jan/27/egyptian-museum-gluing-tutankhamun-beard-conservation-cairo

how important the spread of data really is (**Tassie *et al.*** Chapter 3 and **Owens** Chapter 13). A digital failure would be unthinkable in this data age: the revolution would probably not have happened without it. And yet, it would appear, it is quite possible that Egyptian heritage could potentially follow this example. If it were not for Internet social media campaigns, the world would be virtually unaware of the damage being done to sites, to monuments/artefacts[26] and to Egypt's alarmingly dwindling Belle Époque urbanscape (**Tassie *et al.*** Chapter 3 and 9). Yet this largesse of potentiality has not been fully realised. Access to detailed information and records is of seminal importance to all cultural heritage projects, and the aftermath of the revolution has made it tragically apparent that previous projects and administrations have failed to keep pace with the escalating tempo of recovery and archiving (**Cohen** Chapter 4 and **Tassie** Chapter 12). As a result, the best-meaning cultural rescue projects in the world would not be able to identify specific looted objects, or be able to reconnect them with their original magazine/museum/site.

One thing that the cultural heritage community could (and should) do is institute immediate changes to the manner in which archaeological and heritage remains are excavated (**Tassie** Chapter 12), recorded and archived (**Cohen** Chapter 4), and should work with museum curators, Egyptian heritage professionals and all other related parties to ensure that any looted or misplaced artefact will be immediately traceable. While publication of every single excavated piece would be someway beyond the bounds of reason, systematically updated, amended and immediately accessible databases will go a long way towards ensuring that looters' hands will be essentially tied by cultural red tape that will make looting difficult, and resale/export impossible. At the other end of the process, the desire for antiquities must be addressed from the head down. This will be achieved through imposing a structured system of anti-looting publicity, and financial and judicial penalties to collectors and auction houses, whose resulting caution will neutralise the need for looting. Of course there must also be practical solutions on the front line, to defend at-risk sites from unwanted attention (**Tassie *et al.*** Chapter 3), environmental transformations (**Tassie *et al.*** Chapter 9), land reclamation (**Huyge** Chapter 7 and **Tassie *et al.*** Chapter 9) and vandalism (**Owens** Chapter 13), but the only way that real progress can conceivably be made is if those involved in the heritage industry conduct efforts to save Egyptian cultural heritage as a collaborative effort that starts with education, and not with dialogue rife with Draconian threats or penalties.

The greatest and most expensive rescue, excavation and conservation efforts in the world will be utterly futile if no efforts are made to change the host country's public perceptions about the 'past' that has been preserved (see **Krause** Chapter 2; **Hosny and Ghanem** Chapter 11), and how it can be a genuinely productive, useful, and financially rewarding entity, deserving of both respect and protection. Grass-roots efforts to train and educate Egyptians about their past, and encouraging them to undertake jobs connected with the heritage industry – from guiding to catering and site maintenance (see **Tassie *et al.*** Chapter 3) – would lead to a sense of pride, belonging and identity in their heritage, that they would then feel more impetus to protect. It is evident that the seeds of this are very much present in Egyptian society, although a lack of education (see **Krause** Chapter 2 and **Tully** Chapter 5) means that coverage of pre-Islamic history at the school level is decidedly erratic, and there is little engagement with the details of Pharaonic or Ptolemaic history and archaeology. Local populations must be persuaded that heritage is not only for tourists – as is generally believed [see current volume] – but can be a vibrant and living part of everyday life for all Egyptians, who can take pride in showing it to (and defending it from) those who visit in order to see it.

The populace's immediate needs must also be met, and the best means of doing this is to study their reactions to the aftermath of the revolution. Looting aside, the biggest issue was probably land grabs and encroachments, and their urban equivalents. The big issue, as is perfectly obvious, is land and space for Egypt's rapidly expanding population. The Delta, especially, is facing numerous anthropogenic and natural threats (**Tassie *et al.*** Chapter 9 and **Al-Khalil** Chapter 11); the breadbasket of Egypt is thick with archaeological sites, agricultural land and people, all of which are locked in a battle for primacy. And the standoff is worsening. A vicious cycle has ensued by which agricultural land is regularly lost when archaeological remains are discovered on it, but archaeological sites rarely 'become' agricultural land. This, combined with the fact that compensation for those who report new discoveries is often woefully inadequate, means that the general public has become resentful of everything to do with heritage, which clutters up their lifestyles and yields them nothing but problems. The same could be said of protected heritage buildings in Cairo or other cities, where space is at a premium and many people have nowhere to

[26] http://paul-barford.blogspot.co.uk/search?q=egypt

live; this puts old, unused buildings at risk from unethical (and often illegal) development programmes. Funding must be provided to survey and excavate at-risk sites, and to entertain the notion of repurposing sites for agricultural development if they possess insufficient historical significance or potential as tourist attractions to be conserved *in situ*. In cityscapes, this would entail the restoration and repurposing of culturally valuable buildings, to provide accommodation or other functions that are needed by the local population. This, combined with an improved compensation system, a reduction in motivation to loot, and the incorporation of hitherto disengaged people into the world of heritage management will presage the improvement of conditions for all parties concerned.

Finally, one must also remember that the revolution itself gave rise to heritage that is worthy of preservation both in terms of its historical importance and also its social implications for the development of Egyptian culture. The graffiti that was such a vital part of the revolution and its' aftermath has been targeted by both governmental and military agencies, threatening one of the scant means of communication that have been available to the disenfranchised throughout this entire troubled period (see **Owens** Chapter 13). While recognising the problems that graffiti can potentially pose to heritage buildings (etc.) upon which it may be emblazoned, this must not be used as an excuse to destroy or whitewash genuine socio-political concerns that pose no threat to extant heritage. This, again, is an opportunity to exploit the data age: to create immediate archives (see **Cohen** Chapter 4 and **Tassie** Chapter 12) of wall art, and to use a updateable database to upload new images from across Egypt so that some record remains of this fragile and vital part of Egyptian culture. The same system could also be turned to the conservation and mapping of ancient rock art (**Huyge** Chapter 7), although this does of course raise concerns about site security if GIS data were available to vandals or art thieves (**Tassie *et al.*** Chapter 3). The diversity of papers that are contained within this book also reference the fact that the cultural 'net' is expanding, as both academics and the general public are picking up on previously overlooked, relatively modern or abstruse (**Hosny and Ghanem** Chapter 11 and **Hassan** Chapter 8) tangible and intangible cultural practices that are finally being recognised as a heritage worth both celebrating and preserving.

The continued incorporation of the wider population into these sorts of discourses will create a safety net for both heritage and those who are born to its guardianship. At the end of the day it is the people themselves who have made the difference by creating the culture that surrounds them; it must be the duty, of all who are able to assist, to do whatever it takes to help them conserve and understand it, so that it can be both a useful part of everyday lives as well as a springboard of self-definition and identity, and a source of pride.

Lawrence S. Owens
London
27th January 2015

Chapter 2

Egyptian Cultural Heritage at the Dawn of the Arab Spring – a Future for the Past

Kelly Krause

ABSTRACT

Since the start of Egypt's January Revolution in 2011, several heritage sites, ancient monuments and artefacts exhibited in Egypt's museums and storehouses have suffered from negligence or worse. At the same time, many of these places and objects have served as important symbols of the evolving Egyptian cultural identity, where several communities and countless individuals have acted to protect and preserve Egyptian cultural heritage amid chaos, violence and an overall lack of security. Though this cultural heritage can serve to generate a new and positive Egyptian identity within Egypt's changing society, it is also a platform for dispute and argument within and between administrative bodies, heritage professionals and local populations. The author examines the relevance of 'place' within Egyptian communities and current operational and theoretical practices in Egyptian heritage management and what this indicates for the future of the practice and its contribution to the Egyptian people.

INTRODUCTION

Culture is the soul of a people, of a society, a country. When a country or a nation is in the midst of revolution and has to re-define itself, it has to start with its soul in order to understand where they are coming from and what the future holds for them. The idea of a fixed identity is often an illusion; identities in any one place are often fluid and blurred, constantly changing and merging over time through a cumulative process. Similarly, Egyptian cultural identity has continued to evolve through the January Revolution and now continues to influence Egyptian politics and social development as Egyptians' understanding of their identity takes root within their larger society.

Although physical surroundings have been important over the course of the Revolution (landmarks, buildings), place has been much more so, serving as a network of understanding between people and their environment, their fellow citizens and their history. Moreover, place can change and be permeable to new ideas, new practices and new people. Cultural identity demands that in a changing society, a revolutionary society, we try and hold on to what is important from the past and adopt the best features of the new (Davis 1999: 40).

Beyond symbolizing certain values and beliefs, the very transformation of cultural places, objects and practices into heritage is a process whereby identity is defined, debated and contested. Hassan argues that our sense of "identity", at least in modern times, has been largely influenced by a "nationalist" ideology, often 'legitimated by invoking the achievements of our ancestors and a glorious past' (Hassan 1998: 213). Where cultural heritage could be considered as generating a consensus for the development of a new and positive Egyptian identity, it is also the subject of differences and conflicts within Egypt's current institutional context (the Ministry of Antiquities, the Ministry of the Waqf, the Supreme Council of the Armed Forces).

Heritage is a contested concept, with many different types of people participating in several ways, all for various reasons. Multiple groups have a vested interest in heritage and how it is used, preserved and developed. Egypt is a pertinent example of this, given the diversity of places that are designated as heritage; these are inherited 'artefacts' but they gain an active influence in the present by way of the various popular meanings and official sanctions ascribed to them. While a physical place or site is still important, what goes on at these places is all the more relevant. It is the sum of the values in and connections to these social expressions that allow Egyptians to reflect not only on who they are, but who they will become as the country embodies a new vision of itself within the context of an increasingly globalized world.

People and Place: Identity, Heritage and Community in Egypt

Recognizing the bond between cultural sites and local populations is the first step in defining the community in Egypt and in creating mechanisms for genuine participation and collaboration in research and management. At many places in Egypt this bond is already visibly recognized and demonstrated by local people protecting their heritage. The exclusion of local populations from the heritage management process or any resulting opportunities, however, can cause communities to feel disenfranchised and lead to growing resentment, as has been witnessed at several sites and monuments across the country during the January Revolution (Abusir, Dahshur, Gerza, Saqqara, Cairo, Abydos, Tell el-Hibeh, and Tell el-Maskhuta), with magazines being broken into at Buto, Luxor and Qantara. This relationship can be reconciled, and even strengthened, through the welcoming of local initiatives to actively engage in the presentation of local and national heritage.

Figure 2.1: The Nahdet Misr (Renaissance of Egypt) Monument by Mukhtar now located in front of Cairo University. It is the icon of the 1919 movement for independence and the development of modern Egypt, which shows the mix of Egypt's cultural heritage (photograph John H. Hamer ca. 1930).

Foremost is a frequent need of effective communication. Archaeologists and other heritage professionals often lack cultural sensitivity and knowledge of traditional cultural practices and, perhaps more so, a practical understanding of community needs and problems. They tend to dominate discussion and decision-making processes, while local peoples often find the 'experts' to be impractical, confusing and unclear in their objectives and approach. Their experiences have made local communities in Egypt wary, and due to their marginalization in social and political systems they are often unaware of legal and bureaucratic situations and of available support systems. This regularly means frustration and failure for their efforts. Other efforts like the Community Archaeology Project at Quseir, however, situated on Egypt's Red Sea coast, have been very successful, building a strategy that has involved employment and training, public presentations, interviews and oral histories, educational resources and community controlled merchandising. Addressing identity, heritage and citizenship, the Quseir example highlights how the integration of local groups in planning and decision-making processes can help to overcome the ill-feelings and suspicions often created by institutions and heritage agencies (Glazier & Jones 2009).

Despite its many problems heritage plays an essential role 'in husbanding community, identity, (and)... history itself' (Lowenthal in Davis 1999: 13). Egyptians still have been determined to guard their country's heritage amid protests and clashes between authorities and activists over the course of the Revolution, most memorably when citizens linked arms to form a human shield around the Egyptian Museum to protect it from looters and vandals in January 2011.

It was at this time that thousands of jailbreaks and large-scale looting were also deliberately orchestrated by then President Hosni Mubarak; the majority of these criminals are still at large in Egyptian communities. Some of these career criminals have re-organized their gangs and continue to systematically loot sites, such as Abu Rowash, Abusir, Abydos, Tell el-Hibeh, Saqqara and Abu Gurob. These criminals not only damage sites but hold local communities in fear. These acts of looting are compounded by systemic corruption, where local police accept bribes to turn a blind eye toward looting activities, intimidation and even violence. This lack of law and order is one of the biggest threats to Egypt's people and heritage alike.

Much of the culpability for the lack of security and protection at Egypt's heritage places may be placed on the country's then de facto ruling body, the Supreme Council of the Armed Forces (SCAF): according to Article 6 of the UNESCO declaration concerning the intentional destruction of cultural heritage, "A State that intentionally destroys or intentionally fails to take appropriate measures to prohibit, prevent, stop, and punish any intentional destruction of cultural heritage of great importance for humanity, whether or not it is inscribed on a list maintained by UNESCO or another international organization, bears the responsibility for such destruction, to the extent provided for by international law."[1] In other words, the Egyptian state - personified by the SCAF for the better part of eighteen months between February 2011 and August 2012 - is responsible for any wilful loss, damage or destruction of cultural property.

But what about the institutions created specifically to guide the direction, development, safeguarding, protection and preservation of Egypt's cultural heritage? How have they served Egyptians and how do they operate presently within Egypt's current social context? Moreover, what are the implications of their actions for Egypt's identity and cultural environment as the country continues to transition through its revolutionary period?

HERITAGE MANAGEMENT IN EGYPT – EGYPTIAN HERITAGE FOR EGYPTIANS

Egypt's Supreme Council of Antiquities (SCA) was originally founded as the *Service des Antiquités Egyptiennes* by French Egyptologist Auguste Mariette in 1858, though Egyptians sometimes look back to Mohammed Ali's decree of 1835 as the true founding of Egypt's Antiquities Service and the Egyptian Museum (Reid 2002: 55-6).[2] In the ensuing period of Egypt's colonial rule, all administrators were appointed from England or were non-Egyptian; Egyptians were deprived of even minor political and administrative roles. This exclusion is matched by the almost total absence of Egyptians from positions of academic significance in the field of Egyptology. After Mariette, the directorship of the Antiquities Service remained a French and British sanction until 1952 when Mustapha Amer was appointed the first Egyptian Director of the Service. Notwithstanding, it may still be debatable if Egyptian heritage is for Egyptians.

Elsheshtawy has argued that the danger for developing countries like Egypt and others in the Middle East is no longer from external forces (Orientalists, colonialists, imperialists, etc.) but from the inside: in viewing the public as a threat that has to be dealt with and contained, local decision-makers preclude a large segment of the population from certain rights (socializing in urban historic areas, enjoyment of outdoor activities) which become symptomatic of more serious infringements leading to their disenfranchisement and potentially dangerous drawbacks (i.e. fundamentalism, Islamisation) (Elsheshtawy 2006: 297).

Figure 2.2: The tomb of Auguste Mariette in the grounds of the Museum of Egyptian Antiquities, Cairo (photograph L. S. Owens).

In the past, the SCA (now part of the Ministry of Antiquities) and other government bodies have offered little to no co-ordination or consultation with the Egyptian public or even necessarily informed them as to what is happening. Restoration projects have provided little if any on-site information on the proposed restorations, schedule or methods. Neither have they sought public support or funding.[3]

Cultural heritage sites have been especially at risk from uncontrolled development and environmental degradation in urban areas. Development at/around heritage sites can be and has been positive when it is executed with a long-term vision and in a *sustainable* way with careful consideration for the property and the local community around it. Unfortunately, many developments and restoration projects in Egypt merely use heritage to develop tourism - the tourism sector accounts for more than a tenth of Egypt's gross domestic product and is the source of income for approximately 20 per cent of the labour force in the country[4] - with little to no regard for local residents or the integrity of the property.

In this occurrence, upgrading is expensive, and it has been easier for the Egyptian government to evict residents and small businesses. The notion of evacuating shops, for example, which are the property of the Ministry of Religious Endowments, represents a grave violation of the idea of *waqf* (endowment; pl. *awqaf*), one of the most important bases of Islamic civic and spatial organization.[5] Since 1952, the Ministry of Awqaf has acted as the administrator of a considerable number of buildings throughout Egypt, most of which are classified as historic monuments and also actively integrated into the community in both a spiritual and secular way (either residential or commercial or as services). Conversely, the SCA has functioned to limit the use of these same buildings within a definitive, regulated framework and through imported international standards rather than through social consensus.

Since the start of the January Revolution, the SCA, then under the umbrella of the Ministry of Culture, swung between a Ministry of Antiquities (MA) and an independent SCA body affiliated to the Egyptian cabinet. Eventually, the Supreme Council of the Armed Forces established the National Rescue Government in November 2011 and the Ministry of State for Antiquities was formally and firmly recognized as the guiding body of Egypt's antiquities, even after several name change, including the dropping of State.[6]

Despite the fact that the decision-making now resides with the MA, the new ministry relies heavily on international archaeological investment for both fieldwork and preservation. Lack of funding and losses in the tourism sector have greatly impeded the immediate implementation of the ministry's plans, though budgets for large projects like the Grand Egyptian Museum (GEM) and the National Museum of Egyptian Civilization (NMEC) have been largely provided for by UNESCO and the Japan International Cooperation Agency (JICA).[7] For now, the MA plans to continue to allow foreign teams to continue working in Egypt, though admittedly with the anticipation that they will educate and train more Egyptians in excavation, restoration, museology and heritage management.

CONCLUSIONS

Ultimately, the future of heritage management in Egypt cannot depend solely on foreign investment and the highly volatile tourism industry[8], but on the policies and practice of the new MA and its minister Mamdouh el-Damaty.[9] Even more so, it will depend on Egypt's new political regime: in June 2012, Mohammed Morsi of the Freedom and Justice Party, an offshoot of the Muslim Brotherhood of Egypt, was announced as the winner of Egypt's first democratic election in decades. The new Egyptian president surprised many, reaching out to a range of states in pursuit of international legitimacy while neutralizing the SCAF, which had controlled Egypt since the fall of deposed President Hosni Mubarak.[10] Morsi himself was deposed after a popular uprising on the 30th June 2013, and General Abdul-Fattah el-Sisi took control, eventually being elected president in May 2014 (Kingsley 2014). Further parliamentary elections are due in Spring 2015.[11] Of course, sustainable heritage management in Egypt also depends on stable economic and social growth.

We can recognise the extent to which deviation in the objectives and interests of the main institutions and stakeholders responsible to the conservation of Egypt's cultural heritage can generate paradoxes and contradictions, and particularly the absence of collective results between their actions. This implies an integrated approach where social and infrastructure problems are treated simultaneously with problems of preservation/conservation to ensure that Egyptian society retains its identity without endangering its cultural heritage. Active participation by the general public must consequently form part of state policies for the protection of Egyptian cultural heritage. Rather than being simply "informed" by archaeology or cultural institutions, communities need to be fully involved to drive collaboration and the negotiation of multiple identities and narratives, positioning archaeologists and other heritage professionals as *partners* rather than "leaders" and local populations as the owners and caretakers of their heritage (Tully 2009: 75).

Heritage management in Egypt may also benefit operationally through the initiation of education measures in order to arouse and develop respect and affection for the remains of the past, including: the development of a policy and plans that aim to give cultural heritage a function and meaning in the life of local communities; community participation in local excavations, training programmes and other heritage initiatives; the organization of guided tours, lectures and exhibitions dealing with issues related to cultural heritage (excavation, preservation, ownership, management); the clear, informative and engaging display of monuments and heritage sites; and the publication of written guides, books and other media.

Furthermore, large archaeological expeditions will have to divert funds and energy into contributing something at the local level. Archaeologists and other heritage professionals will have to consider the place of local museums, heritage centres, and educational facilities. This process would take place at the local level, where foreign institutions contribute to the initial construction of museums and local authorities administer and benefit from their operation; people can learn to appreciate the inherent values of the past without necessarily having to identify with them in any personalized way (Meskell 2000: 150).

The January Revolution continues to bring out the best in the Egyptian people. Unfortunately, the persistent damage inflicted on Egypt's sites and monuments is also symptomatic of the violence and neglect the country and its heritage continue to face under the administration of those directly responsible for its protection, development and proliferation, both Egyptian and foreign.

Most of us either visit Egypt or practice Egyptian archaeology as if we still encountered an ancient landscape, ignoring the living people, their traditions, practices and ideologies. There are exceptions, but they remain somewhat unique in the wider sphere of practice in Egypt. Rather than asking who *owns* the past, the better question may be how we can *make use* of the past to redress inequalities and promote development and mutual understanding (Hassan 2010: 271). Those of us working with Egypt's heritage need to revise our research agendas and provide policy makers and the public with materials that focus on the social and cultural dynamics of Egyptian civilization, from most ancient Egypt to the present (Ibid.). The archaeological community and heritage industry must become more 'theorized' about their activities and their implications and more active in their negotiations in a fuller global setting — and that includes the local level. Protecting cultural heritage in a revolutionary state is not only an investment in the pride that citizens will have in who they are as a people, but also into the driving force Egypt needs for growth and development. Only when this level of involvement is achieved can we truly enter discussions about responsibility and ethics and make our proper contribution to the social sciences and, more importantly, to the people of Egypt.

ENDNOTES

1 UNESCO declaration concerning the intentional destruction of cultural heritage: http://portal.unesco.org/en/ev.php-URL_ID=17718&URL_DO=DO_TOPIC&URL_SECTION=201.html

2 Reid, D. M. 2002. *Whose Pharaohs? Archaeology, Museums, and Egyptian National Identity from Napoleon to World War I.* Cairo: AUC Press. Under the 1835 decree, antiquities were to be sent to Rifaa al-Tahtawi, director for the School of Languages in Ezbekiyah. Al-Tahtawi and Yusuf Hekekyan were to inspect the proposed site for a museum next to the school, and Hekeyan, an engineer, was to design the building; unfortunately the plan never took hold, and Mariette was to start afresh twenty-three years later.

3 A glaring exception is the project to revive the Hellenistic library in Alexandria independent of the SCA with the aim of enhancing and renovating the historical cultural heritage of the city (see Butler, 2003).

4 Tohamy, S. and Swinscoe, A. 2000. *The Economic Impact of Tourism.* Cairo: The Egyptian Center for Economic Studies (ECES). Including indirect effects, the total contribution to output reaches $ 9.6 billion (11.6 percent of GDP).

5 Williams, C. 2006. Reconstructing Islamic Cairo: forces at work, in D. Singerman and P. Amar (eds), *Cairo Cosmopolitan: Politics, Culture, and Urban Space in the New Globalized Middle East.* Cairo and New York: AUC Press, pp. 269-294. Traditionally, *waqf* has functioned as a system whereby wealthy patrons deeded the profits from various urban and rural properties they owned to provide for the building, staffing, and maintenance of religious and civic foundations which became part of the public-municipal domain.

6 The SCA is still operating as a separate body, though some of the MA's planned reforms will include the rescheduling of the SCA's mission and a decision on whether or not it will be part of the ministry. Mustafa Amin has served as the SCA secretary-general since September 2011.

7 El-Aref, N. 2012. Heritage at what cost? *Al-Ahram Weekly Online* 1080: http://weekly.ahram.org.eg/2012/1080/eg42.htm As of January 2012, the MAS was in debt to more than LE1 billion to construction companies in charge of restoration and development projects, in addition to a LE350-million sovereign loan given by the government to the ministry to aid its financial recovery.

8 Sakr, M. and Massoud, N. 2003. *International tourism volatility with special reference to Egypt.* Cairo: The Egyptian Center for Economic Studies (ECES). Although the economic impacts of tourism downturn are immense, particularly when indirect and secondary effects are taken into consideration, Egypt's tourism industry is resilient and responds quickly to crises and regains momentum over a relatively short span.

However, this fast recovery is often due to drastic price cuts which cause sluggish growth of tourism receipts in relation to tourist arrivals, and aggravate the adverse impacts on the business sector as well as the macro-economic implications of tourism downturns.

9 El-Damaty is the fifth minister of the MA, succeeding Mohamed Ibrahim and chief archaeologist and former secretary-general of the SCA Zahi Hawass, who was sacked from the post in July 2011 after rising dissent against his alleged ties to President Hosni Mubarak's regime. See *A Short History of the Antiquities Service* at the back of this book for a fuller history of the comings and goings of the Secretary Generals of the SCA and Ministers of Antiquities.

10 In August 2012 President Morsi dismissed SCAF leader Field Marshal Mohammed Hussein Tantawi and his second-in-command, General Sami Annan. Morsi has also attempted to reverse the "supplemental constitutional articles" that the military issued just before the recent presidential election, an act which purports to restore presidential and legislative powers back to those elected bodies.

11 The first of a two phases of parliamentary elections will be held on the 22-23rd March 2015. Egypt sets dates for parliamentary polls, *Al Jezeera* - http://www.aljazeera.com/news/middleeast/2015/01/egypt-sets-dates-parliamentary-polls-201518202648567559.html

REFERENCES

Butler, B. 2003. "Egyptianizing" the Alexandrina: the contemporary revival of the ancient mouseion/library, in J. Humbert and C. Price (eds), *Imhotep Today: Egyptianizing Architecture*, London: UCL Press, pp. 257-280.

Davis, P. 1999. *Ecomuseums: a Sense of Place.* London: Leicester University Press.

El-Aref, N. 2012. Heritage at what cost? *Al-Ahram Weekly Online* 1080: http://weekly.ahram.org.eg/2012/1080/eg42.htm

Elsheshtawy, Y. 2006. Urban transformations: social control at a-Rifa'i mosque and Sultan Hassan square, in D. Singerman and P. Amar (eds), *Cairo Cosmopolitan: Politics, Culture, and Urban Space in the New Globalized Middle East.* Cairo and New York: AUC Press, pp. 295-312.

Glazier, D. and Jones, A. 2009. 'Not just Egyptians; Not just Europeans: Different Cultures, Working together…' Examining the Heritage of Quseir, Egypt, in F. A. Hassan, G. J. Tassie, A De Trafford, L. S. Owens & J. van Wetering (eds.) *Managing Egypt's Cultural Heritage: Proceedings of the First Egyptian Cultural Heritage Organisation Conference on: Egyptian Cultural Heritage Management.* London: Golden House and ECHO Publications, pp. 27-37.

Hassan, F. A. 1998. Memorabilia: archaeological materiality and national identity in Egypt, in L. Meskell (ed.) *Archaeology under Fire: Nationalism, Politics and Heritage in the Eastern Mediterranean and Middle East.* London: Routledge, pp. 200-216.

Hassan, F. A. 2010. Egypt in the memory of the world, in W. Wendrich (ed.) *Egyptian Archaeology.* Oxford: Wiley-Blackwell, pp. 259-273.

Kingsley, P. 2014. Abdel Fatah al-Sisi won 96.1% of vote in Egypt presidential election, say officials, *The Guardian* June 3 - http://www.theguardian.com/world/2014/jun/03/abdel-fatah-al-sisi-presidential-election-vote-egypt

Meskell, L. 2000. The practice and politics of archaeology in Egypt, *Annals of the New York Academy of Sciences*, 925: 146-169.

Reid, D. M. 2002. *Whose Pharaohs? Archaeology, Museums, and Egyptian National Identity from Napoleon to World War I.* Cairo: AUC Press.

Sakr, M. and Massoud, N. 2003. *International tourism volatility with special reference to Egypt.* Cairo: The Egyptian Center for Economic Studies (ECES).

Tohamy, S. and Swinscoe, A. 2000. *The economic impact of tourism.* Cairo: The Egyptian Center for Economic Studies (ECES).

Tully, G. 2009. Ten years on: the community archaeology project Quseir, Egypt, *Treballs d'Arqueologia*, 15: 63-78.

UNESCO declaration concerning the intentional destruction of cultural heritage: http://portal.unesco.org/en/ev.php-URL_ID=17718&URL_DO=DO_TOPIC&URL_SECTION=201.html

Williams, C. 2006. Reconstructing Islamic Cairo: forces at work, in D. Singerman and P. Amar (eds), *Cairo Cosmopolitan: Politics, Culture, and Urban Space in the New Globalized Middle East.* Cairo and New York: AUC Press, pp. 269-294.

Chapter 3

Egypt's Heritage in Times of Conflict and Crisis

G. J. Tassie, A. De Trafford and J. van Wetering

ABSTRACT

The Egyptian revolution of 25th January 2011 brought the authoritarian regime of Hosni Mubarak to an end and gave hope of greater social, political and economic freedom to millions of people. However, the lack of administrative continuity, government funding, disappearance of the police and enforceable laws and regulations in the field of cultural heritage management over subsequent years left Egypt's cultural heritage highly vulnerable. Museums and magazines were attacked and robbed, and hundreds of sites looted, often by well organised criminal gangs wielding automatic weapons. Terrorist attacks and sectarian violence have resulted in the destruction of museums, churches and other historic buildings, as well as illicit and illegal encroachments onto both protected and unprotected archaeological land, often as a ruse to conceal looting activity. The population of Egypt is booming; however, reclaimed desert has been neglected as a venue for construction, with developers favouring convenient archaeological sites, or historic Belle Époque buildings that have been razed for the construction of tenements. This is not only destroying the aesthetics of the great cities, but strikes at the very heart of Egypt's multiethnicity.

Many individuals –both heritage workers and the general public – have come together to protect their heritage from the unscrupulous, from forming human chains around vulnerable monuments to the formation of social media campaigns to warn against the imminent destruction of cultural heritage, and to demand greater security at sites and monuments. This is an opportunity for greater cooperation between Egyptian and international archaeologists, and with the general public who live beside these sites and monuments. It is an opportunity to create new systems of administration and laws to protect cultural heritage, and to listen to the voices of the modern Egyptians in formulating heritage management and values.

INTRODUCTION

Recent events in Afghanistan, Egypt, Iraq, Libya, Syria, and Tunisia have provoked considerable dialogue concerning the protection of cultural property in times of armed conflict, civil unrest and national disasters (Kila 2013). The Arab Spring, of which Egypt was a part, has had a serious effect on cultural property: 'bad as things were before 2011, never has the damage been as sustained, extensive and methodical as since the region tumbled into violence at the beginning of the Arab Spring' (Athanasiadis 2014). The cultural heritage of Egypt is a finite resource: if we do not do something to stop the looting and destruction, most sites in Egypt will be gone in 25 years (Parçak, in Vergano 2014).

The Egyptian revolution of 25th January 2011 resulted in the end of Hosni Mubarak's tenure as president, and also witnessed the disappearance of police from their posts, and a state of lawlessness that left many archaeological sites open to looting, vandalism and illegal building activities. The Central and Eastern European transitions from communism to democracy saw similar lawlessness in the 1980s to 1990s, with widespread destruction, armed conflict, vandalism and theft. Some of the main challenges to protecting the cultural property were the lack of administrative continuity, government funding, and enforceable laws and regulations in the field of cultural heritage management. Despite the recurrence of these trends, not only in Egypt, but throughout North Africa and South-western Asia as many countries try to change from authoritarian regimes to greater social, political and economic freedom, it would appear that both national and international measures are ineffective in these situations.

Although thefts from museums are a serious problem, these items have – in principle – usually been studied and registered, and so are easier to track. However, even the Museum of Egyptian Antiquities, Cairo, where the Registration and Collection Management Department has been creating a database of the museum's vast collection since 2007 and has records for almost all registered museum objects, the objects' specific location [in the museum's galleries], is not always known (Keshk 2012a). Most of the items kept in magazines (storehouses) are typically uncatalogued or have only sparse records, and so are prime targets for thieves (Tresilian 2014). At some sites, an overflow of objects are kept in undecorated tombs that are then bricked-up to safeguard them. Worst of all is site looting, for this leaves cultural heritage without context, destroying sites for future investigation, and the items looted from these sites cannot easily be traced (see Fig. 3.1). Although looting is not new and has been undertaken in Egypt for millennia, an increase in the illicit trade in antiquities is noticeable since the time of the eighteenth-century 'Grand Tour'. There have been some high profile cases of looting and antiquities smuggling such as those of Frederick Schultz and Jonathan Tokeley-Parry and the Abd el-Rassul brothers (Brodie 2014; Doole 2002; Gerstenblith 2002; Tassie 2007; Wilson 2002) however, since 2011 there has been a dramatic increase in the scale and organisation of looting. This is also the case with the illegal encroachments on archaeological sites. In February 2006, the *First Conference on Encroachments on Archaeological Sites* was held in Egypt. This conference highlighted the problems of encroachments and their impact on sites and monuments as well as artefacts. Over ten years ago agriculture and urban development, particularly illegal constructions, were encroaching on archaeological sites up and down Egypt. Even the most famous of sites, i.e. the Giza Pyramids, Luxor, and Hierakonpolis were not free from this encroachment. Since the revolution cases of illegal encroachment have increased ten-fold, with sites such as Abu el-Hummus, Abusir, Abydos, Atfih (Aphroditopolis), Akhmim, Antinoupolis, al-Bordan, Borg el-Arab Dahshur, Fustat, Gebelein, Gerza, Heliopolis, Izbat al-Jabri, al-Khatib, Lisht, Maadi, Saqqara, Tell Aziz, Tell el-Hibeh, and Wadi Digla – to name but a few – all suffering incursions of one form or another.

The scale of looting and theft is of course connected to Egypt's depressed economy, lack of security and meteoric unemployment, which ran at 12.7% in 2012, with over a quarter of all people living beneath the official poverty line at 25.2% (Brederova 2014).

The decrease in tourism since 2011 has also had a major impact, as the industry had been steadily rising since the mid-1990s and by the mid-2000s accounted for more than 12% of Egypt's gross domestic product (GDP) and 12-14% of total employment (Ashton 2013). In 2010 14.7 million tourists visited Egypt, contributing $13.63 billion to the economy (11% GDP); this was down to 9.8 million in 2011, recovering slightly to 11.57 million tourists in 2012, but falling again in 2013 to 9.5 million with with revenues of $5.9 billion (6.7% GDP) as a result of governmental warnings to avoid the country post-Morsi (Kingsley 2014a). The recovery in 2014 has been good, jumping 112% to 2.8 million tourists contributing $2 billion in the third quarter of 2014 (compared to 1.6 million tourists generating $900 million in the same quarter in 2013 [Ahram Online 2014; Mostafa 2015b]). There was also an increase in domestic tourism in the latter part of 2014 (Mostafa 2015a).

There are 65 magazines located around the country, the ex-Minister of Antiquities Dr Mohammed Ibrahim estimated that in the first 16 months after the January 25th revolution 2% of the artefacts once held in these storehouses were looted = 50,000 artefacts (Joseph 2012), although this figure had changed in 2014 to 4,000 artefacts (Brederova 2014), the discrepancy reflecting once more just how databasing efforts have failed to keep up with the flow of archived remains. Increased security has seen a decrease in thefts, but an increase in illicit digging that has been estimated at 100 times the pre-2011 rate (5697 illicit digs in 2012). Related crimes have also risen, to include 1,467 cases of illicit trading in antiquities, 150+ attempts to smuggle antiquities abroad, and at least 35 deaths related to looting (Hendawi 2012). Recent research by the *International Coalition to Protect Egyptian Antiquities* (ICPEA) suggests thefts at archaeological sites in Egypt have rocketed by between 500% and 1,000% since the Arab Spring uprisings of 2011. Monica Hanna – who works with the ICPEA – states that the team using satellite imagery have counted more than 200 sites that have been affected by looting, and that there has been an increase by about 300% in the past three years in instances of grave robbing. The team estimates that between 100 and 150 objects have gone missing every day since 2011 (DW 2014). "The illegal trade of Egyptian antiquities is a worldwide problem, but the U.S. is one of the target markets," says Andrew Moore, the president of the Archaeological Institute of America´ (Shaw 2014a).

THE THREATS TO CULTURAL HERITAGE

The 1954 UNESCO *Convention for the Protection of Cultural Property in the Event of Armed Conflict* was designed to protect cultural property during periods of conventional war, but has proven to be inadequate in dealing with the issues that have arisen in Egypt since 2011. It should be noted that the 1954 Convention came into being as a result of World War II, and it is perhaps unsurprising that it has not adapted to the changing face of modern conflict and social breakdown. It therefore behoves us to reassess the procedures in place to protect the world's cultural heritage (Eichberger 2010; Forrest 2014; Schipper and Eichberger 2010). The 1954 Hague Convention includes these peacetime measures against future conflict:

- Registration on 'International Register of Cultural Property under Special Protection'
- Training of specialised military personnel to secure respect for cultural property
- Cooperation of military with the civilian authorities responsible for safeguarding it
- Cooperation between archaeologists, heritage managers, politicians and the military

What role can cultural heritage play in forming new Egyptian identities, and how will it be protected during reconstruction and development? Central and Eastern European revolutions prompted the UNESCO International Decade for Natural Disaster Reduction (IDNDR), established to develop management strategies for cultural heritage at all levels, to include:

- Improved cultural heritage stewardship and integration in disaster management
- Making disaster planning a national priority
- Skill development and professional training
- Media promotion cultural issues to governments and the general public
- 'Blue Shield' markings to denote protected status
- Cooperation and contact between domestic and international organisations
- Establishing a special tax to fund disaster planning, mitigation and relief
- Encouraging private and public partnerships

However, despite various UNESCO visits to Egypt from 2011 onwards, these strategies proved to be ineffective due to the lack of administrative continuity, government funding, enforceable cultural heritage laws and regulations, and absent security at sites, magazines and museums.

Egypt's cultural heritage has emerged as one of the main casualties of both the revolution and Egypt's fast-growing population's demand for housing. Ambitions of developers aside, there is a misplaced but enduring belief that modernity is attainable through high-rises, factories and large-scale development projects (Athanasiadis 2014). This building (or agriculture) often takes place on 'grabbed' land belonging to the Ministry of Antiquities (MA).

'The people responsible for these takeovers include contractors who might appropriate significant amounts of land to divide up and resell for multiple purposes, or even villagers and townspeople who live in settlements abutting the archaeological areas. The latter group tends to acquire land at a much smaller scale than the former. Acquisition involves hastily constructing a wall around a piece of land, or quickly tilling the soil and planting or claiming to plant something there. The most effective ploy used to keep the newly acquired land, if immediate construction is untenable, is to use the area as a cemetery, or at least give the appearance that this is its new function' (Ikram 2013: 366).

This is primarily a ploy by contractors, whereas local people often regard these areas as lying empty and unused, and therefore believe that they are finally being utilised. This raises the issue of community archaeology and education, as increased engagement in planning and community archaeology incentives will involve local inhabitants and lead to greater public and private engagement with heritage.

Looting may be one of the oldest professions, but has achieved new heights – or depths – since 2011. The absence of policing and adequate legislation has shown just how vulnerable Egypt's resources are. During the initial demonstrations at the end of January 2011 only a few looting attempts were reported, the most high profile being that of the Egyptian Museum of Antiquities, Cairo. Military personnel were deployed to protect not only the museums, but the thousands of sites around the country. After the overthrow of the Mubarak regime the military personnel were redeployed, and the Tourist and Antiquities Police that normally protect the archaeological sites and magazines did not – or could not – return to their posts owing to public disfavour. Only a few small groups of site guards (*ghafirs*) steadfastly remained at their posts, although some of these were held-up at gunpoint. The 16 months of interim government saw the most widespread loss of cultural property, mainly from antiquities storerooms and archaeological sites, and there was a lack of coordinated efforts to prevent this. Security breakdowns were followed by the collapse of continuity within the MSA (now the MA). After the resignation of Zahi Hawass as the Minister of Antiquities in July 2011 a lack of administrative continuity ensued, for there were rapid changes of personnel in positions of power within the Ministry of State for Antiquities (now the MA) (Keshk 2011a).

Since Hawass' resignation there have been three ministers for antiquities – Ahmed Eissa, Mohamed Ibrahim and Mamdouh el-Damaty (as of June 2014) – but the disruption in the antiquities department combined with the long initial absence of the guards created a security vacuum that led to greater organisation within the looting community, a situation exacerbated by the release of numerous criminals from prison early in 2011. What happened next suggests that the majority of cultural property loss is a by-product of the civil unrest rather than being the direct result of armed conflict, as testified to by several millennia of looting in Egypt (Ikram 2013).

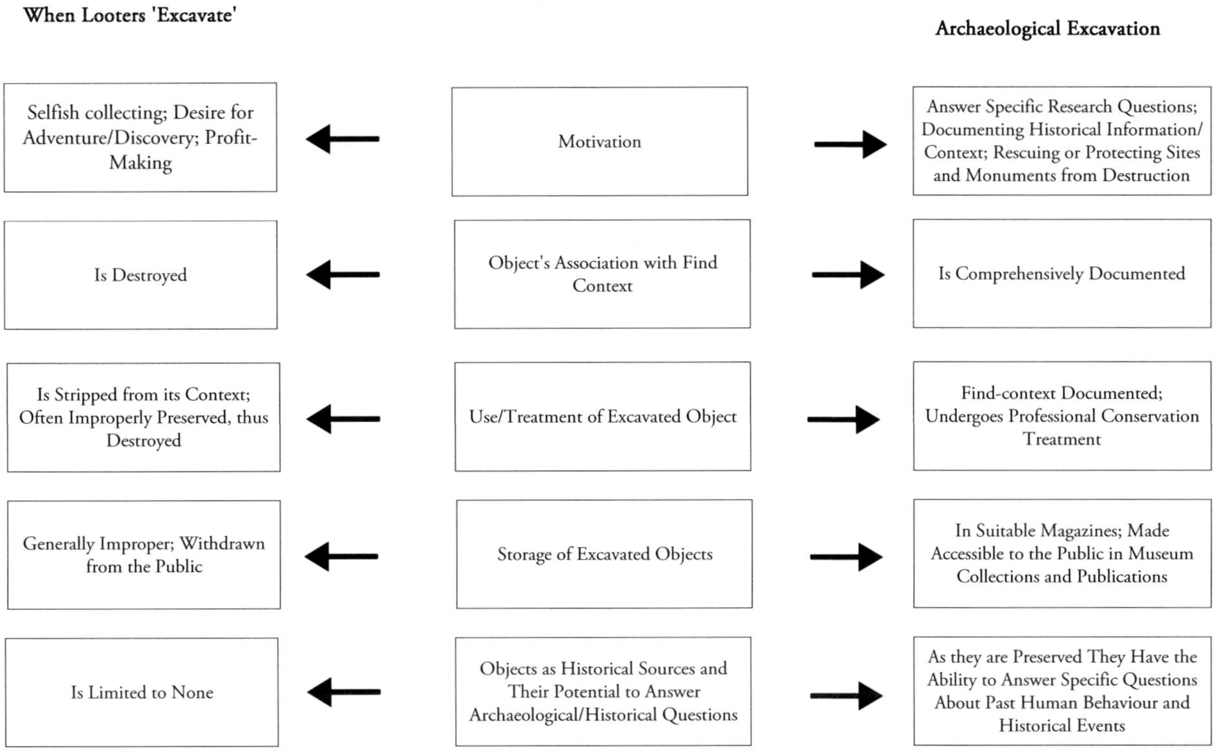

Figure 3.1: Illicit digging vs. archaeological excavation (adapted from Fasold, Stutzinger and von Kaenel 1995: 26).

> 'However, under the Morsi administration and its Islamist allies, the country suffered from a systematic lack of interest towards the archaeological and cultural heritage of Egypt, the total lack of political will to protect and enhance the archaeological areas, and even an ideological tendency to de-legitimize the pre-Islamic past as an essential component of national identity' (Hanna 2013b: 372).

During Morsi's reign hardline preachers – both on television and in mosques – openly encouraged looting of sites and destruction of cultural heritage, perhaps owing to their pre-Islamic nature, with one particularly radical Salafist leader advocating the destruction of the pyramids of Giza. While el-Sisi's administration has seen some improvements, the structure of command and exercise of power has suffered. However, when the organised looters strike they can outnumber the guards by as many as 15:1, and be heavily armed (Ikram 2014). In 2014 tanks and armoured vehicles are still a permanent fixture outside the Coptic Museum as well as the Egyptian Museum, stationed there to protect them against any further civil unrest that may occur.

Various scales and types of looting can be identified, such as professional organised looting and the opportunistic robbers. These organised gangs consist of:

> '…an individual with connections to facilitate the disposal of stolen antiquities controls the professional "mafia" of looters. His underlings acquire, transport, and see to the nitty-gritty of the operation. Often the "king-pin" will hire thieves on an *ad hoc* basis, or opportunistic robbers will go to him to sell artefacts as they do not have the connections to dispose of them' (Ikram 2013: 367-8).

Two categories of organised looters can be observed: violent and relatively non-violent. The violent looters, often consisting of career criminals that were let out of prison early in 2011 are relatively new, and is a direct result of the recent increase in the traffic in arms in Egypt. These violent looters employ guards with guns while hired diggers loot sites. However, the latter category have been well established in Egypt for many years, digging random pits in the hope of finding gold and other valuables. Some of these well-armed looters have killed the poorly armed site guards that remained on the sites after the better equipped police left. 'Prior to 2011, these guards were generally sufficient to intimidate prospective robbers as the guards were in positions of authority, and the fear of reprisal when caught was a sufficient deterrent to the thieves. However, the absence of a clear authority, coupled with weaponry, made looters feel relatively invincible, even those who were opportunistic and not part of a larger organization' (Ikram 2013: 368-9).

In the years since the 2011 revolution, well-armed "mafia" groups have targeted archaeological sites and, sometimes with the aid of a bulldozer, have dug up monuments and artefacts, and taken them to sell on the black market, usually to powerful dealers. The illicit antiquities are either shipped abroad immediately, or held in a safe house for dealers to view and buy what they believe they can sell on. Some of these groups seem to have read archaeological reports and may possibly be using geophysical prospecting to target their nefarious activities. The unarmed gangs or as Hardy (2015a) terms them subsistence diggers, follow a similar pattern in disposing of their loot. Many of this latter group are driven by the rampant inequality and poverty and are oblivious to the destruction of their cultural heritage, only wishing to feed their families. Large portions of land under World Heritage List protection have been occupied on several occasions at Dahshur, Saqqara, and Lisht, and reused for constructing modern cemeteries, which are a cover for looting (Hanna 2013a; Ikram 2013).

Prior to 1983, legal antiquities dealers operated in Egypt; Law 117 (1983) changed this, with most dealers moving overseas, ceasing business, or going underground creating the conditions for rampant abuse (Waxman 2008: 120-6). Trew (2014) suggests that the illicit antiquities business stretched to the top echelons of government under the Mubarak regime, prominent families colluding with dealers, diplomats, security forces and ministries to obtain items and remove them from the country via truck, boat or plane. Hawass' work to undo this damage in the 2000s has been set back by the 2011 revolution and its aftermath (Smith 2014 passim; Waxman 2008: 125), and this deficit is one of the new government's greatest challenges. The Egyptian antiquities laws are already sufficient in this respect; they just need to be properly enforced (Mostafa 2014c).

Satellite imagery by Parçak among others has revealed extensive illicit digging across the country, with tens of thousands of looting pits dotting the landscape, many of them very recent (Moustafa 2014; Vergano 2014). However, these satellites do not reveal the excavations being undertaken beneath houses or the walls of tombs and temples that are being attacked in order to remove decorated blocks, as has been attested in Saqqara and sites in the Delta (i.e. Behbet el-Hagar and Kom Abu Billo), Middle Egypt and Luxor. The combined loss of information on past human activity is enormous (Ikram 2013)[1]. Antiquities Law No. 117 of 1983 (amended by Law No. 3 of 2010), which prohibits looting or any encroachment on archaeological sites (Ikram 2011), has failed to stem the tide. Corruption, wealthy oligarchs, funding issues, bureaucratic lethargy and risk-avoiding attitudes may all play a part (Kila 2013: 320). It is apparent that the security forces are considerably better at catching looters than either they – or governmental policy – are at preventing the looting in the first instance.

Inadvertent damage by terror attacks also threatens cultural heritage, such as the car bomb that caused substantial damage to the Islamic Museum of Art in Cairo in January 2014, damaging mosques and the fabric of local buildings as well as the intended target (a police station). The manuscripts it contains had to be hastily removed, with inevitable conservation issues. In January 2915 the Al-Arish Museum in the Sinai also suffered serious damage during a terrorist attack on the nearby security directorate. A similar situation transpired at the Institut d'Egypte (Egyptian Research Council) in 2011, where an arson attack destroyed 10,000 books and damaged 20,000 more; the full fate of the remaining archives is still unknown (El Aref 2015; Cairo Observer 2014; Fangary and Wahba 2012). Further lootings and arson have damaged the Villa Casdagli (Midan Simon Bolivar) in 2013, and the Villa Kevork Ispenian (Pyramids Road) in 2011 and 2012 (Tresilian 2014), while the important Coptic areas of Abu Mina and the Wadi Natrun were attacked and looted by well-armed radical militias in 2014. It is understood that they also aim to grab archaeological land for illegal construction and agriculture activities (Egypt's Heritage Task Force 2014). In sum, cultural heritage is suffering in the face of sectarian vengeance, poor economic infrastructure, and the existence of the illicit trade in antiquities (Brederova 2014).

[1] It should be noted than Egypt is not unique in this respect. Around 78.5% of 3009 archaeologists surveyed in 2013 had encountered looting or evidence thereof in their fieldwork (Proulx 2013: 119). This is universal, with particular increases in South America, North Africa and Southwest Asia.

VALUES OF CULTURAL HERITAGE

The need for cultural heritage conservation begs the question: what are the cultural constraints determining why, how and for whom an archaeological site is preserved (Mason and Avrami, 2002:18)? It would generally appear that cultural heritage 'value' equates with archaeological 'value' (Gestrich 2011), and thus on public interest rather than economic. According to the World Bank and the IMF, there is a positive correlation between World Heritage (WH) Listing and tourism growth, with a resulting increase in long-term GDP growth: tourism thus generated increases growth per capita by around 10.4% (Lehr 2014). The cultural wealth of Egypt is such that it is in danger of becoming a WH-sponsored open air museum for tourists and the government. However this is clearly unsustainable: cultural heritage cannot merely be regarded as a commodity (i.e. visitor attraction), for it does not include the non-use values, and these socio-cultural values must also be considered when assessing a site's significance to various groups, both current and future. Therefore, the aesthetic, historic, scientific, religious, symbolic, educational, economic, and ecological values all need to be considered when assessing the values of cultural heritage (Agnew 1997; Klamer 2014). World Heritage Listing does not only raise the economic value of sites and monuments, but adds a layer of legal protection to what essentially constitute not only a cultural resource but also the country's living memory (Keshk 2011a).

This protection is clearly needed. Rural sites are part of the landscape, with fields surrounding and overlaying them, while urban sites found during the construction of new buildings are built upon, sealing them for future generations (Huisman 2012); only rarely are they important enough to prevent modern construction. When archaeology is discovered during the course of constructions it is often destroyed, surreptitiously sold to dealers, or just built over rather than notify the proper archaeological authorities (Waxman 2008: 125). Most developed countries have legislation requiring developers to fund any such necessary work before any new developments destroy any archaeology present. This usually takes the form of an archaeological assessment, and any necessary excavations conducted and paid for by the developers (Stapp and Longenecker 2009). Although legislation exists in Egypt to compel developers to permit archaeological investigations prior to building activities in registered archaeological areas, this is often ignored, or when investigations are conducted they consist of test-pits dug by unskilled labours with action only taken if architectural remains or a statue is discovered. The regulations that do exist need to be not only rigorously enforced before significant damage has been done, but significantly expanded and improved upon to take in the whole country (Tassie and Hassan 2009).

Once the use and non-use values of a site have been assessed, some sites may be turned over to the local population. The fact that most traditional building techniques do not use deep foundations means that the archaeology may remain undamaged, and accessible to future generations. However, more ambitious underground construction (i.e. car parks) and anything with more ambitious foundations – especially in a city – is less forgiving to the archaeology. It is of course undeniable that more land is needed for housing and agriculture, but it is also necessary to balance the needs of the past and present, and to establish better relations between governmental departments and the general public. When archaeology is discovered during the course of constructions it is often destroyed, surreptitiously sold to dealers, or just built over rather than notify the proper archaeological authorities, for they think their land will be confiscated with insufficient compensation (Waxman 2008: 125). Both better education to make people aware of the worth of their cultural heritage and greater and fairer rewards are needed to rectify this situation.

Cultural heritage management needs to be flexible; it needs to be inclusive of all the stakeholders. 'The key to making a change to site management in Egypt is to shift the focus in conservation and site management from the site itself to the local community and to society at large' (Fushiya and De Trafford 2009: 49)'. This sentiment, is echoed by Fushiya (2010) who highlights the fact that the local communities have often been given limited access to knowledge, and limited opportunities to become involved in the archaeology, with the modern living standards of everyday Egyptians often restricted in order to protect national heritage, leading to discord and resentment. This is a failure on the part of cultural heritage planners, for the failure to recognise the relationship between archaeological sites and modern society will condemn both and serve none. The past cannot be hermetically sealed in the present, and the needs of the modern population cannot be ignored (Agnew 1997). Amongst the various factors that have negatively impacted on cultural heritage in Egypt is the failure to recognise the relationship between the archaeological sites and the present society — both the local community and other stakeholders. Local involvement is an essential element of successful archaeological site management. Recognition of the role of the local community could make a great contribution in improving the present critical situation of many archaeological sites worldwide (Pyburn 2014; Schadla-Hall and Larkin 2014).

This issue is particularly visible in Egypt, owing to the way in which the missions tend to excavate. Academic archaeology relies upon seasons of several months of fieldwork per year, reflecting funding patterns and teaching obligations, whereas contract archaeology is only undertaken in response to a specific threat to cultural heritage, and continues until the site has been investigated and recorded. Contract archaeology at present only accounts for a very small percentage of the archaeological work undertaken in Egypt. Research sites are therefore often worked at for only a fraction of the year, and are reliant upon the good will of the local community for their preservation or protection in the archaeologists' absence. It therefore behoves the archaeologist to always involve local groups in their work, to communicate the results of their endeavours, so that they are part of the process of exploration and learning. The combined experience of the local population and the archaeologists, consisting of a thorough knowledge of local circumstances, the region, its landscape, and its history, is important in the process of understanding the history of a site. Not only is this a pragmatic function, but is also a socially requisite one, given that local groups may have genetic, social and cultural connections with the site, and are also bound to inherit its custodianship once archaeological works there have ceased. As Wendrich (2006: 186) states:

> "Stimulating the interest of the local population in nearby antiquities and creating a heightened awareness of their cultural value will help to preserve the ancient remains. Direct economic interest of the local community in the local antiquities will strengthen this effect considerably. For archaeologists, important issues are at stake. To have the support of the local population in the protection of an archaeological site is as important as legal and government protection. Archaeologists can have an important role in stimulating such support by aiding the development of sustainable tourism. They can provide the knowledge to make an unglamorous archaeological site into a fascinating narrative… By involving the local population directly in the excavation and adding a training component and site management plan to the archaeological work, an unglamorous mud-brick site might change from a useless section of off-limits land at the fringe of a community to a source of pride and potential income."

Lower Egyptian Cultural Heritage in Times of Conflict and Crisis

Lower Egypt's cultural plight since the revolution needs some further elucidation. Magazines were targeted from 2011 onwards – at sites including Tell el-Fara'in, Tell el-Dab'a, Qantir, Saqqara and Mit Rahina (2013) – in the widespread belief that they contained gold and similar valuables, when they found that they only contained pottery and bones they smashed the seemingly valueless remains in anger and (Al Rawi 2011; Ikram 2013). Between 2011 and 2012 sites in the Memphite necropolis (Abu Roash, Abusir, Dahshur, Giza, Saqqara, Saqqara South and Tarkhan) and the Delta (tomb of Kenamun in Tell el-Maskhuta, Tell el-Basta, Tell Tenis, Tell el-Yahudiya, Sa el-Hagar [Sais], San el-Hagar [Tanis] and Zoulien) were also looted or attacked (Al Rawi 2011; Hanna 2013b; Looting Database Archives). Throughout 2014 and into 2015 a sharp increase has been recorded in illegal excavations being undertaken by citizens living in the slums of the province of Alexandria (Egypt Independent 2015a).

> 'The reasons behind this large-scale loss of antiquities are poverty, greed, and ignorance. The dramatically escalating cost of living in Egypt, the increasing number of available and desirable commodities ranging from foodstuffs to electronics, the lack of jobs, and the poor pay, especially in the public sector, all contribute to people's attempts to supplement their income whenever possible' (Ikram 2014).

Collector demand for illicit antiquities, along with the illicit antiquities dealers and the middlemen who hire local villagers to dig for them must bear the greater responsibility, as the middlemen and dealers are the ones who make the greatest profits (Brodie 2011; 2014; Brodie *et al.* 2000; 2006; MacKenzie 2011).

Land grabbing incidents are also increasingly common. Notable examples include Al-Bordan in the west Delta, where residents from Al-Hamman bulldozed Graeco-Roman structures in order to construct summerhouses[2], and the site of Tarkhan, where much of the Early Dynastic and later tombs have been covered by a modern cemetery, two houses, and ploughed fields (Ikram 2014). An illegal landfill has existed on the archaeological land of north Abusir since 2007. This land is owned by the MA and is registered on the UNESCO World Heritage List as part of the archaeological land of the Memphite Necropolis.

[2] Contractor Yasser Khalil and truck driver Mohamed Abdel-Sattar were accused of damaging the archaeological site, but they denied all charges (El-Aref 2013a). The armed gang returned in early 2014, but were successfully repelled.

Unfortunately, the site is currently in such a bad state that fumes from burning garbage reach to the nearby archaeological monuments (ECHO Website). The area around the pyramid and other monuments at Abu Roash has also become a dumping ground (Fushiya and De Trafford 2009), as have the barracks of Mohammed Ali built to protect the Citadel (Schwartzstein 2014).

Another such site used as dumping ground was the Masalla section of Al Matariya district, which is the location of ancient Iwn or Heliopolis and contains one of Egypt's few remaining freestanding obelisks. The area behind the Dynasty XII obelisk of King Senusert I had been turned into a garbage dump picked over by sheep and goats, and a nearby spot where remains of a Middle Kingdom temple lies was used as a swimming pool for dogs. Subterranean water had leaked into the archaeological pit where the remains lie, filling it with water, and dogs are taking a plunge to escape the summer heat. If obdurate, archaeological remains are often destroyed to make way for land grabs. In June 2013 the Gate of Ramsis IX of the Ramesside Temple of Ra in Arab al-Hisn in ancient Heliopolis was set ablaze. This resulted in severe damage to the inscriptions. The people responsible for this act of arson wanted to seize the land on which the ancient temple lies. This act seems to have been part of a systematic campaign in the region, for there had been previous attempts to break another gate at the site, that of Ramses II, as well as attempts to burn the site. This group had also built small huts and converted part of the area into a parking lot and car wash area. However, Monica Hanna led a campaign later that June to clean up the ancient site of garbage that had been dumped there, and in the same month launched a campaign called *Egypt's Heritage Task Force*, which is a crisis management team to keep an eye on ancient sites during times of civil unrest. It should be noted that local residents are not solely responsible for this form of damage. Clerical and administrative error led the Ministry of Endowments to bulldoze archaeologically valuable remains near Souq al-Khamis while laying the foundations of a large wall to surround the market. This destruction and also further encroachments in the area was only stopped after much damage had been done (El-Aref 2012; 2013a; Hanna 2013c).

There is not a case in Egypt that would not benefit from greater and better efforts to educate and engage communities in the importance of their local heritage. The case of Dahshur is a good example. This UNESCO World Heritage site is home to two of Egypt's oldest and best-preserved pyramids, surrounded by very economically deprived areas, exacerbated by poor farmland quality[3], population increases and burgeoning poverty and unemployment. Between 2006 and 2007, Fekri Hassan undertook the development of a site management project for Dahshur and the Memphite Pyramid Fields (and Dahshur lake), which in 2009 became the UN project *Mobilization of the Dahshur World Heritage Site for Community Development.* The project spanned five UN agencies and five governmental institutions, to include the UN World Tourism Organization, UNESCO, the Supreme Council of Antiquities and the Egyptian Environmental Affairs Agency, among others (Galla 2012; Hassan 2013). Local residents were surveyed in order to assess their knowledge and understanding of the archaeological remains: the fact that 41% of all woman and 27.3% of all men were unaware of the remains' cultural significance (Hassan 2013) testifies to the lack of cultural involvement that appears to be endemic in Egyptian society. The project aimed mainly at preserving the cultural heritage of Dahshur, enhancing local economic development and creative industries, raising local awareness of the importance of cultural heritage, protecting the area's natural resources and promoting the development of sustainable tourism in the area. Governmental authorities and the local community could engage with the UN on an environmental and cultural programme. The programme also targeted Dahshur Lake as a part of the development project, with many studies being undertaken and a request submitted for the Environment Ministry to define it as a protected area.

Goals:

- Expand employment opportunities in UNESCO World Heritage sites
  - Supporting local production of arts
  - Promoting the development of creative industries and small tourism businesses
  - Particular focus on women and youths
- Build capacity for cultural management and protection of World Heritage cultural assets;
- Promote public awareness of the social value of WH sites and natural resources
- Provide forums for cross-cultural exchanges.

Achievements:

- An integral tourist plan for Dahshur

[3] Climate change and the building of the Aswan High Dam have badly affected the quality of agricultural.

    - 50 million EGP allocated by tourism ministry for basic infrastructure
    - 4.4 million EGP to build a visitors centre.
    - A master plan of the area
- Quality environmental assessment and a protected area report.
    - Area declared as "environmentally managed"
    - Control of hunting and protection of biodiversity
- More than 3,000 people received training in a variety of potential tourist industries
    - Basic hospitality, horse cart driving, tourist guides
    - Trained artesans have produced prototypes of products to be widely marketed
    - More than 300 people received specific training on entrepreneurship.
- 294 loans of <3,000 EGP were disbursed through the BEST foundation, 25 % of them to women.

Galla (2012)

This project – which continued until 2013 – was severely impacted upon by the aftermath of the 2011 revolution. Minor looting escalated to an orchestrated land grab by an armed gang accompanied by villagers from Ezbet Dahshur and some local residents, hastily erecting 30+ white cement block tombs in front of the Black Pyramid of Amenemhat III (a Dynasty XII necropolis, under investigation by a German mission). This initial group were quickly joined by people from nearby villages not wanting to miss out on the action. The intruders, in total disregard of the legal processes, refused to move and expanded their operations to hundreds of new tombs that were then sold to villagers who used them to loot whatever was beneath (Hanna 2013a: 24; Kingsley 2013). Appeals by archaeologists and UNESCO were unsuccessful. The response by local residents was heartening – dozens of Egyptian youths and Manshiyet Dahshur residents protested at the footstep of the Bent Pyramid, demanding that the authorities put an end to the looting and construction, holding placards with messages such as "God does not bless a nation that ruins its heritage," "Heritage is our past, present and future", and "Let's protect it with love and respect." These protests prompted the government to provide improved security at the site, and the land grab contractor was arrested. Guilty parties' pleas that they claimed 'empty' land owing to the reticence of the ministry in allocating new cemetery plots were dismissed; appropriate land had already been allocated, and has been handed over pending archaeological review (El-Aref 2013a). The MA has taken legal steps against the few remaining intruders, and is now collaborating with the Tourism and Antiquities Police to expel them by force in line with Law 117 and its 2010 amendments (El Aref 2014e). As of early 2015 the illegal modern cemetery was still in place; although it seems to have been abandon as vegetation is now reclaiming the land (see Fig. 3.2).

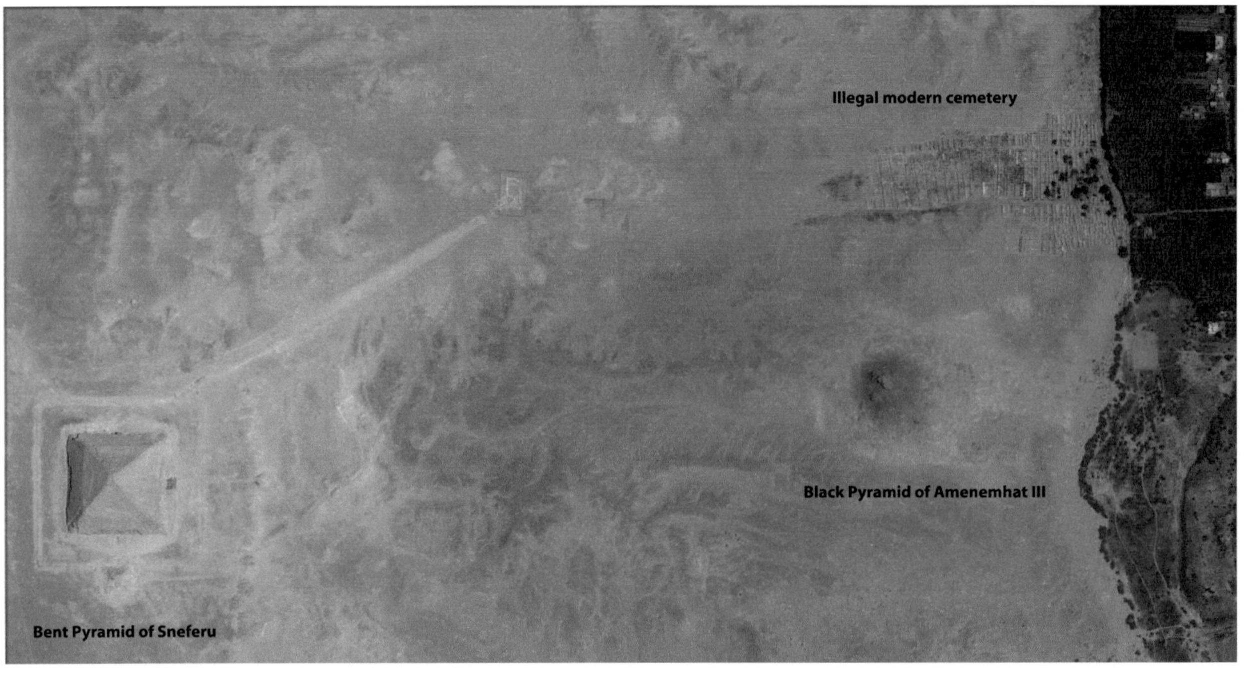

Figure 3.2: Google Earth image of the illegal cemetery/looting at Dahshur, January 2015 (Source: Google Earth).

After these encroachments, as part of the *Mobilization of the Dahshur World Heritage Site for Community Development* programme Fekri Hassan undertook the final part of the project. From April to May 2013, around 60 local villagers (from Manshiyet Dahshur, Ezbet Dahshur, Zaweiyet Dahshur, Manshiyet Kasseb, and Mazghuna) were trained in guiding, archaeology, ecology and cultural heritage management, and thus became qualified "heritage guardians", entitled to act as guides and teachers for local people, and to educate them about the importance of Dahshur. A further programme was devoted to enhancing the awareness of local youths of the significance and values of the heritage resources in their vicinity, and to encourage them to take part in protecting and conserving heritage at risk from looting, neglect and development (Hassan 2013: 68). In all, over 91 individuals attended these training sessions, to include a number of SCA/MA inspectors. Those with the highest overall marks were awarded the title "chief heritage guardians", prompting a sentiment of pride, achievement and – most important of all – involvement. This community archaeology project is one of the key means of engaging with communities that are presently excluded from the management of Egypt's cultural heritage (Hassan 2013).

THE HISTORIC URBAN CENTRES OF CAIRO AND ALEXANDRIA IN TIMES OF CONFLICT AND CRISIS

Land grabs were not solely a rural affair in the aftermath of the 2011 revolution. However, what was at threat was less archaeological and more architectural. Laws 178/1961 and 144/2006 were introduced to protect historically or architecturally valuable buildings (antiquities in general are protected by Law 117/1983); the buildings in question pertain to Egypt's 'Belle Époque', a catch-all term that describes the multiplicity of 19th to early 20th century architecture in the baroque, Roman-Byzantine, Ottoman, European, Art Déco and Art Nouveau styles, especially in Cairo and Alexandria. Theoretically any building over 100 years is regarded as a historic monument, even if it is not registered with the antiquities authorities, and thus cannot be damaged or dismantled without due process. Such buildings receive further protection from listing with the National Organisation for Urban Harmony (NOUH), established in 2006 to prohibit the demolition of buildings of distinguished architectural value, and to guarantee the protection of the country's eclectic architectural heritage. However, a lack of policing and the pressures of a swelling population with nowhere to live has led to extensive circumventing of these guidelines. The roof of a protected Art Déco building in Al-Sayeda Zeinab was destroyed, and this was used as evidence to show it was structurally unsound, and therefore suitable for demolition. The former villa of the world famous singer Umm Kulthum in Zamalek, as well as several distinguished villas in the Cairene suburbs of Heliopolis and Mohandessin – and in Alexandria – were also demolished under similar pretexts (El-Aref 2014a).

Since 2011 the destruction of these historic buildings has increased due to the lack of a strong central authority. Ikram (2013: 367) stats that:

> 'Many buildings in urban contexts have been hastily destroyed and new ones are quickly being put in their place. Although in time it is hoped that the due process of law will penalise their owners, the original monuments are lost forever, often with no documentation in the form of plans or photographs'

Quite aside from the loss to Egypt's cultural heritage, the constructions that replace these Belle Époque buildings are almost invariably hastily-constructed and badly – even dangerously – made: the use of cheap materials and untrained labour means that they regularly collapse (Guerin 2014; Maqbool 2013). The rate of deterioration and urban densification due to corruption in municipal government and the security apparatus combined with the power of the construction mafia is nowhere more apparent than in Alexandria. Thirty-six historic buildings have been struck from the heritage registry in recent years – a carte blanche to demolish them – and another 90 (to include Lawrence Durrell's villa) are pending court approval for destruction by developers. The city's iconic modernist building housing its municipality was torched and destroyed during the early days of the revolution (Cairo Observer 2014). In January 2012, news that the famous Art Déco Cicurel Villa had been removed from the protected heritage site list led to protests and sit-ins by members of the AHAC[4], along with other concerned groups and individuals, eventually resulting in the villa's status being reinstated. The group currently aim to prevent the demolition of Alexandria's Greek Club building (Keshk 2012c).

The rate of heritage destruction, the damage to modernist buildings by the 2011 events, and the proliferation of badly made modern replacements means that Alexandria's decline is irreversible (Cairo

[4] Architectural Heritage of Alexandria Committee (an affiliate of the NOUH).

Observer 2014). Internet and social media campaigns (i.e. *Walls of Alexandria* website) have raised awareness of Alexandria's vanishing heritage, but have so far failed to stem the tide. There is a sense that "...the whole building environment is deteriorating, because there is just no vision" (Aboelkhier of the *Save Alexandria* campaign, in Schwartzstein 2014), and that too little is being done, and too late. Plans have now been drawn up by Alaa al-Habashi and Mohamed Awad to restore the Villa Aghion that was partially (and illegally) destroyed in 2009 (Keshk 2012c).

Figure 3.3: The partially restored house of Gamal al-Din al Dhahbi in Old Cairo.

While Alexandria has achieved the most media coverage, Cairo has also been affected by this growing trend, notably the ancient district of al-Darb al-Ahmer where numerous buildings have been destroyed dating from the sixteenth to the nineteenth centuries. Other examples include the Ottoman house of Matsh-Merza in Boulaq that was illegally damaged by a contractor in 2013. He was arrested by the police, but – presumably emboldened by the paltry fine of LE500 that was imposed – returned immediately to the house and completed the work of destruction, unhindered by the police, the SCA or even the MA (El-Aref 2013a). Manshiet Nasser – now one of Cairo's largest slums – contains countless elegant fifteenth-century tombs and mausoleums that are now blackened by the burning of refuse. The fact that Old Cairo (which contains over 600 historical sites of interest) is on UNESCO's world heritage list has not helped their survival, as the entire area currently faces destruction from an ever-growing population (Ahram Online 2012), looters eager to exploit the lack of security, and the massive increase in illegal construction (notably in Manshiet Nasser). Ex-Minister of Antiquities Mohamed Ibrahim issued one-hundred-and-ninety-two demolition orders, but administrative zeal has not been matched by implementation on the ground. A mixture of lethargy, administrative entanglement and corruption has led to utter disregard for both the law, and the historic buildings the laws are designed to protect. It is probable that the most positive effects will be brought about by public campaigns such as *Save Cairo* (run by Omneya Abdel Barr), *Save Alexandria* and *Save Mansura*, reinvigorating conservation of old buildings and rally private donors to buy and renovate old buildings and sites before they are destroyed. These groups have submitted the following petition:

"We will use all legal and judicial means – and if we have to use our bodies to shield Egypt's material heritage and to protect its history we will use them" to the public prosecutor to take on their case against the heads of Cairo's historic districts and the Cairo Governorate (Davis 2014).

Figure 3.4: Bab el-Nasr, the northern gate of the old city walls of Cairo, being restored in 2003.

Al-Muizz Street and its monumental edifices suffered from negligence, theft and encroachment by motor vehicles and temporary roadside cafes following the events of 2011 (Keshk 2011b). Matters came to a head in 2013 when an Ottoman gate was destroyed, prompted general outcry and an enquiry. Possibly as a result of this, the MA (in collaboration with Cairo Governorate and the Ministry of Tourism) began a three-phase restoration project in late 2013, aiming to return the street to its pre-revolution condition (including rubbish clearance, replacement of information panels and damaged granite tiles, and the clearing of both encroachments and graffiti [El-Aref 2014b]).

This destruction of the built urbanscape occurs both within and outside the law, which is in itself tragically prone to changeability. The loss of the building is exacerbated by the loss of the archaeology that lay beneath it, and which also suffers from modern foundation construction. In particularly old sites such as Alexandria and Heliopolis, this results in the loss of remarkably rare and intact deep urban stratigraphies that could have informed modern and future archaeologists about the country's history. If physical heritage is destroyed, then memory of what once was is all that remains. Memory, however, is a notoriously fallacious and flexible tool, subject to revisionist narratives and strategic manipulation. If the last palpable, visible traces of a multiethnic and multireligious heritage are eradicated, future generations will be prevented from developing a rich, nuanced national and cultural identity, for once a culture is deracinated – and surrenders to modernity – it fades (Athanasiadis 2014).

It appears that there are few mobile items that are safe from the attention of looters. Architectural ornaments – from doorknobs to entire doors, ceilings and pulpits – are routinely ripped out and sold, usually overseas in markets such as Qatar and Abu Dhabi (Cairo Observer 2014), and it seems redundant to observe that this has also increased in prevalence since 2011. Important objects are often lost this way, such as the star-shaped bronze decoration bearing the name of Sultan Barquq from the entrance gate of the

Sultan Farag Ibn Barquq funerary complex (Cairo Observer 2014), and the furniture and fittings from the Mausoleum of Mohamed Sherif Pasha in Old Cairo (ECHO Website). The vast majority of crimes go unsolved, and few of the captured perpetrators are prosecuted. We will never know the full extent of these thefts, due to the lack of databasing, the lack of central organisation, the erratic nature of site management, and the flawed relationships that exist between these buildings and neighbouring communities.

Figure 3.5: The Barquq Complex (Al-Muizz Street) being restored in 2003.

Building damage may come from unexpected sources. A group of Copts known as Zabbaleen had provided a cheap, efficient and environmentally friendly refuse collection service in the area, feeding organic waste to their pigs and recycling almost everything else. With the culling of their pigs in the last years of Mubarak's reign – purportedly due to the threat of swine flu – they largely abandoned this job, resulting in proliferation of waste that threatened various heritage sites. This culling of pigs was compounded with the employment of Italian and Spanish multinational garbage companies being hired to clean Cairo's streets. A prominent example is the historic Mosque of Ibn Tulun, built in 876 AD, which has been extensively damaged by waste water around the external walls. Restoration work in 2002-4 had repaired some damage, but drainage water has subsequently affected the Imara House[5] behind the main *qibla* of the mosque. Another example is the Early Islamic site of Fustat (Ezbet Kheirallah), which was looted and encroached upon by armed gangs and vandals following the revolution. Although the encroachments were cleared, the house garden had by early 2014 become a dumping ground for local residents (El-Aref 2014c). Under El-Sisi this army of 70,000 Zabbaleen are now starting to return, although much damage has already been done. The pigs, which gobble up the organic waste, are now kept out of sight. The government is putting the Zabbaleen on the municipal payroll for the first time and ending the effort undertaken by Mubarak regime to contract rubbish collection services to foreign companies (El Wardany 2015).

[5] The Imara house – one of four that used to surround the mosque – is notable for its wooden halls and highly decorated ceilings (El-Aref 2013a).

Figure 3.6: The restored wakala of Bazabah in Old Cairo.

Protesters are asking the government to freeze all construction licences in Old Cairo for a year, remove illegal buildings and extra floors, and refuse to provide illegal buildings with drainage systems or electricity. They have asked the government to work in collaboration with civil society and local councils in order to protect Old Cairo as well as historical buildings all over the country. "The problem will not be solved unless the relationship between the government and its responsibility to protect these historical buildings and the desire of their owners to make their property a lucrative investment is fine-tuned," said Mohamed Abu Seada, head of the NOUH. The owners of historic buildings need to be given incentives to maintain them, possibly in the form of tax exemptions, ability to increases rental fees, or the provision of free maintenance. The government could also offer owners land in return for expropriating their property. This would greatly facilitate the development of the NOUH's Architectural Heritage List. Over the last ten years, various legal loopholes have led to important buildings being removed from the NOUH list (El Aref 2014); amendments to Law 144 of 2006, and the unified construction law have now covered these loopholes. On 11th June 2012, a protocol agreement for a preservation and management project for Historic Cairo was reached between the NOUH and the UNESCO Cairo office, on behalf of the UNESCO World Heritage Centre. A project for the elaboration of a conservation/regeneration plan for Historic Cairo, called Urban Regeneration for Historic Cairo (URHC), was initiated by the UNESCO World Heritage Centre, dedicated to the safeguarding of cultural heritage and aiming to define more appropriate and efficient site management systems. A new authority was established in late 2014, consisting of representatives from the Antiquities, Tourism, Endowments and Construction ministries, as well as the Cairo governorate, with the aim of regenerating Historic Cairo by 2022. The new authority aims to remove all encroachments, pave all the streets, transform certain governmental buildings into galleries, hotels and cultural centres, and to blend recent architecture to match adjacent historic monuments (Abdelhafez, 2014; El-Aref 2014f). These initiatives will be strengthened by the forming of a ministerial committee to create a joint fund to complete stalled renovation projects in many mosques and other Islamic sites, as well as tackle the bureaucracy and obstacles that inhibit the completion of Islamic heritage development projects (Mostafa 2015c). Other actions that could be taken include:

1) Creating an inventory of all historic buildings;

2) Preservation of those buildings that are deemed important, allowing controlled modern refurbishments of certain historic buildings, demolition – and land reuse – in extreme cases.

3) Finding modern roles for underused historic buildings, to serve local needs. Demolition of a Belle Époque house and replacing it with a short-lived tenement block is not sustainable. Many of these historic buildings, if refurbished, would make excellent housing for Egypt's urbanites.

Upper and Middle Egyptian Cultural Heritage in Times of Conflict and Crisis

Upper and Middle Egypt fared just as badly – if not worse – than Lower Egypt. In the first sixteen months after the revolution numerous sites and magazine were attacked, notably including Abydos, where 200+ pits <8 m deep were dug, mummies were ripped to pieces and numerous tombs were ransacked (Hessler 2013). Smaller scale looting occurred all over the West Bank at Birket Habu and Kom es-Samak, and at Esna where people were caught digging beneath their houses near the Temple of Khnum. Hierakonpolis was also attacked. The atmosphere of opportunistic theft resulted in various ludicrous attempts on oversized sculptures, including the 6-metre-tall sculpture of Ramses the Great in a southern Aswan granite quarry, and the Merenptah stele in Gebel el-Silsila. In Middle Egypt, looting was noted at Tuna el-Gebel, the open-air museum at Ashmunein, Tell el-Hibeh and Abusir el-Maleq; security personnel managed to repel a similar attack on the magazine at Bahnasa. The Faiyum saw attacks on el-Lahun and Gerza, and an unsuccessful attack on the magazine at Kom Aushim. Hundreds of <5 m deep pits were dug into the non-elite cemeteries at Gurob, and the Harem Palace. Looting was also reported in the Western Desert oases of Bahariya, Dakhla and Kharga (ECHO Website; Hiel 2013a; Looting Database Archives; Tresilian 2014; Al Rawi 2011).

Figure 3.7: Modern encroachment on the Pyramid of Amenemhat I at Lisht.

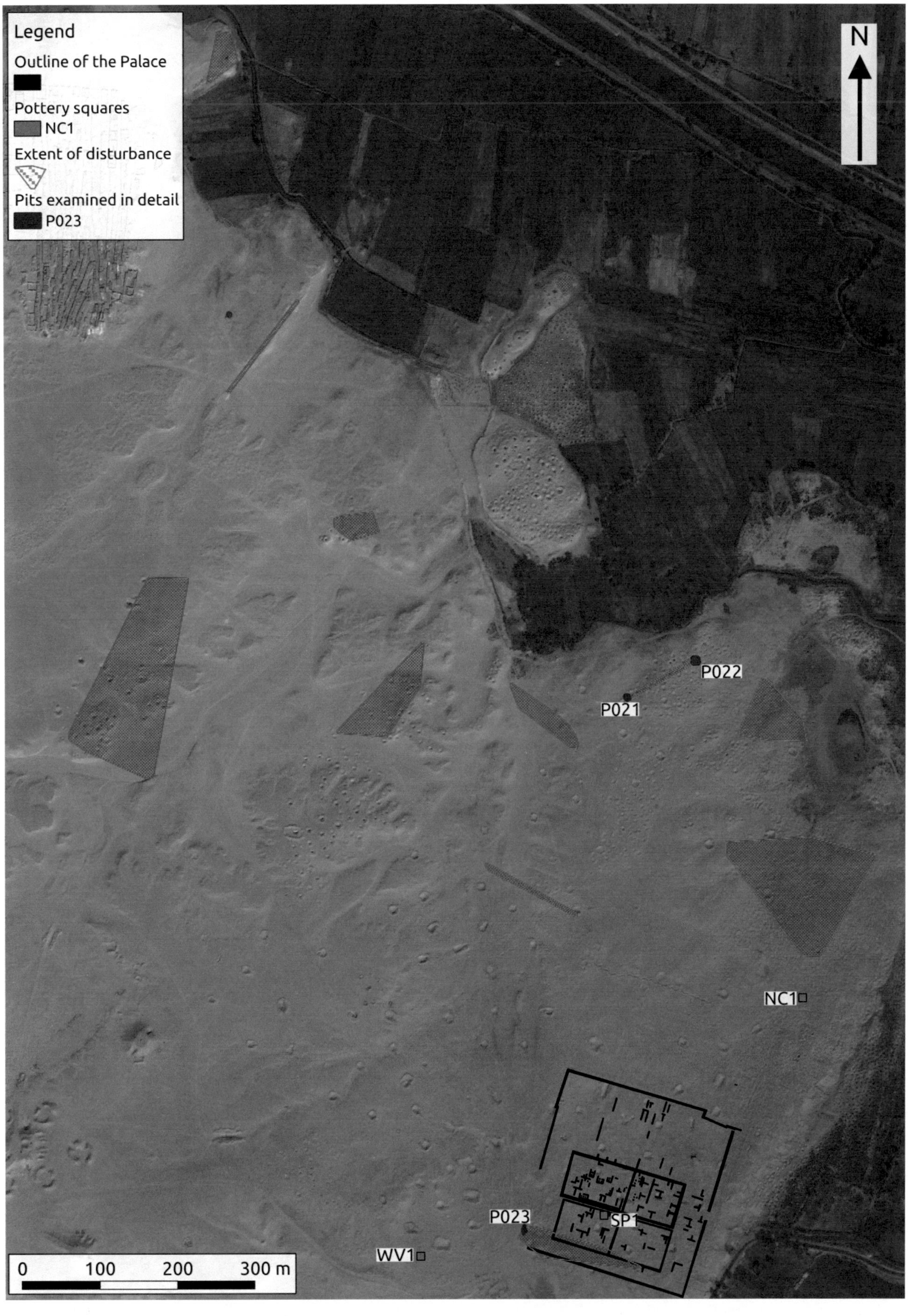

Figure 3.8: The extent of the looting activities at Gurob (photograph Ian Shaw).

Figure 3.9: The inspection of a looter pit into a non-elite shaft tombs at Gurob (photograph Ian Shaw).

Figure 3.10: A modern cemetery being built next to the ancient cemetery at Gerzeh.

There was a commensurate boom in the looting and sale of small portable objects, notably in Beni Suef – and particularly in Al-Wasta – where Hanna and Ikram (2013) note that trade occurs '…in most of the public cafés…all one has to do is to sit in a café, look like a stranger and wait to be approached by someone who has artefacts for sale'. Much of this material probably comes from Al-Hibeh and Abu Sir Al-Maleq, and includes sarcophagi and coffins, *ushabtis*, amulets, glazed ceramics, pottery vessels, bead necklaces, bead bracelets, and chunks of inscription hacked out of limestone walls. While larger objects are available, these are less economically viable owing to the difficulty in exporting them undetected; there is therefore a premium on smaller pieces (Hanna and Ikram 2013). 'Dealers of various levels are clearly coming to buy objects here, and then taking them to their stores or distribution points in both rural and urban locations' (Hanna and Ikram 2013).

The loss of archaeology at Tell el-Hibeh (ancient Teudjoi/Ankyronpolis) is particularly unfortunate. Looted by an antiquities dealer in 1995, the site, which covers about two square kilometres still offered an unparalleled opportunity to investigate the character, layout and development of a provincial town (Redmount 2014). The site includes cemeteries and the ruins of a walled ancient provincial town with a limestone temple, industrial facilities, houses, a possible fort and governor's residence. The remains date from the Third Intermediate Period, with further elements from the Late, Graeco-Roman, Coptic and early Islamic periods (Redmount 2012; 2014). Since early 2011 its potential to provide a better understanding of the TIP – notoriously one of the most complex and confusing periods in Egyptian history – has been reduced to a pockmarked moonscape of shattered mummies, smashed sarcophagi, broken pottery and jumbled mud-brick. Clearly significant structures that were previously unknown are now exposed. The site has not only been looted – it has been actively destroyed, with looters deliberately defacing and demolishing unsaleable objects with a startling level of violence. The organiser – a heavily armed career criminal who was later killed by the security forces in late 2012 – appears to have inspired further efforts, as looting has not ceased at the site, but it is not being undertaken with such ferocity and pace. The director of the American mission at the site has started a *Facebook* page[6] entitled Save El Hibeh Egypt, in order to raise awareness to the plight of the site (Cecca and McLerran 2013; Redmount 2014), while Nadia Ashour – general director for antiquities in the region – has mounted a campaign to visit local villages, where they spread awareness with the elders, who then pass on the genuine value of preserving cultural heritage to other people in the village. Redmount (2014) is optimistic that it may yet prove possible to salvage some archaeological data.

Figure 3.11: Extent of looting activities at Tell el-Hibeh (Source: Google Earth).

[6] https://www.facebook.com/groups/337119989673652/

Figure 3.12: The aftermath of the looting activities at Tell el-Hibeh (photography: Carol Redmount).

The archaeological site of Abusir el-Maleq lies 10 km south of Meidum. It covers 500 acres of land and was inhabited from at least 3,250 BC until about AD 700. Unfortunately, its importance has not saved it:

> 'Once gently undulating sand, the site is now a pock-marked lunar landscape with dense scatters of mummy wrappings pulled off bodies, and huge piles of bones. Wrapped limbs and heads of people who were buried here more than 2,000 years ago now lie dismembered and scattered about the site. Obviously, several artefacts have been recovered from here; the pillagers hide their loot on-site in convenient tombs and covered by desiccated reeds and maize stalks'. (Hanna and Ikram 2013).

Looters appear to come from every walk of life, both local diggers and organised gangs from elsewhere. Regardless of their origin, however, the destructive effect they are having on their own heritage is appalling, given that the site has never been fully mapped, explored and recorded. The site's potential may only now be realised through salvage archaeology, which must be undertaken with alacrity before we lose all the evidence of Egypt's rich past in this area (Hanna and Ikram 2013). A similar plaint should be made for Atfih, where the sacred cow necropolis and surrounding area (to a radius of 1 km) has been cratered by looting, while walls and chapels (and their contents) have been smashed beyond recognition. Cultivation is also creeping nearer the site from the west. Antinoupolis (aka. Sheikh 'Ibada) located north of Mallawi, was built by the Emperor Hadrian in AD 130 to commemorate his beloved Antinous. There are also New Kingdom and Coptic remains at the site. The southern sector of Antinoupolis was dominated by a famous hippodrome, paralleled only by the Circus Maximus in Rome. Since 2011, this site has also suffered looting, removal of architectural blocks, cratering and destruction.

The national thirst for land means that illegal encroachment is also a problem. Attempts at Abydos and Hierakonpolis have been rebuffed, but the village of Deir el-Ballas has become a city and covered most of the archaeological site, destroying the workmen's village, many of the houses, and the façade of the South Palace (presumably looking for treasure) and collapsed a big part of the facade. Local SCA inspectors are hoping to persuade the governor to build a wall around what remains (Ikram 2014). A similar issue exists at Atfih (Aphroditeopolis) and Antinoupolis, where new houses have been built where a famous triumphal arch, documented in *La Description de l'Egypte*, once stood (Hanna 2013a: 125). Modern tombs have been illegally constructed on the on the east side of the city and the north part of the hippodrome, while the city's enclosure wall and a Roman cemetery have also been bulldozed for agricultural purposes (Hanna 2013a: 125). Bulldozers were also used at Gebelein and Gerezia, while Nubian disenfranchisement combined with the depressed economy has led to looting at Aswan, Qasr Ibrahim (Egypt's Heritage Task Force) and – most recently, Gharb (West Aswan) where four New Kingdom tombs were discovered and claimed by a Nubian group in 2013. One of the tombs pertained to Wesir, (Mayor of Abu [Elephantine]) and his wife, Tuyu, while others appear to have been defaced, perhaps by the owner, reflecting social mores under Akhenaten. The MA finally gained control of the tombs in 2014. Further looting has also been observed at Qubbet el-Hawa (El-Aref 2013b).

Figure 3.13: The empty cases in the Mallawi National Museum after the theft and ransacking (Photograph Monica Hanna).

Modern trends have also dictated the terms of theft. Morsi's ousting in mid-2013 led to 'revenge' attacks – although principally motivated by poverty – on cultural property, including the Mallawi National Museum. This museum, which lies about 200 miles south of Cairo, was gutted mid-August 2013 by several gunmen: 1,050 objects out of a total of 1,089 were taken or destroyed; all that was left was broken pottery, shattered glass and charred remains of priceless wooden pieces. Although the majority of these artefacts have now been recovered, the conservation work on both the museum and artefacts continues (Hanna 2013a; 2013b). There has also been increased sectarian violence against over 50 historic churches and monasteries in Middle Egypt and the Faiyum. Sufi mosques and shrines (in many cases by Salafist extremists), were attacked in the Alexandria, Qalyubia, and North Sinai governorates. These destructive elements are by no means universal: the sight of Muslims and Christians holding hands to form a human chain around churches to stop them from being attacked was an encouraging one. At the time of writing, only 10% of the vandalised Coptic churches had been restored and yet more were being attacked (Fayek 2014; Hanna 2013a; 2013b; Hiel 2015), although UNESCO has undertaken to provide funds and expertise for their restoration. Ansina is a particularly urgent case in fact. Believed to be where the holy family stopped while fleeing Roman persecution, the wealth of the site manifested itself as an entire rock-cut settlement with churches, monasteries and caves Some of the local Muslim villagers believe the rock-cut monastic settlement houses gold treasures, and used dynamite (in the fourth century cave church of Saint Kolta) in order to locate it, but this only resulted in damaging a wall and creating a hole in the floor. The southern monastic complex that is built of mud-brick has been partially bulldozed and its western side has been taken by orchestrated land grabs. Iconography – notably crosses – has been hacked, with varying level of success, from the walls, while looters dig by day, looking for small items to sell (Hiel 2013b).

THE ART MARKET

Looters take advantage of the tolerance created by the selling off of old collections to supply a market with clandestinely looted remains, which account for perhaps 95% of the market (Neil Brodie cited in Smale 2014). That said, the secretive nature of the trade means that estimates are hard to cast accurately, although the conclusion that looting is both globally pervasive and commonplace is inescapable (Proulx 2013). Looting and trafficking from Egypt, Libya, Syria and Iraq has increased dramatically since 2011, and perhaps $3-6 billion worth of Egyptian antiquities have illegally left the country in that time. Official import figures echo this trend, with $10.7 million worth of Egyptian archaeological, historical and ethnographic goods entering the US in 2013, up 105.5% on 2012. These figures do not include undocumented, smuggled objects (Shaw 2014a). Control is near impossible. There are 7-10 illicit excavations per day, and dozens of small, unsecured ports, various land borders and various airports that enable the objects to be removed to brokering houses in Switzerland and elsewhere. The objects are then given a false provenance and offered for sale in London, New York, Geneva or Paris (the major centres of antiquities consumers), or leave for private collectors in Eastern Europe, the Gulf states of Qatar or Abu Dhabi and the Far East (Hanna 2013a; Ikram and Hanna 2013; Shaw 2014b). Egyptian antiquities provably looted since 2011 are already appearing on the public markets in the West, and also most definitely the private ones as well (Hardy 2013; 2015b). Wealthy collectors fuel this market, and can build museum-quality collections of mostly illegal antiquities with seemingly perfect provenance. Although several countries already have stringent heritage laws, a tightening of these laws so that documented provenance for any object entering or leaving the country are required along with dealers being required to show a valid export permit from the source of the piece's origins when entering a country (Hammerstein 2014; Smale 2014).

While looters are rightly condemned for their actions, most are in fact barely able to survive and are driven to looting by circumstance. They sustain themselves on a steady trickle of small finds (coins, jewellery, vases, figurines etc.) and only rarely find pieces that are deemed worthy of being exported through middlemen to the international market at hugely inflated prices (Hardy 2015a; Thompson 2014). Particularly fine pieces may also be kept for many years by these dealers in illicit antiquities to obscure the date of their acquisition and allow them time to fabricate a false provenance. The collectors are of course far more culpable in creating a demand for these items. The illicit trade in cultural objects can be harmful in several respects, but 'is often justified by destination museums, collectors, and academics on the grounds that it rescues "art" or "knowledge" for the public benefit. In consequence, the trade enjoys considerable support from wealthy individual and institutional collectors, who are reluctant for the trade to be investigated too closely and who often will not support or adopt policies or practices aimed at impeding it' (Brodie 2011: 411). In the same spirit as 'blood diamonds', the chain of ownership must be demonstrated to be flawless, and not dependent upon the economics of modern desperation. Being shown the damage done to archaeological sites through searching for ancient coins for example, may sway their consciences of some (Elkins 2014), or collectors could be encouraged to fund and participate in sanctioned archaeological excavations as a means of channelling their love for ancient artefacts. Targeted regulatory changes could be made to decrease the financial incentives that motivate some collectors. In the U.S.A. the Internal Revenue Service should refuse to allow tax deductions for charitable donations of antiquities without documentation of legal export, on the grounds that these antiquities are most likely looted or stolen (Thompson 2014). The public must also demand due diligence from publically funded institutions like museums. There needs to be more and better research, more efficient policies and greater coverage, that recognises that antiquities trafficking is not just a matter of preservation of cultural heritage, but one of economics and even security, given the use of illicit antiquities sales to fund extremist and radical ideologies (Davis and Bowman 2014).

Entre ports are the gateways for the trade, which must be tackled there. There must be greater use of the ICOM Red List, which highlights genres of at-risk objects rather than individual items, and gives guidelines concerning how to deal with suspected antiquities trafficking (Keshk 2012a; Tresilian 2014). One would assume that auction house staff already possess the knowledge to differentiate between established old collections and recently excavated illicit material. Ebay has already reneged on its 2013 promise to not sell stolen Egyptian antiquities (Trew 2014), although most of the materials offered are in fact fakes. Out of the three large auction houses – Christies, Sotheby's and Bonhams – only the former is showing any signs of increased vigilance and responsibility regarding items of questionable provenance (Mostafa 2014), instead placing the onus on the MA. A dedicated repatriation team tracks eBay listings and the catalogues of large auction houses on a daily basis. At the time of writing, eBay is indifferent to documentation and provenance concerns, and so leaves itself open to abuse by – and, indeed, is passively supporting – dealers in looted antiquities. International laws must be amended to land the responsibility for repatriation of each looted object on the auction house (or site), rather than the MA or the Egyptian government. If eBay and other e-auctions such as CataWiki were forced to cover the costs of repatriating the objects to the source countries and running the repatriation units, the financial threat would make them much more vigilant.

Information exchange and greater transparency between the MA, museums, antiquities dealers and Egyptologists is of the utmost importance in combating the illicit trade in antiquities and defining what is and is not legal. Many of the stolen and looted artefacts are not put on the Art Loss Register due either to those responsible for the objects not wanting to admit what they have lost, or have not recorded what they have lost (Richards and Summerscale 2014).

A NEW HOPE

It would be easy to become demoralised at this seemingly endless reiteration of theft, looting, land-grab, illegal building, corruption and destruction of cultural property, yet among the chaos there are heartening indications of an increasingly prominent group who are dedicated to the preservation of Egypt's cultural heritage. Following Mubarak's overthrow, protesters in Cairo grouped together to protect the Egyptian Museum from looting after an initial break-in on the 28th January 2011; one of the strongest images to emerge from the Egyptian revolution is of a group of protesters encircling the museum to protect it from would-be looters. Similar crowds surrounded and protected the Bibliotheca Alexandrina, the site of San el-Hagar (Tanis) and the temples of Karnak in Luxor. Vigilante groups patrolled the sites of Luxor's West Bank and apprehended robbers or prospective thieves (Ikram 2013: 370), while there also been various street-cleaning and refuse-collecting campaigns designed to protect Egypt's cultural heritage (Hanna 2013c).

Social media is perhaps the peoples' greatest asset in the battle to save Egypt's cultural heritage. Spreading news of nefarious acts results in a network of opinion makers, community leaders, and protesters to concerned citizens, thus forcing change in site and heritage protection policy. It has also led to the most vital of dialogues: that between archaeologists and the general public (Shaw 2013; Varner 2014). While there is enormous pressure on archaeologists to publish academically (for this is what gains them credibility and jobs), it is vital that academics not overlook the potential for engagement in non-professional media, for those that engage in it are literally potential allies against a common foe (i.e. the *Saving Antiquities for Everyone* (SAFE) website). In recent years the ECHO website and *Facebook* page have been joined by many new sites, blogs and Twitter accounts, some created by young Egyptian archaeologists, others by established Egyptologists and yet others by concerned citizens frustrated with the government's failure to prevent the destruction of their heritage (Gill 2014, and this volume). Monica Hanna (*Egypt's Heritage Task Force*), Yasmin El-Dorghamy (*Stop the Heritage Drain*) and Carol Redmount (*Save El Hibeh Egypt*) have all come to prominence this way, as have their messages (Durham 2013; Fabian 2014; Redmount 2014). El-Dorghamy is also the editor of *Rawi Magazine* (launched in 2008), a glossy and informative publication about Egyptian history and heritage that has found its way to national newsstands and the international community (Keshk 2012b). Other cultural heritage protection groups include *Treasures of Egypt at Risk*, the *Front for Saving Egyptian Antiquities*, *Megawra Built Environment*, *Save al-Muizz Street*, and the *Heliopolis Heritage Initiative* (Keshk

2012b), some of which '…took part in the writing of the new Egyptian constitution and presented a re-draft of the articles to ensure better protection for Egyptian heritage in the future' (Hanna 2013b: 375).

Attempts to safeguard Egyptian heritage have extended overseas. Egypt has requested a bilateral Memorandum of Understanding (MoU) with the US, urging congress to adopt new rules that would empower Immigration and Customs Enforcement officials to seize looted Egyptian antiquities; currently Egypt is excluded from the list of countries from which customs may seize undocumented artefacts. As probably the biggest market, this import ban would create a ripple effect that would reduce market demand and thus the incentive to loot. An MoU with the United States would also serve to stimulate engagement among local communities and public educational programmes in Egypt, and to support important long-term foreign policy goals over a broad range of issues between the U.S.A. and Egypt. Yet even here there are obstacles. Numismatists have called for an exemption of coins from the proposed restrictions, arguing that coins were mass produced only from the Graeco-Roman period, were designed to be traded and were in such wide circulation that the country of origin (as opposed from minting) is not easy to define. It is true that metal detecting of coins is not the most pressing of problems in Egypt, and it does not contribute greatly to the more dramatic looting and destruction of sites and monuments. Yet archaeological associations are still important, and coins add to that context. The issue was debated by the Cultural Property Advisory Committee (CPAC) – headed by antiquities law expert Patty Gerstenblith – and will make recommendations to the State Department (Vergano 2014). The Egyptian antiquities minister simultaneously signed a public-private partnership agreement with the International Coalition to Protect Egyptian Antiquities (members include the Capitol Archaeological Institute at GWU, the Archaeological Institute of America, the American Schools of Oriental Research and the National Geographic Society), which support the emergency sanctions, and aim to provide heritage management training for Egyptians. Eight of the eleven presenters spoke in support of the MoU, a ninth speaker abstained and two opposed the inclusion of coins. The MoU is predicted to pass, and to be adopted in Spring 2015 (TNN 2014).

CONCLUSIONS

At the beginning of the January 25th Revolution a 'large number of non-Egyptian archaeologists and Egyptologists, including many who work in Egypt regularly... bravely voiced their support for the protests while expressing their concern for the well-being of friends and colleagues in the country' (Schadla-Hall *et al.* 2011: 1). In the various statements from scholars of ancient Egypt there was often a marked reluctance to condemn the vandalism at the Egyptian Museum, Cairo and other sites, and to couch criticism of the looting of various sites in the context of the international trade in illicit antiquities and the power of rich Western collectors. There seems to have been a sense that to highlight the vandalism and looting would harm the protestors cause. However, some people and groups did raise concern about the scientific stability of the objects in the Egyptian Museum, Cairo in view of the political 'chaos' occurring outside their institutional home (Carruthers 2015). As Schadla-Hall *et al.* (2011: 2) observe:

> 'The key question is whether, when faced with conflicts that threaten both human rights and heritage, archaeologists should respond as part of a community of heritage professionals, or as concerned humanitarians and therefore as individuals. To focus concern and resources on heritage in the midst of a violent conflict is an affront to human decency. However, for scholars to ignore heritage in these circumstances would be an abrogation of their (our) core ethical and professional responsibilities'.

Four years on from the revolution the situation is a lot clearer and the destruction of cultural heritage is no longer being rationalised, even by political pragmatists. Those culpable of committing crimes against cultural heritage are rightly being criticised and some are even being prosecuted. In these four years Egyptian heritage has come under serious pressure. The aftermath of the 2011 revolution was exacerbated by the lack of administrative continuity, government funding, and enforceable laws and regulations in the field of cultural heritage management. National and international efforts to reclaim antiquities, and the removal of illegal buildings, iconoclastic activity and illegal land grabs are doubtless worthy, but serve to show us just how vulnerable these resources are. New technology such as satellite surveillance of archaeological sites using imagery from DigitalGlobe and Google Earth is being utilised to identify hot spots. Identifying regions where looting occurs may help law enforcement and other officials to track looted artefacts before they turn up for sale. The satellite imagery allows the extent of damage at sites to be ascertained – not only to get a sense of numbers of looting pits, but also to track changes to a particular site over time. Locating the looting activity at various sites will help auction houses and traders scrutinise objects up for sale more closely. Since many objects are known to be from a particular region or era of history, activity in an archaeological site could raise flags before sales even happen (Boyle 2014; Moustafa 2014). At sites that have been severely affected by looting rescue archaeology projects need to be immediately implemented. It is imperative that the archaeology that remains at these sites is documented and saved before it is lost forever (Tresilian 2014). One such rescue project is currently being undertaken by a Polish team at the site of Gebelein (Ejsmond 2014), but this needs to be expanded to sites such as Abusir el-Maleq and Tell el-Hibeh, with a large team of security personnel provided to protect the archaeologists.

The Giza Plateau was once isolated from the modern metropolis, but is now surrounded on three sides by Cairo's encroaching urban sprawl. The controversial wall erected around the pyramids area, unpopular when erected by Hawass in 2008, is now looking like foresight and a sensible precaution. Similar walls were also erected at Abydos, Buto, and Malkata, and while they disfigure the landscape and only offer protection to the cultural properties within, they have cut down the amount of local looting and encroachment (Shaw 2014a). However, these walls are only a short- to medium-term solution, and more inclusive management strategies need to be sought in the long-term. One new strategy was undertaken at a minor step pyramid at Edfu , whereby a wall 1.2 m high and 0.4 m wide was built around the monument, with information boards provided in both Arabic and English. Breaks permitted passage through the area. Local people are thus informed about the site, which is delineated as an archaeological monument, without being barricaded in (Marouard 2013).

Figure 3.14: The wall around the Giza archaeological area.

Reactions must be replaced by preparations. Remedial actions will not replace the irreplaceable – the information and context from which remains were ripped, or that were destroyed by illegal building activity. First, rescue archaeology projects must be immediately implemented at recently looted sites, so that any remaining data can be salvaged and documented before it is lost forever (Tresilian 2014). Wider approaches must also be taken. To be able to effectively protect a country's tangible cultural heritage it is essential to know the amount of cultural property within a country, therefore large-scale surveys need to be conducted (Agnew 1997; Tassie and Hassan 2009). Proactive security measures and emergency strategies need to be embedded in cultural heritage management policies and legislation. The security vacuum should have been replaced by the military: if there is ever a repeat of 2011, policy must dictate that this be the case.

Archaeological sites and museums protection should accord with international standards, including risk management, and the provision of the necessary equipment, experts, and funding. The 12,000 security personnel entrusted with protecting Egypt's cultural heritage should be provided with appropriate training and know-how, and there must be a move to implement new building and development legislation incorporating more rigid protection of cultural heritage, and must include archaeological impact assessments. The implementation, revision, and introduction of new laws and legal measures should be in accordance with articles 47, 49, and 50 of the 2014 Egyptian constitution. New organisational structures need to be developed with closer integration of the governmental agencies in charge of cultural heritage. Three other actions that could be undertaken are:

- The creation of a full national register of sites and monuments for Egypt and registration of all objects in the museums and storage magazines (Tassie and Hassan 2009). Many of the museums and magazines do not have complete registers, and many of those that do exist are inadequate paper records. Therefore, it is a priority that digital databases be created nationwide.
- The hosting of a looting website by UNESCO or ICOM that provides detailed GIS data concerning looting status, and gives a list of stolen artefacts. The website should also be a hub for wider international and national legislation on cultural heritage protection. Relevant news items and publications should also be posted on the site, which should operate as a safeguard against further looting and illicit sales of objects thus derived (Wolfenberger 2014).
- Security devices including CCTV must be installed nationwide in vulnerable museums, magazines or sites. Motion sensors may also be appropriate. Electronic tagging of artefacts is in its infancy, but should be considered as more technology and funding becomes available. These tools have the potential to revolutionise the way that both sites and monuments, along with moveable cultural property are protected in the future.

Social alienation is a major cause of the sprawl of illegal building since 2011, as well as organised crime and loss of respect for security forces. It is apparent that Draconian sentences – while intimidating – do not work, and may serve to cause further social resentment. People's reluctance to report antiquities on their land has a great deal to do with the meagre compensation they are likely to receive; if people got a reasonable price for finding antiquities, they would have no need to sell them to middle men in the black market, thus losing them to the art world forever. Stubborn myths concerning the presence of gold and 'red mercury' (a substance that is supposed gives the person who consumes it dominion over all creatures and that local superstition holds is found in the throats of mummies) on archaeological sites must be dispelled as a matter of urgency, as they are a notable cause of site destruction. These folktales even require a local sheikh to expel *jinns* (evil spirits) from ancient tombs before they are looted (Mostafa 2015d). Person and community-led incentives are crucial in this period of political and cultural democratisation, particularly where there is little security or in isolated locations. Participatory planning and community archaeology have been practiced on a small-scale, but should be expanded across the whole country. Low security sites, or those in isolation, cannot rely upon constant control by authorities – their security must be self-sustaining through the local communities. Outreach efforts must be part of every project's proposal:

> 'they need to invite representatives of the communities, such as the *omdas*, school teachers, and state officials, to a tour of the site, explaining to them the importance their work holds not only for the welfare and identity of the communities themselves, but also of the nation as a whole' (Lazaridis and Helmy 2011).

Young Egyptian archaeologists and heritage managers are trying to raise awareness of the importance of cultural property and 'national pride rooted in the richness of Egypt's heritage amongst Egyptians who, prior to 2011, had given little thought to their past' (Ikram 2013: 371).

The high walls that separate some local communities from their own heritage environment are only a temporary measure, and inclusive strategies need to be developed. . At many sites that are not under excavation and so do not give employment to local workers, and where tourism does not have a direct impact on the local communities, there is no economic benefit to motivate the local people to protect these sites (El-Dorry 2011). The tourist industry gave ordinary Egyptians a stake in their heritage, not because of emotional or societal reasons but for economic reasons: providing a job for thousands of Egyptians (Reid

2002: 296). At present that safeguard no longer exists, and that is one of the main reasons heritage is in danger – no tourists, no foreign revenues – no jobs – no financial rewards emanating from heritage! It is essential to engage in coordinated discussions with the various groups of stakeholders. This is a key opportunity for professional archaeologists and heritage managers to create partnerships with local communities, so that both can be involved in decision making and tourism activities, and participate in training and public awareness so that they can help monitor dangers and propose solutions (Aas *et al.* 2005). The heritage tourism market in Egypt needs to expand its horizons, with the 'heritagization of the everyday past, the value of authenticity, branding heritage places, the spread of cultural routes, intersections between heritage and other forms of tourism, and the heritagization of non-traditional heritage spaces' (Timothy 2014: 30).

It is imperative to define the needs from an educational, touristic, intellectual, private and public point of view. This is also a chance to define new concepts in heritage value, identity and participation, from as early an age as possible. New intellectual, conceptual and applied engagements with cultural heritage values need to be explored; recognising cultural plurality on the basis of equity, and viewing heritage as the outcome of social processes and cultural dynamics that have shaped a sense of self and identity. The school system appears to have perpetuated cultural isolation from modern students' ancestors. Although some school classes cover Egypt's ancient history, the Mubarak regime effectively divorced archaeology from history, and there was limited emphasis on the importance or value of cultural heritage in defining cultural identity (Hanna 2013b; Keshk 2012d). Museums and visits to monuments provide some school context, but education is usually erratic or selective, emphasising the evil characteristics of previous invaders (i.e. the Hyksos or Romans), the glory of some pharaohs (those who built the awe inspiring stone structures found in Luxor and Giza), and almost nothing about the mud-brick remains found at the edge of many villages (Keshk 2012d) although these are in fact both fascinating in their own right, and the key to a greater understanding of ancient Egyptians (Wendrich 2006: 185). Egyptians are accustomed to believing that 'their cultural heritage belongs to the state and it is for the exclusive use of tourists and foreign archaeological missions' (Hanna 2013b: 375). It is thus an elite possession, and nothing to do with the ordinary people of Egypt; so the future chief stakeholders of Egypt's antiquities are those who are the least engaged with them. How can people be expected to appreciate and protect something they do not feel responsible for in the first place? Even signage was written only in English and French until relatively recently:

> 'Egyptology and related disciplines were born as Orientalist disciplines, with all the implications of colonial terminology. Egyptian-born specialists have always struggled to get into the field. Academic resources, which are still primarily written in foreign languages, are difficult to access' (Hanna 2013b: 375).

For years the signage at many sites was only in French and English, although this is gradually changing at places such as the Valley of the Kings and Saqqara, where Arabic is also used. In practical terms, the Egyptians have only had anything to do with their own cultural heritage for the last sixty years or so (Colla 2007: Reid 2002), even though Arabic scholars had been studying it for several hundred years previously (El Daly 2005). As Hanna (2013a: 23) observes:

> 'The value of Egyptian heritage lies in commemorating the country's past and defining its collective identity and cultural memory. With widespread looting and destruction, both culture and identity become diluted. People use spaces and objects both to define themselves and to teach new generations about the failures and successes of the past, all of which have formed the reality of their present'.

The voices of modern Egyptians must be heard in formulating heritage management and values, and to thus address their needs while also halting demolition, looting and encroachment. A campaign needs to be instigated to enhance public awareness of the meanings, values, and significance of cultural heritage and its role in development to all sectors of society, including policy makers. The MA has created a new cultural awareness department, which will target schools and universities, with printed material supporting a brief syllabus taught by professional archaeologists. Booklets on the history of every governorate in Egypt will also be published and taught in the relevant schools (El Aref 2014e), thus intellectually empowering the next generation of people to become aware of their cultural heritage, at both a national and local level. One might also suggest pamphlets handed out to people living near sites, to give a site history of the site and describe what archaeological activities have revealed.

Heritage (cultural) and ecological tourism has fallen by 95% since 2011[7]. Revenues fell from 3bn Egyptian pounds (£250m) in 2010 to a projected 125m (£10.5m) in 2014. The drop has left the MA – which derives most of its income from tourist revenues – struggling to pay the 44,000 staff on its books, let alone embark on grand projects of reform (Kingsley 2014b; 2014c). As such, only very few Egyptian run excavation projects are now funded by the state; the funding for excavation work has largely been diverted to pay for the construction of new museums, such as the Grand Egyptian Museum or the National Museum of Egyptian Civilization, and even this funding has stalled, requiring UNESCO's help (Keshk 2011a; Mostafa 2014b). At present the antiquities inspectors are usually assigned the task of supervising the work of foreign missions, registering newly discovered artefacts and securing antiquities storehouses. Even conservation projects, previously the focus of the MA's work, are being put on hold due to the slowdown in tourism (Ayyad 2015; Egyptian Independent 2015b; Keshk 2011a). All this has resulted in many of the MA's staff suffering 'from apathy with very few incentives to engage with antiquities as cultural heritage. Pressured by weak salaries and bad employment conditions, they have lost any cultural interest in the value of antiquities and hence have little incentive to develop research or raise public awareness' (Keshk 2011a). Therefore, more sustainable methods of growth need to be sought. In inhabited areas these should include Environmental Impact Assessments, including clauses stipulating that the developers pay for archaeological investigations prior to and during the development process (Stapp and Longenecker 2009). This would allow development to proceed whilst also ensuring that the archaeology was documented, and at the same time provide more jobs and money for SCA inspectors.

The manner in which Egyptology has traditionally been taught, combined with the colonial overtones of European involvement with studies of the Egyptian past, means that perhaps 95% of SCA inspectors are unaware of the mechanics of scientific excavation (Zahi Hawass cited in Keshk 2011a). Western methods and standards are widely published, and this now needs to be turned into Arabic, and widely disseminated throughout the field. Personal and business relationships must also be created, with more Egyptian personnel included in foreign missions and vice versa, greater use of fieldschools to teach modern archaeological practice (AREA 2013), and more exchange programmes between universities. This would be invaluable in temporally contextualising ancient studies, elevating technical skill levels and learning about new theoretical and scientific approaches (Lazaridis and Helmy 2011). The new wave of Egyptian archaeologists will thus end up being competent in archaeological field methodology, osteology, and conservation, and should have a great impact upon subsequent generations as well as making the MA more effective and efficient (Kingsley 2014c). Developer-funded projects could go a long way to alleviating many of the problems within the MA, and would create an atmosphere for its personnel to gain knowledge of modern archaeological techniques and the universities to teach them (possibly in collaboration with foreign institutions).

There must be a clear and consistent stand against looting by all heritage organisations and museums (Wolfenberger 2014), and greater cooperation between Egyptian security personnel, the tourism sector, local communities, ICOM, ICOMOS, ANCBS and UNESCO in order to protect cultural heritage, and address the problem of looting. Technological advances must be pioneered and shared, while security measures and community archaeology must be implemented in order to protect the sites, and, more importantly, show Egyptians that they have a vested interest in so doing. Social and economic systems must be reviewed, and the issue of illicit antiquities be addressed from the top down in order to purge the underlying reasons for the looting and destruction of cultural heritage. The installation of a stable government may support the regeneration of the tourist trade and help alleviate the economic burdens on Egyptian society, and in the process help to protect Egypt's world heritage.

References

Aas, C., Ladkin, A. & Fletcher, J. 2005. Stakeholder collaboration and heritage management, *Annals of Tourism Research* 32(1): 28–48.

Abdelhafez, A. 2014. Urban planners aim to restore Cairo, Al-Monitor November 23 - http://www.al-monitor.com/pulse/culture/2014/11/cairo-urban-development-khedive-traffic-egypt.html##ixzz3K4elR2q7

AERA 2013. Fieldschools, *AREAWEB* - http://www.aeraweb.org/field-school-program/

[7] Red Sea tourism, while affected, has not suffered nearly as badly

Agnew. N. 1997. Preservation of Archaeological Sites: A Holistic Perspective, *Getty Conservation Institute Newsletter* 12(2): 1-6.

Ahram Online. 2012. Egypt population reaches 91 million, grows 18 per cent in eight years, *Ahram Online, Thursday* 30 Aug 2012 - http://english.ahram.org.eg/News/51634.aspx

Ahram Online. 2014. Egypt tourism revenues more than double in third quarter, *Ahram Online,* December 8 - http://english.ahram.org.eg/NewsContent/3/12/117437/Business/Economy/Egypt-tourism-revenues-more-than-double-in-third-q.aspx

Andrén, A. 1998. *Between Artifacts and Texts: Historical Archaeology in Global Perspective.* New York: Plenum Publishing.

El-Aref. N. 2012. Building blunder prompts discovery of pharaonic stele in Cairo, *Ahram Online* - http://english.ahram.org.eg/NewsContent/9/40/52528/Heritage/Ancient-Egypt/Building-blunder-prompts-discovery-of-pharaonic-st.aspx

El-Aref. N. 2013a. From rumour to bulldozer, *Al Ahram Weekly* Issue No. 1147, 9 May - http://weekly.ahram.org.eg/News/2525/-/-.aspx

El-Aref. N. 2013b. Aswan tombs attacked, *Al Ahram Weekly* Issue No. 1153, 20 June - http://weekly.ahram.org.eg/News/3028/47/Aswan-tombs-attacked.aspx

El-Aref. N. 2013c. Egypt asks for return of artefacts listed on eBay London, *Ahram Online* - http://english.ahram.org.eg/NewsContent/9/0/82614/Heritage/0/Egypt-asks-for-return-of-artefacts-listed-on-eBay-.aspx

El-Aref. N. 2014a. Protecting architectural heritage, *Al Ahram Weekly* Issue No. 1194, 24 April - http://weekly.ahram.org.eg/News/6040/47/Protecting-architectural-heritage.aspx

El-Aref. N. 2014b. Restoring Al-Muizz Street, *Al Ahram Weekly* Issue No. Issue No.1195, 1 May - http://weekly.ahram.org.eg/News/6105/47/Restoring-Al-Muizz-Street.aspx

El-Aref. N. 2014c. Threats to Fustat? *Al Ahram Weekly* Issue No. Issue No.1195, 1 May - http://weekly.ahram.org.eg/News/6104/47/Threats-to-Fustat-.aspx

El-Aref. N. 2014d. Illegal excavations foiled in Sohag's Akhmim, *Ahram Online* - http://english.ahram.org.eg/News/103108.aspx

El-Aref. N. 2014e. Temple run, *Al Ahram Weekly* Issue No. 1204, 3 July - http://weekly.ahram.org.eg/News/6686/17/Temple-run.aspx

El-Aref. N. 2014f. A new authority to develop and restore historic Cairo, *Ahram Online* September 9 - http://english.ahram.org.eg/NewsContent/9/43/110354/Heritage/Islamic/A-new-authority-to-develop-and-restore-historic-Ca.aspx

El-Aref, N. 2015. Al-Arish Museum badly damaged by Sinai violence, *Ahram Online* January 30 - http://english.ahram.org.eg/NewsContent/9/44/121776/Heritage/Museums/AlArish-Museum-badly-damaged-by-Sinai-violence.aspx

Aston, J. 2013. Camels, sand, and pyramids: Struggles with tourism in the golden land of the pharaohs, in *Proceedings of The National Conference on Undergraduate Research (NCUR) 2013, Held at the University of Wisconsin La Crosse, WI April 11-13, 2013.* La Crosse: University of Wisconsin, pp. 521-528.

Athanasiadis, I. 2014. It's time to stop the destruction of Middle East Heritage, *American Al Jezeera* May 5 - http://america.aljazeera.com/opinions/2014/5/middle-east-heritagearabspring.html

Ayyad, M. 2015. Antiquities ministry requests EGP 488m to continue projects: Cabinet spokesman, *Daily News Egypt* January 20 - http://www.dailynewsegypt.com/2015/01/20/antiquities-ministry-requests-egp-488m-continue-projects-cabinet-spokesman/

Boyle, K. 2014. Egypt turns to technology in effort to protect ancient treasures from looters, *The Guardian* June 1 - http://www.theguardian.com/world/2014/jun/01/egypt-museum-theft-satellite-technology

Brederova, B. 2014. *The Looting and Deliberate Destruction of Cultural Heritage During Social and Political Unrest of the 21st Century: The Search for Solution.* Unpublished Masters Dissertation, Reading: The University of Reading, Department of Archaeology.

Brodie, N. 2011. Congenial bedfellows? The academy and the antiquities trade, *Journal of Contemporary Criminal Justice* 27(4) 408-437.

Brodie, N. 2014. Provenance and price: Autoregulation of the antiquities market?, *European Journal on Criminal Policy and Research* 20: 427–444.

Brodie, N., Doole, J., & Watson, P. 2000. *Stealing History: The Illicit Trade in Cultural Material.* Cambridge: McDonald Institute.

Brodie, N., Kersel, M. M., Luke, C., & Tubb, K. W. (eds) 2006. *Archaeology, Cultural Heritage and the Antiquities Trade.* Gainesville: University Press of Florida.

Cairo Observer. 2014. 11 Recent cultural disasters in Egypt, *Cairo Observer* February 2 - http://cairobserver.com/post/75403717693/11-recent-cultural-disasters-in-egypt#.U5RwycsU-P9

Carruthers, W. E. 2015. What we are talking about when we talk about Tutankhamun's beard, *The Max Webber Programme Blog* - http://blogs.eui.eu/maxweberprogramme/2015/01/29/what-we-are-talking-about-when-we-talk-about-tutankhamuns-beard/

Cecca, L., & McLerran, D. 2013. Travesty in Egypt, *Popular Archaeology* - http://popular-archaeology.com/issue/09012013/article/travesty-in-egypt

Cleere, H. (ed.) 1984. *Approaches to the Archaeological Heritage: A Comparative Study of World Cultural Resource Management Systems.* Cambridge: Cambridge University Press.

Coban, L. 2011. Why Egyptians preserve their cultural heritage, *The Huffington Post* - http://www.huffingtonpost.com/larry-coben/egypt-cultural-heritage_b_827872.html

Colla, E. 2007. *Conflicted Antiquities. Egyptology, Egyptomania, Egyptian Modernity.* Durham: Duke University Press.

El Daly, O. 2005. *Egyptology: The Missing Millennium. Ancient Egypt in Medieval Arabic Writings.* London: UCL Press.

Davis, T. 2014. Activists warn Egypt's historical sites will be destroyed if government doesn't step in, *The Huffington Post* May 2 - http://www.huffingtonpost.com/2014/05/02/egypt-historical-sites_n_5254069.html

Davis, T. & Bowman, B. A. 2014. Egypt's history is being lost to criminals, *The Huffington Post* April 30 - http://www.huffingtonpost.com/tess-davis/egypts-history-is-being-l_b_5240549.html

Doole, J. 2002. In the News, *Culture Without Context* 10: 13-21.

El-Dorry, M.-A. 2011. Why do people loot? The case of the Egyptian revolution, *Al Rawi: Egypt's Heritage Review* 2: 20-21.

Durham, K. 2013. People of the Year. Monica Hanna: Connecting Egyptians with their heritage, *Egypt Today* December: 56-57.

DW 2014. Egypt ups efforts to protect cultural heritage, *DW* - http://www.dw.de/egypt-ups-efforts-to-protect-cultural-heritage/a-17691553

ECHO Website - www.e-c-h-o.org

Egypt Independent. 2015a. Campaign, alarmed by surge in illegal excavations, promotes awareness, *Egypt Independent* January 27 - http://www.egyptindependent.com/news/campaign-alarmed-surge-illegal-excavations-promotes-awareness

Egypt Independent, 2015b. 13 Archaeological projects suspended due lack of funding, *Egypt Independent* January 12 - http://www.egyptindependent.com/news/13-archaeological-projects-suspended-due-lack-funding

Egypt's Heritage Task Force - https://www.facebook.com/EgyptsHeritageTaskForce

Eichberger, H. 2010. Preparing for the protection of cultural property in the event of armed conflict and natural disaster: Developing new dimension standards for sheltering moveable objects, *Present Pasts* 2(1): 177-193.

Ejsmond, W. 2014. Polish archaeologists found tombs dating back four thousand years in Egypt, *PAP: Science and Scholarship in Poland, News of Polish Science* - http://www.naukawpolsce.pap.pl/en/news/news,400863,polish-archaeologists-found-tombs-dating-back-four-thousand-years-in-egypt.html

Elkins, N. T. 2014. Why coins matter: Trafficking in undocumented and illegally exported ancient coins in the North American marketplace, *Saving Antiquities for Everyone* - http://www.savingantiquities.org/why-coins-matter-trafficking-in-undocumented-and-illegally-exported-ancient-coins-in-the-north-american-marketplace

Fabian, M. 2014. Egypt's Heritage Task Force: Mit Köpfchen und Facebook im Einstaz für die Monumente, *Papyrus Magazine* 1: 25-27 - http://papyrus-magazin.de/Papyrus_online/2014_Heft01/index.html

Fangary, A. A. H. & Wahba, M. N. 2012. January 25th: A great revolution between a period of unrest, an invaluable heritage at risk and a better future, *e-dialogos - Annual Digital Journal on Research in Conservation and Cultural Heritage* 2: 8-15.

Fasold, P., Stutzinger, D. & von Kaenel, H.-M. 1995. Raubgrabungen zerstören archäologische Erbe. *Begleitheft zur Ausstellung Fundort: Unbekannt – Raubgrabungen in Hessen.*, Wiesbaden: Archäologische Denkmäler in Hessen 127.

Fayek, M. 2014. One year after Morsi's ouster, looted Coptic churches turn into trash dumps, *Muftah* August 21 - http://muftah.org/one-year-morsis-ouster-looted-coptic-churches-turn-trash-dumps/#.U_bsP8sg_4j

Forrest, C. 2014. Safeguarding cultural heritage in times of war, *World Politics Review* - http://www.worldpoliticsreview.com/articles/13958/safeguarding-cultural-heritage-in-times-of-war

Fushiya, T. 2010. Archaeological site management and local involvement: A case study from Abu Rawash, Egypt, *Conservation and Management of Archaeological Sites* 12(4): 324-355.

Fushiya, T. & De Trafford, A. 2009. From site to society: From a garbage dumping place to a local heritage site, in F. A. Hassan, G. J. Tassie, A De Trafford, L. S. Owens & J. van Wetering (eds.) *Managing Egypt's Cultural Heritage: Proceedings of the First Egyptian Cultural Heritage Organisation Conference on: Egyptian Cultural Heritage Management.* London: Golden House and ECHO Publications, pp. 38-58.

Galla, A. 2012. Dahshur villages in community development: Memphis and its Necropolis – the Pyramid Fields from Giza to Dahshur, Egypt, in A. Galla (ed.) *World Heritage: Benefits Beyond Borders.* Cambridge: Cambridge University Press, pp. 267-278.

Gerstenblith, P. 2002. United States v. Schultz, *Culture Without Context* 10: 27-31.

Gestrich, N. 2011. Putting a price on the past: The ethics and economics of archaeology in the marketplace. A reply to "What is Public Archaeology", *Present Pasts* 3(2): 80-82.

Gill, D. W. J. 2014. Looting Matters: Blogging in a research context, in D. Rocks-MacQueen & C. Webster (eds) *Blogging Archaeology.* London: Landward Research Ltd in Association with Succinct Research and DIGTECH LLC, pp. 44-59.

Gould, P. G. & Burtenshaw, P. 2014. Archaeology and economic development, *Public Archaeology* 13(1–3): 3-9.

Guerin, O. 2014. Egypt: Cairo flats collapse kills 17 people, *BBC News* November 25 - http://www.bbc.com/news/world-middle-east-30191425

Hammerstein, K. von 2014. Dubious provenance: Pressure grows for museums to return stolen objects, *Spiegel Online International* December 10 - http://www.spiegel.de/international/world/pressure-grows-for-museums-to-return-stolen-objects-a-1007523.html

Hanna, M. 2013a. Losing heritage, losing identity, *Al Rawi: Egypt's Heritage Review* 5: 22-25.

Hanna, M. 2013b. What has happened to Egyptian heritage after the 2011 unfinished revolution? *Journal of Eastern Mediterranean Archaeology & Heritage Studies* 1(4): 371-375.

Hanna, M. 2013c. Ancient Heliopolis under threat, *Daily News Egypt* June 19 - http://www.dailynewsegypt.com/2013/06/19/ancient-heliopolis-under-threat/

Hanna, M. & Ikram, S. 2013. Looting Egypt: Abu Sir Al-Maleq, *Daily News Egypt* June 5 - http://www.dailynewsegypt.com/2013/06/05/looting-egypt-abu-sir-al-maleq/

Hardy, S. A. 2013. Egypt: the boutique business of looting and smuggling antiquities in conflict, *Conflict Antiquities: Illicit Antiquities Trading in Economic Crisis, Organised Crime and Political Violence* - https://conflictantiquities.wordpress.com/2013/05/06/egypt-the-boutique-business-of-looting-and-smuggling-antiquities-in-conflict/

Hardy, S. 2015a. Virtues impracticable and extremely difficult: The human rights of subsistence diggers, *Ethics and the Archaeology of Violence. Ethical Archaeologies: The Politics of Social Justice* 2: 229-239.

Hardy, S. A. 2015b. Antiquities looted during unrest in Egypt are reaching public markets in the West, *Conflict Antiquities: Illicit Antiquities Trading in Economic Crisis, Organised Crime and Political Violence* - https://conflictantiquities.wordpress.com/2015/01/06/egypt-antiquities-looting-australia-antiquities-auction/

Hassan, F. A. 1997. The cultural heritage of Egypt: a world legacy, in *African Cultural Heritage and the World Heritage Convention: Second Global Strategy Meeting.* Addis-Ababa: UNESCO, pp. 86-91.

Hassan, F. A. 2013. Training of local community youth in Dahshur, Egypt, as local tour guides and heritage guardians, in Erasmus Mundus (ed.) *Proceedings of the International Conference Tourism Management and Sustainability of Heritage Sites: the Role of Education and Training.* Assisi: Hercules, pp. 68-78.

Hendawi, H. 2012. In Egypt's turmoil, thieves dig up treasures, *The Bulletin* - http://www.bendbulletin.com/news/1372369-151/in-egypts-turmoil-thieves-dig-up-treasures#

Hessler, P. 2013. The Buried. Excavating the Egyptian revolution, *The New Yorker* November 18 - http://www.newyorker.com/reporting/2013/11/18/131118fa_fact_hessler

Hiel, B. 2013a. Experts heartbroken by raiding in Egyptian area near Nile, *Tribune-Review* June 16 - http://triblive.com/usworld/betsyhiel/4206114-74/antiquities-ancient-hibeh#ixzz33sT8r7Fr

Hiel, B. 2013b. Coptic Christian history lost to thieves in Egypt, *Tribune-Review* December 24 - http://triblive.com/news/editorspicks/5311919-74/egypt-says-christian#axzz2oapHBUqj

Hiel, B. 2015. Egypt's churches charred to shells, *Tribune-Review* January 19 - http://triblive.com/usworld/betsyhiel/7570943-74/church-christian-churches#axzz3PBV6NaMC

Huisman, D. J. 2012. Deep impact: What happens when archaeological sites are built on? *Conservation and Management of Archaeological Sites* 14(1): 60-71.

Ikram, S. 2011. Collecting and repatriating Egypt's past: Toward a new nationalism, in H. Silver (ed.) *Contested Cultural Heritage: Religion, Nationalism, Erasure, and Exclusion in a Global World.* New York: Springer, pp. 141-154.

Ikram, S. 2013. Cultural heritage in times of crisis: The view from Egypt, *Journal of Eastern Mediterranean Archaeology & Heritage Studies* 1(4): 366-371.

Ikram, S. 2014. The loss and looting of Egyptian antiquities, *The Epoch Times* http://www.theepochtimes.com/n3/648156-the-loss-and-looting-of-egyptian-antiquities/?utm_source=dlvr.it&utm_medium=gplus

Ikram, S. & Hanna, M. 2013. Looting and land grabbing: The current situation in Egypt, *Bulletin of the American Research Center in Egypt* 202: 34–39.

Joseph, M. 2012. Minister: 2% of artifacts stolen during security vacuum, *Egypt Independent* - http://www.egyptindependent.com/news/minister-2-artifacts-stolen-during-security-vacuum

Keshk, F. 2011a. Egyptian antiquities suffering due to turmoil at the top, *Egypt Independent* August 17 - http://www.egyptindependent.com/news/egyptian-antiquities-suffering-due-turmoil-top

Keshk, F. 2011b. Restored Moez Street needs rescuing again, *Egypt Independent* September 25 – http:/www.egyptindependent.com//new/restored-moez-street-needs-rescuing-again

Keshk, F. 2012a. Can the Red List protect Egypt's cultural heritage? *Egypt Independent* April 3 - http://www.egyptindependent.com/news/can-red-list-protect-egypts-cultural-heritage

Keshk, F. 2012b. Independent heritage initiatives: A first step to linking communities to their own histories, *Egypt Independent* May 9 - http://www.egyptindependent.com/news/independent-heritage-initiatives-first-step-link-communities-their-own-histories

Keshk, F. 2012c. Cosmopolitan Alexandria endangered, *Egypt Independent* May 29 - http://www.egyptindependent.com/news/cosmopolitan-alexandria-endangered

Keshk, F. 2012d. Despite rich past, history fails to interest Egyptian students, *Egypt Independent* August 30 - http://www.egyptindependent.com/news/despite-rich-past-history-fails-interest-egyptian-students

Khaled, R. 2012. Dahshur lake under threat: Residents complain of state's disinterest, *Egypt Independent* November 5 - http://www.egyptindependent.com/news/dahshur-lake-under-threat-residents-complain-state-s-disinterest

Kila, J. D. 2013. Inactive, reactive, or pro-active? Cultural property crimes in the context of contemporary armed conflicts, *Journal of Eastern Mediterranean Archaeology & Heritage Studies* 1(4): 319-342.0

Kingsley, P. 2013. Egyptians grab ancient land of the pharaohs to bury their dead, *The Observer*, Sunday 28 April - http://www.theguardian.com/world/2013/apr/28/pyramid-tomb-dahshur-egypt-archaeology

Kingsley, P. 2014a. Tourist desert – Egypt desperate to woo back visitors after years of unrest, *The Guardian*, Tuesday 11 February - http://www.theguardian.com/world/2014/feb/10/egypts-tourist-resorts-ghost-towns

Kingsley, P. 2014b. Egypt's tourism revenues fall after political upheavals, *The Guardian,* Friday 29 August - http://www.theguardian.com/world/2014/aug/29/egypt-tourism-revenue-falls-95-percent

Kingsley, P. 2014c. New generation of archaeologists takes ancient Egypt into 21st century, *The Guardian,* Thursday 23 October - http://www.theguardian.com/world/2014/oct/23/egypt-archaeology-restoration-pyramids

Klamer, A. 2014. The values of archaeological and heritage sites, *Public Archaeology* 13(1-3): 59-70.

Lazaridis, N. & Helmy, M. 2011. Revolutionizing Egyptology: The sociopolitical changes in Egypt and their impact on Egyptology, *Hellenic Society for the Study of Ancient* Egypt - http://www.eemaa.eu/node/229

Lehr, D. 2014. Digging out of tourism downfalls: Egypt's archaeology takes the stage, *Huffington Post* December 17 - http://www.huffingtonpost.com/deborah-lehr/digging-out-of-tourism-do_b_6341104.html

Looting Database Archives - http://www.egyptological.com/looting

Mackenzie, S. 2011. Illicit deals in cultural objects as crimes of the powerful, *Crime, Law and Social Change* 56 (2):133-153.

Maqbool, A. 2013. Egypt's illegal construction time bomb, *BBC News* January 25 - http://www.bbc.com/news/world-middle-east-21192988

Marchant, J. 2911. Spring comes to ancient Egypt, *Nature* 479: 464-467.

Marouard, G. 2013. Construction of a protective fence at the Edfu step pyramid, *ARCE Bulletin* 203: 26-35.

Mason, R. & Avrami, E. 2002. Heritage values and challenges of conservation planning, in J. M. Teutonico & G. Palumbo (eds) *Management Planning for Archaeological Sites: An International Workshop Organized by the Getty Conservation Institute and Loyola Marymount University, May 2000* Los Angeles: Getty Conservation Institute, pp. 13-26.

McManamon, F. P., Barnes, J. A. and Stout, A. 2008. Contemporary archaeological resource management and the "liberals' dilemma." in F. P. McManamon, A. Stout, & J. A. Barnes (eds) *Managing Archaeological Resources: Global Context, National Programs, Local Actions.* Walnut Creek, [CA]: One World Archaeology 58, Left Coast Press, pp. 17–34.

Mostafa, R. 2014a. Smuggled Egyptian artifacts retrieved from Christie's Auction House, *The Cairo Post* June 10 - http://thecairopost.com/news/114306/news/smuggled-egyptian-artifacts-retrieved-from-christies-auction-hous

Mostafa, R. 2014b. UNESCO seminar to fund Egypt's stumbling archaeological projects, *The Cairo Post* October 8 - http://thecairopost.com/news/126643/travel-antiquities/unesco-seminar-to-fund-egypts-stumbling-archaeological-projects

Mostafa, R. 2014c. Antiquities crimes should be a felony: Zahi Hawass, *The Cairo Post* October 10 - http://thecairopost.com/news/126768/travel-antiquities/antiquities-crimes-should-be-a-felony-zahi-hawass

Mostafa, R. 2015a. Domestic tourism booms in Luxor and Aswan in mid-year holiday, *The Cairo Post* January 7 - http://www.thecairopost.com/news/132512/travel-antiquities/domestic-tourism-booms-in-luxor-and-aswan-in-mid-year-holiday

Mostafa, R. 2015b. Tourism booms at Christmas, *The Cairo Post* January 4 - http://www.thecairopost.com/news/132195/travel-antiquities/tourism-booms-during-christmas

Mostafa, R. 2015c. Ministerial committee to safeguard Islamic heritage, *The Cairo Post* January 11 - http://www.thecairopost.com/news/132974/inside_egypt/ministerial-committee-to-safeguard-egyptian-islamic-heritage

Mostafa, R. 2015d. Grave robbers employ sheikhs to counter jinns in tombs, *The Cairo Post* January 14 - http://www.thecairopost.com/news/133369/inside_egypt/grave-robbers-employ-sheikhs-to-counter-jinn-in-tombs

Moustafa, N. 2014. Fear and looting in Egypt - visible from space, *American Al Jezeera* February 13 - http://america.aljazeera.com/watch/shows/techknow/blog/2014/2/13/fear-and-lootinginegyptvisiblefromspace.html

Proulx, B. B. 2013 Archaeological site looting in "glocal" perspective: Nature, scope, and frequency, *American Journal of Archaeology* 117: 111-125.

Pyburn, K. A. 2014. Preservation as 'disaster capitalism': The downside of site rescue and the complexity of community engagement, *Public Archaeology* 13(1–3): 226–39.

Al Rawi. 2011. The state of Egyptian Heritage, *Al Rawi: Egypt's Heritage Review* 2: 8-19.

Redmount, C. 2012. Massive looting and destruction at ancient Egyptian archaeological site, *Popular Archaeology* - http://popular-archaeology.com/issue/june-2012/article/massive-looting-and-destruction-at-ancient-egyptian-archaeological-site

Redmount, C. 2014. El-Hibeh: a plundered site, *Egyptian Archaeology* 45: 13-17.

Reid, D. M. 2002. *Whose Pharaohs? Archaeology, Museums, and Egyptian National Identity from Napoleon to World War I.* Berkeley - Los Angeles - London: University of California Press.

Richards, G. & Summerscale, T. 2014. *Gleaming in the Dust: An Audio Documentary.* London: Square Bracket Productions - http://gleaminginthedust.com/

Schadla-Hall, T. & Larkin, J. 2014. Forward, *Public Archaeology* 13(1–3): 1-2.

Schadla-Hall, T., Moshenska, G. & Thornton, A. 2011. Editorial, *Public Archaeology* 10(1) 1-3.

Schipper, F. T & Eichberger, H. 2010. The protection of cultural property in the event of armed conflict: the cultural property protection officer as a liaison between the military and the civil sector, *Present Pasts* 2(1): 169-176.

Shaw, A. 2014. No consensus on tackling Egypt looting, *The Art Newspaper* - http://www.theartnewspaper.com/articles/No-consensus-on-tackling-Egypt-looting/3256

Shaw, G. 2013. Egyptians tweet to save their heritage from looting, *The Art Newspaper* - http://www.theartnewspapper.com/articles/Egyptians-tweet-to-save-theirheritage-from-looting/30307

Shaw, G. 2014a. Controversial security walls help protect Egypt's antiquities, *The Art Newspaper* - http://www.theartnewspaper.com/articles/Controversial-security-walls-help-protect-Egypts-antiquities/32560

Shaw, G. 2014b. Egypt tracks down suspected looted works to Europe, *The Art Newspaper* - http://www.theartnewspaper.com/articles/Egypt-tracks-down-suspected-looted-works-to-Europe/32917

Smale, A. 2014. Stemming a tide of cultural theft, *New York Times* December 17 - http://www.nytimes.com/2014/12/18/arts/international/stemming-a-tide-of-cultural-theft.html?_r=1

Smith, C. 2014. The power of corrupt political environments and its effects on museums: A look at Egypt's modern-day 'Indiana Jones': Dr. Zahi Hawass, *History Theses.* Paper 27 - http://digitalcommons.buffalostate.edu/history_theses

Stapp, D. & Longenecker, J. 2009. *Avoiding Archaeological Disasters: A Risk Management Approach.* Walnut Creek: Left Coast Press.

Schwartzstein, P. 2014. Egypt's population boom threatens cultural treasures, *National Geographic* - http://news.nationalgeographic.com/news/2014/04/140418-egypt-population-heritage-conservation-threats-world/

Tassie, G. J. 2007. A trade older than the pyramids, *ECHO Website* - http://www.e-c-h-o.org/tombrobbery.php

Tassie, G. J. & Hassan, F. A. 2009. Sites and monuments records (SMRs) and cultural heritage management (CHM), in F. A. Hassan, G. J. Tassie, A De Trafford, L. S. Owens & J. van Wetering (eds.) *Managing Egypt's Cultural Heritage: Proceedings of the First Egyptian Cultural Heritage Organisation Conference on: Egyptian Cultural Heritage Management.* London: Golden House and ECHO Publications, pp. 191-205.

Thompson, E. 2014. Egypt's looted antiquities, *New York Times* May 30 - http://www.nytimes.com/2014/05/31/opinion/egypts-looted-antiquities.html?smid=fb-share&_r=1

Timothy, D. J. 2014. Contemporary cultural heritage and tourism: Development issues and emerging trends, *Public Archaeology* 13(1-3): 30-47.

TNN. 2014. US to impose restrictions on smuggling Egyptian antiquities, *TNN* November 25 - http://www.tnnegypt.com/us-to-impose-restrictions-on-smuggling-egyptian-antiquities/

Tresilian, D. 2014. Egypt's heritage crisis, *Al Ahram Weekly* Issue No. 1207, 24 July - http://weekly.ahram.org.eg/News/6818/32/Egypt%E2%80%99s-heritage-crisis.aspx

Trew, B. 2014. Egyptian tomb-bobbing market explodes on eBay, *The Daily Beast* May 31 - http://www.thedailybeast.com/articles/2014/05/31/egyptian-tomb-robbing-market-explodes-on-ebay.html

Varner, T. 2014. Saving cultural heritage, one tweet at a time, *Saving Antiquities For Everyone* - http://www.savingantiquities.org/saving-antiquities-one-tweet-time/

Vergano, D. 2014. Archaeologists warn of pillaged Egypt as U.S. weighs tougher antiquities laws, *National Geographic* June 3 - http://news.nationalgeographic.com/news/2014/06/140603-egypt-looting-hearing-law-state-coins/

El Wardany, S. 2015. Why Cairo recycles better than New York City in waste-picking tale, *Bloomberg* January 19 - http://mobile.bloomberg.com/news/2015-01-20/why-cairo-recycles-better-than-nyc-in-waste-picking-tale-cities.html

Watson, P. 2002. The investigation of Frederick Schultz, *Culture Without Context* 10: 21-26.

Waxman, S. 2008. *Loot: The Battle over the Stolen Treasures of the Ancient World.* New York: Times Books, Henry Holt and Company, LLC.

Wendrich, W. 2006. Archaeology and sustainable tourism in Egypt: Protecting community, antiquities, and environment, in N. Agnew and J. Bridgland (eds) *Of the Past, for the Future: Integrating Archaeology and Conservation.* Los Angeles: The Getty Conservation Institute, pp. 184-190.

Wolfenberger, J. 2014. *Avoiding the Mummy's Curse: How Museums Can Work to Raise Awareness and Prevent Looting in Egypt.* Unpublished Masters Dissertation. Pleasant Hill [Cal.]: John F. Kennedy University.

Chapter 4

Creating Egyptian Archives and the Production of Perfect Paperwork?

Nathalie Cohen

ABSTRACT

This paper examines some of the issues relating to project archiving, which result from developer-funded archaeological investigations in England and also archives generated by research projects and academic institutions in Egypt will also be considered. The types of media used and the methodologies developed to archive material will be discussed. Some of the problems associated with the process of compiling and depositing an archive will be raised, and the benefits of undertaking the task will be demonstrated.

INTRODUCTION

When Auguste Mariette first formed the *Service d'Antiquités* in 1858, he should have also initiated a Central Archive and a Sites and Monuments Records (SMRs), following the practice of record keeping in Europe at the time. This oversight has meant that the records of survey and excavation work conducted in Egypt over the past 150 years are now scattered throughout the world. Although the *Annales du Service des Antitquités de L'Egypte* (*ASAE*) and Amleek form a good core of archaeological work conducted in Egypt, they are by no means a complete archival record.

Archaeologists have many ethical obligations to cultural heritage, to other archaeologists, and to present and future generations. Their fundamental obligation to cultural heritage is to preserve it for future generations, and thereby to protect it from the threats posed by the modern world. Although a small amount of sites may be preserved for showing to the public, site archives remain the only primary surviving evidence of the site. The site itself will have been stripped of the cultural and environmental indicators of human activity, apart from the iconographic record and the structure itself. It is therefore vital that we preserve the site archives in their entirety, for without this original record of the excavation it would be impossible to reconstruct the human activity that was conducted at the site. Unfortunately, however, publication of interim and final reports has often been lackadaisical or altogether absent, and we may wait for over twenty years for a final report that never materialises. We are thus failing in our duty to cultural heritage, for records are the only evidence of the archaeological work conducted, and also comprise the only means by which future academics can re-interpret the site.

At present, no archaeological material can leave Egypt without the written permission of the Ministry of Antiquities (MA). Intact objects are usually deposited in local magazines or local museums, with the finest examples going to museums in Cairo, Luxor or Alexandria. However, the written, drawn and photographic record is more important than any of these physical remains. The archival material must be researched by archaeologists and specialists, then transformed into monographs of their research projects. Once the projects are 'finished' and the results published, the original archival material is often dispersed to institutional repositories (i.e. museums, universities and other institutions) around the world. Unofficial repositories may spring up to in cases where museums or other institutions cannot or will not take archival material, and many private archives are held by individual site directors. Although some of the archival material created by Egyptian-run projects will either be deposited in the local *tafftish* (MA offices) or the central offices in Cairo, these institutions cannot cater to archival material's specific requirements. The fire that destroyed the archives at the *Institut d'Égypte* (Egypt Scientific Institute [ESI]) in 2011 underscores the importance of creating a specialised central repository (perhaps with regional centres) that would be fire resistant, containing archives kept in environmentally controlled conditions (de Vartavan, 2011). This fire also illustrates the importance of the digitisation of archives, and placing them in separate repositories.

What are archives and why are they important? The exact meaning of an archive should perhaps be addressed. Archives are contemporary transactional records, which can be divided into various categories: professional, education, museums and galleries, archaeological, business, local government, religious, charities, national, medical, performing arts, film and estates. The physical archives may be held in governmental buildings, mosques, universities, hospitals or private institutions. Archaeological archives are the complete record of the excavation or survey of a site – the written, photographic, drawn, artefactual and ecofactual – without which archaeologists cannot understand the range of human activities that were conducted in their research area (Tassie & Owens 2010).

Archives will result from all kinds of archaeological investigations including evaluation, excavation, watching briefs, building recording (including epigraphy) and survey. Every aspect of the assessment and analytical process will also create its own archive of paper and digital data. Finally the artefacts and environmental samples collected from the site must be catalogued and stored in appropriate repositories.

This brief paper will examine some of the issues relating to the archiving of projects that result from developer-funded archaeological investigations in England. Archives generated by research projects and academic institutions will also be considered. The types of media used, and the methodologies developed to archive material, will be discussed. Some of the problems associated with the process of compiling and depositing an archive will be raised, and the benefits of undertaking the task will be demonstrated. This information will then be used to propose the development of an Egyptian archiving system.

Notification and Dissemination

Until recently, notification of archaeological work in England took the form of separate documentation submitted to the local Sites and Monuments Record office (SMR) and the National Monument Record centre (NMR), thus informing regional and national bodies that the work had taken place. However in 2004, a new initiative by the Archaeology Data Service (ADS at http://ads/ahds.ac.uk) largely replaced this system with a single form, the On-Line Access to the Index of Archaeological Investigations (OASIS). The information submitted by archaeological units or research bodies thereby became directly accessible by interested parties, via the Internet. Details entered onto the form include locational details (including the National Grid Reference), the names of supervisors, project managers and funding bodies, the type of work undertaken and a brief summary of the results of the investigation. It is also possible to submit copies of 'grey literature' (unpublished reports produced for clients) to the ADS, which can then be downloaded by researchers.

The next step in more widely disseminating the information gleaned from excavation is publication. Every archaeological intervention undertaken in London by MoLAS and other contracting units is published in the form of a short summary document, which is sent to the local journal *London Archaeologist*. Summaries are also sent to the relevant period journals (i.e. *Britannia, Medieval Archaeology* and *Post-Medieval Archaeology*). For sites outside Greater London, summaries are also sent to the local county archaeological journals. For larger and more complex sites, a variety of other publication avenues can be explored. These can include short articles in local and period journals, academic study series papers and monographs, and popular books and leaflets.

However, the majority of sites do not receive sufficient funding from developers or research funding bodies to allow for publication, other than a summary note. Indeed, many may not merit stand-alone publication due to a lack of evidence retrieved from the site. Sometimes the site director may die before they get round to publishing the information they generated from the site, without appointing a subordinate to carry out the work in their stead. In is therefore vital that the archive be completed and deposited to in order to allow for future reinterpretation and publication.

Archiving and Deposition

At the beginning of any project, an appropriate repository able to accept the documentary and artefactual archive should be identified, and any costs associated with deposition must be included in any project design and costings. The London Archaeological Archive and Research Centre (LAARC) was set up to accept archives generated by projects in the Greater London area (see Swain, 1999). The nature of the archives accepted by LAARC varies in accordance with the nature of the projects, from excavation, post-excavation, survey, fieldwalking, standing structure recording, and research. In order to match extant materials, each archaeological project must create on-site or temporary archives that follow a certain standard and format (see Tassie and Owens 2010). If a recording system is not computerised, the artefacts, drawings, photographs, contexts and features should be typed up and cross-referenced. These, in addition the site and artefact drawings and photographs, human skeletal records, sampling data and analytical reports on artefacts, structures, stratigraphy and environmental data, go to form the site catalogue/archive.

In order to accept archives from such a disparate range of bodies, LAARC has produced detailed guidelines for deposition with regard to the way in which the material is to be presented (Grew 1998). In practice, this means that every archive must contain the following information:

- Site plan
- Survey and levels data
- Deposit survival form (outlining surviving remains of deposits; height of natural ground surface)
- A brief summary of the fieldwork

Other items may include site registers, a range of recording sheets (context, masonry, timber, trench, worked stone), original site drawings, (plans, sections and elevations), a matrix, photographs, miscellany (historic maps and drawings, site notes, correspondence etc.) and unpublished documentation or 'grey literature' (project designs, reports and desk based assessments etc). In addition to the stratigraphic archive, there will also be paperwork associated with finds and environmental analysis. Larger sites generate more data; LAARC have designed extra checklists to catalogue this material.

Some archaeologists divide the archives into a primary archive and a research archive. The primary archive, as outlined below, is simply a record of all data collected, whereas the research archive is the data in standardised format with artefactual and environmental reports and an interpretation and history of the site (Drewett, 1999: 176). A site archive normally consists of:

- Survey reports (e.g. drill core, geophysical, documentary)
- Base plan of site at 1:100, showing location of trenches
- Site notebooks, area folders, and diaries
- Recording sheets and indices
- Original photographs
- Site drawings
- Records of conservation and scientific analyses undertaken during fieldwork
- Computer discs and printouts.
- Original sample records, including dating catalogues
- A site matrix with the complete stratigraphic sequence
- Original skeleton records
- Skeletal material
- Artefacts and ecofacts, including bulk finds

The last two categories of course have to stay in the designated local museum or in a regional or central magazine, whereas the rest of the site archive will usually stay with the institution of the principal investigator. A duplicate of the site archive should be presented to the centralised archive for curation, detailing where the skeletal and artefactual material has been stored, and the relevant entries made in the National Register detailing the site and whereabouts of the site archive.

Irrespective of where the archive is to be stored, the archival material must be presented in a stable condition. This means that all metal paper clips and staples need to be removed and the documents should be held together with plastic-ended treasury tags. The use of adhesive tape and glue should also be avoided. The paperwork should be filed in acid-free wallets and boxes, and paper and film archives should be boxed separately. Site plans should be printed on film or stored in Melinex pockets, and should not be rolled but must be stored flat. These drawings, documents and objects, along with the photographs, are best stored in the dark, in a temperature range of 13° – 20° and a relative humidity of 45-50% - maintaining an environment that is moderate and stable (Drewett, 1999: 176).

There are several other issues associated with transfer and deposition:

Microfilming – At present, microfilming of paper archives is still widely used for security copying (Handley, 1999). Three copies are usually produced, a silver (or master) copy and two diazo copies. The master and one diazo copy are lodged with the NMR in Swindon and the other is placed with the LAARC. Although it seems likely that this expensive and time-consuming method of security copying the original paperwork may eventually be superseded by advances in digital recording and scanning; for the time being issues with refreshment and data migration of digital archives (see below) means that microfilm copying is still the most stable and durable medium.

Digital archive – increasingly, archaeological archives contain a large component of digital data. This may relate mostly to office-based post-excavation work in the form of reports, relational databases and CAD/GIS projects, but may also include elements generated at the site itself, such as digital photographs and electronic survey data. While the use of the digital medium undoubtedly speeds up the archaeological process, and allows for rapid and accurate recording and analysis, the creation of a digital archive may lead to problems with deposition. The issue of suitable storage must be assessed by both the creators and the repository, as must the preservation format of files prepared for deposition. Metadata needs to be created in order to provide front-end indexing for the archive, and strict version control needs to be exercised by the creators of the archive. Once deposited, the archive will need to be refreshed and migrated in order to ensure stability and prevent obsolescence (Bell and Walford 2002, 40-41). There are three important international organisations that set data standards for computerised data archives: International Standards Organisation (ISO), the Open Archival Information (OASIS) and the International Council of Archives Committee on Electronic Records across the Globe (ADS 2001; Roskams 2001: 82).

Legal issues – in England, two major legal issues need to be addressed regarding archive deposition: Transfer of Title, and Copyright. Transfer of Title concerns the ownership of artefacts retrieved during excavation: these legally belong to the landowner of the site and written agreement must be obtained from this individual or group before the finds can be deposited with a museum. This obviously has an impact on museum collections, as decisions regarding selection and retention of artefacts can only be made by the museum once they legally own the material. With regard to Copyright, the creators of the documentary archive must agree to be bound by the Conditions of Copyright Agreements outlined by the museum or accepting repository, and ensure that the Copyright of material from other sources is recognised and can be respected (through the submission of a Copyright Schedule).

WIDER ISSUES

"The purpose of archaeology is to achieve, for the benefit of society, an understanding of the human past through the study and interpretation of its material remains. Therefore, at the core of archaeology lies the long-term preservation of the past for present and future benefit: this preservation occurs in situ or as an archive of finds and records in an archive repository."

(Society of Museum Archaeologists, 1995).

This section aims to address the issue of "preservation by record" as a central concern for archiving projects created through the agency of developer-led archaeological investigations and other forms of rescue archaeology, and shall also question the problems and benefits of the current system.

One of the major problems with archiving is attitude. "Archivists, like the archives in their care, still have an image problem . . . this woeful situation will not be changed overnight but as a nation we should be striving to change it" (RCHM 1999, 8). This view may be seen as somewhat overstating the case, but the issue is nonetheless a serious one. The archaeological process is often protracted, particularly for larger sites, which may undergo several phases of investigation over many years and a post-excavation and publication process of equivalent length. Archiving obviously comes at the very end of the process and it can be difficult to summon up the enthusiasm (and more importantly the time and funding) to complete the project and deposit it with a museum. "Unless archives have a determined champion on council, committee or board, the danger is that they have a very low profile indeed and command little support when it comes to the allocation of budgets. It seems to be all too widely assumed that archives can get along on a shoestring budget under officers at the lowest tier of management" (RCHM 1999, 8).

National Planning Policy Framework – NPPF – lays out specific guidelines for developer-led archaeological work in England is an example of centralised bodies' failure with regards the current issue, for while it specifies that contractors and developers should provide for publication, no mention is made of archiving requirements. The fact that NPPF[1] defines preservation by record as a 'second best option' – seemingly unaware that it may be the only option for the overwhelming majority of archaeological projects

[1] This framework replaces Planning Policy Statement 5: Planning for the Historic Environment (PPS5), which replaced Planning Policy Guidance Note 16 – or PPG16.

– serves to illustrate just how poorly archiving is served (and, unfortunately, perceived) by current policy, both official and within the field.

In general, the following, largely interlinked, nationwide problems have been identified as the result of surveys of archaeological archives:

1. A lack of identified repositories
2. A lack of space for archive holdings
3. Deposition backlogs held by fieldworkers
4. Issues with finds ownership and copyright
5. Selection and disposal criteria
6. Digital archives
7. Dissemination of information and access to archives

One of the central failings of the developer-funded publication programme is that wider research aims are not included in project designs. It is therefore vital that the archives be deposited with a museum, so that the material is available to researchers who can then undertake some of the onus of publication However, the lack of funding and personnel to support and maintain archaeological archives means that a great amount of material remains unarchived, and that researchers cannot readily access what archives there are.

Benefits of Archive Deposition:

1. **Use of older archives**

Research and re-evaluation of old archives can lead to re-interpretation of hypotheses, and may influence new fieldwork. The benefits of re-examination of archive material have been clearly demonstrated by the Grimes London Archive Project, in which the archives generated by Grimes (partially published in 1968) – head of the Roman and Medieval London Excavation Council (RMLEC) – was re-examined and published in the 1990s. This included the publication of a gazetteer listing all of his excavations in the City, site-specific studies of major excavations at St. Bride's Church and the Mithraeum, and an area study of the northwest corner of the City of London. This re-examination of excavated material and documentary archives not only led to redefinition and re-dating of sites, but also to new work including re-examination of pottery typologies and the generation of new fieldwork at several sites.

2. **New Research**

Other recent research projects based around archive reviews include GIS (Geographical Information System) reviews of archaeological deposits of different dates in the City of London, and a detailed examination of the London waterfront.

3. **Reconstructions**

Without detailed archive records, projects involving the reconstruction of structures excavated on sites would not be possible.

4. **Education and Outreach**

LAARC also hosts outreach events such as Open Days for members of the public, seminars for students and 'big digs' (using sand boxes and real artefacts) for children.

EGYPTIAN ARCHIVES

Egyptian excavations and archives bear both similarities and differences to their British counterparts. After archival material has been analysed and the final report published, it is usually deposited with the directors' nominated repository such as a museum or university, in the absence of central and regional repositories. As a result, the archives of archaeological projects undertaken in Egypt have been scattered throughout the world. There should always be a backup archive – preferably in Egypt – in order to enable scholarly access, and also to protect the work in case the primary record is damaged or destroyed. Governments may also seek to control the flow of information, and further copies of the archive are therefore called for.

As with all archival processes, location of repository and format of archive are primary considerations. Although some archaeological missions may wish to archive their data in a digital format, logistical considerations mean that it is unrealistic and impractical to expect all archaeological missions to do so. Archives must therefore be able to accept digital and paper copy, must possess the facilities for transforming one format to the other, and must also have the facility to provide access to researchers and other stakeholders[2]. In practical terms, it may be advisable to fuse CultNat's archaeological computing expertise with the MA's expertise in archaeological fieldwork, in order to establish a joint centralised archive. The hard-copy archives could be held in a section of the *Biblioteque Alexandrina* or the *Grand Egyptian Museum*, although – given the specialised needs of these archives – it may be better to build new dedicated structures to house this invaluable archaeological resource.

Once repositories are built, new protocols and guidelines will be needed to ensure that archives are created and deposited in a standardised and orderly manner[3]. The creation of regional and central archives will add further weight to MA directives requiring that archaeological projects be published within five years of their completion. As stated above, central archives will allow researchers to more easily compare primary data from various projects, and will also ensure that records pertaining to Egypt's cultural heritage are maintained in the country instead of being scattered around the world.

SPECIFIC POLICIES FOR EGYPT TO INSTIGATE

There are many actions that can and should be instigated to protect and house the archives of archaeological work undertaken in Egypt. Some general actions include the creation of all the archaeological sites that have been investigated in Egypt; this means not only researching the published data in journals such as the *ASAE,* but also the unpublished grey literature. Other specific actions can be divided into several areas:

1. *Local Exploration work undertaken by Egyptian Inspectors and other Researchers*
Old Excavations: Locate the present whereabouts of all archival material, whether in local, regional or central MA buildings, or even with individual inspectors or their families. This archival material should then be conserved before depositing it in the repository, and must also be registered on new, specially-designed forms. Sites should be revisited to gather as much missing information as possible.

New: All current and future archives must be deposited following the new protocols. New MA staff should be trained for the documentation and curation of archival material. A department should be established for the collection and collation of old archival material from both local and foreign expeditions. MA excavation policies must be restructured to include the creation and maintenance of archives.

2. *Research Undertaken by Foreign Missions*
Old: Trace old archives and assess their present state of preservation. Have these archives been digitised? If so, the MA should hold (or have access to) copies of the digital archives. The institutions holding the original site archives should fill out specially-designed forms, and to file copies of these with the MA. MA personnel should revisit any sites possessing incomplete archives, and missing information must be filled out where possible.

New: All current and future missions must use the new system. The forms and provisional archival material must be deposited with the regional/central archive before the mission leaves Egypt, followed by copies of the full archive once the project has been completed; these archival deposits must be approved by the Chief Inspectors. The archives must be sent for evaluation to a special scientific committee headed by the Minister of Antiquities and consisting of the Secretary General of the SCA, the heads of the Upper and Lower Egyptian antiquities service, and expert consultants such as Manfred Bietak, Mark Lehner, David O'Connor, James Allen, Barry Kemp, Attiya Radwan, Mohammed Abdel Nour el-Din and the directors of the French, German, Dutch, American and other institutes. The committee will vote to either accept the archive, or to recommend amendments where necessary. This quality control will ensure the quality of the archives, and also guarantee closer cooperation between foreign missions and the MA.

Current MA policy of digitising the records of artefacts held in the Egyptian Museum collections should be extended to all magazines throughout the country, enabling cross-referencing of all new and old collections. This policy should also be extended to international collections, so these can also be cross-

[2] It is essential that hard copies of archives also be held in the repositories

[3] The legal issues also need to be addressed, but this should not prove to be an insurmountable problem.

referenced. This process will be greatly facilitated by a recent trend towards digitisation by many of the world's more forward-thinking museum – such as the Petrie Museum, the Medelhavsmuseet Stockholm, the British Museum and the Louvre – which will also serve to combat illegal looting and trade, as well as providing an international support network to catch and prosecute the offenders.

CONCLUSIONS

Deposition of the archive is a fundamental part of archaeology. Excavation is by its very nature a destructive process, and the records created on the site and during post-excavation analysis represent the only surviving remains of the original archaeology. Despite this, logistical and image issues have conspired to hinder the adequate development of a standardised recording and cataloguing process, resulting in a worrying backlog of material that is now unavailable for research. It is abundantly clear that archive depositories must be established in Egypt for the good of the country's cultural heritage, and that present and future archaeologists must be held to standardised guidelines for creating and depositing their archival material. While it is probable that universally-accessible centralised digital data storage systems will eventually become the way forward for this field (Jacobs and Holland 2007; Whitcher Kansa *et al.* 2007), current logistical issues and the diverse nature of the datasets (as well as a general mistrust in digital-only storage) means that regional and national archives are the best current solution to this issue.

Glossary of Terms

Base Plan – Single-context planning produces a large amount of plans; to help make sense of these plans they need to be positioned in their exact provenience in a scale plan of the site. The plan on which field data are placed is called the base plan, a plan that depicts the whole site at 1:100 scale (1:20 can be used for small sites and 1:500 or more for large sites). The base plan must show the site grid, site datum, any temporary bench marks (control points), the positions of the trenches along with their coordinates and reference numbers and letters of any excavation sub-units.

CAD – Computer aided design.

Diazo Copy – A photomechanical copy, usually of a line drawing, in which black or coloured lines appear on a white background.

Ecofact – Any organic/environmental non-artefactual material that has been modified by humans - such as felled trees, food remains, shellfish middens, animal bones, cereal grains, coprolites and teeth - but not used as artefacts.

GIS - Geographic Information System, a spatial database.

Matrix – A site matrix, i.e. a large Harris Matrix of the site's contexts shown graphically.

Melinex Pockets – Archival Polyester Sheets (Melinex) for the transparent protection of manuscripts and other documents.

Metadata – Descriptive data about data or data content.

Plastic ended Treasury Tags – Treasury tags are short pieces of string with orthogonal plastic cross-pieces, used to thread through the holes in a stack of documents or cards and then inserted into a female tag at the other end to form a loop, so binding the documents.

Refreshing and Migrating of Archives – An act whereby digital archives are migrated to newer file formats to stop them becoming obsolete.

Relational Databases – An interrelated data stream made up various smaller databases such as can be constructed in *Access*.

References

ADS 2001. Digital archives from excavation and fieldwork *Guide to Good Practice,* 2nd Edition. (http://ads.ahds.ac.uk/project/goodguides/excavation/).

Bell, M. and Walford, K. 2002. Digital Archiving for the (Still) Terrified in *The Archaeologist*, Number 44, 40-41.

Brown, A. and Perrin, K. 1999. *A Model for the Description of Archaeological Archives* English Heritage.

de Vartavan, C. T. 2011. Curators: Digitise1 Digitise! Digitise! And spread! *AEC Egyptology Newsletter* 21: 1.

Drewett, P. L. 1999. *Field Archaeology: An Introduction.* London: UCL Press.

Ferguson, L. and Murray, D. 1995. *Archaeological documentary archives* Institute of Field Archaeologists Paper No. 1 RCHME/IFA.

Grew, F. 1998. *General Standards for the Preparation of Archaeological Archives Deposited with the Museum of London.*

Handley, M. 1999. *Microfilming archaeological archives* Institute of Field Archaeologists Paper No.2, RCHME/IFA.

Jacobs, P. and Holland, C. 2007. Sharing archaeological data: The distributed archive method, *Near Eastern Archaeology* 70(4): 197-200.

Malek, J. 2003. We have the tombs. Who needs the archives? in N. Strudwick & J. H. Taylor (eds.) *The Theban Necropolis Past, Present and Future.* London: British museum Press. pp. 229-43.

Perrin, K. 2002a. Unlocking the box: the future for archaeological archives in *CFA News*, 1.

Perrin, K. 2002b. *Archaeological Archives: Documentation, Access and Deposition. A Way Forward* English Heritage.

Pickering, P. 2002. Learning from ten years of PPG16 in *London Archaeologist*, Volume 10, No. 3.

RCHM. 1999. *Archives at the Millennium: the 28th Report of the Royal Commission on Historical Manuscripts 1991-99.*

Roskams, S. 2001. *Excavation.* Cambridge: Cambridge University Press.

Tassie, G. J. & Owens, L. S. 2010. *Standards of Archaeological Excavation: A Fieldguide to the Excavation Methodology, Recording Techniques and Conventions.* London: ECHO Publications and Golden House Publications.

SCOLA. 1995. *Archaeology and Planning in London: Assessing the effectiveness of PPG16.*

Swain, H. 1998. *A Survey of Archaeological Archives in England: a report prepared for English Heritage and the Museum and Galleries Commission.*

Swain, H. 1999. 'Taking London Archaeology to Londoners' in *London Archaeologist*, Volume 9, No.1, 3-5.

Whitcher Kansa, S., Kansa, E. C. and Schultz, J. M. 2007. An open context for Near Eastern archaeology, *Near Eastern Archaeology* 70(4): 188-194.

Chapter 5

Contemporary Egyptian Dialogues: Collaborative Approaches to Museum Displays of Ancient Egypt

Gemma Tully

ABSTRACT

Contemporary perceptions of ancient Egypt are unquestionably influenced by two centuries of Western research tradition, which focused primarily on monuments, death and the elite over narratives of daily life. This, allied with the tendency to define living Egyptians as disconnected, 'Oriental' or 'other' means that current understandings of ancient Egypt continue to disenfranchise modern Egyptians from the past, and to replicate powerful stereotypes. This exclusivist approach to Egyptology is inconsistent with twenty-first century archaeological methodologies, which aim to collaborate with diverse communities – 'source', visitor and academic – in order to enhance understanding of the past.

Following a four-year collaborative project with members of the modern Egyptian community, expert Egyptologists and non-experts, this paper aims to reveal current Egyptian perspectives on the ancient Egyptian past. Addressing centuries of Western 'tunnel vision', the Egyptian voices presented here offer suggestions for the future of Egyptological scholarship and museum display that can be integrated alongside the needs of Western audiences and academics. Finding a means of negotiating ancient and modern Egypt, identity and academia, East and West, this research is essential if we are to engage Egyptology with contemporary debate, and to address issues of ethics and multivocality in the furthering of knowledge.

INTRODUCTION

> *It is better for philosophy to err in active participation in the living struggles and issues of its own age and times than to maintain an immune monastic impeccability, without relevancy and bearing in the generating of ideas of its contemporary present.* (John Dewey 1916: 62)

This opening quote by the American philosopher and psychologist John Dewey encapsulates arguably the most important issue to modern scholarship – contemporary relevance. Egyptology, following more than two hundred years of Western research tradition, continues to focus on the mystery and grandeur of the ancient civilisation, marginalising daily life themes and the views of living Egyptians (Reid 2002; Assman 2003; Moser,2006). While Egyptologists are beginning to refocus research on the lives of 'ordinary' people in ancient Egypt, alongside pressure from post-colonial theorists (Gero *et al.* 1983; Gero 1985; Layton 1989; Pinsky & Wylie 1989; Atkinson *et al.* 1996; Franklin 1997; McDavid & Babson 1997; Meskell 1998), and despite the fact that the Egyptian authorities are promoting collaboration, changes are not communicated effectively in the public arena. The problem is perhaps most apparent in the museum sphere where 21st century audiences (like their 18th century counterparts) may well stare in awe at 'wondrous curiosities' (Moser 2006), but struggle to make personal connections between ancient Egyptian lives and their own. Similarly, modern Egypt is invisible within this relationship because contemporary museum images – following the style of early Western landscape painters in Egypt (Clayton 1982; Conner 1983; Jacobs 1995) – continue to focus on unpopulated desert ruins or archaic scenes of rural life. This – and Western media portrayals – means that the realities of modern Egypt are little known beyond the country's borders. This may be exacerbated by the power of lingering Orientalist ideology, which used the arrival of Islam in Egypt as a means of divorcing the population from their ancient heritage.

This chapter aims to explore the variety of roles ancient Egypt plays in Egyptian life today. Challenging multiple stereotypes of Egypt, ancient and modern, the following dialogues will reveal how collaboration with Egyptian communities can help displays of daily life in Egypt compete with – and complement – the visual qualities of monumental architecture and mortuary paraphernalia. This research aims to convince practitioners that non-traditional partnerships of this form are mutually beneficial, and that greater collaboration between curators, 'source' and visiting communities can imbue historical displays with modern life and generally engage with contemporary debate in a manner that will enable the museum to retain a place of value in society.

ORIGINS

In late January of 2006, I was visiting Egypt as part of the University of Southampton's Community Archaeology Project in Quseir (henceforth CAPQ), a collaborative venture between British archaeologists and the local community that had been developing since 1998 (see Peacock *et al.* 2000; 2001; 2002; 2003; Moser *et al.* 2002). I had recently met Richard Parkinson from the Department of Egypt and the Sudan at the British Museum (now Oxford University), who informed me of plans to redisplay some of the museum's 'greatest treasures', the eighteenth dynasty tomb-chapel paintings of Nebamun. The aim was to use the tomb-chapel scenes, which contained lifelike depictions of social activities (from elite festivities to peasants herding cattle) to address the imbalance in public knowledge and museological representation between 'ordinary' and 'elite' ancient Egyptian lifestyles (fig. 5.1). In order to explore the absence of 'everyday' themes in Egyptology exhibitions, and to pursue a community archaeology approach (Pardoe 1992; McDavid 1997; Herle 2000; Field *et al.* 2000; Moser *et al.* 2002; Smith 2004; Tully 2007), I took images of the exhibition to Quseir and shared them with my Egyptian colleagues. Our discussion of the British Museum's plans and their perspectives on the representation of ancient Egypt in the West made it immediately clear that further such research was necessary to address the obvious disparity between different forms of Egyptological knowledge - expert and public, Egypt and West.

In late January of 2006, I was visiting Egypt as part of the University of Southampton's Community Archaeology Project in Quseir (henceforth CAPQ), a collaborative venture between British archaeologists and the local community that had been developing since 1998 (see Peacock *et al.* 2000; 2001; 2002; 2003; Moser *et al.* 2002). I had recently met Richard Parkinson from the Department of Egypt and the Sudan at the British Museum, who informed me of plans to redisplay some of the museum's 'greatest treasures', the eighteenth dynasty tomb-chapel paintings of Nebamun. The aim was to use the tomb-chapel scenes, which contained lifelike depictions of social activities (from elite festivities to peasants herding cattle) to address the imbalance in public knowledge and museological representation between 'ordinary' and 'elite' ancient Egyptian lifestyles (fig. 5.1). In order to explore the absence of 'everyday' themes in Egyptology exhibitions, and to pursue a community archaeology approach (Pardoe 1992; McDavid 1997; Herle 2000; Field *et al.* 2000; Moser *et al.* 2002; Smith 2004; Tully 2007), I took images of the exhibition to Quseir and shared them with my Egyptian colleagues. Our discussion of the British Museum's plans and their perspectives on the representation of ancient Egypt in the West made it immediately clear that further such research was necessary to address the obvious disparity between different forms of Egyptological knowledge - expert and public, Egypt and West.

The Quseir dialogues raised five points regarding the transformation of ancient Egypt from a completely 'dead' culture to one with resonance with the present.

1) Working with Egyptian and Western museum audiences in the exhibition development process to create dynamic display methods
2) Encouraging the co-representation of daily life and the more popularly presented theme of death
3) Showing a range of elite and non-elite lifeways in ancient Egypt through the combination of tomb-chapel scenes and artefacts, and seeking modern equivalents, in order to address the invariably elitist and 'distant' nature of ancient Egyptian culture
4) Creating an atmospheric exhibition that would resonate with audiences' own lives while provoking the reconsideration of perceptions of ancient and modern Egypt
5) Contextualising ancient and modern Egyptian narratives, to present Pharaonic Egypt as part of a continuum rather than an isolate, revered at the cost of living culture[1].

These principal aims led to the development of a methodology embedded in postmodern theories of relative history concepts (Assman 2003: viii), explicitly acknowledging that archaeology and associated practices 'construct the past' (Moser 2003: 3) and thus play a powerful role in the mediation of modern identities (Ames 1992; Coombes 1994; Bennett 1995; Lidchi 1997; Caulton 1998; Hein 1998; Hooper-Greenhill 2000; MacDonald 2002). My research was governed by 1) The perspectives of the Egyptian community, 2) The desires of Western museum visitors, and 3) Visual analysis of current Western Egyptological exhibitions. It should therefore be remembered that while Egyptian dialogues provide the

[1] These themes bear a striking resemblance to those raised in recent Western museological debates surrounding more general issues of archaeology exhibitions (Flynn, 2009: 20-25) and the 'new museology' (Layton 1989; Karp & Lavine 1991; Karp *et al.* 1992; Kaplan 1994; Kreps 1998; 2003; Hooper-Greenhill 2000; Peers & Brown 2003).

focus of this chapter, these also relate to the traditions of Egyptology exhibitions, and of course must also consider the needs of contemporary needs of all agents involved in the drive towards museological change (Tully 2010).

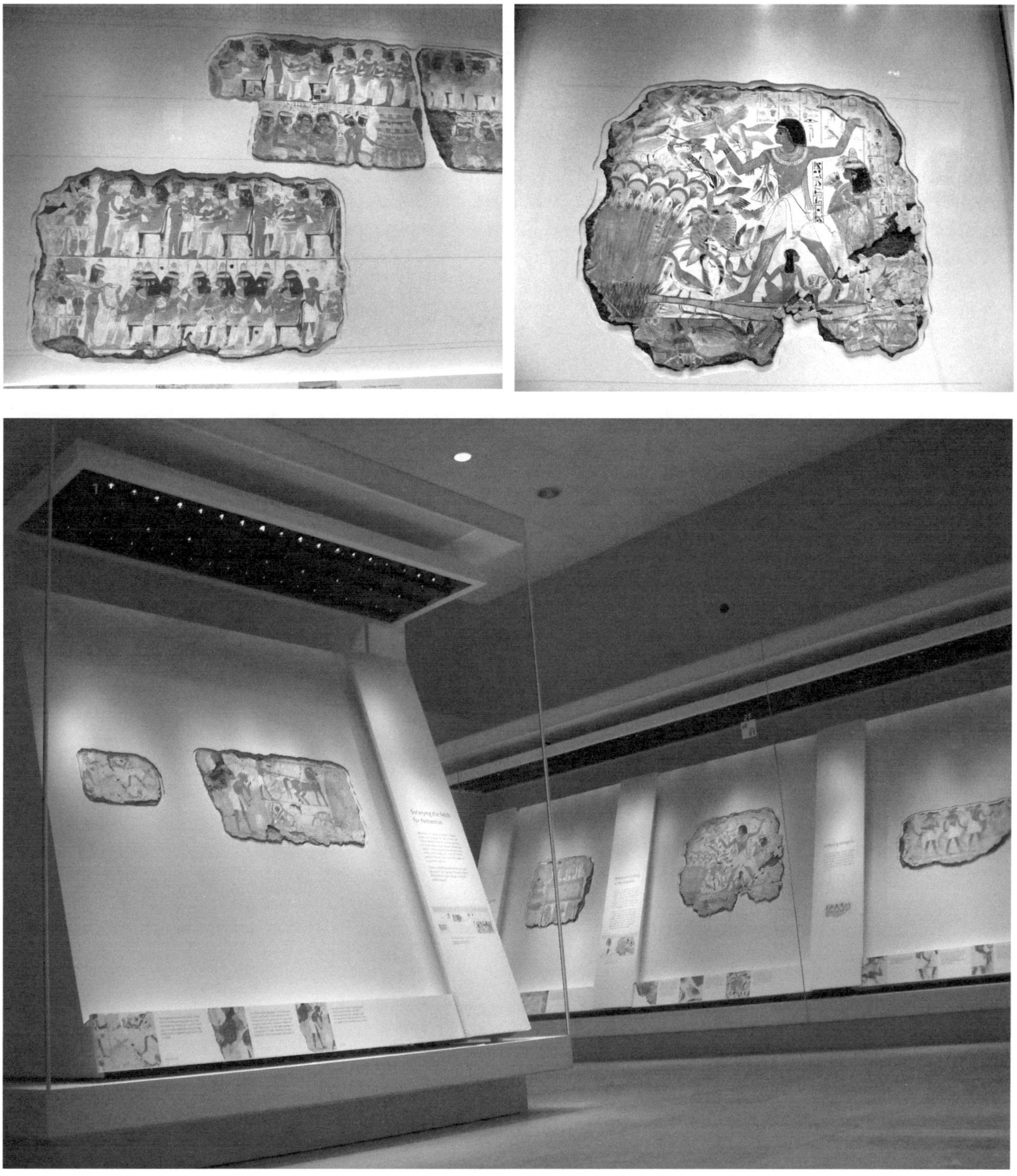

Figure 5.1: The Nebamun exhibition at the British Museum (photographed by Gemma Tully)

METHODOLOGY

Engagement with members of the Egyptian community took place over a six-month period[2], during which I hoped assess Egyptian voices' power to reposition Egyptological practice and perception in museum contexts. Following the principles laid out in Tully (2007), I interviewed 150+ individuals

[2] From January to June 2007

concerning their perception of Egyptian identity, and ancient and modern Egyptian heritage. The sample was balanced between professional and non-professional, was geographically disparate (Alexandria to Aswan), and were self-defined as being as one or a combination of Egyptian, Arab, Nubian, Bedouin, Muslim, Christian and Atheist. I made it clear that all participants were to be cast in the role of expert, and that all opinions were valid. This 'archaeological ethnography' approach (Meskell 2007) revealed personal perspectives on the modern role of ancient Egypt, the West's perspective on Egyptian culture past and present, and how Egyptology should be displayed.

OPENING DIALOGUES

Questions involving the role ancient Egypt plays in shaping individuals' identities provided a powerful opening point for discussion. Although there was by no means universal consensus, the majority of interlocutors stressed connections between the history of their country and modern Egyptian identity. Whether through direct links to the ancient Egyptians or as part of a general continuum, the past was clearly tied up with the present. Those who were directly involved in working with sites and antiquities felt direct ancestry with ancient groups, and perhaps reflects the personal internalisation of lived experience. One of the guards at the Cairo Museum said: 'these are my ancestors; this is not a job for money. You talk to any of the guards and most of them feel the same.' Many locals from the Qurna area (Luxor West Bank) stressed the importance of traceable descent. A tomb guard from Deir el-Medina said that, 'families have always lived here, for hundreds of generations…they were the original Egyptians and anyone who says otherwise hurts us.' These are evidently fairly widely held sentiments. Mohammed (owner of the Sennofer Café and Guest House in Qurna) believed that people and the tombs 'are all tied together; they have always been and should stay that way', an opinion shared by a temple guard at Peshedu in Deir el-Medina ('the tombs and the life are entwined'). These sentiments may be genuine measures of affinity, yet may also have been forcibly voiced in the hope of asserting local rights to remain in an area due to be transformed into the *Tombs of the Nobles Tourist Park*. However, there are also indications that such interest is not entirely mercenary. Omar, a tour guide who had never lived in Qurna, believed that a small number of tombs should be sacrificed if 'people could remain' and 'life could continue', while Mohammed and Omar (two young men working in a local alabaster factory) told me that while they enjoyed living in modern houses at New Qurna, they felt that they had lost their history and their relationships with the people and tombs of 'Old' Qurna. These feelings are echoed by those who have grown prosperous and moved away, such as my translator Mahmoud, who was born in Qurna in a house built over an Egyptian tomb in which his family often slept during hot summer months. In his own words:

> Qurna is a difficult one, and so personal. I think that the people should have been made to leave because the water was damaging the tombs, but that the government should have left some of the houses as they were part of the bigger history of Qurna. I have spent so many years with tourists and I know they would have been interested to see the continuation of life. People lived in the same place for thousands of years – lived – it was not only a site of death and I think removing the history is a big mistake.

Mahmoud's comments on 'living' tombs and 'removing history' through house clearance were echoed in the Sennofer Café guestbook, which contained hundreds of messages, articles and copies of letters sent to the Egyptian government, as pleas for the Qurna area to remain unchanged. This would tend to suggest that tourists are open to 'real life' experiences, not a purely dead ancient Egypt. This is also a professionally held view: Dr Meguid (Nubia Museum, Aswan) argued that '…now, tourism is different, people come to see the people...they don't only come for the antiquities but to see people like themselves.' Such statements reflect the need to reassess the stories museums tell and the voices that speak the narrative.

In so far as the continuum of history is concerned, the hybridist nature of modern identity was expressed by numerous individuals, including Dr Eldamaty, ex-curator of the Egyptian Museum in Cairo and now the Minister of Antiquities:

> Egypt is Egypt, it has a long history from ancient through all periods. It is one timeline. We are derived today from so many people: Hyksos, Kushites, Persians, Greeks, Romans; it is a mixing jar but we are all Egyptian…Today's identity is a result of all of this, not only one part of our history but all, and we need to find our modern identities in relation to all of our history. We are not only the sons of Pharaohs and they were not the only success of our nation.

Elham Salah Eldien (Coptic Museum, Cairo) sees this continuum as '…a ring, a chain of evolution and continuation' within which all periods of history should be considered equally, as even if some eras appear weak in terms of overall heritage, each era 'played a part in shaping the next and was shaped by what went before.'

It was not only museum professionals who expressed such views. Haytham, a Masters student at the AUC (American University in Cairo), told me:

> It is difficult to discuss the connection between modern Egyptians and ancient Egyptians because of so much change from ancient Egypt, to the Copts, to the Islamic period and modern Egypt. Current society is a culmination of all of these civilisations and this is what is great about Egypt, you can see history everywhere. We should not separate it all out in museums as we will lose our sense of history; it needs to be understood as a whole.

The issue of communication has also been raised, notably the feeling that historical narratives are not communicated effectively beyond the country's borders was also addressed by Myrium, an AUC student:

> There are two very different ways of understanding Egypt. In the West it is logical and scientific but focused on just one era. Here history all melds into one. Egyptians care about different elements for different reasons. The past exists and all Egyptians take pride in their history and this is something that is not seen by the outside world.

The divide between Western pigeonholing of Egyptian history and Egyptian promotion of amalgamation and succession is most evident within the museum sphere, where Western traditions tend to promote an unbalanced narrative of Egyptian past and present. Owing to a long-term fascination with the Dynastic period, Roman, Coptic and Predynastic periods are marginalised while the Islamic period is either absent or spatially distanced and integrated into a general Arab-Islamic history. This issue has been addressed by many contemporary Egyptian museums (Doyon 2007; 2008), that promote a more balanced, non-Orientalist rhetoric than has historically been the case (Reid 2002).

There has thus been a trend towards Egyptian museology's incorporation of different periods and cultures, even within seemingly specialised museums – such as Luxor – which spans the Predynastic to the Islamic period (see Doyon 2007: 105). Reda Salah (Egyptian Museum in Cairo) points out that even though exhibits are specific, the museum is used to promote 'all eras of history' to school groups. By reinventing themselves as a cultural palimpsest, Egyptians are reclaiming their heritage from the West and thus promote all kinds of their history as essential partners that transcend the bounds of exclusivist Western discourse.

Numerous individuals expressed concern at the lack of exhibition communication between Egyptians and Western museums, professionals and local communities. As Dr Meguid (Nubia Museum), put it:

> The roles of the museum and the archaeological community need to be mutually complementary. We need to be in touch with our communities to let them know what we are doing and to understand their feelings toward us.

Dr Meguid also saw the need for a parallel approach in terms of the presentation of Egypt beyond the country's borders, saying:

> When museums present other cultures it is mostly from a Western point of view. We need to keep ideas open. Museums should not be about imposing ideologies. Curators often live on different islands to visitors and communities, and this needs to change.

The need for collaborative strategies in Egyptological representation was also addressed by many university students. Haytham perhaps articulated this most clearly:

> We all read and learn about ancient Egypt from a Western point of view. There are Egyptian books that address these issues but we are not encouraged to read them, so the Western view has

> a huge influence... Ancient Egypt needs to find this modern Egyptian perspective in the West to create a balance.

Stereotypes and unchanging images of Egypt were also raised as both reasons for (and hindrances to) cross-cultural collaboration. Haytham called for further co-operation between Western and Egyptian society, arguing that 'our ancient history is the only thing that is promoted; even the ministry of tourism here only focuses on ancient Egypt.' Haytham's point is certainly a valid one – the international view of Egypt has proved remarkably resistant to change. As Mernat from the Coptic Museum put it, 'those in the West see ancient Egypt much like the Egyptians do.' This is due in part to what Dr Meguid called the 'old Egyptologists' way', which focuses almost exclusively on religion, mortuary practice and the pharaohs. I tested this assertion with the assistance of AUC students. I also involved a number of non-Egyptians, asking them whether perceptions of ancient Egypt had changed since coming to live in the country. The majority of students said no; of those that said yes, the dominant change was only in terms of the most superficial misconceptions. As one 21 year-old female American student of Middle Eastern history stated, 'my opinion of ancient Egypt has changed as I've realised that Egypt is not all about mummies and pyramids; there is a very rich social and political history too!'. However, most AUC student views reflected a widespread lack of in-depth understanding of Egypt, a result duplicated in the British Museum (see Tully 2010).

AUC students were interviewed in order to assess their perception stereotyping concerning ancient Egypt. While many students voiced concern about stereotyped western views of modern Egypt, only a minority voiced similar concerns for ancient perceptions. One 22 year-old Egyptian female anthropology student wrote, 'I don't believe my opinion of ancient Egypt is any different to the West'. It became clear that understandings remain coloured by Western preconceptions of Egyptological knowledge, despite the fact that most of the AUC students had directly experienced ancient Egypt. This inconsistent duality of perception and training can be seen at the very highest levels. Egypt's image of a land of the elite, shrouded in mystery and preoccupied with death, is one that will not be shaken. In a lecture at the American University in Cairo, Dr Zahi Hawass[3] addressed his predominantly Egyptian audience with phrases such as 'the adventure and thrill of discovery…mummies have magic and secrets' and 'the Valley of the Kings - the place that has magic'. This paean to heritage tourism is a direct contradiction of Hawass' official website, which has a distinctly more sombre approach to issues such as mummy relocation to the new National Museum of Egyptian Culture in Fustat, where 'they will be displayed for educational purposes rather than for thrills.'[4] These inconsistencies have bedevilled the subject, and the chances of finding 'the real people' of Egypt – ancient or modern – are small indeed unless we can cut 200 years of monomaniac Egyptomania (Curl 1982; 1994). Certainly, the international attitude towards (and understanding of) Egypt is less than encouraging (Glazier 2005; Doyon 2007; 2008). As Loutfy Abd Elhamid from the Egyptian Museum told me:

> People in the West don't know that much about ancient Egypt but they really don't know much about modern Egypt. Tourists are often shocked when they come here and see that we're not living in the desert like the Bedouin. You mustn't forget that many people in the East also think like this about modern Egyptians, it's not just a Western thing. The problem is that we always focus on ancient Egypt for tourism and never on modern Egypt, so people only see the same images of sand, camels and monuments.

Sherif, a civil engineer in Cairo, added that many of Egypt's problems are created by the outside world, as the simplification of culture makes it easier for those in the West to extract views that enhance their own scholarly, political and socio-economic position. Contemporary artist Khaled Hafez also raised the issue of inaccurate external representation, attributing many of Egypt's problems to the West's appropriation of the East, and the recycling of themes in its exhibits. Thus death and the Pharaohs embody ancient Egypt, while identity, sexuality and gender define the modern Middle East. Sherif suggested a route out of this unhealthy relationship:

> We need to make our future and stop focusing on the past, we need to modernise and overcome stereotypes. Many people here only see the negative side of the West and the war in Iraq and it is

---

3 18th of April, 2007

4 See http://guardians.net/hawass/news/new_mummy_room_at_the_cairo_museum.htm

> the same with many in the West thinking of Muslims as uneducated religious fanatics. Poverty is our main problem and television is a problem for the world as it is only one view and creates hatred.

One way to achieve a greater balance of representation and overcome the multidirectional flow of stereotypes is by dealing with people cross-culturally and incorporating 'real people', both past and present, into the museum sphere. Rashid, a shop owner in Luxor, suggested:

> We need to show the real Egypt of now in museums also, to show change and that we don't all ride camels around the desert. We need to spread this kind of knowledge and interest, tying in Egypt today and talking about people and normal life from all generations, taking into account differences and similarities.

The need for more historically and experientially contextualised representations of Egypt was promoted further during discussion on Egyptology displays. For example, various individuals expressed a desire to know how the Nebamun tomb-chapel paintings came to be in the British Museum. Lamiaa, one of the staff at the Egyptian Museum, suggested that, 'it is good to recreate the tomb but along with this you must tell people its whole history from ancient Egypt up to today to show people who cannot visit Egypt.'

The need for dramatic interpretation of atmosphere, or 'mood', frequently arose in these surveys, especially in connection with contextualising ancient Egyptian artefacts. Egyptian artist Elhamy Naguib told me that 'the feeling is the most important element to recapture'. When asking how individuals would like to experience the tomb-chapel paintings, the majority opted for a recreated tomb as it would: 'create the right feeling/atmosphere', 'be more authentic/realistic', 'help you to imagine how the ancient Egyptians thought/what life was like', 'be more visually interesting/eye-catching' and 'provide clearer meaning.' Naguib also discussed the potential for cross-temporal display as a means of communication. Using the Whitney Museum in New York as an example, he said:

> They [Whitney Museum] used various things to unite American culture between 1945 and 1995 and a great amount of time and energy has gone into finding relationships between items. This concept of pulling together all elements from a certain material culture is a good approach as every visitor can find something that fascinates him. This will be the same in Egyptology exhibits if you can find things and link the past to people's experiences today.

Loutfy Abd Elhamid emphasised the importance of revealing 'the people behind the tombs, normal people' through the inclusion of original tools and objects that express both similarities and differences in activities and mentalities to today. Moving away from the traditionally aloof nature of the ancient Egyptian past to focus on elements of the everyday, Dr Meguid also expressed the need for new approaches:

> We have to forget the old ideas, we need to talk to real Egyptians living now and connect now to Egypt's past – not only kings and queens but more daily life, people are getting bored of kings, daily life is new!

Numerous individuals stressed the importance of the daily life theme as a means of making ancient Egyptian history more accessible in museum displays. New dialogues centred on everyday lives offer a way to address all of the issues raised here, and to reposition the museum as a forum for cross-cultural dialogue that can move beyond centuries of stereotypes.

SUMMARISING COLLABORATION

The Egyptian perspectives presented here offer a means of re-focusing museological methodology. While there is obviously more research to do, what we have learned so far underscores the fact that the past plays a vital role in the shaping of Egyptian identity and the representation of Egypt, both within and beyond the country's borders. Greater collaboration between Egyptians and museum professionals, Egypt and the West, is essential to relate ancient Egypt to the modern country. Repopulating both Egypts through both living voices and the theme of daily life will enable museums to find resonance with people's lives in the present. The research also reflects the ethical role museums could play in the presentation of Egyptian heritage to benefit contemporary Egyptians, rather than acting as objects of power within 'modern Orientalism'. International attitudes towards Egypt, both within the country and overseas, support Egyptian calls for change (Tully 2010). Discussions of context, atmosphere, familiarity, the unification of past and present, Egypt and West, and life and death, all emphasised the same themes within the specific context of Nebamun's tomb-chapel. Recent changes in Egyptian museology circles suggest that the role of ancient Egypt in the formation of modern Egyptian identities has now transcended traditional Western arguments of exclusion. It is also apparent that Egyptians have interests in their own past that transcend the purely mercenary (i.e. political and economic) and that the old claim that Islam has driven a non-negotiable wedge between two polarised Egyptian identities cannot be substantiated. It is also evident that Western museum exhibits of Egyptology can be enhanced through collaboration with Egyptian agents, whose voices must no longer be ignored. While the current research may not do full justice to the multiplicity of Egyptian understandings of their past, these perspectives provide a crucial departure point from which to engage Egyptology with contemporary debate, and to address the role of museums in the furthering of knowledge.

REFERENCES

Ames, M. 1992. *Cannibal Tours and Glass Boxes: The Anthropology of Museums.* Vancouver: University of British Columbia Press.

Assman, J. 2003. *The Mind of Egypt: History and Meaning in the Time of the Pharaohs.* New York: Metropolitan Books.

Atkinson, J., Banks, I. and O'Sullivan, J. (eds) 1996. *Nationalism and Archaeology.* Glasgow: Cruithne Press.

Bennett, T. 1995. *The Birth of the Museum.* London: Routledge.

Caulton, T. 1998. *Hands on Exhibitions: Managing Interactive Museums and Science Centres.* London: Routledge.

Clayton, P. A. 1982. *The Rediscovery of Ancient Egypt: Artists and Travellers in the 19th Century.* London: Thames and Hudson.

Conner, P. (ed.) 1983. *The Inspiration of Egypt. The Influence on British Artists, Travellers and Designers 1700-1900.* Brighton: Brighton Borough Council.

Coombes, A. 1994. *Re-inventing Africa: Museums, Material Culture and Popular Imagination in Late Victorian and Edwardian England.* New Haven: Yale University Press.

Curl, J. S. 1982. *Egyptomania: The Egyptian Revival. An Introductory Study of a Recurring Theme in the History of Taste.* London: George Allen and Unwin.

Curl, J. S. 1994. *Egyptomania: The Egyptian Revival: A Recurring Theme in the History of Taste.* Second Edition. Manchester: Manchester University Press.

Dewey, J. [1916] 1966. D*emocracy and Education. An Introduction to the Philosophy of Education.* New York: Free Press.

Doyon, W. 2007. *Representing Egypt's Past: Archaeology and Identity in Egyptian Museum Practice.* Masters of Art: University of Washington.

Doyon, W. 2008. The poetics of Egyptian museum practice, *British Museum Studies in Ancient Egypt and the Sudan* 10: 1-37.

Field, J., Barker, J., Barker, R., Coffey, E., Coffey, L., Crawford, E., Darcy, L., Fields, T., Lord, G., Steadman, B. and Colley, S. 2000. 'Coming back': Aborigines and archaeologists at Cuddie Springs, *Public Archaeology* 1(1): 35–48.

Flynn, T. 2009. Revealing all, *Museums Journal,* September: 20-25.

Franklin, M. 1997. Power to the people: Sociopolitics and the archaeology of the Black Americans, *Historical Archaeology* 31: 36-50.

Gero, J. M., Lacy, D. and Blakey, M. L. (eds) 1983. *The Socio-politics of Archaeology.* Ameshurst, Massachusetts: University of Massachusetts research report, series 23.

Gero, J. M. 1985. Socio-politics of archaeology and the woman-at-home ideology, *American Antiquity* 50: 342-350.

Hawass, Z. 2007. *Recent Discoveries.* 18th April, Ewart Hall, Lecture given at the American University in Cairo.

Hein, G. 1998. *Learning in the Museum.* London: Routledge.

Herle, A. 2000. Torres Strait islanders' stories from an exhibition, *Ethnos* 65(2): 253-274.

Hooper-Greenhill, E. 2000. *Museums and the Interpretation of Visual Culture.* London: Routledge.

Jacobs, M. 1995. *The Painted Voyage.* London: British Museum Press.

Kaplan, F.E.S. 1994. *Museums and the Making of Ourselves: The Role of Objects in National Identity.* London: Leicester University Press.

Karp, I. and Lavine, S. D. 1991. *Exhibiting Cultures: The Poetics and Politics of Museum Display.* Washington: Smithsonian Institute Press.

Karp, I., Kreamer, C. M. and Lavine, S. D. 1992. *Museums and Communities: The Politics of Public Culture.* Washington: Smithsonian Institutional Press.

Kreps. C. 1998. Museum-making and indigenous curation in central Kalimantan, Indonesia, *Museum Anthropology* 22(1): 5-17.

Kreps. C. 2003. *Liberating Culture. Cross-cultural Perspectives on Museums, Curation and Heritage Preservation.* London: Routledge.

Layton, R. (ed.).1989. *Who Needs the Past? Indigenous Values and Archaeology.* London: Unwin Hyman.

Lidchi, H. 1997. The poetics and the politics of exhibiting other cultures, in S. Hall (ed.) *Representation: Cultural Representation and Signifying Practice.* London: Sage, pp. 151-224.

MacDonald, S. 2002. *Behind the Scenes at the Science Museum.* Oxford: Berg.

McDavid, C. 1997. Descendants, decisions and power: The public interpretation of the archaeology of the Levi Jordan plantation, *Historical Archaeology,* 31(3): 114–131.

McDavid, C. and Babson, D. W. (eds) 1997. Introduction: The realm of politics: Prospects for public participation in African American plantation archaeology, *Historical Archaeology* 31(3): 114-131.

Meskell, L. (ed.). 1998. *Archaeology Under Fire.* London: Routledge

Meskell, L. 2007. Falling walls and mending fences. Archaeological ethnography in the Limpopo, *Journal of South African Studies* 33(2): 383-400.

Moser, S., Glazier, D., Philips, J., El Nemer, L. N., Mousa, M. S., Richardson, S., Conner, A. and Seymour, M. 2002. Transforming archaeology through practice: Strategies for collaborative practice in the community archaeology project at Quseir, Egypt, *World Archaeology* 34(2): 220-248.

Moser, S. 2003. Representing archaeological knowledge in museums. Exhibiting human origins and strategies for change, *Public Archaeology,* 3: 3-20.

Moser, S. 2006. *Wondrous curiosities. Ancient Egypt at the British Museum.* Chicago: Chicago University Press.

Pardoe, C. 1992. Archers of radii, corridors of power: Reflections on current archaeological practice, in B. Atwood and J. Arnold (eds) *Power, Knowledge and Aborigines.* Melbourne: La Trobe University Press, pp. 132-141.

Peacock, D. P. S., Blue. L., Bradford, N. and Moser, S. 2000. *Myos Hormos, Quseir al-Qadim: A Roman and Islamic Port on the Red Sea Coast of Egypt.* Interim report for Supreme Council of Antiquities, Cairo, Egypt: Department of Archaeology, University of Southampton.

Peacock, D. P. S., Blue. L., Bradford, N. and Moser, S. 2001. *Myos Hormos, Quseir al-Qadim: A Roman and Islamic Port on the Red Sea Coast of Egypt.* Interim report for Supreme Council of Antiquities, Cairo, Egypt: Department of Archaeology, University of Southampton.

Peacock, D. P. S., Blue. L. and Moser, S. 2002. *Myos Hormos, Quseir al-Qadim: A Roman and Islamic Port on the Red Sea Coast of Egypt.* Interim report for Supreme Council of Antiquities, Cairo, Egypt: Department of Archaeology, University of Southampton.

Peacock, D. P. S., Blue. L. and Moser, S. 2003. *Myos Hormos, Quseir al-Qadim: A Roman and Islamic Port on the Red Sea Coast of Egypt.* Interim report for Supreme Council of Antiquities, Cairo, Egypt: Department of Archaeology, University of Southampton.

Peers, L. and Brown, A. K. (eds) 2003. *Museums and Source Communities: A Routledge Reader.* London: Routledge.

Pinsky, V. and Wylie, A. (eds) 1989. *Critical Traditions in Contemporary Archaeology.* Cambridge: Cambridge University Press.

Reid, D. M. 2002. *Whose Pharaohs? Archaeology, Museums and Egyptian National Identity from Napoleon to World War One.* London: University of California Press.

Smith, L. J. 2004. *Archaeological Theory and the Politics of Cultural Heritage.* London: Routledge.

Tully, G. 2007. Community archaeology: General methods and standards of practice, *Public Archaeology* 6(3): 155-187.

Tully, G. 2010. *'Answering the Calls of the Living': Collaborative Practice in Archaeology and Ancient Egyptian Daily Life Display in Western Museums.* Unpublished PhD thesis: University of Southampton

Chapter 6

Egyptian Antiquities on the Market

David W. J. Gill

ABSTRACT

Several million dollars' worth of Egyptian antiquities are sold on the market every year. The majority of these items seem to have surfaced for the first time since 1973, the date of the Archaeological Institute of America's 'Resolution of the Acquisition of Antiquities by Museums'. Some of the material appearing on the market appears to have been removed from archaeological stores in Egypt. There is also clear evidence that reliefs and other items are being removed from recorded tombs. Many other items, such as the Akhmim stelae, come from previously unknown sites, and their removal has led to a loss of knowledge about the original contexts. The scandals surrounding the return of antiquities to Italy has resulted in more rigorous acquisition policies being developed by North American museums. This is likely to suppress the market for Egyptian objects that do not have recorded collecting histories.

INTRODUCTION

Several thousand Egyptian antiquities appear on the market each year, prompting a series of questions: are they from old collections? Are they recently surfaced finds? Have they been illegally exported from Egypt? Are they modern fakes? Egyptian antiquities have been collected in modern times since at least the eighteenth century (Fagan 2004). It is unrealistic, and indeed undesirable, to call for a universal ban on the sale of archaeological material that has contextual origins in Egypt. The main concern must be to discourage the looting of unknown archaeological sites in order to provide new material for the market. The scale of looting in some parts of the world such as the southern Aegean (Gill and Chippindale 1993) and southern Italy (Elia 2001), is now being quantified (Chippindale *et al.* 2001). However, there has been no detailed study of the scale of looting in Egypt, although it seems to have greatly increased since the 25th January Revolution.

THE SCALE OF THE MARKET

The value of the antiquities market has almost certainly been exaggerated. It has often been placed third after drugs and weapons. So far there has been no attempt to calculate the scale of the antiquities market, though at a conservative estimate it is probably in the region of several hundred million dollars a year (Gill and Chippindale 2002: 51-53). The seizure of the stock of London-based dealer Robin Symes, consisting of approximately 17,000 objects, has been valued at $250 million (Watson 2006: 94). However, it is unclear if this 'snapshot' of stock in hand is an accurate one, and whether the size of these holdings can be considered to be representative of all dealers in antiquities. In 1997 Sotheby's decided to stop selling antiquities in London following the disclosure and publication of internal paperwork (Watson 1997). The sale of antiquities was consolidated in New York and a study of the subsequent sales shows that Sotheby's sold some $306 million worth of antiquities from June 1998 to December 2010 (29 sales in total). Over $64 million of this (i.e. 21%) was obtained from the sale of Egyptian antiquities. Christie's New York sold over $169 million worth of antiquities between 1999 and December 2010. There has been a marked downward trend in the percentage value of Egyptian antiquities at Sotheby's. Some years (i.e. 1998) saw Egyptian antiquities fetching over 40% of the value of the sale, while recent years (i.e. 2007 and 2009) shown the proportion to be closer to 12%.

A single raid in the Geneva Freeport in August 2003 saw the confiscation of over 200 Egyptian antiquities, to include two mummies and several sarcophagi. This was apparently the result of a six-month investigation into an international 'smuggling ring' that included Swiss, Canadian, German and Kenyan nationals. The subsequent trial (in 2004) saw ringleader Tariq al-Suwaysi sentenced to 35 years in prison, and nine others to 15 years *in absentia* (see Meier and Gottlieb 2004). In October 2004, 619 Egyptian antiquities were seized at Heathrow after being consigned from Switzerland. In another incident, an Australian antiquities dealer was detained at Cairo in December 2008 as he tried to leave on a flight for Thailand with a selection of antiquities.

The percentage of Egyptian antiquities passing through Sotheby's in New York in the last decade suggest that approximately two-thirds do not appear to have a recorded collecting-history that can be traced back to the period before 1973, the date of the Archaeological Institute of America's 'Resolution of the Acquisition of Antiquities by Museums'. This date has been used for previous studies (Gill and Chippindale 1993; Chippindale and Gill 2000; Chippindale *et al.* 2001) and it marks a point when professional archaeologists as well as museum curators, collectors and those involved in the antiquities market, will have been reminded of the importance of checking collecting histories. Secure collecting histories are important, as London-based dealer Rupert Wace recently commented, 'Good Egyptian antiquities with good provenance are selling really well' (Harris 2010). The reason is self-evident: a documented collecting history will avoid possible future disputes and claims.

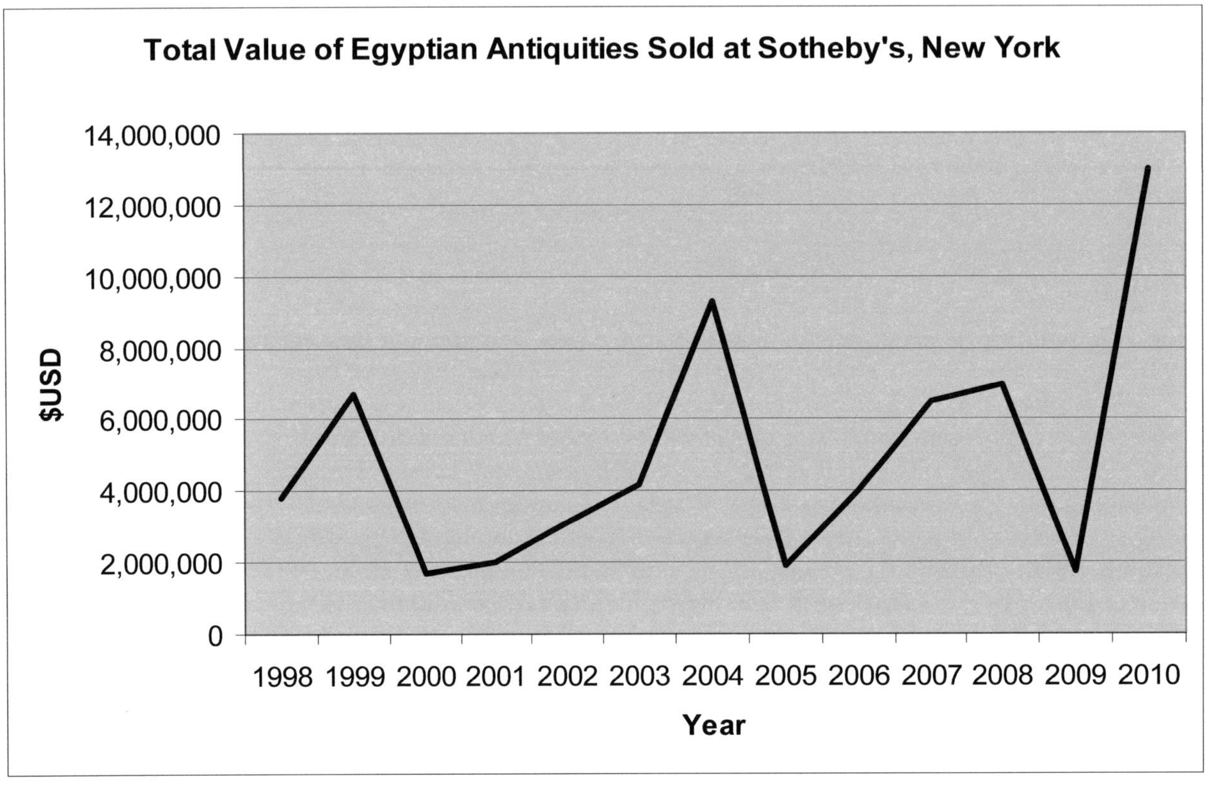

Figure 6.1: Value of Egyptian antiquities sold at Sotheby's, New York.

REMOVALS FROM ARCHAEOLOGICAL STORES

It is a matter of concern that thefts from archaeological stores in Egypt have provided material for the market. Sometimes these stores have been closed for several decades, and the thefts have gone either unnoticed or unreported. In one case, 27 Egyptian papyri excavated from the Sacred Animal Necropolis in North Saqqara turned up at the British Museum for identification (Watson 2002). These thefts underscore the vital necessity for the MA (Ministry of Antiquities) to undertake the development of an object management system.

The St Louis Museum Mummy Mask

In 1998 the St Louis Art Museum (SLAM) acquired a 19th Dynasty Egyptian mummy mask from Phoenix Ancient Art for $499,000 (Amineddoleh 2009). Since then, the ex-Minister for Antiquities, Zahi Hawass, has called for its return. Two parallel and contradictory collecting histories have emerged from the ongoing debate (Gay 2006; Gill 2009c: 94; Waxman 2008: 23-24). It seems that there is agreement that the mask was excavated at Saqqara in 1952, not least because it appears in photographs of the excavations. SLAM, along with the mask's vendor, suggests that the mask was sold by the original excavator, Mohammed Zakaria Goneim (d. 1959). Egyptian authorities reject the suggestion that Goneim would have acquired the piece and rather propose that the mask was removed from the Saqqara store during the 1980s. The museum has claimed that it 'exercised' appropriate due diligence (Cuno 2008: 169 n. 4). This included checking with the Art Loss Register (ALR) to see if the mask had been reported as stolen, as well as writing to staff at the Egyptian Museum in Cairo. The case has not yet been resolved.

The Ducks from the Pyramid of Amenemhet III

In 2007 Christie's in New York handed over a Middle Kingdom alabaster duck to Egyptian officials. It had apparently been excavated in 1979 at the pyramid of Amenemhet III (Hope 2007), and was subsequently removed from the archaeological store at Saqqara. Dieter Arnold of New York's Metropolitan Museum of Art recognised the piece and alerted the authorities.

A second duck (from the same context) appeared in the London gallery of Rupert Wace Ancient Art (Handwerk 2006; Waxman 2008: 23), and was exhibited in New York in January 2006. The provenance was described as being 'a private collection in France'. Hawass later revealed that the previous owner was not an individual but a consortium of four French dealers known as PIASA. It has not been disclosed how the duck came into the possession of the French auctioneers, or why a London dealer chose to describe a consortium as 'a private collection'.

The Ma'adi Museum

The majority of artefacts excavated by Cairo University from the sites of Heliopolis and Ma'adi were originally stored in the Ma'adi Museum. The museum was raided in September 2002, and approximately 370 objects were removed (Brodie 2005). Eighty of the pieces surfaced in a Texas dealership in 2003, and were traced back to a US Army helicopter pilot who had served in Egypt for part of 2002. The pilot apparently claimed that the pieces had been acquired in Egypt by his grandfather during the 1930s and 1940s. The objects were subsequently consigned to North American and European galleries. The pilot was arrested 'on charges relating to his sale of stolen Egyptian antiquities' in 2008. Seventy-nine objects were recovered as a result of this arrest, thanks to collaboration between the SCA and ECHO with Luc Watrin, who supplied a dossier on the objects held in the Ma'adi Museum up to 1996 (Watrin 2005a; 2005b).

Figure 6.2: One of the photos of the vitrines in the Ma'adi Museum supplied by ECHO (Photograph: Joris van Wetering).

Other pieces were identified as they emerged onto the market. Egypt was able to recover seven lots due to be auctioned at Bonham's London on 28th October, 2004. The objects had been provided with a collecting history that traced them back to the 1930s through a Joseph Garnish. In June 2004, Christie's

New York offered a single rose granite vessel that claimed to pertain to the 'J. Garnish Collection, acquired in Egypt in the 1930s' (lot 99). It sold for $6,573, and was then offered on loan New York's Metropolitan Museum of Art by the buyer. Another piece passed through Sands of Time Antiquities, also claimed to be derived from the collection of Joseph Garner (sic.), and originally collected in Egypt during the 1930s. A further eight pieces were returned by a Swiss private collector in 2009. A further 200 stolen pieces therefore remain in circulation.

THEFTS FROM RECORDED ARCHAEOLOGICAL SITES

Thefts have also been taking place at recorded sites. In some cases the items – such as the decoration from tombs – may have been well recorded and published, and the theft demonstrated.

The Eye of Amenhotep III

The eye of a colossal statue of Amenhotep III was discovered at the pharaoh's mortuary temple at Kom el-Hettan in 1970. It appears to have been stolen from the site in 1972 and then formed part of the Norbert Schimmel collection in North America (Muscarella, 1974). The eye subsequently passed through Sotheby's New York (16 December 1992: lot 87) and into a German collection. It was donated to the Antikenmuseum in Basel, Switzerland, by a Swiss collector in 2002. The eye was returned to Egypt in October 2008.

The Tomb of Tetaki (TT15)

The tomb of Tetaki pertains to an official who lived during the reign of Ahmose (1550-1525 BCE). It was investigated by Lord Carnarvon in 1908 but due to thefts had to be closed by Arthur Weigall, the then Chief Inspector (Hankey 2001). The tomb was reopened in 1924 and a full record of the tomb-paintings was made (Davies 1925). Further work on the tomb was conducted in the 1990s.

The Louvre acquired four reliefs in 2000 and 2003; the identity of the vendor has not been disclosed. One of the pieces appears to have surfaced in the London market during the 1980s. Approaches to the museum by Zahi Hawass were ineffectual, and as a result sanctions were imposed by the Egyptian authorities (Schemm 2009; see also Gill 2009c: 94). These included the suspension of the Louvre-sponsored expedition to Saqqara and the cancellation of a lecture in Cairo by Christiane Ziegler, a former curator at the Louvre (see also Waxman 2008: 19, 84). Intervention by the French Minister of Culture, Frederic Mitterrand, led to a panel determining that the reliefs should be returned to Egypt (October 2009). The related press statement stressed that the Louvre had made the acquisitions 'in good faith'. A statement (7th October, 2009) from the French Ministry of Culture noted: 'It wasn't until November 2008, after archaeologists rediscovered the tomb from which the frescoes appear to have come, that serious doubts emerged about the legality of their removal from Egyptian territory'.

The route by which the reliefs passed from the tomb to the market and thence to the Louvre has yet to be divulged.

The Tomb of Mutirdis (TT410)

In May 2008, Bonham's London withdrew a fragment of an inscription that came from the tomb of Mutirdis in the Asasif (Gill 2009c: 84). It was reportedly acquired by an Australian seafarer, perhaps in the 1940s. However, the tomb was only excavated in 1969, and an image of the fragment offered in the sale features in the tomb's publication (Arnold 1977). The Egyptian authorities identified the lot and requested its return. It is perhaps significant that a translation of the text was provided in the sale catalogue, but even so it was not realised that this fragment came from a published tomb; the name of the translator was not provided. It was claimed that the vendor had purchased the fragment 'in good faith', though the precise collecting history has not been revealed.

The Naos Fragment of Amenemhet I

In 2009 New York's Metropolitan Museum of Art purchased a Middle Kingdom naos fragment of Amenemhet I from a North American private collector, and immediately handed it over to Egyptian authorities. It was recognised that the fragment had originally formed part of a monument from Karnak. It appears that the museum purchased the fragment from the anonymous owner purely to return it. The route by which the fragment arrived in the private collection has not been disclosed. It appears that there may have been a political motive behind the return, as stated in the press release (October 2009) issued by from MMA Director Thomas Campbell:

> The Metropolitan Museum is delighted to be able to assist in returning this granite fragment to its original home. Though the fragment is small, its return is a larger symbol of the Museum's deep respect for the importance of protecting Egypt's cultural heritage and the long history of warm relations the Museum enjoys with Egypt and the Supreme Council of Antiquities.

The museum was perhaps wanting to present itself in a new light following the return of the Euphronios krater and other antiquities to Italy (Gill 2010b).

The Tomb of Imep-Hor

In March 2009 Josep Cervello from the Universitat Autonoma de Barcelona raised concerns about an inscribed limestone block (and seven other pieces) on display in a Madrid art gallery. The block apparently belonged to a Barcelona *galerista*, Félix Cervera. The fragment appears to come from Saqqara where Cervello had worked. He specifically noted the presence of disruptive looting there in 1999. The *galerista* claimed that the pieces had been acquired on the London market. The matter is unresolved and the SCA has indicated that it would like the block to be returned to Egypt.

The Temple of Isis, Behbeit el-Hagar

A number of granite reliefs from the temple of Isis, Behbeit el-Hagar, have surfaced on the market (Favard-Meeks 1991; Favard-Meeks 2002). The site was surveyed and reliefs recorded in 1977; however it has been noted that several pieces have appeared on the market since 1993 (Favard-Meeks 2002: n. 1). Further fragments from the temple seem to have been offered at auction in New York in 2002 and 2004.

Figure 6.3: Blocks from the Temple of Isis, Behbeit el-Hagar (photographs G. J. Tassie).

Thefts from Unrecorded Archaeological Sites

The number of thefts from unrecorded archaeological sites is hard to quantify. In 2000, Vivian Davies gave evidence to the UK Parliamentary Committee on Culture, Media and Sport and stated (UK Government 2000: 218, Q642; quoted in Gill and Chippindale 2002: 53):

> The destruction in countries like Egypt is catastrophic. As I know from my own experience of working in the field there and talking to my colleagues in Egypt, Egypt is not alone but it is probably uniquely rich in antiquities. Massive destruction is being done to archaeological sites in Egypt on a daily basis. Objects are finding their way out through various laundering systems. Some find their way to the United Kingdom. We have to play our part in countering this.

A written statement was issued by the ambassador of the Arab Republic of Egypt, drawing attention to the 'substantial and irrevocable damage to Egypt's cultural heritage' (UK Government 2000: 385, appendix 66; quoted in Gill and Chippindale 2002: 53).

The Head of Amenhotep III

The greywacke head of Amenhotep III was found at an undisclosed site in Egypt and is reported to have passed into the hands of Ali and Touori Farag. Jonathan Tokley-Parry acquired the piece and removed it from Egypt. The head was covered in a resin and painted so that it appeared to be a garish piece of *kitsch* sold to an undiscerning tourist. Tokeley-Parry subsequently gave the head the fictitious 'provenance' of the Thomas Alcock collection, reported to have been formed in the 1920s (Gertsenblith 2002). This air of authenticity was enhanced by the addition of fabricated labels.

Tokeley-Parry sold the head to the New York dealer Frederick Schultz (Watson 2002; Gertsenblith 2006: 70-71). It was then sold in 1993 for $1.2 million to Gawain McKinley, and thence to the London-based dealer Robin Symes (Watson 2004). Tokeley-Parry later described the head as 'quite simply, a world masterpiece that's been snatched from the concrete mixer' (Tokeley 2006: 202). He added: 'I am very proud to have been there, and to have saved it'. This echoes the oft-repeated view that de-contextualised antiquities are somehow 'saved' when they pass from the antiquities market to collectors or public museums (see also Gill 2009a). The head was returned to Egypt in 2008.

The Akhmim Stelae

Three limestone stelae were found at Akhmim during construction work in 1994 (Meier and Gottlieb 2004; Meier 2004). One of the stelae was inscribed with the cartouche of the 26th Dynasty rule, Psamtek I. The builders chose not to declare the pieces to the authorities but instead sold them to Egyptian dealer Ali Farag; it is reported that they initially asked for $70,000. Jonathan Tokeley-Parry recorded the find in his journal for 23 June 1994 (Tokeley 2006: 202-03):

> Ali's returned from Akhmim, having visited the 'Stelae Hoard' site. The contractors wrapped his head in a towel, and took him a roundabout route (so he could never find the site himself, and denounce them, if it all turned sour). But once he was inside the hoardings, they showed him everything. The architect was there, and provided a scale drawing of the site, with the proposed building, and the find spots of each stele.
>
> It even showed how they'd been lying when they were found.

Tokeley-Parry also noted that 'the owners seem to be a consortium of lawyers'. Ali Farag then seems to have approached Tokeley-Parry to handle the stelae. They had worked together since 1988: 'Mr. Tokeley-Parry says that by the summer of 1994, their six-year partnership had produced a formidable record: more than 60 trips between Egypt and England, more than 2,000 objects smuggled without incident' (Meier and Gottlieb 2004; see also Watson 2002). It was reportedly Tokeley-Parry who arranged for the stelae to leave Egypt.

One of the stelae was authenticated by Jaromir Malek (Oxford University's Griffith Institute) upon being approached by lawyer Kim Pegler, acting on behalf of a client. Malek identified the stelae as pertaining to the scribe Pasenenkhons. The result of the confirmation, which had not elicited any response from the authorities, allowed Tokeley-Parry to approach Frederick Schultz, a dealer in New York with whom he had had previous contact. It is reported that Schultz paid $52,000 to Tokeley-Parry. During 1997 three of the Akhmim stelae (one belonging to Pasenenkhons, and two others) apparently passed through the Zurich Freeport and the storage facility of an untraced 'H.H. Antiques'. A person linked to the shipping agency described H.H. Antiques as 'a fantasy company ' (Meier and Gottlieb 2004). The three stelae were then transferred by lorry to Geneva and passed into the hands of Phoenix Ancient Art that at the time was run by Sleiman Aboutaam. Images of the stelae were checked against the Art Loss Register, which confirmed that they had not been reported as stolen. At the same time an academic article on the stelae was prepared by Massimo Patanè of the University of Geneva (Patanè 1998).

In 1998 the set of stelae were purchased by a Paris-based dealer Bernard Blondeel, for around $500,000 (Meier and Gottlieb 2004). In the autumn of 1998 the stelae were displayed at the Biennale Internationale des Antiquaires in Paris. The Pasenenkhons stele was subsequently purchased for $210,000 by H. Henry Elghanayan of New York. However, in 2002 the stele was recognised from the papers seized by British police at the home of Tokeley-Parry, and was removed from Elghanayan 's apartment and returned to Egypt. Elghanayan was reimbursed by Blondeel, and Blondeel by Phoenix Ancient Art.

Recently Surfaced Antiquities

An Egyptian coffin was confiscated in Miami in October 2008. The coffin dated to the 21st Dynasty and pertained to an official named Imesy. The piece had been consigned by a Barcelona *galerista*, Félix Cervera, who was the proprietor of Arqueología Clásica. The coffin had been sent from Spain via Ireland, apparently as part of a consignment of agricultural materials. No papers accompanied the coffin, and Cervera was unable to provide a documented collecting history. According to the court papers (dated 7 October 2009), the importer was a Joseph A. Lewis II, who was also unable to demonstrate the collecting history. The piece was returned to Egypt in March 2010 at a press conference attended by Zahi Hawass.

Cervera was a one-time member of the International Association of Dealers in Ancient Art (IADAA). This raises serious issues about the conduct of members and their handling of recently-surfaced antiquities (see Ede 2006), especially in the light of Palladion Antike Kunst and its association with objects returned to Italy (Gill and Chippindale 2006: 325, B7, B10). Cervera was also cited (in January 2007) as being linked to the Italian investigation into antiquities from Sicily as part of Operation Ghelas.

Antiquities from Other Museums

While many of the examples have been drawn from material that has been removed from Egypt, thefts from international collections of Egyptian antiquities have also been proven to be cause for concern.

Egyptian antiquities stolen from Amsterdam's Bijbels Museum in July 2007 re-emerged at an unidentified major New York auction house. The items were identified by the Art Loss Register and were confiscated by agents of the US Immigration and Customs Enforcement (ICE). However, there was concern that they would not be returned to Amsterdam as the insurance money had already been paid out.

In December 2008, Christie's New York offered a series of Egyptian antiquities (reports suggest a total of nine), stating that they were from 'the collection of Barry Stern' (9th December, 2008: lots 8, 27, 33, 36, 40). The collecting history for the lots stated: 'Acquired by the current owner's parents, circa 1955'. It later transpired that Stern had deaccessioned the pieces from the Long Island University Art Museum, where he had worked as director. Computerised records were also allegedly deleted. Stern was sentenced in October 2010.

The appearance of such material in auction-houses can only be unsettling for the legitimate market. O'Keefe has commented on the purpose of auction-houses (O'Keefe 1997: 7-8):

> The primary interest ... is to have a stock of antiquities for sale without any legal problems attaching to the transaction form the way in which the antiquity was obtained. Consequently, this group will want access to the sources of antiquities to be as free as possible. At the same time, they will want to avoid adverse publicity arising from possession of antiquities alleged to have been obtained in dubious circumstances. In particular, they do not want clients facing claims by governments or other collectors for return of an antiquity following theft or unlawful export. This is bad for business and bad for the reputation of the dealer or auction house.

In spite of these cautionary words, recently surfaced antiquities do continue to appear on the market with alarming regularity.

Engaging with Museums and Collectors

Museums with established holdings of Egyptian antiquities may wish to develop their holdings, and private collectors will want to expand their collections. However, it is important that both be able to collect not only legally, but also ethically. This issue has come to the fore in recent years, especially in

North America, driven in part by the so-called Medici Conspiracy that related to recently-surfaced antiquities from Italy and Greece (Watson and Todeschini 2006). A series of prominent North American museums – including the Cleveland Museum of Art, Boston's Museum of Fine Arts, the J. Paul Getty Museum, New York's Metropolitan Museum of Art, and the Princeton University Art Museum – voluntarily returned some 120 high-profile objects (Gill and Chippindale 2006; Gill and Chippindale 2007; Gill 2009b; Gill 2010b). It has since become clear that Italy could have asked for substantially more items, but instead appears to have chosen a representative selection. In return, Italy offered significant loans of archaeological material to North American collections.

At an institutional level, the Association of Art Museum Directors (AAMD) formulated new guidelines on the acquisition of archaeological material. These new guidelines chose 1970 – the date of the UNESCO Convention on the Means of Prohibiting and Preventing the Illicit Import, Export and Transfer of Ownership of Cultural Property – as the benchmark for acquisitions[1]. According to AAMD guidelines, museums must place details of all acquisitions on an online object register so that interested parties may examine the object, research its background and, if appropriate, make a claim. One of the consequences of these new guidelines is that North American museums are much more reluctant to acquire Egyptian antiquities with incomplete collecting histories, a reluctance compounded by the highly publicised interventions of Zahi Hawass and the aggressive policy of the MA. As a secondary result, objects with genuine, full and documented collecting histories now achieve much higher prices at auction.

The Italians were able to make this impact due to the extensive photographic archives seized from dealers in Switzerland and Greece (Watson and Todeschini 2006; Gill 2009b), and which were used to support their successful claims. If such photographic archives exist for Egypt, they are yet to be identified. However, there should be a worldwide call for all museums to use 1970 as the minimum original collection date for acquisitions, and that this should also apply to dealers and auction-houses.

Conclusion

One of the issues to emerge from a study of the market is that galleries, dealers, auction-houses, museums and private collectors need to exercise more rigorous due diligence, especially in the aftermath of wholesale looting in Egypt since the 2011 revolution. This situation has been exacerbated by the raiding of antiquities magazines (storehouses) and museums, such as the well-documented raid on the Cairo Museum on the 28th January, 2011. There is clearly an issue to address: how can the market for newly surfaced Egyptian antiquities be suppressed? In late 2011, Egypt joined the ranks of countries to possess a ICOM Red List, designed to classify endangered archaeological objects in the most vulnerable areas of the world as works of art, in order to prevent them being sold or illegally exported. It could be argued that the creation of such a list will put undue pressure on those who trade in any one specific group of cultural objects, yet it is hard to see how those who deal with the same materials that ICOM is sworn to protect should not recognise this potential problem. It also follows that auction houses, galleries and dealers must adopt a more rigorous due diligence procedure concerning the material they handle.

However, the fact that a piece may not be mentioned on the Red List or Art Loss Register does not mean the piece has not been removed illicitly from an archaeological site; it merely suggests that the piece was not previously known or recorded: if an object is unseen for 3000 years and is then ripped from its context, it will not appear in an electronic database. Over-reliance on image registers should be avoided; greater attention needs to be paid to the careful documentation of collecting histories (Gill 2010a), to ensure that shadowy and fictitious collection records are not created in order to circumvent the 1970 UNESCO Convention. The association of the (newly created) 'Amarna princess' in the (obscure) 1892 Silverton Park sale only created a (false) sense of authenticity (Hardwick 2010). The problem of modern creations posing as recently-surfaced (and high value) Egyptian antiquities may also be a significant problem (Watson 1997: 134-41; Stock 2009). The term 'provenance', which is widely used in the market, should be replaced with specific accounts that point to both original archaeological context and the collecting history for the piece.

The debate about recently surfaced antiquities can – yet should not – be confused with long-standing historic claims on cultural property: it is perfectly apparent that the removal of the Rosetta Stone from Egypt during the Napoleonic Wars (Fagan 2004: 53-55) is ethically distinct from the 21st century looting of an inscribed stele from an unexplored site in Egypt. Yet James Cuno, president and director of the Art Institute of Chicago, has used the Rosetta Stone as an example of how an object not derived from a

[1] The US signed up to the agreement in 1983, while United Kingdom became a signatory in 2002

scientific excavation can be key to the study of ancient Egypt: 'The practice of Egyptian archaeology is only meaningful today because of our knowledge of Egypt's history as made possible by an unexcavated antiquity that has been housed and studied in a British museum for over two hundred years' (Cuno 2009: 10; see also Cuno 2008: xii-xv). This is not to say that iconic objects for the study of Egyptology should not be more appropriately displayed in Cairo than in Berlin, London or Paris.

This raises the issue of universal (or encyclopaedic) museums that embrace a range of world cultures (Cuno 2004; Lewis 2004; MacGregor 2009). There is a place for collections of Egyptian antiquities, and there is no reason why these (often obtained through the system of partage) should not be displayed outside Egypt in order to encourage an understanding of – and interest in – ancient Egyptian culture (e.g. Gill 2005; Moser 2006). However, it is difficult for museums to create an Egyptian collection *de novo,* as they would be expected to acquire objects with documented collecting histories that could be traced back to before 1970. It should be noted the 'Declaration on the Importance and Value of Universal Museums' that was passed in December 2002. The chair of the International Council of Museums (ICOM) Ethics Committee noted: 'The real purpose of the Declaration was, however, to establish a higher degree of immunity from claims for the repatriation of objects from the collections of these museums' (Lewis 2004). The 2002 Declaration included this statement:

> Calls to repatriate objects that have belonged to museum collections for many years have become an important issue for museums. Although each case has to be judged individually, we should acknowledge that museums serve not just the citizens of one nation but the people of every nation. Museums are agents in the development of culture, whose mission is to foster knowledge by a continuous process of reinterpretation. Each object contributes to that process. To narrow the focus of museums whose collections are diverse and multifaceted would therefore be a disservice to all visitors.

Yet in spite of this, five of the nineteen signatories have returned antiquities to source countries – including Egypt, Greece and Italy – since the Declaration. It is also surprising that so many undocumented Egyptian antiquities continue to surface on the market. Auction houses must exercise more rigorous due diligence to sales, and by museums and private collectors prior to purchase.

Acknowledgements

This research is part of a larger project on collecting antiquities conducted with Christopher Chippindale and Christos Tsirogiannis. I am grateful to Paul Barford, Marc Fehlmann, and Kasia Szpakowska for their comments on various aspects of this paper.

Websites

A list of objects either returned to Egypt or on a wanted list appears under 'Recovering Stolen Treasures': www.sca-egypt.org and a list of sites looted during and since the revolution is available at 'Egyptological Looting Database': http://egyptopaedia.com/2011/.

References

Amineddoleh, L. 2009. Phoenix Ancient Art and the Aboutaams in hot water again, *Art & Cultural Heritage Law Newsletter* 1: 13-15.

Arnold, D. 1977. *Das Grab der Mutirdis.* Grabung im Asasif: 1963-1970, vol. 6. Mainz: von Zabern.

Brodie, N. 2005. In the news, *Culture Without Context* 16: http://www2.mcdonald.cam.ac.uk/projects/iarc/culturewithoutcontext/issue16/news.htm

Chippindale, C., and D. W. J. Gill. 2000. Material consequences of contemporary classical collecting, *American Journal of Archaeology* 104: 463-511.

Chippindale, C., D. W. J. Gill, E. Salter, and C. Hamilton. 2001. Collecting the classical world: first steps in a quantitative history, *International Journal of Cultural Property* 10: 1-31.

Cuno, J. 2004. The object of art museums, in J. Cuno (ed.), *Whose muse? Art museums and the public trust.* Princeton: Princeton University Press. pp. 49-75.

Cuno, J. 2008. *Who owns Antiquity? Museums and the battle over our ancient heritage.* Princeton: Princeton University Press.

Cuno, J. (ed.) 2009. *Whose Culture? The promise of museums and the debate over antiquities.* Princeton: Princeton University Press.

Davies, N. d. G. 1925. The tomb of Tetaky at Thebes (No. 15), *Journal of Egyptian Archaeology* 11: 10-18.

Ede, J. 2006. Who owns objects? A view from the antiquities trade, in E. Robson, L. Treadwell, and C. Gosden (eds), *Who owns Objects? The ethics and politics of collecting cultural artefacts.* Oxford: Oxbow, pp. 77-81.

Elia, R. J. 2001. Analysis of the looting, selling, and collecting of Apulian red-figure vases: a quantitative approach, in N. Brodie, J. Doole, and C. Renfrew (eds), *Trade in Illicit Antiquities: the destruction of the world's archaeological heritage.* Cambridge: McDonald Institute, pp. 145-53.

Fagan, B. 2004. *The Rape of the Nile: tomb robbers, tourists, and archaeologists in Egypt*, 3rd edition. Boulder (Co.) and Oxford: Westview Press.

Favard-Meeks, C. 1991. *Le temple de Behbeit el-Hagara: essai de reconstitution et d'interpretation.* Studien zur altägyptischen Kultur. Beihefte, vol. 6. Hamburg: H. Buske.

Favard-Meeks, C. 2002. The present state of the site of Behbeit el-Hagar, *Britism Museum Studies in Ancient Egypt and Sudan* 3: 31-41.

Gay, M. 2006. Out of Egypt, *Riverfront Times,* February 15: http://www.riverfronttimes.com/2006-02-15/news/out-of-egypt/full/

Gertsenblith, P. 2002. United States v. Schultz, *Culture Without Context* 10: http://www2.mcdonald.cam.ac.uk/projects/iarc/culturewithoutcontext/issue10/gerstenblith.htm

Gay, M. 2006. Recent developments in the legal protection of cultural heritage, in N. Brodie, M. M. Kersel, C. Luke, and K. W. Tubb (eds), *Archaeology, cultural heritage, and the antiquities trade.* Gainesville: University Press of Florida, pp. 68-92.

Gill, D. W. J. 2005. From Wellcome Museum to Egypt Centre: displaying Egyptology in Swansea, *Göttinger Miszellen* 205: 47-54.

Gill, D. W. J. 2009a. Electronic review of James Cuno, *Who Owns Antiquity? Museums and the Battle Over Our Ancient Heritage* (Princeton University Press, 2008), *American Journal of Archaeology* 113: 104.

Gill, D. W. J. 2009b. Homecomings: learning from the return of antiquities to Italy, in N. Charney (ed.), *Art and Crime: exploring the dark side of the art world.* Santa Barbara: Praeger, pp. 13-25.

Gill, D. W. J.2009c. Looting matters for classical antiquities: contemporary issues in archaeological ethics, *Present Pasts* 1: 77-104.

Gill, D. W. J. 2010a. Collecting histories and the market for classical antiquities, *Journal of Art Crime* 3: 3-10.

Gill, D. W. J. 2010b. The returns to Italy from North America: an overview, *Journal of Art Crime* 3: 105-09.

Gill, D. W. J. and Chippindale, C. 1993. Material and intellectual consequences of esteem for Cycladic figures, *American Journal of Archaeology* 97: 601-59.

Gill, D. W. J. and Chippindale, C. 2002. The trade in looted antiquities and the return of cultural property: a British parliamentary inquiry, *International Journal of Cultural Property* 11: 50-64.

Gill, D. W. J. and Chippindale, C. 2006. From Boston to Rome: reflections on returning antiquities, *International Journal of Cultural Property* 13: 311-31.

Gill, D. W. J. and Chippindale, C. 2007. From Malibu to Rome: further developments on the return of antiquities, *International Journal of Cultural Property* 14: 205-40.

Handwerk, B. 2006. Egypt's antiquities chief combines passion, clout to protect artifacts, *National Geographic News* 24 October: http://news.nationalgeographic.com/news/2006/10/061024-hawass.html

Hankey, J. 2001. *A Passion for Egypt: Arthur Weigall, Tutankhamun and the 'Curse of the Pharaohs'*. London: I.B. Tauris.

Hardwick, T. 2010. A group of art works in the Amarna style, in S. H. D'Auria (ed.), *Offerings to the Discerning eye: an Egytpological medley in honor of Jack A. Josephson*. Leiden: Brill, pp. 133-51.

Harris, L. 2010. Collectors' focus, *Apollo*.

Hope, B. 2007. Stolen Egyptian artifact handed over to consulate, *New York Sun* 10 August: http://www.nysun.com/new-york/stolen-egyptian-artifact-handed-over-to-consulate/60264/

Lewis, G. 2004. The Universal museum: a special case?, *ICOM News* 57: 3.

MacGregor, N. 2009. To shape the citizens of "that great city, the world", in J. Cuno (ed.), *Whose culture? The promise of museums and the debate over antiquities*. Princeton: Princeton University Press, pp. 39-54.

Meier, B. 2004. Antiquities gallery will return two limestone monuments to Egypt, *New York Times* 2 April 2004: 3.

Meier, B., and M. Gottlieb. 2004. An illicit journey out of Egypt, only a few questions aksed, *New York Times* 23 February 2004: 1.

Moser, S. 2006. *Wondrous Curiosities: ancient Egypt at the British Museum*. Chicago: University of Chicago Press.

Muscarella, O. W. 1974. *Ancient art: the Norbert Schimmel Collection*. Mainz: P. von Zabern.

O'Keefe, P. J. 1997. *Trade in Antiquities: reducing destruction and theft*. London: Archetype Publications; UNESCO.

Patanè, M. 1998. Trois steles egyptiennes de Basse Epoque, *Göttinger Miszellen* 166: 57-63.

Schemm, P. 2009. Egypt cuts ties with France's Louvre museum, *Associated Press* October 7: http://article.wn.com/view/2009/10/07/Egypt_Cuts_Ties_With_Frances_Louvre_Museum_i/

Stock, J. 2009. Falsche Pharaonin, *Der Spiegel* 20 July: http://www.spiegel.de/spiegel/print/d-66133689.html

Tokeley, J. 2006. *Rescuing the Past: the cultural heritage crusade*. Exeter: Imprint Academic.

UK Government, Culture, Media and Sport Committee. 2000. *Cultural property: return and illicit trade*. London: House of Commons.

Watrin, L. 2005a. The sacking of the Archaeological Museum at Ma'adi, *GREPAL* - http://www.grepal.org/english/sac_maadi.php

Watrin, L. 2005b. Part II: The Museum robbery: The Ma'adi affair, investigation into the theft and trafficking of objects from the Ma'adi Museum, *GREPAL* - http://www.grepal.org/english/sac_maadi2.php

Watson, P. 1997. *Sotheby's, the Inside Story*. London: Bloomsbury.

Watson, P. 2002. The investigation of Frederick Schultz, *Culture Without Context* 10: 21-26.

Watson, P. 2004. The fall of Robin Symes, *Culture Without Context* 15: http://www2.mcdonald.cam.ac.uk/projects/iarc/culturewithoutcontext/issue15/watson.htm

Watson, P. 2006. Convicted dealers: what we can learn, in N. Brodie, M. M. Kersel, C. Luke, and K. W. Tubb (eds), *Archaeology, Cultural Heritage, and the Antiquities Trade*. Gainesville: University Press of Florida, pp. 93-97.

Watson, P., and C. Todeschini. 2006. *The Medici Conspiracy: the illicit journey of looted antiquities from Italy's tomb raiders to the world's great museums*. New York: Public Affairs.

Waxman, S. 2008. *Loot: The Battle Over the Stolen Treasures of the Ancient World*. New York: Times Books.

Chapter 7

"Battered Bulls" Again: Destruction and First Attempts at Conservation of Rock Art in Egypt

Dirk Huyge

Abstract

Largely eclipsed by the extraordinary remains of Pharaonic civilisation, Egyptian rock art has not received much interest from the general public and the scientific community alike. Consequently, very little has thus far been undertaken to safeguard this immense but highly vulnerable patrimony consisting of many hundreds of sites and thousands of images, the vast majority of which are of prehistoric age. Through recent surveys, it has become clear how much rock art destruction must have taken place in the past, especially as a consequence of large-scale quarrying operations for building materials along the Nile and in the Eastern Desert. This destruction is ongoing, but some recent, spectacular rock art discoveries have contributed to a growing awareness among the Egyptian antiquities authorities of the scientific potential of rock art, its fundamental cultural value and possible economic relevance. As a consequence, some tentative attempts have been made in recent years to protect rock art sites by installing fences and/or putting local guards in place.

Introduction

The destruction of rock drawings is not a new phenomenon. It was reported as far back as 1912 in the Wadi Abu Agag, north of Aswan in Upper Egypt (Schweinfurth 1912), a long time before any general awareness regarding the scientific potential and fundamental cultural value of rock art. Here, quarrying activities in 1907 led to the breaking-up of a sandstone boulder covered with anthropomorphic representations and a variety of symbols. This was followed by further destruction at the same site (as feared by Schweinfurth) around thirty years later (Dunbar 1941). Among the victimised drawings was a rare representation of a camel that had been attributed (erroneously, in all probability) to the late Old Kingdom, on the basis of an accompanying hieratic inscription. Smith warned of further threats and imminent destruction of rock art sites through quarrying for building materials in the area of Gebel el-Silsila (Smith 1967). Iconoclasm of a more organised nature was reported by Mayer (1981) and Lauwers (1995) in the Wadi Abu Subeira, about 12 km north of Aswan, where a number of sites seemed irrevocably threatened by the systematic industrial exploitation of Nubian sandstone escarpments. Since I first published a brief report on rock art destruction in *African Archaeological Review* in 1998 (Huyge 1998), relating the obliteration of some exquisite Pharaonic petroglyphs representing sacrificial bulls at Elkab in Upper Egypt, several more cases of rock art devastation have come to light (i.e. Hendrickx & Gatto 2009).

These few reports on the destruction of rock art and warnings of threats against it concern only the southernmost part of the Upper Egyptian Nile Valley, and are evidently only the tip of the iceberg. There are various threats to rock art, such as vandalism, modern graffiti, pollution, weathering, and modern development projects. The opening up of the desert to tourists also causes its own problems, with people carelessly disposing of litter, purposely touching the rock art and leaving their names on the rock faces. Much unknown rock art has undoubtedly disappeared in complete silence (and will continue to do so). It is probably not a coincidence that the first attempts at rock art conservation and management also concern this Upper Egyptian area, which has been far more intensively explored for rock art during the past few years than any other part of the country[1].

Quarrying and Mining Threats

One of the major threats to rock art is stone quarrying, both large- and small-scale. Large-scale stone quarrying along the flanks of the Nile Valley has been ongoing for at least five millennia, and it is beyond doubt that a considerable amount of prehistoric and Pharaonic rock art must have disappeared because of the intensive quarrying activities in antiquity (Klemm & Klemm 2008). The major destructions in this respect, however, must have happened in the second part of the 20th century, especially in the sandstone

[1] For the situation in the Western Desert of Egypt, which is not considered here, see Riemer 2009

area between Esna and Aswan (and farther south). There are various reasons for the modern intensification of quarrying in this part of Egypt, one of them being the construction of many new settlements to house the Nubians displaced as a result of the construction of the Aswan High Dam and the creation of Lake Nasser in the 1960s. Furthermore, the past three decades have witnessed an explosive expansion of existing towns and villages all along the Nile Valley (in which traditional mud-brick masonry gives way to building in stone, since it is now no longer permitted to exploit the Nile riverbanks for mud). In this area, small-scale artisanal operations alternate with large industrial quarries. The el-Hosh area, for instance, on the west bank of the Nile and about 30 km south of the town of Edfu, which presents one of the highest densities of rock art in Egypt (see Huyge *et al.* 1998), was heavily quarried for sandstone using explosives in the 1960s and 1970s (Fig. 7.1). Hundreds, probably even thousands, of petroglyphs must have been destroyed as a consequence of this (Figs 7.2-3). Elsewhere, such as in Wadi Abu Subeira (see Storemyr *et al.* 2008), the main threats to rock art are the innumerable clay mines. While these are subterranean exploitations, the mining process means that the whole vicinity of the mineshafts is thoroughly turned over and covered with spoil (Fig. 7.4).

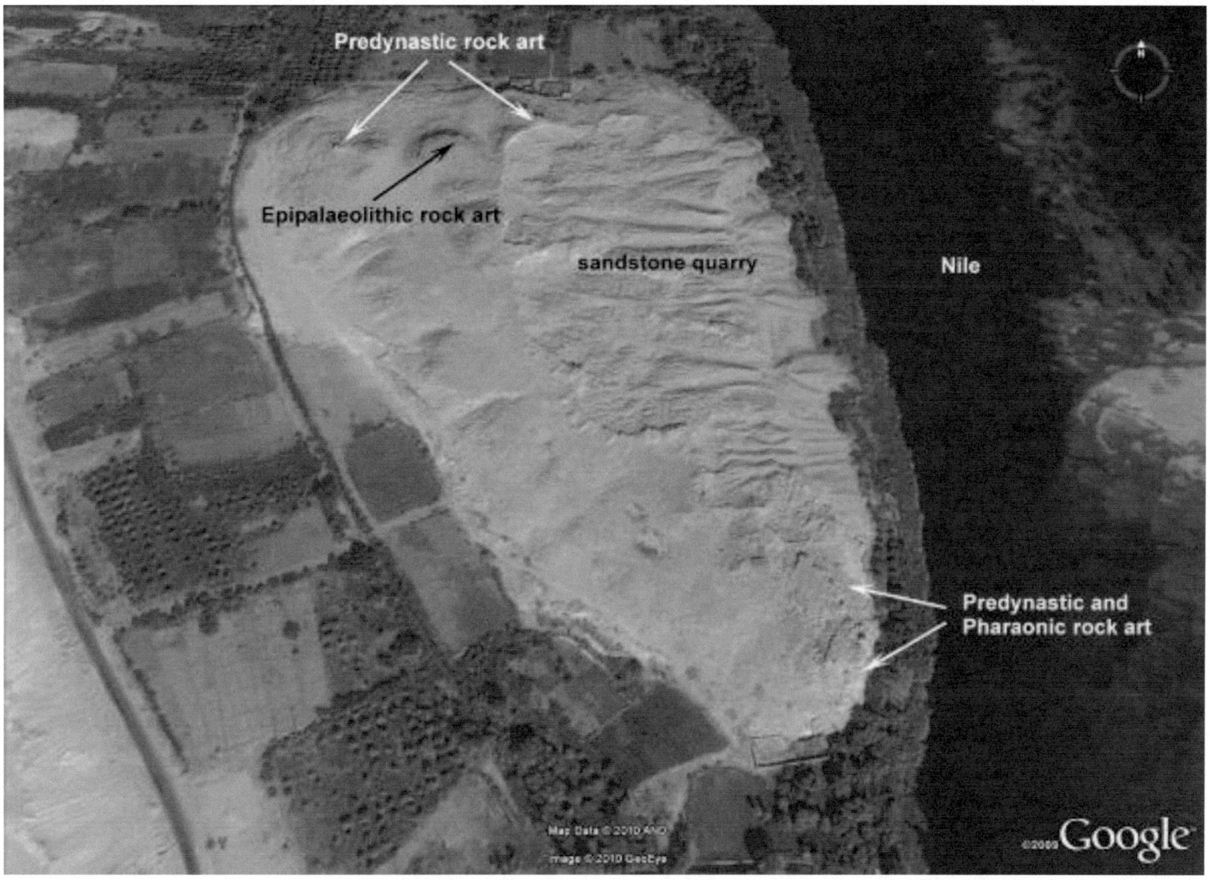

Figure 7.1: Almost half of the site of Abu Tanqura Qibli at el-Hosh has been quarried away using explosives in the 1960s and/or 1970s. In view of what remains (rock art locations indicated), a considerable amount of petroglyphs must have disappeared (modified after Google Earth 2010).

In other parts of Egypt, such as in the limestone area from Cairo to Esna, the situation is less well known, but is unlikely to be much different. The transformation of the Red Sea coast into a near-continuous chain of holiday resorts since the 1980s will certainly have caused extensive rock art devastation. In the latter area, because of the lack of archaeological surveys, our archaeological knowledge is highly biased, but the reconnaissance of the Wadi Deir (Dittmann 1990: 95-121), the hinterland of the port of Quseir (Prickett 1979) and the Marsa Alam area (Tratsaert 2000), all seem to indicate that it is also a highly sensitive area as far as rock art is concerned.

Figure 7.2: A view of the Abu Tanqura Qibli quarry towards the south. Along the edge is broken-up rock art. The panel illustrated in fig. 7.3 is in the foreground (photograph: D. Huyge/RMAH).

Figure 7.3: A broken-up rock art panel at Abu Tanqura Qibli with Predynastic depictions of an antelope and an elephant (photograph: D. Huyge/RMAH).

OTHER THREATS

There are several others threats to Egyptian rock art. Because of newly constructed roads, both along the Nile Valley and traversing the Eastern Desert, and the intensification of four-wheel-drive off-road traffic, human presence at the rock art locations has substantially increased during the past few years. Several cases of deliberate destruction and vandalism have been witnessed (Fig. 7.5) (see, e.g., Bahn 2010: 178-179). While some examples of theft are known, this seems to be a relatively minor issue when compared to other parts of North Africa, such as Morocco (Salih 2007). Large-scale fertilising projects and the implantation of a huge industrial infrastructure, notably for the production of phosphates, are rapidly transforming the lower desert areas along the Nile Valley into featureless plains and pockmarked wasteland. At Elkab in Upper Egypt, for instance, an ever-expanding phosphate plant is now threatening several important rock art sites, including the famous Borg el-Hamam with dozens of Predynastic drawings and hieroglyphic rock inscriptions (Huyge 1984; Hendrickx & Huyge 1989: No. 77). Unless local antiquities authorities take immediate, urgent action, these sites are doomed to disappear in the short-term.

Figure 4: A view of Wadi Abu Subeira with localisation of the Late Palaeolithic rock art site CAS-6 and a modern clay mine in operation (photograph: P. Storemyr).

SOLUTIONS AND PROSPECTS

A substantial increase of rock art research along the Upper Egyptian Nile Valley during the past decade has led to some remarkable discoveries that have contributed to a growing awareness among the local antiquities authorities of the scientific relevance of rock art and its important cultural value. These discoveries include the finds of sophisticated Pleistocene, Late Palaeolithic rock art at Qurta in 2005 (see Huyge 2008, 2009; Huyge & Claes 2008) and Wadi Abu Subeira in 2006 and 2010 (see Storemyr *et al.* 2008; Kelany in press). These finds, particularly those at Qurta, have been widely covered by both the international and local media. The Qurta sites, which are not open to the general public because of their fragility and difficult accessibility (but discussed already in the latest edition of *Lonely Planet* and other travel guides), have been visited by select tourist groups that pay a substantial fee to view them. The positive side to this is that the Egyptian antiquities authorities are now also starting to recognise the previously underestimated touristic and economic potential of that part of their heritage. Both the Qurta and Wadi Abu Subeira areas, comprising several rock art sites, are currently under permanent guard. They are, to the best of my knowledge, the only 'pure' rock art sites in Egypt that have this privilege (all other guarded sites with rock art, such as the Wadi Hammamat sites in the Eastern Desert, also comprise Pharaonic antiquities, which is the prime reason they are being protected).

Figure 7.5: Detail of a rock art panel with Predynastic and later imagery at Wadi Barramiya in the Eastern Desert. The chalk inscriptions were done sometime between 2007 and 2009 (photograph: W. Claes/RMAH).

Evidently, it is not possible to protect all rock art sites in this way. There are simply too many and they are too widely distributed over the country. Only in exceptional cases can the possibility be considered of taking rock art away from its original location and storing it in a museum or storeroom, even though, as Bahn (2010: 150) correctly states, "… it is catastrophic to remove rock art from its original site and transport it to museums – this 'kills' it". In the case of a rock art panel at the el-Hosh site Abu Tanqura Bahari 14, representing the most complex geometric figure ever found in Egyptian rock art and most probably of Epipalaeolithic age (c. 9,000 years old?) (Fig. 7.6), there was no other option (see Huyge & Storemyr 2012). Part of it had already been damaged and leaving it in place would definitely have led to its complete destruction. Depriving the rock art of its context and surroundings should be avoided at any price but, in this particular case, it can only be hoped that the display of the panel in a much-frequented museum, which has been proposed with some insistence to the Egyptian antiquities authorities, may contribute to a growing awareness among the general public and professionals alike.

Figure 7.6: Complex Epipalaeolithic geometric design (height: 35 cm) in situ at Abu Tanqura Bahari 14 at el-Hosh. The sandstone block with the motif (inset), the upper left part of which is broken, was removed from the site in 2010 and is currently stored in the SCA storeroom at Kom Ombo (registration number 2062) (photograph: D. Huyge/RMAH; tracing inset: I. Therasse/RMAH).

Figure 7.7: The Late Palaeolithic rock art site CAS-6 in Wadi Abu Subeira has been recently fenced off with barbed wire to keep mining companies out (photograph: P. Storemyr).

In view of the many threats to this fragile patrimony, every effort should be made to preserve and protect what can still be saved. Archaeological missions active in rock art-sensitive areas should consider it a priority to carry out an exhaustive survey of the region they are working in. Rock art sites should be inventoried and individual drawings copied as thoroughly as time and resources permit, by photography or by any other means (the development of new digital recording techniques will undoubtedly prove to be of immense value in this respect; see Curci *et al.* 2012). An excellent example of such an undertaking is the QuarryScapes project (2005-2008) (see Abu-Jaber *et al.* 2009 and www.quarryscapes.no), part of which was conducted in the Aswan area in Upper Egypt. While this project essentially focused on ancient quarries, rock art occurrences were also systematically surveyed (see, e.g., Storemyr 2008, 2009). The training of Egyptian archaeologists in rock art recording and conservation is of vital importance as is the development of a national strategy for rock art management. Ongoing is the Wadi Abu Subeira Archaeological Survey, directed by A. Kelany (in press) of the Supreme Council of Antiquities (SCA Aswan), that has led to the discovery of several extremely important rock art sites, some of which are definitely of Pleistocene age (see above). This project, carried out exclusively by Egyptian colleagues, is aimed not only at locating and recording, but also at conservation of rock art sites in the form of directing mining companies away from archaeological areas. This has been pursued with success and at least one of these sites has been fenced (Fig. 7.7) and the whole wadi's lower course is currently officially guarded by the SCA. Such extremely valuable actions, attesting also to a growing interest in rock art among native archaeologists, provide most welcome reasons for hope.

ACKNOWLEDGEMENTS

My thanks are due to Paul G. Bahn and Per Storemyr for commenting upon a first draft of this paper.

REFERENCES

Abu-Jaber, N., Bloxam, E. G., Degryse, P. and Heldal, T. 2009. *QuarryScapes: Ancient Stone Quarry Landscapes in the Eastern Mediterranean.* Geological Survey of Norway Special Publication 12. Trondheim: NGU Geological Survey of Norway.

Bahn, P. G. 2010. *Prehistoric Rock Art. Polemics and Progress.* Cambridge: Cambridge University Press.

Curci, A., Urcia, A., Lippiello, L. and Gatto, M. C. 2012. Using digital technologies to document rock art in the Aswan-Kom Ombo region (Egypt), *Sahara* 23: 75-86.

Dittmann, A. 1990. *Zur Paläogeographie der ägyptischen Eastern Desert.* Marburger Geographische Schriften 116. Marburg/Lahn: Marburger Geographischen Gesellschaft e.V.

Dunbar, J. H. 1941. *The Rock-Pictures of Lower Nubia.* Cairo: Government Press.

Hendrickx, S. and Gatto, M. C. 2009. A rediscovered Late Predynastic-Early Dynastic royal scene from Gharb Aswan (Upper Egypt), *Sahara* 20: 147-150.

Hendrickx, S. and Huyge, D. 1989. *Elkab IV. Topographie. Fascicule 2. Inventaire des sites archéologiques.* Bruxelles: Fondation Égyptologique Reine Élisabeth.

Huyge, D. 1984. Horus Qa-a in the Elkab area, Upper Egypt, *Orientalia Lovaniensia Periodica* 15: 5-9.

Huyge, D. 1998. "Battered bulls": rock art destruction in Egypt, *African Archaeological Review* 15: 3-11.

Huyge, D. 2008. Côa in Africa: Late Pleistocene rock art along the Egyptian Nile, *International Newsletter on Rock Art (INORA)* 51: 1-7.

Huyge, D. 2009. Late Palaeolithic and Epipalaeolithic rock art in Egypt: Qurta and el-Hosh, *Archéo-Nil* 19: 108-120.

Huyge, D. and Claes, W. 2008. 'Ice Age' art along the Nile, *Egyptian Archaeology. The Bulletin of the Egypt Exploration Society* 33: 25-28.

Huyge, D., De Dapper, M., Depraetere, D., Ismail, M., Marchi, E., Mommaerts, R., Regulski, I. and Watchman, A. 1998. Hilltops, silts, and petroglyphs: the fish hunters of el-Hosh (Upper Egypt), *Bulletin des Musées royaux d'Art et d'Histoire* 69: 97-113.

Huyge, D. and Storemyr, P. 2012. A 'masterpiece' of Epipalaeolithic geometric rock art from el-Hosh, Upper Egypt, *Sahara* 23: 127-132.

Kelany, A. In press. More Late Palaeolithic rock art at Wadi Abu Subeira, Upper Egypt, *Annales du Service des Antiquités de l'Égypte.*

Klemm, R. and Klemm, D. D. 2008. *Stones and Quarries in Ancient Egypt.* London: The British Museum Press.

Lauwers, R. 1995. Egypt: rock art in danger, *Bollettino del Centro Camuno di Studi Preistorici* 28: 10.

Mayer, W. 1981. Felszeichnungen bei Assuan, *Mitteilungen des Deutschen Archäologischen Instituts, Abteilung Kairo* 37: 313-314.

Prickett, M. 1979. Quseir regional survey, in D. S. Whitcomb and J. H. Johnson, *Quseir al-Qadim 1978. Preliminary Report.* Cairo: American Research Center in Egypt, pp. 257-352.

Riemer, H. 2009. Prehistoric rock art research in the Western Desert of Egypt, *Archéo-Nil* 19: 31-46.

Salih, A. 2007. Rock art patrimony of Morocco: an endangered cultural property, in J. Deacon (ed.), *African Rock Art: The Future of Africa's Past.* Nairobi: Trust for African Rock Art, pp. 71-76.

Schweinfurth, G. 1912. Über alte Tierbilder und Felsinschriften bei Assuan, *Zeitschrift für Ethnologie* 44: 627-658.

Smith, P. E. L. 1967. A preliminary report on the recent prehistoric investigations near Kom Ombo, Upper Egypt, in *Fouilles en Nubie (1961-1963).* Cairo: Service des Antiquités de l'Egypte, pp. 195-208.

Storemyr, P. 2008. Prehistoric geometric rock art at Gharb Aswan, Upper Egypt, *Sahara* 19: 61-76.

Storemyr, P. 2009. A prehistoric geometric rock art landscape by the first Nile cataract, *Archéo-Nil* 19: 121-150.

Storemyr, P., Kelany, A., Negm, M. A. and Tohami, A. 2008. More 'Lascaux along the Nile'? Possible Late Palaeolithic rock art in Wadi Abu Subeira, Upper Egypt, *Sahara* 19: 155-158.

Tratsaert, B. 2000. Inscriptions in danger, *Egypt Revealed* 1: 18.

Chapter 8

Purity, Power and Nudity: Social Dynamics of Hammams in History

Fekri A. Hassan

ABSTRACT

Hammams are one of the many manifestations of public bathing that made this act a forceful social event and a potent personal experience. Through control and management of the body society maintains its structures, norms, and discipline. In several religions water became a currency of faith and the medium by which God is approached and through it one may taste his mercy and benevolence. Cleanliness thus not only brings one in contact with the substance of life and death, but also with the divine. Unlike both Roman and Greek bathing houses, which were large, bright and noisy, the hammams were quiet places. The hammam recalled the tranquillity of the garden and was a place of relaxation, of amicable social exchanges, and rejuvenation. Its lengthy sequence with exposure to different temperatures, positions, and activities awakened the senses in a measured and protracted pace to ensure a peaceful transition from the daily stress to a state of pleasant and calm reinvigoration. Under the Mamluks and Ottomans hammams flourished throughout North Africa and South-west Asia, with rich patrons building these intuitions, some attached to mosques others in their homes and for the public as charitable institutions, reinforcing their status and social standing. Nowadays, the number of hammams, as in Cairo for example, has dwindled and the remaining hammams can hardly keep up with the rising costs of water and fuel. They have been deserted by the more affluent in society not because of the introduction of private baths, but because of a change in the ethos of community and the cultivation of the practice of a nuclear family with hopes for partaking of "modernity". One of the main elements of modernity (once represented by an electric fan and a refrigerator) is the possession of a modern bathroom.

INTRODUCTION

The hammam, an institution of public bathing of Turkish origin, is one of many manifestations of public bathing. The hammam has a long history with origins that can be traced back to Greek and Roman public baths. Public baths ("onsen") in Japan represent a parallel development. I wish here to examine the hammam in a historical perspective in order to grasp its deeper symbolic meanings and social significance. Although hammams and other public baths are ostensibly about washing and cleanliness, I submit here that the public bath in general and the hammam in particular have a transcultural appeal because of a convergence of elements that make public bathing a forceful social event and a potent personal experience. I submit that the key elements that make public bathing such a powerful and potent experience are partial or total nudity under the gaze of others and the sensations involving water and steam in an architectural design.

The body is our interface with others and with nature, and it is through it that we learn about ourselves and it is through its control and management that society maintains its structures, norms, and discipline. Accordingly, the body is the object of religious codes and the instrument of political indoctrination. In Islamic Turkey and the countries that were at one time under Ottoman rule (including Syria, Jordan, Egypt, Tunisia, Algeria and Morocco) activities, practices, and dress codes are entangled in religious discourse. The same applies to the Jewish public baths, which were adopted from the Romans. In ancient Rome and Greece, and in Victorian England, the hammam was an institution of nation building and political discourse.

One of the earliest descriptions of hammams in Egypt is by Abel-Latif Al-Baghdadi, who lived in Cairo in AD 1200 (see Al-Baghdadi 1964; 1998). He devoted a relatively lengthy section of his book to hammams, and devoted his observations mostly to the first room in the hammam and the fireplace:

> *I have never seen any bathhouses that are better than the Egyptian hammams in as much as they are built, the way they are decorated, and the way they are run. At first, the basins accommodate between two and four riwya (water fillings) or more. Two pipes feed the basin with hot and cold water which are mixed to flow into the large basin. Almost one quarter of this basin is above ground. The rest of it is underground. The bather descends into*

this basin to be submerged. There are cabins with doors in the hammam. The Maslakh, also has cabins for the high order individuals (Arbab Al-Takhasus) so that they may not mix with the commoners (Al-'awam) and so that they would not show their private parts. This Mislakh with its cabins is pleasant in its appearance, "handsome" in its architecture. There is a pool of marble in its centre under a dome supported by columns. The roof is decorated. The walls are plastered and white-washed with marbled varicoloured floor. The marbling on the inside is better than that of the outside, and is, nevertheless, luminous, and highly polished. Its materials are of different colors, saturated in hue so that if you enter you will not wish to leave.

Its fire-place (Mawqid) is a wonder. The fireplace (Beit al-Nar) has an open dome to which the flames reach. On its platform are arrayed four cauldrons made of lead. They are connected at the top with pipes so that water runs from the water flowing from the well to the fountain (Fasqyia) and from that to the first cauldron where it is cold. It runs from the first to the second where it is warmed, then to the third, where it is further heated and subsequently to the fourth where it becomes very hot. Hot water then issues to the conduits of the hammam. As such water flows hot at a little expense, efficiently, and in a very short time. ... These cauldrons require to be refilled since water in the first cauldron is redacted at a rate twice that of the last cauldron.

The floor of the fireplace (Aton) is covered with about fifty ardebs of salt since salt conserves heat (My translation).

In 1481, Mushullam ben Menhaem noted that "*There is no other place that has Public Baths better than those of Cairo.*" About the same time in 1450, Gilles le Bouvier stated that "*to go to the hammam was one of the great pleasures of Cairo ladies because in addition to bathing they were also beautified. After the bodies were scrubbed with a glove made of rough wool, they took part of the food brought from their homes by their servants. Afterwards they rested for an hour or two. They were attended by a beautician called "Ballana" who dyed their hair using henna with great care so that the dye did not soil their foreheads or necks. Henna gave their hair a lovely reddish lustre. The blondes dyed their hair black because Egyptians were not fond of blonde women unless when the Sultan had a blonde princess, whom the commoners would then imitate. Women also removed their body hair using a paste made from orpiment [yellow arsenic sulphide] and lime which left their skin fair and soft*[1]. *This was followed by manicuring nails and massage. Afterwards, they took a bath in tepid or cold water for relaxation, which was followed with the consumption of sweets and fruits (Mazaheri)*" (Volkoff, 1971).

Almost four centuries later, a detailed ethnographic description of the hammams in Cairo was given by Edward Lane in his *An Account of the Manners and Customs of the Modern Egyptians*, first published in 1836. He remarked that "*bathing is one of the great luxuries enjoyed by the people of Egypt, and there are a few pleasures in which the women of Egypt delight so much as a visit to the bath, where they frequently have entertainment; and often, on these occasions, they are not a little noisy in their mirth.*" Some hammams were linked to mosques to provide for the necessary cleaning rituals.

HAMMAMS AND BODY POLITICS: TURKISH BATHS AND FOREIGN AFFAIRS

Politics and religion are social institutions that mould people into "subjects". Moreover, political and religious schemata of our bodies and those of "others" do shape our identities. Westerners, once identified religiously as Christians, distinguished themselves from Africans, Asians and Arabs on the basis of difference in colour, facial features, hair, and body build. The Arabs were often identified generically as Muslims, and vice versa, and have been portrayed on occasions with certain facial features, but because many "Arabs" are practically "white" and may pass for many Mediterranean Europeans, they are often characterised by stereotypical attire. Clothing may be regarded as a modification of the body or a means by which the body is presented, framed, extended, re-shaped, or fashioned as a "social" body. Removing one's clothing thus is a mode of "stripping" that teases out the social binders and modifiers that habitually become inseparable elements of both the private and social body and the self.

[1] According to Lane (1836), the name of the delipatory is "noorah" (from the Arabic word "to make luminous") and consists of quick lime and orpiment (about an eighth part). It is made into a paste, with water, before application: it loosens body hair in about two minutes, when it is washed off. This seems to be a very hazardous substance on account of the caustic characteristic of quick lime and may cause severe skin burns if not completely rinsed off before it begins to attack the skin. The use of poisonous arsenic compounds is also another hazard.

The hammam, where one disrobes, was one of the social institutions encountered by Europeans when they first came in contact with Muslims in Turkey. The hammam was thus seen mostly as a means by which Muslims and Christians/Europeans differed. One of the celebrated early European accounts of the hammam is the description given by Lady Mary Wortly Montagu based on a journey undertaken between 1716-18. Srinivas Arvamudan (1995) sees in her accounts the elements of "Levantinisation", a term coined for the characterization of the Levant, which broadly means the Orient as the contamination of European values by supposedly degenerate Levantine influences. The hammam fitted the bill, and was used a paragon of the presumed Oriental licentious sexuality and degeneracy.

This issue became abundantly clear when Turkish baths were first introduced into Victorian England, which totalled at one time 40 individual stand-alone establishments. Intended mostly for the "workmen", the leisured class claimed that the hammam led to indolence and that it would destroy "manliness" which created the British Empire, as it had destroyed the Roman Empire. According to M. Shifrin[2],in 1861, Dr. J. L. W. Thudichum read a paper on Turkish baths to the *Medical Society* in London which aroused much correspondence, including a letter that queried if the active, fox-hunting, cricketing, boating Englishmen bear the same kind of treatment that benefits and gratifies the indolent, languid, luxurious Turk? The editorial of the *British Medical Journal* in the same week went even further:

> *The [Turkish bath] may be adapted to the mental and physical constitution of those lazy Eastern voluptuaries who have cost us so much trouble and so many lives, and the well-fed and fatted contents of their harems.*

The editorial continued with the statement that no healthy person would indulge in hammam as a "slothful pasha". One Dr Henry W. Killmark warned against the threat of effeminacy and degeneracy of "race" cause by the hammam, which it has done with the ancient Romans and the modern Turks.

The hammam, and at its core the "body," was the potent and most sensitive raw material of political identification and distinction. It is indeed rather remarkable that the views expressed by Lady Montagu were still aired in 1861, a full 147 years after she had made her remarks. However, the persistence of that discourse makes sense in light of the clash between Britain, as well as France, with the Ottomans, in the gambit by such Europeans countries to undermine the political hegemony of Turkey with the sole aim of replacing it as a world power that would inherit Turkey's territorial possessions as their colonies.

David Urquhart promoted the idea of Victorian Turkish hammams while serving as a diplomat in Turkey (First Secretary to Viscount Ponsomby, the British Ambassador to Constantinople) in the mid 1830s. Urquhart believed that the hammam was a model to be admired and hoped that it would be copied in order to raise the level of British ideas of personal cleanliness to Turkish standards. Urquhart, however, had his political agenda. He hoped that, by introducing Turkish culture, Britain would be encouraged to adopt a more pro-Turkish, anti-Russian foreign policy[3]. Although he clashed with Palmerston and was dismissed from the diplomatic service, he succeeded in making the Turkish bath a successful business in Victorian England. The first Turkish bath was opened, with Urquhart's financial help in 1857. It was operated by William Potter, whose wife Elizabeth supervised separate sessions for women. In Ireland the first Turkish bath was built by Richard Barter. The success of the hammams was due to the work of well over a hundred Foreign Affairs Committees – consisting of workmen – set up by Urquhart both to influence the government and to spread the news of Turkish bath.

In April 1855, a secretary of one of the committees established a newspaper, *The Sheffield Free Press*, which became the mouthpiece of Urquhart's movements. The paper was not just about pro-Turkish policies, but also on the rights of the working class. Next to articles on Turkish baths were pieces on foreign affairs, including at one time an article on the diplomatic history of the eighteenth century by a writer called Dr Karl Marx. The relationship between Turkish baths and foreign affairs was explained as follows:

> *Some surprise has been expressed that we should make mention of the bath in a political journal...It* [the bath] *is not only a remedy and preventative of disease, a sweetener of the temper and a promoter of thorough cleanliness, but it is an antidote to intemperance and a means of destroying the barriers which now separate entirely the lower from the higher classes.*

[2] See Malcolm@vicotrianturkishbath.org

[3] See www.victorianturkishbath.org

No barrier of ceremony, of pride, or of habit, is so great as that of filth which, in these times, especially in large towns, separates the poor from the rich, as if they were not members of the same state, but as Disraeli has phrased it, "the two nations.

In spite of this, the introduction of Turkish bath was resisted. The original Baths and Wash-houses Acts of 1846 and 1847 precluded the provision of publicly financed Turkish baths. Accordingly, the majority of early Turkish baths were commercial establishments and hence has to raise their fees to break even, let alone make a profit. This meant that Turkish baths were rarely established in poorer areas. In 1864, when one Turkish bath was opened for a few hours on Sunday mornings, the only day when the poor working class can go, pressure from the Church opposed the move.

TRESPASSING GAZES, IMPERIALISM, MALE FANTASIES AND HAMMAMS

The Turkish bath and the Harem were among the saline elements in the representation of the Orient by westerners, as in the works by Delacroix, Ingres and Gérôme[4].

The confrontation between West and East, if we are to frame it in this crude generalisation, was not simply the work of a few politicians. It was, in fact, a product of a cultural transformation for a new Europe that was searching for its identity and "character" as the power of the Church was waning and as "people" – mostly the elite and the intellectuals in their company – began to assert themselves in an age where the power of kings and their authority was being challenged. A new Europe was appropriating symbols of power (i.e. obelisks) and in the meantime dissociating itself from its main opponent, the Ottomans. It was artists and writers who were the intellectual soldiers of a new Europe. In addition to extolling national landscapes and domestic scenes, they have also become preoccupied with the female body as a means of returning to "humanised nature" since women have, in different mythologies, been linked to rivers, springs, the seasons, trees, lakes, and the sea, as well as a way by which artists, mostly males, were playing with the sexual fantasies that were often excluded or neutralised by social and religious codes. The 18th and 19th centuries were ages of liberation and freedom – the depiction of nude females was rooted both in mythologising women as well as in the trespassing gaze.

Around 1817-19, Ingres' *Turkish bath* invites you almost through a peep-hole to spy on women who are depicted in languid and suggestive positions that seem to have little to do with cleanliness or bathing but are mostly focused on the sensuality of the nude female body.

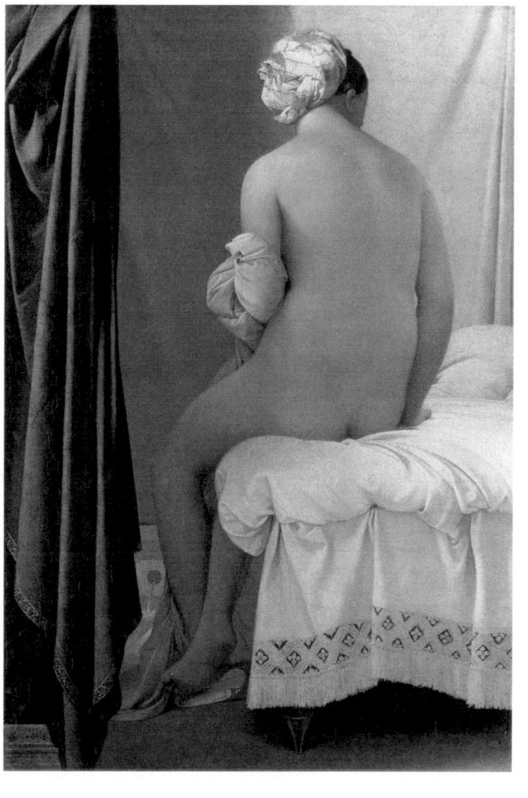

Ingres discovered the theme of the Turkish bath in the letters of Lady Montagu (see above). Her description of the bath at Hadriapole appealed to his fantasy of voluptuous pleasures of the female body that he presented in his Venus Anadymene (1848, Oil on canvass, Chantilly Musé Condé), in which he refers to Botticelli. He completed the Turkish bath in 1859. It was modified in 1860 from its original rectangular shape. The bather in the foreground is corpulent and lascivious, an ode to the flesh. We are also treated to a back [dorsal] view that we also see in the Bather of Valpinç (1808, oil on canvass, Louvre, Paris). In the background Ingres painted a medley of luscious female bodies accompanied by a black slave playing the tambourine. Bathing in Ingres' Turkish bath, beneath its evocative sexual overtones not only invoke deep mythological icons of women, dance and music, but also the role of the female body in setting cultural boundaries and identities (ethnic, religious, national and personal).

Gaudibert (1971: 30) takes notice of the light that isolates the group in the foreground whose bodies seem to be irradiated by an inner glow. It is light which breaks up the space in the canvass. This light recalls the glow of

[4] Delacroix, Eugene, *Women of Algiers in their apartments*, oil on canvass, 1834, Musee du Louvre, Paris; *Gerome Jean-Leon*, Moorish Bath, oil on canvas, 1880, Mildred Anne Williams Collection, Victor Spark, New York; Ingres, Jean-August-Dominique. *Turkish Bath*, oil on canvas fixed to panel, 1863, Musee du Louvre, Paris.

heavenly bodies, of goddesses in a celestial realm. In this scene, the light and fair complexion of "white" women is markedly contrasted with the two black women, often interpreted as slaves. This theme of contrasting bathing women with black slaves is evident in the *Small Bather* (interior of a Harem, 1828, Oil on canvas, Louvre, Paris, 35 x 27 cm), and was similarly used by Delacroix in his painting "Women of Alger in their apartments" produced in two versions dating to 1834 and 1849 (Bacholle 2001).

Delacroix, Ingres and other painters have unveiled the Orient. Then and now, the presentation of the body is heavily entangled in a web of significations. Orientalists McMaster and Lewis (1998) note that the image of veil, both in paintings, photographs and texts is strategically placed to signify religious, social and cultural practices which include purdah, the harem, polygamy, a repressive order based on the subjugation of women, sadism and lasciviousness. They also conclude that the depiction of veils in post-colonial times has increased in western media in tandem with the growing dissemination of a political agenda, after the collapse of the Soviet Union, that trumpets and fuels fears of a global Islamic threat. Today as in the past, the media are marshalled or become the proponents of political schemes. According to MacMaster and Lewis (1998), the facility with which the media have been able to deploy stereotypes of veiling owes its efficacy to the resonances that are rooted in an older Orientalist [Imperialist] tradition.

The harem and the hammam, often conflated, can be viewed from a different perspective situating these institutions within historical and cultural traditions that allow women to engage in activities from which males are segregated and forbidden (see Ahmed 1982, pp. 521-534). In a hammam or harem, women, as in the gathering of forty or fifty women in Yemen every afternoon, engaged in smoking, chewing qat (a mild narcotic), telling stories playing music, dancing, and engaging in satire, ridicule, and disrespect for males and the ideals of the male world. I suggest that (1) social practices are often complex and cannot be dismissed or challenged without a full understanding of their ramification and history, and (2) that media in the west have employed prejudicial, stereotypical views of the certain aspects of the Islamic world since the 18th century in a context of a clash of political and economic interested that have recently been depicted to the benefit of current political schemes as a "clash of civilizations" (Macmaster & Lewis 1998).

THE HAMMAM: CLEANLINESS AND FAITH

The appeal by David Urquhart to "cleanliness" as a key aspect of the Turkish bath, which was overlooked in Victorian England in favour of its "degenerate" influence, is rooted in one of the most important aspects of water- its potential to remove dirt, grime and filth from the body with attendant sensations of being refreshed, revived and revitalised. In a sense, cleanliness by water – especially a shower or a bath with cold water in hot weather and warm water when it is cold – has a blissful effect that is not lost on any one who goes to a hammam, especially when bathing is done in a sequence that accentuates the changes in the temperatures of the water and the mode by which it is applied (i.e. immersion, dipping, plunging, showering, dowsing). These sensations are captured in recent accounts disseminated in several websites such as:

> *"The heat lulled me into a torpid sweat. I sagged against the wall splashed cool water on my face and listened to the women's voices bounce off the wall. (http:seattlepi.nwsource.com/lifestyle/moroccohammam).*

> *"I tilt my head back and the water pours over me; I am struck by how much I welcome the sensation of streams of cool water rinsing away the hot beads of sweat that had collected… I feel my body start to relax." (http://www.bootsnall.com/articles /04-12/moroccan-hammam-at-a-cairo Spa).*

> *"After the decadent rubadub we get rinsed down again with the lovely warm water. They help us stand up (we are so relaxed we need help by this point as we feel like jelly!) and pour more water over our heads. I hear Jess scream, and my guy is thoughtful enough to ask first if I want the cold water tossed over me. First I say no, then*

reconsider. I also give a yelp but it feels good after all the heat. A little more steamy water and then they towel us dry."

(http:/steegar.wordpress.com/2007/05/07hammam-heaven)

The revitalising power of water did not only originate with the sensory perceptions of water but also with its scarcity and critical importance in arid lands where springs, rivers and rain were literally the source of life. This is not only evident in the way water was regarded in remote antiquity among the Egyptians and the inhabitants of Mesopotamia, but is also clear in biblical scripture.

In Islam, cleansing oneself with water is practiced every day five times before the daily prayers. This ritual washing or ablution makes it necessary to have a water fountain next to the mosque or in its courtyard. Sometimes water is provided from a well. Bathing is required before and after sexual intercourse or after any impurities from nocturnal emissions. Water purifies, cleanses and re-vitalises. Bathing amounts to the daily practice of baptism, and links it with the procreative acts. For Muslims, *Al-Nazafa min al-Iman.* ["Cleanliness is essential (a part of) faith]. Where water is scarce and household and private supply of water is not available, the institution of the public baths in the Byzantine world, as in Egypt and Syria, where Muslims replaced the governing elite, the hammam was appropriated. As the Greeks modified the Roman baths, so did the Muslims.

During an examination of the relationship between water and religion, it became clear to me that the idea of God, as well as that of deities or other supernatural elements in other religions was invariably structured in relationship to Nature in which water played a major role. This may also be said of indigenous religious beliefs that predate world religions (see for example: www.indigenouswater.org; Tuzin 1977; Rinne 2001; Scarborough 1998).

Although foragers, hunters and gatherers are at the mercy of rainfall, there was no motivation to harness or control water under a peripatetic mode of existence with high seasonal and daily mobility. By contrast, farmers who appeared about 10,000 years ago began the first systematic attempts to channel, drain, and manage water resources. Their livelihood depended on it and their fears and anxieties were alleviated through religious rituals and practices that encompassed both begging the gods for mercy and controlling the metaphysical world through the action of religious functionaries. With the emergence of divine kings, the king became the supreme intermediary who ensured the return of floods or plentiful rainfall (Hassan 2006; Scarborough 2003).

In Egypt, for example, village chiefdoms emerged at ca. 4500 BC and were succeeded by petty kingdoms and principalities by 3800 BC, coalescing into regional kingdoms by 3500 BC. Between 3300 and 3200 BC, a process of national unification led to the rise of a nation state headed by a king who was regarded as the incarnation of a living god (Horus), who is descended from a family of gods that included an ancestral king of Egypt (Osiris), an earth god, a sky goddess, a god of air, and a goddess of moisture. This family was created by a Creator God (Atum) who appeared on a hill from the primordial water of creation (Assmann 2002).

Osiris was associated with the summer drought that revived Egypt after its seasonal drought. One of the king's functions was to intervene on behalf of the people to the gods in order to ensure a plentiful flood and a good harvest (Assmann 2002). Amenemhat I (1991-1962 BC), the first pharaoh of the Middle Kingdom proclaimed:

"The Nile greeted me in every valley,
None went hungry in my years, none thirsted then
Men dwelt in peace, through that which I wrought, conversing of me'.

By the fourteenth century BC, one of the Egyptian pharaohs, Amenhotep IV [Akhenaton](1353-1335 BC) composed this hymn to the Nile (Pap. Chester Beatty V and Ostracon Ramesseum 92, UC 33007):

Hymn to the flood, Hail flood!
Emerging from the earth, arriving to bring Egypt to life,
Hidden of form, the darkness in the day,
The one whose followers sing to him, as he waters the plants
Created Re to make every herd live,
Who satisfies the desert hills removed from the water,
For it is his dew that descends from the sky

He, the beloved of Geb, controller of Nepri,
The one who makes the crafts of Ptah verdant.

Lord of fish, who allows south marsh fowl,
Without a bird falling from heat
Maker of barley, grower of emmer grain
Creator of festivals of the temples.
When he delays, then noses are blocked,
Everyone is orphaned. . .

In Mesopotamia, with a cultural development parallel to that of Egypt, the rulers were not regarded as gods; but some had a priestly function. The gods in Mesopotamia controlled rain. One of main gods, Enki (literally production manager) was also known as "Owner of the river" and the "Source" (of ground water). The role of gods in ensuring sufficient water supply and prosperity was clearly spelled out in a hymn to Rim-Sin, King of Larsa, dating to ca. 1822 BC (Postgate 1992).

In Judaism (developed mostly during the first millennium BC in contact with Egypt and Mesopotamia) and Islam (7th century AD), God replaces earthly divine kings and pre-Judaic deities in their capacity to send or withhold water.

He (the Lord) sendeth the springs into the valleys--
They give drink to every beast of the field:
The wild asses quench their thirst.
By them shall the fowls of the heaven have their habitation
He watereth the hills from his chambers--
He causes the grass to grow for the cattle,
And herb for the service of man:
that he may bring forth food out of the earth."
Psalm (104:10-13)

Both in Judaism and Islam, God, as Creator, is regarded as "Maker" who created a living world and who is capable of reviving the dead and dead lands with the power of water. The planets, mountains, hills, brooks, animals and plants rejoice and proclaim his blessings. As a medium of creation, water figures prominently in the chain of divine actions.

In Psalm 65, God visits the earth in the rain showers, watering its furrows abundantly blessing its growth. The earth responds with overflowing abundance: "*The hills gird themselves with joy, the meadows clothe themselves with flocks, the valley decks itself with flocks. the valleys deck themselves with grain, they shout and sing together for joy.*"

In the Koran (22:5), "*And you see the earth barren and lifeless but when we send down water upon it, it thrills and swells and puts forth every joyous kind of growth.*"

God in the Judeo-Christian-Islamic tradition is not identifiable with nature. God transcends nature and material existence. He created and commands nature, and the contemplation of the visible things the processes of nature, and its order leads to the recognition of God.

> *"It is He who sends down water from the sky and with it we bring forth the buds of every plant. From these we bring forth the thick-clustered grain, palm trees laden with clusters of dates within reach, vineyards and olive groves and pomegranates (which are) alike and different). Look upon their fruits when they bear fruit and upon its ripening surely in these there are signs for true believers"* (Koran 6:99).

Water thus becomes a currency of faith and the medium by which God is approached and through it one may taste his mercy and benevolence. Cleanliness thus not only brings one in contact with the substance of life and death, but also with the divine. According to Cherie J. Lenzen, (1998, the GreenCOM Project), all three monotheistic religions revere water. What differentiates Islam from Christianity and Judaism is that the ultimate control of life support resources rests with God (*`Allah*), and that rain is a sign of his mercy and benevolence on earth; the divine realm and a heavenly paradise is a garden with flowing water fountains and rivers. The garden in Islamic countries was both a public and private realm, murmuring fountains, verdant foliage and fruit trees as a microcosm of Heaven on earth.

The palaces and gardens of the Islamic world were places for contemplation and reflection rather than a place for debates and congregation. The main religious focus of the public space was the mosque, which was one of the means to address one's personal relationship with God. Ablutions were an integral part of this, preparing one to face the creator and the source of all life on both Heaven and Earth. The garden celebrated the rewards for the faithful, reflecting an everlasting afterlife in Paradise. Drinking fountains (*sebils*) and public baths were provided by the rich, in order to earn God's blessings and also to allow the poor to enjoy the bliss of water, a sign of God's mercy. It is apparent, therefore, that the Turkish bath differed from the Roman bath, which functioned as a forum for social engagements, political dealings and business transactions.

In Islam and Judaism, the association between divine power and water was embedded in a pastoral paradigm of shepherds and farmers, tied to nature and the agricultural cycle. For the Romans, by contrast, the focus was not on a pastorally associated abstract deity, but on city life, civic conduct and public affairs. There were still water-connected pagan deities, but they were associated with "social water" in manmade pools, rather than a natural spring, and piped water rather than rain. In this way the Romans elevated the city to the status of a temple of life, while public baths became venues for the laving of bodies with urbanised water, eventually becoming a source of civic pride and an arena for the exertion of power and influence (Hassan 2000).

The Roman bath was large, bright and noisy, contrasting strongly with the hammam's emphasis on tranquillity, silence and relaxation, a venue for amicable social exchanges and rejuvenation. The lengthy bathing sequence involved exposure to different temperatures, positions and activities, designed to awaken the senses in a measured manner, and to distance oneself from the rigours of daily stresses. Unlike the Greek bath, there was no emphasis on violent exercise and athletics. As Twigg (2000) notes, the objective of the Roman bath was to instil a sense of civic community. It was also used to promote the notion of equality, which was necessary for the military ethos of both Romans and Greeks. After undressing, the bather would undertake muscular exercises like running, wrestling, active sports or gymnastics. The bathers also engaged in mental exercises, such as talking, reading, singing and debating. The notion of a sound mind in a sound body was instrumental to the Greek gymnasium; the baths were believed to be restorative, regular attendance a vital means of maintaining good health. This "classical" paradigm and belief that communal bathing led to character-building, "manliness" and good community spirit is still maintained in public[5] schools, military barracks and locker rooms (DeLaine and Johnston 1999).

The baths were places for sensory delights, where bathers could enjoy the pleasures of large, well-lit rooms under airy vaults, involve in social transactions and even carry out business and shopping. It was such a fundamental part of Roman life that it served as a marker of the civic life and urbanity required to 'become' Roman. DeLaine (1999) suggests that the spread of bathing throughout the Roman Empire reflects the distinctiveness of this "imperial civilisation" in the eyes of non-citizens. The bath's manipulation of the body thus became a part of a "civilising process" in the sense used by Elias (1982), the requirements being the result of careful control of the body: short hair, all bodily hair removed or trimmed, teeth cleaned, body washed and properly dressed in an enveloping toga. Physical appearance and bodily image are at heart of "culture", and is reflexively believed to reflect character in national, imperial, military and religious orders, including Islam. These institutions also regiment their members through control of their sexuality and diet, so the baths have a particularly potent symbolism for Islamic society; this is best illustrated by the fact that the hammam is a site for hair removal, bridal beautification and grooming[6].

The importance of Roman baths is reflected in the complexity and cost of the construction and servicing of the baths (see DeLaine 1999; DeLaine & Johnston 1999). Vast quantities of water were supplied through an elaborate system of pipes and aqueducts running from the main water canal. The expense of constructing and operating the baths made it primarily an elite concern; controlling bathing facilities was the means by which wealthy patrons legitimised their power in the community, using their "Romanness" to ensure their position as guardians of the empire.

Of course, the baths were also an economically important enterprise. They were built by individuals or communities either as free public institutions, or as a source of income to both owners and operators. Although constructing and running a bath was prohibitively expensive and thus precluded most members of the community, Delaine (1997) has noted that building and running baths provided employment opportunities to both skilled and unskilled workers; perhaps as many as 16,000 people were employed in the construction of the baths of Caracalla, almost as many as were employed in the building of the Giza pyramids.

---

5 In the British sense (i.e. elite private schools).

6 Bouhdiba (1985) provides a detailed discussion of body treatment in the hammam.

The earliest examples of Islamic baths were constructed by caliphs and the elite in the Jordanian desert, and date to the Umayyad and `Abbasid periods. Examples of these "Desert Castles" have been excavated at Azraq, As- Sarakh (part of the Qasr Hallabat complex) and the world heritage site of Qusayr `Amr, famed for its bath frescoes. The investment in these structures was evidently considerable, given the scale of cut-stone water cisterns, wells and reservoirs that supplied as-Sarakh and Qusayr `Amr.

The Turkish hammam as we know it, however, is a social institution that developed under the Ottomans and the Mamluks during the Medieval period, at a time when communal bathing had died out in Europe. Reintroduced by Crusaders following their return from the Middle East, baths increased in popularity throughout Europe from the 13th to 15th centuries. Although bathing enjoyed considerable public acceptance in cities like Paris – where bath owners even formed a guild – the church strongly disapproved of bathing, which they regarded as a sinful indulgence when compared to Christianity's idealised asceticism. This could not have differed more from Islam, where bathing was a means of approaching the divine (see above), and baths also served as a major social and business venue. Accordingly, baths flourished, with maybe as many as 1500 in Cairo during the 10th century AD. These were run by both philanthropists and merchants with a sense of civic duty, who made themselves responsible for the construction and maintenance of public buildings. One of these merchants, Al-Rou'i (1600s AD), is memorialised in the name of the quarter he developed: Azbakia (Hanna 1997).

The role of the elite in the construction of hammams echoed that of the Roman elites some centuries before (see above). While not usually built on the same scale as the large Roman baths, the construction of hammams was costly, and supplying them with water and fuel was also not cheap. While they were often run by businessmen, however, there was generally considered to be a sense of moral positivity in the hammam business. The elite constructed and maintained public bath facilities free of charge, in accordance with the Islamic belief in the veneration of water as a divine substance. This also gave them the opportunity to appear pious and righteous, as they were doubtless aware that the provision of a hammam earned them high status as community leaders. This philanthropic attitude regarding bathing did not translate well to a European context – David Urquhart's efforts to encourage Turkish baths for the poor were somewhat unsuccessful..

The social role of the hammam has changed considerably into the present day. There are very few hammams still in operation in Cairo – for instance – and those that remain can barely keep up with the rising costs of water and fuel. This is partly an economic issue, but is primarily social: they have been deserted by the more affluent strata of society due to a change in the ethos of community, and an aspiration towards the nuclear family and "modernity". One of the main elements of modernity (once represented by an electric fan and a refrigerator) is the possession of a modern bathroom, while the spa is perceived to be a modernised water institution with emphasis on swimming, athletic exercises and fitness. The spa has therefore taken over the role of the hammam, maintaining a much-needed link with water at a scale not possible at home, and at the same time providing a sense of exclusivity and distinction because of the cost of the service. Hammams are thus almost solely utilised by those who have no other option, and as there is no longer any social kudos to be gained from their construction and maintenance, their standards of sanitation are declining (at least from our current perspectives). The hammam is now maligned not by western travellers and artists, but by people within the community who judge the hammams to be dens of deviance and licentious behaviour, just as they were originally perceived to be by the Church. This is doubly unfortunate, for the hammam is one of the few venues where women could convene socially, away from the gaze and interference by men. The fact that the hammams are now being condemned by those who take a narrow view of religious mores and who no longer see water as a sign of god's mercy and beneficiation is sad indeed.

Nudity, Exposure and Society

The voluntary self-exposure involved in the use of a hammam says something about the nature of the society which created it, while the attitudes of outsiders to public (semi)nudity is also potentially informative. In the present day, various concerns about nudity and protocol in hammams have been raised in a number of venues:

> *"I was in the middle of dropping my drawers when I looked up to find a room full of people staring at me. I flushed red ad stopped, pants at mid-thigh, my half naked-lily-white arse hanging out for all to see. The women scattered around the room whispered among themselves and grinned in my direction. I smiled back weakly, face burning crimson, and reluctantly finished my striptease.*

Not since junior high gym class had I felt like this. Never mind the fact that my state of near nudity was perfectly apropos for my current location—a Muslim bathhouse known as a hammam—I still felt like I was caught in one of those dreams where you suddenly find yourself standing naked in the frozen-food section of the grocery store" (http:seattlepi.nwsource.com/ lifestyle/ moroccohammam).

Winda Benedetti, Seattle post-intelligencer reporter

Sources concerning nudity was also expressed by a would-be traveller to Morocco in a *Lonely Planet* chat forum (http://thorntree.lonleyplanet.com/message post).

"Hi I am planning a 1-month trip to Morocco… I'm female and I am concerned about hammam protocol. I am not comfortable being naked around others. Sounds silly, but there are good reasons for me to keep some underwear on…" In response she was assured by others that she could keep on her underwear.

But even with underwear on, Tanalee Smith (www.bootsnall.com/articles/04-12/morrocan hammam- at a Cairo Spa.) narrates how "*Moments after I settle (sic.) into my personal 2x1 meter steam room, there is a light knock on the door and a questioning, "OK?" I am joined by Suzanne, a squat Moroccan woman wearing a black one-piece bathing suit and a sweet smile. I try to act nonchalant. But honestly, it isn't everyday that I meet a new person when I am wearing nothing but a pair of beige nylon panties which I realize now are soaked through from the condensed steam and the wet mat I am resting on"*

Almost a century and half ago, UK social conventions meant that nudity was also a concern for male bathers. Erasmus Wilson wrote in his book "The Eastern, or Turkish Bath," that a costume was indispensable. "Without a costume in the presence of others, the bath is not the bath- it is an evil, and as an evil it should be suppressed with the utmost severity." Usually, bathers were partially covered by towels, though most swam in the plunge pool in the nude. At the London hammam, modesty tents were lowered over bathers as they left the pool[7]. For women, "Penelope" wrote in the Rochdale Times that "*there is something contrary to feminine instinct in the gregarious nature of a public Turkish bath.*" An architect, Robert Own Allsop, stated that many British women, unlike their French counterparts, preferred not to get undressed or take showers in communal areas. He recommended the use of private dressing and reposing rooms, as well as private shampooing recesses.

The act of bathing invariably implies the total or partial removal of clothing, whether private or public. This act of "denudation" involved the presence of "others", mostly strangers, and this has significant psychological implications connected to the personality of the bather and social conventions governing nudity and dressing in public. My thesis is that denudation is an act of "exposure" which unveils the physical aspects of a person, which include: 1) sex, 2) age, 3) deformities, 4) state of health, 5) body configuration, 6) fitness and maintenance, and 7) body treatment and modifications. Denudation is paradoxical because on the one hand it involves removal of the attire which is, after all, a social prop for the "self" as social actor; removing clothes therefore involves an element of release from "pretence" or social controls. On the other hand, the way the body is maintained, groomed, or neglected reveals many aspects both about personality and adherence to social norms, which shape expectations.

Denudation thus accentuates our body in order to transmit self-identifying messages concerning who and what we are, making us vulnerable and bare of any embellishment or masquerade. Being in a new and unfamiliar social field with new terms of reference and abnormal social encounters inevitably causes anxieties, which are dealt with socially through ritualised behaviour and perhaps rationalisation. The hammam, however, lies within and outside society. Social encounters in the hammam will have implications for the world outside, which cannot be shed as easily as our underwear. This liminality, the in-between situation, the node between here and there, now and then, is compounded with the deeper symbolic meanings of the setting of the hammam as a paradoxical and transformative place where purity and filth coexist, where dead skin is scrubbed away like that of a snake shedding its former self. The hammam contains the primordial elements of water and fire, comprising a cosmically reductive microcosm of earth, water and heaven. Hammam architecture reiterates this notion, roofed by a dome with sparkling stars of light – or perhaps, more appropriately, rays of moonlight (they are called *qmariat*

[7] www.victorianturkishbath.org

[moony] in Arabic) – over a tiled floor with a water pool, the primeval water of creation in which we are immersed in order to be reborn. The hammam's shifts of temperature could be considered to be symbolic of seasonal change, while the dim light and reduced noise are reminiscent of the expectation-filled silence preceding an important announcement or event, or perhaps the hush of the grave or womb, awaiting resurrection. The hammam is an exercise in poetics, which reveal its fundamental nature. While metrics, ecology, economics and other quantifiable elements are important in understanding hammam design and social role, these will be unsuccessful unless one also considers the "objectives" that the hammam serves and the meanings of a "hammam" rather than a spa, gymnasium, private bath, onsen or swimming pool.

As we have seen, the hammam is primarily an "urban" phenomenon, a microcosm of a community in a liminal space that eases the urban woes of finding friends, picking up useful information and hints, making business contacts and finding a suitable bride. The hammam is a place where strangers become friends, where friends renew their friendships and learn to accept one another precisely as they are, without adornments or attire. This takes place within a supra-social context where the light from Heaven shines on moral bodies, wet and naked in a state of nature that the morality of the city is intent upon denying.

Nudity, Water and Sexuality

It is not difficult to understand why a hammam may be construed as a place where sexual encounters are common. Nudity, warm stimulating water, the sight of other naked bodies, and intimate close proximity to others all have sexual undertones. Bouhdiba (1985) examined the notion of the hammam as an eroticised place, and has commented upon the fact that taking a bath (hammam) is a religious requirement after sex, leading to a mental association between hammam and sex. A hammam is also a prelude to sex, which is in turn linked directly to purification. This takes a very specific form with women, who use hammams to boost their physical beauty and accentuate their womanhood. To be scrubbed, bathed, and massaged by a stranger is also potentially loaded with parasexual if not sexual overtones.

These overtones are accentuated by separation of the sexes. In a society where homosexuality is not socially acceptable, encounters between two naked men or two naked women could potentially be a source of tension. Islamic jurists are traditionally suspicious of hammams for this reason (Bouhdiba 1985), especially as hammams are frequently the subject of poems that extolled the love of boys. The slight hysteria surrounding hammams as sexualised environments has led to a popular belief that virgins may get pregnant merely by being in a hammam; prudent women therefore wash the seats for fear of coming in contact with semen (Bouhdiba 1985).

Although it is not unlikely that sexual encounters may be initiated at a hammam, it is probable that the discourse exists because they are cognitively linked, and because a hammam would be the first social institution that makes use of liminality to legitimise and re-enforce proper social conduct. The potency and potential danger involved in sexual experiences requires the "purification" that the hammam brings, and may accordingly stand for keeping up general social conduct. The sexually and socially insecure would find in the hammam an easy target for their condemnation, as would those uneasy about the notion of a degenerate orient, who felt their beliefs threatened (as during the reformation), or those casting covetous eyes at the property. Many of these issues can be illustrated by the example of Paris. Numerous baths were set up in the 12th-13th centuries, 26 of them by 1292, and these all appear to have had some association with eroticism and promiscuity (Vigarello 1978). During the 14th century it was deemed necessary to create a distance between the sexes in the hammam, while the sexes were completely segregated by the 15th century. By the 16th century the baths were suppressed altogether[8]. Darmon (1983) sees this as part of a social trend into the Reformation, the principal cause of the spread of misogyny in 16th and 17th century France. At that time preachers raged against the flesh, and the fact that women's fashions tended to expose the upper half of their breasts. Some preachers even advocated that women should not leave home unveiled. Women were increasingly regarded as lustful with an insatiable desire for sex, and social environments such as hammams were viewed with commensurate suspicion.

There were various other contexts that seemed incongruent with the Islamic ideal of hammam design and usage. Judaism holds that it is necessary to bathe and thus purify women who had given birth or were menstruating; the latter was so threatening that men who come in contact with women during this time would also be considered to be impure. Nakedness was similarly considered to be shameful because it implied poverty and destitution. Female nudity was viewed as a temptation to men, although it was permissible in an all-female context. The definition of 'nudity' was also configured in a manner that

[8] Duerr (1988) disagrees with this, stating that the sexes were always separated

underscores the social tone. Female nudity was more strictly defined than male nudity; a woman was not considered to be dressed unless the whole body (not just the genital area) was covered, including the hair of married women. Indeed, any woman who left her home with her hair uncovered or with a revealing dress could be divorced by her husband without payment of any divorce settlement; any woman who appeared in public without a headdress was deemed to be unrespectable (Hoss 2005).

Muslim ulemas were confronted with the vexing question of whether naked women should be permitted in a hammam. El-Ghazali was opposed, stating that women should be banned unless they were ill or in childbed. 'Uqbani was somewhat more tolerant, but asserted that a husband was perfectly within his rights to forbid his wife to go to one. This all springs from what nakedness actually involved. According to extreme views, nakedness (exposure of "'oura" [from the root for "shame": 'ar]) can literally entail the entire female body. The sexes were therefore separated, and it became forbidden to gaze at persons of the other sex. This became such an issue that Al-Ghazali devoted one full chapter in his book (Ihya) to good manners in a hammam, which concluded that a man should wear two loincloths: one for the genitals, and one for the eyes to prevent accidental viewing of another man's genitalia (Bouhdiba, 1985). This apparent panic at the thought of states of undress reached more salacious assertions in the work of the jurist 'Uqbani, who voiced an apparent hidden anxiety when he claimed that women's hammams were conducive to lesbianism:

> *"Especially when encounters with shameless women are an invitation to expose attractions likely to excite a desire that some find more agreeable to satisfy in contact with other women than in copulation with men."*

In his analysis of Sexuality in Islam, Bouhdiba (1985) concludes that the hammam is a social institution by which Islamic society has managed to come to terms with its centuries-long repressive misogynist Puritanism:

> *"In using the hammam Muslim society has forged a valuable instrument for itself to channel the sexual drives liberated by religion but suppressed by Puritanism."*

It seems, however, that a hammam – with its erotic connotations – is a place for anxiety and fantasy, of pleasurable bodily experiences that do not carry the full consequences of dangerous liaisons or illicit sex, comprising safe parasexual sensations that that are neither a substitute for sex nor a sublimation of sexual drives, but a parallel channel to allow oneself to experience the sensuality of the body. As the self encounters itself in embodied experiences it realizes its gendered identity.

CONCLUSIONS

The hammam and the Roman bath were deployed within a strategy of social empowerment and control, as well as socialisation and enculturation. Both were also primarily urban institutions. While the Roman bath was a form of civic governance and discourse, the hammam developed in the shadow of the mosque and is imbued with religious symbolism.

In cities, where water is scarce and costly, bathing became the preserve of the rich; the elites could choose to exercise highly visible benevolence, charity and magnanimity by making baths available to the common people in Rome and Byzantium, thus currying social favour. There was a change towards the birth of Islam, when an Umayyad caliph founded a hammam in the Jordanian desert for the delectation of himself and honoured guests. Medieval Arab hammams reflected something of the Late Roman, rich merchants founding hammams as charitable institutions, thus reinforcing their status and social standing. The religious overtones are clear: Judaism and Islam both hold that water was a gift from God, so anyone who permitted wider access to it was essentially a religious evangelist. The philanthropic elites in both the Roman and Islamic worlds were plugged into the divine domain that uses water as a metaphor for the parable of creating the world from water, and the provisioning of water as a source of life.

The hammam is a social phenomenon. Its development and spread between cultural contexts and historical periods is enmeshed in complex social dynamics influenced by the experiential qualities of – and social attitudes towards – water, nudity and temperature. The cleansing function of water is also entangled with notions of purity and sanctity, which was seen as being differentially important to different sexes and subgroups throughout history. These functions combine to make bathing a liminal experience. Within a social context the hammam becomes a space both within and outside society, a space for social intimacy and disclosure, which is occasionally implicated in sexual encounters or displays of prudence. In lieu of socially taboo behaviour, the hammam is also the scene for parasexual scrubbing and massage, which imbues it with an aura of eroticism. This is the principal reason why the hammam became one of the main tropes in the encounter between the West and the Islamic World. It is peculiarly poignant that the hammams are currently under attack on various fronts, and that religious extremists have targeted them as places of illicit and forbidden sexual encounters.

REFERENCES

Ahmed, L. 1982. Western ethnocentrism and perception of the harem, *Feminist Studies* 8(3): 521-534.

Al-Baghdadi, A. 1964. *Kitab Al-Ifada wa'l Itibar [The Eastern Key]*. (2nd edn). Trans. by H. Z. Kamal. London.

Al-Baghdadi, A. 1998. *Kitab Al-Ifada wal 'itibar (Book of Bebefitis and Reflection concerning Observations and Events witnessed in Egypt).* (2nd edn). Cairo: Al-Hyia Al-'Ama lil Kitab.

Arvamudan, S. 1995. *Lady Mary Wortley Montagu in the Hammam: masquerade, womanliness and Levantinisation*: http://muse.jhu.edu/journals/elh/ v062.1/aravamundan.htm.

Assmann, J. 2002. *The Mind of Egypt: history and meaning in the time of the Pharaohs.* Boston: Harvard University Press.

Bacholle, M. 2001. *Women in Their Apartment: the trespassing gaze.* West Virginia Philological Papers.

Bouhdiba, A. 1985. *Sexuality in Islam.* London: Routledge.

Culianu, I. P. 1991. A corpus for the body, *Journal of Modern History* 63: 61-80.

Darmon, P. 1983. *Mythologie de la femme dans l'Ancienne France XVIe-XIXe siècle.* Paris: Seuil.

DeLaine, J. 1997. *The Baths of Caracalla: a study in the design, construction, and economics of large-scale building projects in imperial Rome.* Rhodes Island: Journal of Roman Archaeology.

DeLaine, J. and Johnston, D. E. 1999. Roman baths and bathing. Part I. Bathing and Society, *Journal of Roman Archaeology,* Supplementary Series no. 37: 7-16.

Duerr, H. P. 1988. *Nacktheit und Scham: Der Mythos vom Zivilisationsprozess.* Frankfurt am Main: Suhrkamp.

Elias, N. 1982. *The Civilising Process* Oxford: Blackwell.

Gaudibert, P. 1971. *Ingres.* New York: Grosset and Dunlap.

Hanna, N. 1997. *Making Big Money in 1600: The Life and Times of Isma'il Abu Taqiyya, Egyptian Merchant.* Syracuse [NY]: Syracuse University Press.

Abbas, A. N.D. *Tugar al-Qahira in the Ottoman Period, Al-Dar Al-Misryia Al-Lubnaniyia.* Cairo.

Hassan, F. A. 2000. Rain, rivers and fountains: the legacy of water and civilization in the Mediterranean. In *Water Security in the Third Millennium*: Mediterranean Countries Toward a Regional Vision. Forum of the UNESCO International School of Science for Peace, Como, Italy. pp. 213-240.

Hassan, F. A. 2006. Archaeology for our times: Water and Civilisation. Review of: The Flow of Power: Ancient Water Systems and Landscapes, *The Review of Archaeology* 27: 1-9.

Hoss. S. 2005. *Baths and bathing: the culture of bathing and the baths and thermae in Palestine from Hasmoneans to the Moslem conquest.* Oxford: BAR International Series 1346.

Lane, E. 1983 [1836]. *An Account of the Manners and Customs of the Modern Egyptians.* London: Dover edition.

MacMaster, N. and Lewis, T. 1998. Orientalism: from unveiling to hyperveiling, *Journal of European Studies* 28.

Postgate, N. 1992. *Early Mesopotamia: Society and Economy at the Dawn of History*, London: Routledge.

Rinne, E-M. 2001. Water and healing-experience from the traditional healers in Ile-Ife, Nigeria, *Nordic Journal of African Studies* 10(1): 41-65.

Scarborough, V. 1998. Ecology and ritual: water management and the Maya, *Latin American Antiquity* 9(2): 135-159.

Scarborough, V. 2003. *The Flow of Power: Ancient Water Systems and Landscapes.* New Mexico: SAR Press.

Tuzin, D. P. 1977. Reflections of being in Arapesh water symbolism, *Ethos* 5(2): 195-223.

Twigg, J. 2000. *Bathing the Body and Community Care.* London: Routledge.

Vigarello, G. 1978. *Le corps redresse: histoire d'un pouvoir pedagogique.* Paris.

Volkoff, O. 1971. *Le Caire (969-1969), Historie de la ville des "Mille et Une Nuit"*, [*Cairo, City of One Thousand Nights and Nights (969-1969)*]. Trans. into Arabic by Ahmed Slieha. Al-Hiya Al-Misriyia lil-Kitab. 1986, Cairo: IFAO.

Websites

malcolm@victorianturkishbath.org and (www.victorianturkishbath.org) (see M. Shifrin)

http:/steegar.wordpress.com/2007/05/07hammam-heaven

http://www.bootsnall.com/articles /04-12/moroccan-hammam-at-a-cairoSpa

www.bootsnall.com/articles/04-12/morrocan (see Tanalee Smith)

http:seattlepi.nwsource.com/lifestyle/moroccohammam (See Winda Benedetti, seattle post-intelligencer reporter).

http://thorntree.lonleyplanet.com/message (Lonley Planet chat forum)

www.indigenouswater.org

Chapter 9

The Nile Delta in Peril: Cultural Heritage Management in the Delta

G. J. Tassie, J. van Wetering, and A. De Trafford

Abstract

Formed by branches of the Nile in the prehistoric period, the Delta floodplain has seen continuous human occupation and is now is one of the most populated regions in Egypt. Responding to fluctuations in the flood discharge of the Nile, incursion and retreat of the Mediterranean shoreline, as well as subsidence of the land, the floodplain of the Delta is a showcase of how climate change and geological processes can shape landscapes. It was in the context of this moveable, changeable and dynamic landscape that Egyptian civilisation was forged, fuelled by countless external groups from the Levant, Mesopotamia, Persia, Greece, Rome, and Europe, interacting with Egyptians through trade, invasions or population movements. Levantine trading posts, Greek industrial cities, monasteries, mosques, royal tombs, forts, shipyards, orchards, cemeteries, capital cities and much more are witness to a procession of world events. Yet this precious world heritage is now threatened by coastal erosion, fishponds, expanding settlements, and runaway development. Originally inhabited by no more than a million people, the Delta is now home to as many as 43 million, a figure expected to double in the next thirty years. Thousands of villages, hamlets, towns and farmsteads are spreading so fast that they are threatening sites of all periods, from Rosetta with its famous medieval architecture to barely known archaeological sites that were once the majestic capitals of ancient Egypt, such as Sais and Buto. The physical expansion of the Delta dwellers is accompanied by an array of activities that threaten the very existence of ancient sites, from building to the removal of soil, sand and gravel for construction, drowning sites with sewage and effluent water, and turning sites into fish farms. Moreover, the temptation of illicit digging is often irresistible. Climatic changes in the form of sea level rise and fluctuating Nile flood regimes also pose a threat to this vulnerable area.

Introduction

The Nile Delta is today supported at its stem by the grey mass of Cairo, although in the past it was the thriving city of Memphis that fulfilled this role. However, it is not just the varied Delta landscape, with its palm trees, marshlands, fields of maize, cotton, bersim and rice, melting into the desert that makes Lower Egypt special – it is the people that farm the fields, and work in the cities. The population is as vivacious and as active as it has always been, given to as many human frailties as strengths, unified by its sense of internal cohesion, usually at the mocking expense of the southern Sa'idis. This is, again, hardly an innovative perspective: Egypt may have been unified for over 5,000 years, So although Egypt has been a unified state for over 5,000 years, there still seems to be this mental divide between north and south, a divide noted upon by Sinhue in his Middle Kingdom text the *Story of Sinhue*: when Sinhue on finding himself in Asia, 'compares his situation to that of a Delta man seeing himself in Elephantine in the extreme south of Egypt' (Leahy 1995: 226), saying how strange he found it. The divisions and different character of the various areas was also recognised in another Middle Kingdom text *The Teaching for King Merikara* (Wilson 2007: 19-21). Cultural differences in the pottery production of the fifth and fourth millennia BC are well attested, although there may also have been a different dialect as illustrated by the Third Intermediate Period and Late Period names of kings, such as Shoshenq and Psamtek, and in the Coptic dialects, of which Bohairic is the northern version (Wilson 2007: 26).

Two of the most famous of Egypt's historians – Manetho and Herodotus – spent much of their time in the Delta, Manetho even being born there at Samanud (classical Sebennytos) ancient Tjeb-netjer, [Herodotus, of course being a Greek Traveller]. In the first millennium BC the region was home to many thriving cities, including Alexandria, Bubastis, Busiris, Sais, Xois, Papremis, Tanis and Mendes (see Leclère 2008), which were also home to an influx of people from Sub-Saharan Africa, Asia and Europe, lending them a cosmopolitan ambience. Recent underwater discoveries in the area of Alexandria are revealing the splendours of the Delta in the Graeco-Roman Period, the Western harbour of Alexandria contains a wonder of the ancient world (the Pharos), and the Eastern harbour shelters the palaces of Anthony and Cleopatra. The seaboard became a major focus for trade in the Graeco-Roman period, as the long-lost cities of Nicopolis, Taposiris, Canopus, Menouthis and Herakleion are now making apparent (Blue and

Khalil 2010; 2011; Stanley *et al.* 2004). Even the name 'Delta' was given by the Greeks, because of its resemblance to the triangular Greek letter *delta* (Δ).

Figure 9.1: Sunset over a delta village.

Archaeologically, the Delta contains various sites with long excavation histories, including Alexandria, Bubastis, Buto, Merimde Beni Salame, Naukratis and Tanis, amongst many others (Leclère 2008). Despite this wealth, however, the Delta is comparatively unexploited by tourists, as these sites lack the accessibility and high profile enjoyed by Upper Egyptian sites such as the Valley of the Kings, Kom Ombo, Dendera and Abu Simbel. While a challenge, however, the Delta holds rich rewards, not just archaeologically but culturally, socially and environmentally.

Apart from those few sites named above, the Delta has traditionally been overlooked by archaeological investigation, despite its traditional role as one of ancient Egypt's Two Lands (Wilson 2007; 2012b), and while the balance of archaeological excavation and survey has started to be redressed in recent years, it is now more vital than ever that work be increased in this threatened area. Coastal erosion, pisciculture, expanding settlements and runaway development by a population exceeding 40 million (a figure expected to double in the next thirty years) are threatening sites of all periods and types. Thousands of villages, hamlets, towns and farmsteads are spreading in an unprecedented tide of human swell, threatening sites of all periods from Rosetta with its famous medieval architecture to the barely known archaeological sites that were once the majestic capitals of ancient Egypt like Sais and Buto. The physical expansion of Delta dwellers comes with an array of activities threatening the very existence of ancient sites – urban sprawl and land reclamation building over sites, increased agriculture, removing soil, sand and gravel for construction, drowning sites with sewage and affluent water, turning sites into fish farms, and looting.

Figure 9.2: Panoramic view of the Rosetta Branch of the Nile in the Minufiyeh Province.

Figure 9.3: The village of Kom el-Ahmer in the Minufiyeh Province.

Figure 9.4: Daily life in the city of Samanud.

Figure 9.5: The site of Tell Basta (Bubastis) surrounded by the modern city of Zagazig.

Figure 9.6: The site of Tell Basta (Bubastis) surrounded by the modern city of Zagazig.

SURVEYING AND EXCAVATING THE DELTA

Because Upper Egyptian sites are generally easier to excavate and yield better preserved remains, they have attracted the attention of excavators more readily than less prepossessing sites in the Nile Delta (Borghouts 1988: 3). The Nile Valley (from Elephantine/Aswan to Abu Roash) holds the burial grounds of the majority of the ancient Egyptian kings: at Abydos, Giza, Saqqara, Thebes; as well as many of the most impressive religious monuments: the Abu Simbel temples, Temple of Hathor at Dendera, Karnak, and Luxor Temple and the most complete Pharaonic city so far found in Egypt: Amarna. These sites have produced information about Egyptian society on many different levels, supplying material for archaeologists, art historians, philologists and other specialists (Andrén 1998: 41). It is only in recent times that archaeologists have overcome the restrictions imposed by funding bodies and social expectations (Bietak 1979a: 93-4; Borghouts 1988: 3), and are able to take the anthropological perspective.[1]

In the early twentieth century, settlement sites in Lower Egypt were only excavated because of their Biblical or Classical connections (Holladay 1982: 3; Naville 1885; Petrie and Duncan 1906; Trigger 1989: 103), or perhaps their royal links (i.e. Tanis, burial ground for kings of the Third Intermediate Period, to include Amenemope, Osorkon II, Psusennes I, Psusennes II Sheshonq II, Sheshonq III, Sheshonq IV, Siamun, and Takelot I [Montet 1947; 1951; 1960]). Limited survey work was also carried out on the desert edge, levees or turtlebacks (Daressy 1912, 1914a, 1914b, 1930; Junker 1928, 1930) rather than on the alluvial floodplain where the majority of sites were either underwater or deeply buried by alluvium and later occupations, or are now below the water table. While challenging, the issues involved in Delta archaeology are surmountable; the historical emphasis on Upper Egyptian epigraphy-bearing sites is partly a question of agendas, as noted by Yoyotte (1958: 23):

[1] Archaeological excavations were generally funded by museums or private collectors that wanted to possess and display beautiful artefacts, or be associated with great finds.

'...l'égyptologie s'est faite spontanément, au fil de l'histoire. Si elle avait pu se créer a priori, c'est incontestablement par le Delta ancien, plus menacé, touché par l'expansion agricole urbaine, qu'il aurait fallu commencer.'

Since the Nubian Rescue Campaign, Egyptian archaeology has increasingly aligned itself with mainstream archaeological practice, finding equilibrium in the last decades of the twentieth century. Small mounds have yielded unexpectedly important results, for example at Tell el-Dab'a/Avaris (Bietak 1975), and Tell Ibrahim Awad, which revealed a sequence spanning Naqada III to the Middle Kingdom (van Haarlem 2009), a great rarity in Egyptian archaeology. It was in this period that the comparatively untouched Delta came into its own, with its great array of settlement and cemetery sites, often shielded by alluvium or sand dunes.

Despite the opening-up of the area, concern for Delta sites has been growing since the 1950s. Habachi, one of the great Egyptian archaeologists, and an inhabitant of the Delta, had been stressing the importance of exploration in the Delta for many years, and stated this in his report on the work done at Qantir (Habachi 1954: 443-562). In 1962 Georges Posner stated: 'la connaissance insuffisante du Delta en face de tout qu'on sait la Haute Égypte a des effects fâcheux pour l'Egyptologie parce qu'elle désaxe notre vision' (Posner 1962: 639). These sentiments were again repeated and stressed by Manfred Bietak in his 1979b article (p. 60), and also by Shehata Adam in his 1981 article (p. 165-7), both of who elaborated on the modern population, land and pollution pressures on Delta archaeology. At the *Second International Congress of Egyptologists*, held in Grenoble, France, in September 1979, a special resolution was passed giving special priority to survey work in the Delta. At the *Eighth International Congress of Egyptologists* (28th March - 3rd April 2000), members of the International Association of Egyptologists called for a Delta rescue project. Gaballa and Hawass were key members in this plea, the latter even suggesting that non-vital archaeological work should be suspended in the Nile Valley, in favour of working in the Delta. This eventually led to a moratorium on granting new excavation concessions for work in Upper Egypt.

Figure 9.7: The monumental remains at Tanis (San el-Hagar).

This concern led to the instigation of several Delta surveys, addressing a serious deficit in regional studies. Although the Egyptian Antiquities Organisation (EAO [now the Ministry of Antiquities (MA)]) had documentation relating to legally protected and registered sites, there had been no systematic survey to locate sites, to record the types, extent and dates of archaeological material at various locations (Wilson 2009). Over the last 35 years there have been seven major Delta surveys, by missions from Holland, Austria, Italy (East Delta), Canada (Wadi Tumilat), the U.S.A. (East Central and West Delta) and Germany (North West Delta). At present, a 'complete' survey of the Delta is being conducted by the Egypt Exploration Society (EES), including regional surveys of Minufiyeh, Sais and Samanud, in tandem with the Polish archaeological survey of Ash-Sharqiyyah (Jucha 2009). There have also been several seminars held on Delta archaeology, such as:

- *The Archaeology of the Nile Delta, Egypt: Problems and Priorities*
    - Netherlands Institute of Archaeology and Arabic Studies, Cairo
    - 19th-22nd October 1986
- *The Nile Delta in Transition: 4th-3rd Millennium B.C.*
    - Netherlands Institute of Archaeology and Arabic Studies, Cairo
    - 21st-24th October 1990
- *Egypt and the Levant: Interrelations from the 4th Through the Early 3rd Millennium BCE*
    - Nelson Gluek School of Biblical Archaeology, HUC, Jerusalem
    - 1998
- *Landscape Archaeology: Egypt and the Mediterranean World*
    - Geographical Society of Egypt and the French Cultural Centre (CFCC), Cairo.
    - 19th-21st September 2010
- *The Nile Delta as a Centre of Cultural Interactions Between Upper Egypt and the Southern Levant in the 4th Millennium BC*
    - Poznań Archaeological Museum
    - 21st-22nd June 2013

Figure 9.8: Monumental elements and huge mud-brick walls and tell at Tanis (San el-Hagar).

There have also been an increasing number of localised conferences: *Workshop on Archaeological Landscapes of the Egyptian Delta Lakes* (2014, Exeter), *Heracleion in context* (2013, Oxford), *Cleopatra and the End of the Hellenistic World* (2011, Philadelphia), *Maritime Archaeology and Ancient Trade in the Mediterranean* (2008, Madrid), *Archaeology of the Mareotic Region* (2008, Alexandria), *The Trade and Topography of Egypt's North-*

western Delta (2006, Berlin), and *Alexandria: City and Harbour* (2004, Oxford).

In addition to the seminars, there have been three EES/MA Delta Workshops, the first held in 2009 (Bietak 2009: 11), the next in 2011 (Rowland and Spencer 2011: 3), and the third in 2013 (Spencer 2013: 2), with another due to be held in 2015, all hosted by the British Council, Cairo. There have also been study days, such as *Le delta égyptien. Identités géographiques et culturelles d'un territoire* at the Université de Lille 3 in July 2007 or *Alexandria: Past, Present and Future*, held at the Egyptian Educational and Cultural Bureau (London), March 2006.

A short summary of these surveys' achievements is presented here.

1. **The Netherlands East Delta Survey:** the Amsterdam University team conducted a survey of ancient settlements in the Sharqiya Province in the North East Delta, covering an area of 600 km^2, covering 92 sites, 21 of which were free from modern structures or cultivation and available for further investigation (van den Brink *et. al.* 1986: 12-3). The survey was complemented by paleo-geophysical and environmental assessments (Wesemael 1988; deWit 1988). The main goal of this project was to examine the development of settlements and the diversity and functionality of the various sites, as well as to investigate the spatial patterning of the archaeological sites in their natural landscapes, to try and understand the distribution patterning by their position in the landscape (Brink *et. al.* 1988: 7-11). In practical terms, the analysis included aerial photograph reviews, fieldwalking, augering and some soundings. Site preservation, stratigraphy, planning (at 1:2000) and research accessibility assessments were all carried out (van den Brink *et. al.* 1988: 11).

2. **The Italian East Delta Survey:** this survey was part of the Centro Studi e Ricerche Ligabue, Venice project on the dynamics of state formation project, aiming to map Predynastic to Early Dynastic sites in the East Delta between Mendes and Gezira Sangaha to San el-Haggar, an area of c. 435 km^2. The 1987 survey found 32 unexcavated sites, and 5 excavated sites dating from the Predynastic to Roman periods (14 of the unexcavated sites were not on Bietak's map [see 3, below]). The majority of sites were surveyed by fieldwalking, with test pits being dug only at Tell el-Farkha (Chlodnicki *et. al.* 1998).

3. **The Austrian Survey of the East Delta:** the Austrian Academy of Sciences team conducted the largest historical-geographical examination of the East Delta. The survey produced a tentative reconstruction of the Tanitic and Pelusiac branches of the Nile, and other palaeo-water channels, using cartographic and primary and secondary written sources to plot archaeological sites (Bietak 1975: 71-98). The orientation of graves and buildings was also used to assess channel orientation. Where sites were situated along these reconstructed waterways, it gave an indication of date as well as confirming its course (Bietak 1975: 71-98).

4. **The Canadian Survey of the Wadi Tumilat:** the team identified 24 sites along the Wadi Tumilat and a canal running along its southern side initiated by King Nekau II, then expanded by Darius I and Trajan (Redmount 1995). An earlier possible canal made by Senusret was also investigated. Only four of these 24 sites were fully surveyed: Tell er-Retaba, Tell el-Gebel, Tell el-Sahaba and Tell el-Maskhuta, the excavation of the latter also being a focus of the project (Holladay 1982). This survey built on the work of an Austro-German survey conducted in the early 1930s (Schott *et al.* 1932).

5. **The American Survey of Naukratis, West Delta:** this survey took place in the area defined by el-Barnugi to the north and Kom el-Hisn in the south. The survey mainly consisted of fieldwalking with trial trenching at Kom Firin, Kom Dahab, Kom Barud and Kom Kortas, and photogrammetric planning. The survey identified 33 sites in an area of 600 km^2 surrounding Naukratis (Coulson 1988).

6. **The American Mendes Regional Survey, Central Delta:** the survey's aim was to understand the factors contributing to ancient settlement patterns here and elsewhere in the Delta. Forty-one of 48 sites were located though Spot satellite multispectral digital imagery, 18 of which were further surveyed using augering techniques (Brewer *et. al.* 1996). A mathematical model based on Spot and survey data was then used to predict the location of deeply buried sites (Brewer *et. al.*1996).

Figure 9.9: The site of Tell el-Timai (Mendes) surrounded by the modern village.

Figure 9.10: The DAI excavations at Tell el-Fara'in (Buto).

7. **The German Survey of Buto and the West Delta:** this survey – a joint venture between Fachbereich Geographie, Philipps Universität Marburg and the German Institute – aimed to locate possible Predynastic and Early Dynastic settlements in the area between Desuq and Tida, centred on Buto. The survey included the use of Landsat Thematic Mapper scenes, drill coring and a range of geoelectric and refraction seismic methods (Wunderlich 1988: 253). The survey also identified former tributaries of the Nile, and at least seven ancient settlements. Study of the West Delta gezira sands indicated a Holocene date, unlike the Pleistocene sands in the East and South Delta (Wunderlich 1988: 255).

8. **The EES Survey of the Delta:** this ongoing survey was first developed in the 1980s, and aimed to gather data from less well-known or remote sites (identified from pre-1950 Survey of Egypt maps which, show the extent and position of the ancient monuments, *koms* and general sites) using fieldwalking, satellite imagery and local knowledge (Spencer and Spencer 2000: 25). The initial survey was intended to be the basis of future more detailed research to be conducted by other archaeologists (Spencer and Spencer 2000: 27). As such, the survey focuses across the region, including the West Delta (Snape), Samanud (Spencer), Sais (Wilson), Quesna (Rowland) and Kom el-Hisn (Kirby). The results of the survey are combined with published records and entered into a research planning database, which so far holds 735 entries. The survey has continued with work in the provinces of Beheira, Daqahliya, Imbaba, Kafr el-Sheikh, and Minufiyeh amongst others (Rowland 2007; Rowland *et al.* 2009; Rowland and Spencer 2011; Rowland and Wilson 2006; Spencer 2008; Wilson 1998; 2003; 2006b; 2009; 2010; 2011; 2012a; Wilson and Grigoropoulos 2009), and has investigated hundreds of sites and finds spots, several of which were chosen for more detailed research. The Western Delta Landscape Project (a sub-project of the EES Delta Survey) has investigated settlement patterns and ancient watercourses, along with the potential of flattened *koms* for archaeological research (Trampier 2014; Trampier *et al.* 2013).

Mention must also be made of three other innovative projects: 1) the map of Pi-Ramesses; 2) The SEPE East Delta Survey; and 3) the geophysical investigation of the Delta.

1) Magnetometry was used to cover 780,000 m^2 of Pi-Ramesses, detecting mud-brick walls, villas, houses aligned along streets, gardens, wells, lakes and a possible harbour. A potential administrative and gubernatorial centre was also identified. This project also serves to illuminate the methods and practices suitable for Delta topography, although it may have limited value at a multi-period *tell* site (Pusch 2000: 145-6).

2) The Survey and Excavation Projects in Egypt (SEPE) is using satellite imagery to locate new sites (Mumford 2002; 2004; Pavlish *et al.* 2003). Notable among these is Parçak's study of the East Delta (Parçak 2003; 2004), particularly Pharaonic settlements in the regions around Mendes and Tell Tebilla, and with reference to climatic change, riverine regime changes, coastal expansion and floral/faunal fluctuations. Aster, Corona, Landsat TM and Spot images were combined with existing archaeological survey data and maps, attaining a 95% success rate in locating 100+ previously known sites. These location techniques were applied to the identification of previously unknown sites and sites thought destroyed, followed by 'ground-truthing' of the data: this included interviews with the local inhabitants, photography, landscape assessment and artefact registration. Over 60 new (or previously unconfirmed) sites were discovered in this way, dating to the Old Kingdom to the Late Period and Roman eras, and these were added to extant mapping systems along with the environmental data. The results of this survey were also used to calculate archaeological site loss, the anthropology of site destruction, and the general implications for Egyptian archaeology (Parçak 2003; 2009).

3) The Scientific School has been conducting a geophysical survey of the Delta using electric resistivity, and have so far discovered two buried harbours at Tell el-Balamun (Abu Galal), delineated the island of Amun and the River Amun (Gamili 2000: 68), delineated ancient Nile branches around Mendes (Tell el-Roba) and Thmuis (Tell Temai), and various local canals. Their study has also uncovered evidence for two defunct river branches west of the present

> Damietta Branch, and served to delineate the ancient courses of the Canopic, Pelusiac, Tanitic and Mendesian branches (Gamili 2000: 68-9).

Methods such as these are adding to the current arsenal deployed by archaeologists, and many of them will seriously improve current approaches to survey and excavation. Fieldwalking, the standard tool for surveying, is limited on *tell* (or *kom*) surveys, as late finds outnumber early ones by as much as 10 to 1 (Miller-Rosen 1986: 52). This is not only as a result of stratigraphic replacement, but also due to erosion of earlier materials (Miller-Rosen 1986: 52). This bias in favour of the later periods is also true for off-mound sherd distribution. The under representation of the earlier periods and overrepresentation of the later periods can be slightly mitigated by scraping the surface by 5 cm to collect potsherds (Miller-Rosen 1986: 51). However, the Predynastic, Early Dynastic and Old Kingdom sherds will only be expected if the level of these occupations is less than 5 m from the surface (Miller-Rosen 1986: 51). However, in certain areas near the coast the mounds only start in the Ptolemaic period, and may continue to the Ottoman period. Further biases must also be borne in mind when it comes to interpreting site signature from disturbed contexts, such as ploughzones, where the top 0.30 m of archaeology is destroyed, by turning, mixing, breaking and spreading out of artefacts and contexts. Therefore, when undertaking a surface survey in ploughed soil it must be considered that those artefacts collected will only represent 0.3%-15%, and usually only 5-6% of the artefacts present at the site (Steinberg 1996: 368-75). Drill-coring and test pits can help to investigate deeply buried deposits as can various geophysical methods, although the latter can not provide dating evidence. Drill-cores have been used to great effect in both Minufiyeh and Kafr es-Sheikh (Rowland 2007; Rowland *et al.* 2009; Wilson 2006a; 2006b; Wilson and Grigoropoulos 2009).

The early focus on textual material has led to an imbalance between funerary and settlement sites, which are much less frequently excavated (unusual sites such as Amarna excepted) than sites with funerary structures and cemeteries. This has influenced generations of Egyptologists (Bietak 1979b; Giddy 1999), who have not usually received appropriate archaeological training. Pioneers such as Brunton (Badari), Caton-Thompson (Faiyum), Junker (Merimde Beni Salame), and Petrie (Kahun, Naukratis) have pushed the frontiers of settlement archaeology, although little true effect was seen until the 1990s. The use of single context recording – developed in the UK to excavate deeply stratified urban sites (Tassie and Owens 2010) – is now employed to great effect at many Lower Egyptian sites, including Giza (Lehner 2009), Kafr Hassan Dawood (Tassie 2007), Memphis (Giddy and Jeffreys 1991), Quesna (Rowland *et al.* 2013), Saïs (Wilson 2006a; 2006b) and Tell Tebilla (Mumford 2004). Sediment depth is also no longer a concern, as technological advances and equipment is laying open deeply buried or even waterlogged sites such as Buto (Faltings 1998; Hartung 2008) and Saïs (Wilson 2006b). Geological and riverine impacts on life in the Delta are also being investigated, meaning that such evidence can now be used to model the social dynamics of different periods to much greater effect. 'The complexity and multidisciplinary nature of the work and the lack of emphasis on sensational burial finds has, however, limited the public perception of the progress made in delta archaeology' (Wilson 2007: 15).

Blouin (2014: 2, with references) observes that there has also been an increasing number of local studies that compliment the available Hellenistic and Roman papyri and inscriptions from the Nile Delta (for the latter see Bernand 1970). Several doctoral these have also been written on the archaeology of the Delta covering the Predynastic to the Graeco-Roman period (i.e. Razanajao 2006a; Redmount 1989; Redon 2007; Rowland 2004; Tristant 2006). These studies are now contributing to repopulating the region with both sites and people, asserting the regions importance from the Palaeolithic to the Early Islamic period. This recent focus on the Delta has revealed the close links, which existed from the earliest periods between Lower Egypt, South-west Asia and the northern Mediterranean, thereby improving our understanding of the geopolitics of the region. 'In spite of these developments, however, the historical value of this evidence coming from or related to the Nile Delta remains to this day largely unexplored. Yet the potential of available data is great' (Blouin 2014: 3).

Predictive modelling as a Tool for Archaeological Heritage Management, and Research into Site Spatial Patterning, to Protect and Investigate the Archaeological Heritage of the Delta and the Nile Valley

As indicated above, archaeologists need to both protect archaeological sites, and also further the body of scientific knowledge about temporally fluctuating settlement patterns. Predictive Modelling has provided a means for enabling the discovery and understanding of hidden sites. Predictive Modelling (hereafter PM) is *a technique to predict, at a minimum, the location of archaeological sites or materials in a region, based on either the observed pattern in a sample or on assumptions about human behaviour* (Kamermans *et al.* 2009: 9-10). The technique results in predictive maps that indicate where archaeological remains can be expected, an approach that plays a major role in spatial planning throughout the world (Kamermans *et al.* 2009: 10).

Within archaeology, the use of PM has two aims: [1] *to gain insight into former human behaviour in the landscape* (this represents the archaeological research application) and [2] *to predict archaeological site locations to guide future developments in the modern landscape* (this represents the cultural heritage management [hereafter CHM)] application) (Kamermans *et al.* 2009: 10). The archaeological research application will invariably need to *model the locational behaviour of different functional, chronological and cultural types of occupations* whereas the CHM application's goal is to *conserve archaeological remains and limit costs by identifying areas with and without these remains, regardless of their nature* (Verhagen *et al.* 2010: 431). Predictive research maps will therefore have a narrow space-time scale, whereas predictive CHM maps reflect the entire archaeological record. This disparity therefore leads to different methodologies and outcomes (Verhagen *et al.* 2010: 433). In the case of CHM applications, generalised (broad inductive) maps are necessary to represent the complexity of the archaeological record, and reduce it to manageable proportions (Verhagen *et al.* 2010: 433).

PM has its issues, both methodological and theoretical, although a full discussion thereof is beyond the scope of the current work. Many of these reflect the differences between the context for which it was designed and the demands of Egyptian archaeology. Suffice here to say that *much of this criticism is related to the uncritical application of so-called 'inductive' modelling techniques, in which the archaeological data set is used to obtain statistical correlation between the location of archaeological sites and environmental variables such as soil type, slope or distance to water* (Verhagen *et al.* 2007: 203). All the older maps – and many more recent exemplars – are environmentally determinist in their outlook, meaning human behaviour is analysed in purely ecological and economic terms (Verhagen *et al.* 2007: 204).

The potential of CHM-oriented PM is obvious, provided that good predictive models are in place (Verhagen *et al.* 2007: 203-4). The integration of human agency and cultural variables (within a theoretical framework based on middle range theory) is also serving to overcome the environmental biases (Verhagen and Whitley 2012). Extension of PM methods to include Bayesian statistics (Verhagen *et al.* 2010: 434-5) and Dempster-Shafer/DST modelling (Verhagen *et al.* 2010: 435-6) has improved the archaeological applicability of PM significantly. The testability of PM/CHM-derived models means that hypothesis construction and theoretical planning are stronger, thus enhancing our knowledge of the archaeological record and past human behaviour within the landscape (Verhagen *et al.* 2010: 438-9). The methods should find wider acceptance in Egypt. Every *taftish* (local inspectorate) should ideally have an SMR (Sites and Monuments Register) map and a predictive CHM map (map indicating possible archaeological sites) of the territory under their jurisdiction[2]. Regional predictive CHM maps can be used as a means for informing local inspectors about potential archaeological remains in their territory, and encouraging a proactive rather than reactive response to threats of construction developments. Active engagement with both SMR maps and CHM predictive mapping should encourage local inspectors to clarify (and thus improve) the maps, via either desk-based or field assessments. This will increase institutional knowledge within the MA as a whole and within the local inspectorates.

The CHM maps should also be made available to non-archaeological institutions (particularly ministries involved in planning and development) operating in the same territory, indicating low to high probability values for specific zones (based on the clear understanding that low probability does not *ipso facto* mean no archaeological remains). It has become increasingly apparent that looters regularly exploit archaeological publications (see Tassie *et al.* this volume), so distribution must be controlled. Controlled dissemination should be accompanied by a concise briefing concerning the needs and benefits of preserving cultural heritage, and the essential need for proper excavations when archaeological remains are encountered. It must be accessible for non-specialists, should focus on positive benefits (particularly the potential of attracting tourist revenues), and should – of course – be in Arabic. It is anticipated that active participation in the preservation of cultural heritage by non-archaeological institutions should lead to support and understanding of local inspectors' need to carry out watching briefs and, if needed, undertake rescue excavations of archaeological remains found during construction work. The research benefits of multiple collaborating polities armed with CHM maps are self-evident, as they can guard against site loss and damage, can offer numerous analytical routes, and can only lead to better understanding of the Delta and the Nile Valley as a whole.

---

[2] Most if not all of the archaeological information required to prepare these maps is available at the GIS Centre (formerly Egyptian Antiquities Information System [EAIS]) within the MA (www.giscenter.gov.eg/home).

THE DELTA IN PERIL

Academic approaches have changed with the times, and archaeologists are now more conscious of the need to preserve the sites and monuments for future generations, ancient sites are still under threat from many destructive forces such as those summarised below:

1) Acid rain and weathering

2) Pollution

3) Modern agricultural practices

4) Land reclamation

5) Looting

6) Demolition, building and development projects, including land grabs

7) Urban sprawl caused by overpopulation

8) Earthquakes, floods and other natural disasters

9) Tourism

10) Deterioration caused by a change of environment due to excavation.

11) Salinisation

12) High watertable levels

13) Lack of money and resources

14) *Sebakhin*

15) Terrorism and destruction by explosions

16) Vandalism

17) Mining and quarrying activities

Many of the above listed forces of destruction are more prevalent in the Delta than elsewhere in Egypt, and the Delta is particularly susceptible to salinisation, agricultural practices, land reclamation (involving flooding), Se*bakhin* (diggers for ancient mud-brick and mud-brick wash to use as fertiliser) and general demolition/development projects (Borghouts 1988; Spencer and Spencer 2000: Theroux 1997). While nowhere is immune, the sites in the Nile Delta and Middle Egypt seem to have suffered more than those in Upper Egypt, especially since 2011 (see Tassie *et al.* this volume).

Urban sprawl is a trigger for many of these issues, and has raised the need for site protection with immediate effect. This protection needs to become more systematic and enforceable. The population of Egypt has risen 196% to 86 million people since 1960, about half of whom (49.8%) live in the Delta. The total for Lower Egypt, to include Cairo, is 69.2%, marking a growth of 18% since 2006. The US Census Bureau estimates that the population will reach 103.74 million by 2025, perhaps reaching 150 million by 2050 (Schwartzstein 2014). Around 57% of the population lives in rural areas and the rest in urban centres, although population density in Cairo is 46,349 per km^2, making it one of the most densely populated cities in the world (Ahram Online 2012). The population is concentrated in only 7.7% of Egypt's total area, mainly the Nile Valley and the Delta. Alexandria's population has swollen from about one million in the aftermath of World War II to roughly 4.6 million people today. In May 2014 Abdel-Fattah El-Sisi commented that Egypt's increasing population was one of the country's most pressing problems (Ahram Online. 2014). There are worrying demographic concerns for employment, wealth distribution and poverty.[3] According to the World Food Programme, over half of Egypt's population lives

[3] This unprecedented population growth represents very significant and worrying problems for the future, particularly as 60% of the population are under 30 years of age. Government officials recognise the perils of such untrammelled growth, for there is already a widening gap between resource demand and domestic supply. There is a large percentage of the population with little to no work, and prospects for the younger generation are extremely

in poverty, while family planning, education, state services, tourism revenues and treasury budgets are all in disarray.[4] The flow of money from tourism has slowed to a trickle; 13 billion tourist dollars in 2010[5] has now dropped to a fraction of that, hitting an all-time low in 2011 when there was a 45% drop in visitors. It is essential that tourism be re-established along pre-2011 levels and to achieve that Egypt's regime – under its new president – needs to bring calm and order to the country.

Figure 9.11: Waterlogged graves at the Predynastic to Early Dynastic site of Minshat Ezzat (Photographs F. A. Hassan).

Given these figures, the MA's demand for archaeological focus to be Lower Egypt is understandable. Cairo, Alexandria, Mansura and Zagazig's vulnerability to unscrupulous development also necessitates a campaign of rescue archaeology and urban protection. Farmer's increasing – and reasonable – demands for more arable land is pressing archaeological sites ever more, as summarised by van den Brink (1986: 7-8) nearly thirty years ago:

1. Villages are increasing in number and size, requiring ever more mud-bricks that are frequently made from *kom* soil: <10 brick factories were often situated on a single *kom*. This was banned in 1985, a law coming into effect that permitted brick making factories to acquire their material via dredging.

2. The shift from basin irrigation to perennial irrigation has seen a commensurate rise in soil impoverishment, leading to the use of *kom* soil as a field fertiliser.

3. Many of the geziras have been used as sand quarries, thereby destroying settlement remains.

4. It is currently forbidden to build on agricultural land. The Egyptian Ministry of Agriculture is consequently urging the MA to investigate potential archaeological areas under its protection as a matter of urgency, so that the land can be reclaimed. Such assessments are usually done via soundings, although these are often superficial due to the high groundwater level.

Cultural processes of reuse, *sebakh* removal, the capping of older remains by asphalt and concrete, field cutting and ploughing all play their part in destroying or obscuring archaeological remains (Trampier *et al.* 2013: 217-8). In many sites where there were once great mounds (*koms*), there are now only fields or only half a mound. 'Some of the *tells*, particularly the small ones or those near modern towns and cities, have

poor. Now, with popular frustrations intensifying and state services stretched far beyond capacity, effective family planning practices are needed more than ever (Schwartzstein 2014).

[4] The last few years of revolution, election, chaos, removal and prosecution of two presidents, further elections, and terrorists attacks have emptied the treasury, left the country 8% behind its long-term economic projections and compromised the state's capacity to care for its treasures.

[5] UN World Tourism Organisation: http://media.unwto.org/press-release/2011-05-31/tourism-key-economic-recovery-egypt

been levelled for agricultural purposes or swallowed up by urban development...' (Spencer and Spencer 2000: 26). As Hassan (unpublished) notes:

> 'At one time, a huge *tell* (*kom* in colloquial Arabic) covering more than 50 acres, stood where today a cultivated field and an orchard of oranges are a part of the rich fertile plain of the Delta. The *tell* has all but vanished, and the locals have their tales of treasures unearthed and rare objects found by farmers and children. At the surface, still carrying the brutal marks of the blades of the plough, royal jars and skeletons, still in their original burial positions and with all their funerary goods, have now come under the eyes of the Egyptian Supreme Council of Antiquities (SCA). A legal dispute between the land-owner and tenant farmers has brought the subject to the attention of Dr. Mohamed Abdel-Maksoud, who is an energetic dedicated, French-educated Egyptologist, who heads the East Delta Sector. Dr Abel-Maksoud took the initiative to wrench the land from its disputants and put it under the custody of the SCA pending appropriation or rent depending on the availability of funding. In the meantime, in order to provide indisputable archaeological evidence for legal action, he has provided a modest funding for local archaeologists to begin excavations'.

This abstract refers to Minshat Ezzat, an East Delta site that has yielded an impressive and rare Nagada III ceremonial palette, amongst much else (see Fig. 9.11). The conditions that the archaeologists worked in consisted of a hut, for eating, resting, working and storing the artefacts before they were eventually transferred to the central magazine. This is only one instance of many occurring in the Delta, where not only are the archaeological remains threatened, but also the working conditions are untenable for modern scientific research. Another major problem is the lack of trained personnel and resources. Rabie el-Kasim points out that excavations at Silvago are hampered by the lack of a site photographer and conservator, and although there is no mention of the lack of a physical anthropologist, it seems one was absent from the excavation of this cemetery site (el-Kasim 1988: 279-80). El-Kasim (1988: 280) goes on to point out that in the area of Mersa Matruh, research would be greatly helped by the use of a Land Rover, fuel, water tanks and access to a good compass.

Figure 9.12: The site of Ezbet el-Tell (Kufur Nigm) showing the low *kom* (Photograph F. A. Hassan).

There is hardly a site unaffected by development and resultant damage, from Tell Basta (Bubastis) – seemingly always in a race with urban development (Bakr 1982: 154) – to Silvago (el-Wakil 1988: 265). There are many obstacles in the race, however, to include the following as exemplars from Silvago:

- Archaeologists were unaware of the site before the 1960s, by which time much of the site had disappeared; it is therefore difficult to establish the original extent of the cemetery.
- Land reclamation has encouraged the local population to attack the site and prepare it for plantation, causing immense damage to the archaeological remains.
- The vast majority of the tombs found have been seriously affected by groundwater damage.
- Previous excavation results at Kom Firin, which is probably part of the same Graeco-Roman cemetery, have not been published.

Although some of these quotes are over thirty years old, these problems are just as common today, indeed, most of the problems have increased. On a recent visit to the ancient city of Tanis, the effects of *Sebakhin* could clearly been seen on the great mud-brick walls of the city, much of which still lies beneath large unexcavated mounds (see Fig. 9.8; Tassie *pers. obs.*). Indirect action can also harm sites, such as the preparation of adjacent fields, resulting in mean water table raises and the slow seep of chemical fertilisers. This can sometimes assume dramatic proportions. Flooding of an area North of the Kafr Hassan Dawood cemetery resulted in a lake, intended as part of a land reclamation project. However, not only has this action potentially ruined the archaeology – or at least made it harder to excavate – but has also caused the water table to rise, as has the addition of further fields to the other sides of the site. This has ramifications not only for heritage, but also for agricultural productivity, given the salinity that inevitably accompanies such a process. Archaeologists now have the technology, equipment and methodology to investigate these vanishing Delta sites, but lack of funding is seriously hindering all archaeological work in the area.

Figure 9.13: The site of Ezbet el-Tell (Kufur Nigm) showing the low *kom* (Photograph F. A. Hassan).

The struggle for land has led to serious tensions within Egypt. Local populations are understandably frustrated at their inability to farm what appears to be unremarkable (i.e. lacking monuments) archaeological land, while archaeologists are confounded in their efforts to understand these sites by a lack of funding, personnel and resources. Neither side can be utterly victorious: the Delta's heritage must be preserved, and it is impossible to keep the Delta as a permanent open-museum. However, if a site has been fully excavated and published, and is not a touristic draw, should it be kept from cultivation indefinitely? This issue deserves more attention than can be granted here, and should be debated as part of a Delta project (Fushiya and De Trafford 2009: 44-49). The Egyptian Ministry of Agriculture's demand that 'non-productive' areas of land be turned over as quickly as possible can only be addressed in the light of a fully comprehensive survey, so that archaeological sites and data can be saved, and so that the modern population can produce the food and other materials they need. This is the only means we have to combat illegal land appropriation, which would be a 'major tragedy for archaeology as the modifications to the landscape, coupled with the loss of objects and buildings forever destroys our understanding of the site and the history of those who lived there' (Ikram 2013: 367).

Archaeologists working in the Delta should be made aware of these problems, and do all they can to ease frictions caused by the clash of vested interests. It is also an opportunity for academic archaeologists to form outreach programmes to train local groups on how to deal with increased tourism levels, and maximise the revenues thus attained (Wendrich 2006). Public archaeology must be a part of every Delta project proposal, within the framework of Delta-wide sustainable tourism management instigated by the MA and the Ministry of Tourism. This would feed back to improved PM systems, watching briefs and archaeological assessments to constantly moderate and influence development and building programmes in the Delta region. This will of course require the enforcement of special new laws.

GENERAL PRINCIPLES

Ancient Egypt is not just the heritage of one state party but chronicles the development of the human race, it has shaped our modern lives, conditioned our world view. Egypt's sites and monuments are part of the legacy of past human achievement (Hassan 1997), and is thus a shared heritage of humanity. As humanity benefits from Egypt's cultural heritage, so we should all contribute towards it. It is unjust that its current guardians within Egypt be burdened with the task of maintaining it; the responsibility for Egypt's cultural heritage should thus be of concern to the whole world and its governing bodies and institutes (Hassan 1997). The international community has benefitted from Egyptian antiquities colonially, economically and – also – academically. Until very recently, international missions did little to help create the necessary infrastructure in Egypt: facilities and staff to conserve, manage, study, interpret and display Egypt's past or train Egyptian personnel in the field capable of doing so (Hassan 1997: 90; Romer and Romer 1993: passim). Archaeologists now have the ability to restore what has deteriorated, explore what was hitherto unreachable and provide innovative excavation solutions ahead of Egypt's ceaseless expansion. Egypt has recognised the value of assistance and support from international, governmental, intergovernmental, and non-governmental organisations (Hassan 1997: 91), in order to follow the edicts laid down by Farouk Hosny in 1993:

1) Catalogue of the location and condition of archaeological remains to include test excavation and surveying.
2) Documentation of monuments and archaeological sites.
3) Assessment of the environment of sites and monuments to minimise or prevent natural and human-induced threats and hazards.
4) Restoration and preservation of monuments.
5) Establishing a database of the condition and history of monument conservation
6) Dissemination of archaeological knowledge to enhance public awareness and to involve the public in conservation efforts.

Translated from the Arabic by Hassan (1997: 91).

Personnel training was high on this list of priorities. In 1998-1999, a UNESCO Training Programme was held at the Delta site of Kafr Hassan Dawood, and trained many Egyptian and Western students in modern field methods and techniques (Hassan 2000). This was followed by the *Egyptian Human Remains: Retrieval, Conservation and Analysis* Conference in 2000 (Mower and Tassie 2000; Podzorski 2000), and the Delta training programme for SCA staff the same year (Hassan *pers. comm.*). The success of these early fieldschools prompted similar programmes at Sa el-Haqar (training inspectors in finds processing, draughting, surveying and geoarchaeology [Wilson Pers Comm. 2007]), Quesna (training <20 students/inspectors in excavation, surveying, bioarchaeology, conservation and finds processing) and the Giza Plateau Mapping Project (GPMP), which has been running large fieldschools for MA inspectors since 2005. One-hundred-and-forty-six students have been taught in nine fieldschools since 2007, in four main sessions: beginners, advanced, salvage, and analysis and publication (AERA 2013). These programmes must become more widespread, so that the MA can set national standards for documentation, cultural heritage management, conservation, knowledge dissemination and community involvement.

Figure 9.14: The Graeco-Roman remains at Tell el-Muqdam (ancient Leontopolis) showing modern building activities in the background (Photograph F. A. Hassan).

High profile rescue operations have been undertaken in Nubia for over 100 years (Hassan 2009) (Hassan 2009) and in Upper Egypt, particularly the conservation of the tomb of Nefertari (Agnew and Maekawa 1999), and the Theban Mapping Project (Weeks and Hetherington 2014). Although various conservation programmes have been focused upon the Sphinx, it was not until the late 1990s that large-scale conservation and restoration projects started to be undertaken in Lower Egypt, most notably by the Aga Khan Foundation in the Al-Azhar Park (Aga Khan Trust for Culture 2005), the American Research Center in Egypt, particularly in Old Cairo (Danforth 2010), and the Japanese, notably the conservation of the second Khufu boat at Giza. Modern scientific facilities are now available at the Institut Français d'Archéologie Orientale that can be used by various archaeologists and conservators upon request.

There is an element of urgency to this plea of Farouk Hosny, as Delta sites are vanishing faster than ever before. Although the various Delta surveys, conservation projects and fieldschools are an excellent start, a major assessment, conservation and mapping project must be undertaken and a Delta risk map created, followed by research directives addressing particularly important or vulnerable sites.

Cultural protection needs to become more proceduralised, nowhere more so than in the context of rescue archaeology preceding development (new laws need to be passed, procedures established, and government agencies created to implement the system.) Most MENA countries have a significant amount of staff but few established protocols or government staff to oversee development activities. have a significant amount of staff but few established protocols or government staff to oversee development activities. Although these countries normally have antiquities departments, they tend to focus their efforts on known monuments and heritage sites, and while they may not express much interest prior to construction, will be interested if a discovery is made (Stapp and Longenecker 2009). The lack of funding is partially responsible, so if developers were forced to pay for the MA to investigate construction areas and pay for necessary research (to avoid situations whereby developers exert too much pressure on commercial archaeology units, as seen in some European countries), the financial burden on governmental departments could be eased. Countries from all over the world with sufficient financial means and an interest in global archaeology, sometimes based upon previous colonial ties, are archaeologically active in countries such as Egypt – thus interpreting the host country's or local community's heritage from a different, often Western, perspective (Kila 2013: 322). There is however, a budding opposition between global and local archaeology, and heritage studies has created a difficult choice between conducting professional activities according to Western standards versus the incorporation of culturally relevant values (McManamon *et al.* 2008).

Figure 9.15: The remains of the *kom* of Awalad Dawood where there is an Early Dynastic administrative building.

Proactive as well as reactive archaeological practice needs to be instigated, with developers being required by law to undertake full environmental impact assessments that include archaeological impact assessments. This includes doing desk-based assessments, watching briefs and full evaluations before any building or other development is undertaken. Informal systems along these lines have been instigated in Alexandria (by Jean-Yves Empereur and Mohammed Abd-el-Maguid) – involving rescue archaeology with the permission of the developers – but this is a long way from operating within a legally codified framework. In Egypt when construction or other development projects are due to take place on registered or known archaeological sites the law requires that the area to be affected be surveyed, usually by means of test pitting. In 1988, plans for a land reclamation project at Kafr Hassan Dawood led to archaeological prospecting in the area by the local SCA Inspectorate 1988/9. The test pits revealed, according to the excavators, a cemetery dating from the Late Predynastic to Early Dynastic periods. The proposal for a land reclamation project was refused and the land containing the archaeological remains became a protected archaeological site and a decade long excavation project commenced (Hassan *et al.* 2003). In

Spring 2014 plans for a gas pipeline 500 metres away from the protected area of Merimde Beni Salame led to a test pit survey of the area by the local inspectorate (Rowland and Tassie In press). This type of survey, along with desk-based assessments and watching briefs needs to become more professionalised and extended to all areas where development projects are to take place.

Figure 9.16: The large *kom* of Tell el-Dab'a/Qanan.

Figure 9.17: Modern development in the centre of Alexandria.

ENVIRONMENTAL THREATS

The Delta holds two-thirds of the country's rapidly growing population, and produces more than 60% of its food supply. It is the breadbasket of the nation. Pressure is starting to tell, both economically and environmentally. The increasing urbanisation of the Nile Delta is having an adverse effect on the environment. With more people living in the Delta it means more cars, more pollution and less land to feed them all on, just at a time when increased crop production is needed most. Yet the desertification of land through human habitation is only the beginning of the problem. The freshwater of the Nile – which has enabled Egypt to survive as a unified state longer than any other territory on earth – is creaking under the strain of this population boom. Salinity is creeping into the Delta, with one of the worst-affected regions being Kafr el-Sheikh. Coastal farmland has always been threatened by saltwater, but salinity was traditionally kept at bay by plentiful supplies of freshwater flushing out the salt, which no longer occurs due to the Aswan High Dam (Shenker 2009; Torab and Azab 2006). As the Delta substratum becomes more porous seawater has begun to infiltrate the Nile Delta aquifer, a vast source of underground water, which is under increasing pressure from the burgeoning population. Upstream demand has increased, reducing the amount of Nile water reaching the Delta, and increasing the prevalence of sewage, toxins and other impurities in water that does so. Farmers have battled falling fertiliy via the use of chemical fertilisers, or have turned their plots into fish farms (McGrath 2014; Shenker 2009).

Climate change may however be the biggest threat. While controversial at every level, most parties have been forced to agree that the ice caps are melting owing to increases in average land and sea temperatures. The climate and environment of the Nile Delta has been constantly changing throughout the Holocene and before; with an intensification of anthropogenic impacts from the Pharaonic period onwards (Flaux *et al.* 2012; Marriner *et al.* 2013; Stanley *et al.* 2004). 'The Nile Delta has a particularly long history of vulnerability to extreme events (e.g. floods and storms) and sea-level rise, although the present sediment-starved system does not have a direct Holocene analogue' (Marriner *et al.* 2013). In the twenty-first century climate change is set to alter the Nile Delta yet further. The Arab Climate Resilience Initiative (part of the United Nations Development Programme [UNDP]) state that these continuing increases in temperature and sea level will negatively affect biodiversity, food security, water availability, agriculture and tourism (Cattane 2011), while the Intergovernmental Panel on Climate Change (IPCC) declared the Nile Delta to be in the top three of the world's regions most threatened by rising sea level: 'even the most optimistic predictions of global temperature increase will still displace millions of Egyptians from one of the most densely populated regions on earth' (Shenker 2009). The IPCC (2013) predicts a rise of 0.28 to 0.98 metres by 2100; this would destroy at least 12.5% of Egypt's cultivated areas, and displace about eight million people. The higher estimate would see a much more serious result, perhaps in line with McGrath's estimate of 20-30% of the Delta being submerged (2014). Given that much of the Delta coastline lies between zero and 1.0 m a.s.l, any rise in the sea level would see farmland and cities – including Alexandria – transformed into an ocean floor.

Figure 9.18: The Graeco-Roman remains at Kom el-Dikka in the centre of Alexandria.

Agricultural land and the Egyptian population are also threatened by coastal erosion, which is steadily ingesting the country at <175m/yr. The coastal belt of sand (1-10km wide) that has traditionally protected the Delta is being eroded at startling speed, which has accelerated since the construction of the Aswan High Dam. The dam is also causing the Delta to contract, as the estimated 120 million tonnes of silt that used to annually replenish the Delta are now but a memory (Grida 2011; Marriner *et al.* 2013; McGrath 2014; Shenker 2009; Torab and Azab 2006). The sand belt is thus being attacked from without and within; failure of the belt would see inundation of land, destruction of freshwater fish stocks, damage to infrastructure and heritage (i.e. Alexandria and Port Said), serious damage to recreational tourism beach facilities, and salinisation of groundwater. While dykes may provide some protection <0.50m, the barriers must include an impermeable substructure extending from three to 13 metres below sea level to prevent seawater from infiltrating freshwater aquifers, which would itself cause ecological issues (Grida 2011; McGrath 2014). In heritage terms, the fact that many Ptolemaic/Roman and Late Antique cities were built below the 1.0 m a.s.l. contour line means that parts of Alexandria and Rashid, all of Canopus (Aboukir) and Heracleion, numerous small *koms* by Lake Burullus, Kom Tenis (Lake Manzala) and the city of Pelusium have already suffered from sea level rises (Stanley *et al.* 2004; Wilson 2007: 18). A rise of 1.0 m would leave the city centre of Alexandria cut off from the mainland.

All of these are issues that the new Egyptian government will have to tackle in order to avoid a national disaster (Shenker 2009). One final concern is Mubarak's ill-conceived desert reclamation projects, which prompted a bewildering array of canals and pumping stations to draw water from the Nile to irrigate sandy valleys to the east and west. Their water-intensive existence is hastening the demise of the Delta, whose death warrant Mubarak may have signed (Shenker 2009). In terms of heritage, these reclaimed areas are full of archaeological sites that are now under threat, leading to direct conflict between the Ministry of Agriculture and the Ministry of Antiquities. Both Upper and Lower Egypt are being affected in this way, resulting in massive loss of archaeological and heritage remains.

Figure 9.19: Belle Époque buildings in Minufiyeh and Alexandria.

CONCLUSIONS

The Nile Delta is one of the most archaeologically rich, but poorly understood regions of Egypt. Neglected for centuries, the need for investigation is being hurried by multiple threats to its very existence. Preliminary work using innovative techniques and appropriate research paradigms (Tassie and Owens 2010) have revealed extraordinary cultural wealth ranging from Palaeolithic flint scatters to multi-period *koms* to nineteenth century architecture. All of these are being threatened by modern development, which is spiralling out of control owing to the population boom. Standard development threats are accompanied by ecological threats to the coastline (through erosion and rising sea levels), and resultant salinity increases, shrinking land surfaces and the establishment of damaging economic measures such as fish farms. All archaeological work in the Nile Delta should be regarded as rescue archaeology.

Figure 9.20: The site of Tura with a railway line built through the middle of the cemetery (Photograph F. A. Hassan).

Surveys are the most important work that can be carried out to achieve a sense of the scale of the problems involved. Geographic distribution patterns of delta sites, often containing many sites that are not registered by the MA exist (i.e. Trampier 2014; Razanajao 2006a; Tristant 2005). Extant data should be compiled and combined with other work from hitherto unexplored regions[6]; the data must be acted upon, and further investigations undertaken to protect the sites. The survey information as we have it now is very valuable but it is not complete, nor should it be treated face-value, an in-depth understanding of the how each survey was conducted and its methodology is needed to fully understand its results and to comprehensively analyse those results (and very importantly, understand what is not represented in those results!). Excavation projects must be undertaken at important and/or vulnerable sites if the archaeology of the Delta is not to vanish before we can record it. While particularly under threat, Delta priorities should not, of course, be allowed to completely overshadow similar issues elsewhere in Egypt.

Tourism has been damaged by recent events in Egypt, and while numbers are now beginning to increase, there must be a sea change in the way that the past is perceived, handled and benefitted from. The Delta has traditionally failed to benefit directly from tourism, the revenues from which are diverted away, leaving local populations not only socially disenfranchised from their past, but indisposed to protect and cherish their own heritage. Opportunities often present themselves. Recent discoveries at Tell el-Farkha will hopefully presage improvements to this issue. This remarkable architecture would benefit from a visitor center (possibly coupled with a local museum), and can form an economic focus for local people. This may also serve to save the site from urban sprawl and vandalism; by re-creating the site as a tourist attraction, numerous jobs could be created, from site and museum guiding to crafts sales and restaurants.

[6] Temporal distributions of data must also be understood, given the problems of archaeological superimposition. An assessment of the survey areas is needed to determine the gaps in the geographic coverage of the Delta, and instigate surveys in those areas to fill-in the gaps in our body of knowledge.

It is obvious that not every site can be a tourist attraction; sustainable tourist management needs to be formulated within the MA in cooperation with the Ministry of Tourism, to identify the kind of sites that will appeal to visitors and develop these into a Delta-wide network that ensures fair distribution of financial rewards. All involved should ensure that all periods of the Delta's history are represented and established as tourist attractions, and must determine which sites – following full investigation and publication – can be made available for land development. This system must be closely structured and monitored by the MA and other governmental stakeholders to avoid misuse and corruption.

The cultural heritage of Egypt is part of our shared, global cultural heritage and it is the duty of all of us to protect it to inform present and future generations. To help boost the economy of the local inhabitants of the Delta sustainable tourism should be encouraged. It can, in this sense, be 'put to work' in order to reduce the crippling financial burden of caring for it, and its careful maintenance and strategic exploitation can turn it into a source of revenue rather than a financial millstone. It must survive, and it must have a positive social effect: 'tourism and conservation should be natural partners rather than antagonists. Tourism can actually support conservation while still generating income, but quantitative economic analysis is needed for a convincing case to be made for this' (Agnew 1997: 2). The data derived from all forms of study should be advertised through public and academic dissemination strategies, to increase awareness and thus support for this work.

We must use the survey data already derived – and all survey data to emerge in future – to create a pan-Delta CHM map incorporating excavation information, SMRs and predictive maps. This will be a valuable research tool, and will also incorporate protocols to inform future campaigns dedicated to confronting threats to the Delta's archaeological heritage. These will be adaptable, flexible constructs: a protocol on pisciculture, for example, must not make it impossible for fish farms to be established (thus alienating local entrepreneurs), but will provide comprehensible guidelines that lay out why a need for archaeological assessment does not by definition preclude a farms' construction. Pan-conservation of every archaeological site in Egypt is a utopian delusion; we must conflate the needs of the past with those of the present and future, to ensure that field assessment and excavation can coexist with social development and change.

REFERENCES

Abou-Seif, H. 1924. Report on the inspectorate of Tanta from September 1923 to January 1925, *ASAE* 24: 146-150

Adam, S. 1981. Problems related to the preservation of Egyptian Antiquities in Egypt, *Prospection et Sauvegarde des Antiquités de l'Egypte*. Actes de la ronde organisée à l'occasion du centenaire de l'IFAO, 8/12/1981. Cairo, pp. 1965-7.

Adam, S. 1959. Report on the excavations at Ezbet Rushdi, *ASAE* 56: 207-26.

AERA 2013. Fieldschools, *AREAWEB* - http://www.aeraweb.org/field-school-program/

Aga Khan Trust for Culture. 2005. *Al-Azhar Park, Cairo and the Revitalisation of Darb al-Ahmar* - http://www.akdn.org/hcp/egypt.asp

Agnew. N. 1997. Preservation of Archaeological Sites: A Holistic Perspective, *Getty Conservation Institute Newsletter* 12(2): 1-6.

Agnew, N. & Maekawa, S. 1999. Preserving Nefertari's legacy, *Scientific American* 281(4): 75-79.

Ahram Online. 2012. Egypt population reaches 91 million, grows 18 per cent in eight years, *Ahram Online, Thursday 30 Aug 2012* - http://english.ahram.org.eg/News/51634.aspx

Ahram Online. 2014. Increasing population is one of Egypt's main problems: El-Sisi, *Ahram Online* - http://english.ahram.org.eg/News/100291.aspx

Andrén, A. 1998. *Between Artifacts and Texts: Historical Archaeology in Global Perspective*. New York: Plenum Publishing.

Bakr, M. 1982. New excavations of Zagazig University, Colloques internationaux du C.N.R.S. No. 595. *L'Egyptologie en 1979*. Axes prioritaties de recheres, vol. 1, Paris: 153-167.

El-Behary, H. 2013. Almost one-third of Nile Delta to sink by 2030, say experts, *Daily News* - http://www.dailynewsegypt.com/2013/03/05/almost-one-third-of-nile-delta-to-sink-by-2030-say-experts/

Bernand, A. 1970. *Le Delta égyptien d'après les textes grecs* I: *Les confins libyques.* Cairo: Mémoires publiés par les membres de l'Institut Français d'Archéologie Orientale du Caire 91.2.

Bietak, M. 1975. *Tell el-Dab'a II: Der Furdert im Rahmen einer Archäologisch-Geographischen Untersuchung über das Ägyptische Ostdelta.* Vienna, Verlag der Östereiduschien Akademie der Wisseischaften.

Bietak, M. 1979a. Urban archaeology and the town problem, in K. Weeks (ed.) *Egyptology and the Social Sciences.* Cairo, pp. 93-144.

Bietak, M. 1979b. The present state of Egyptian archaeology, *JEA* 65: 156-160.

Bietak, M. 2009. Archaeology of the Nile Delta, *Egyptian Archaeology* 35: 11.

Blouin, K. 2014. *Triangular Landscapes. Environment, Society, and the State in the Nile Delta Under Roman Rule.* Oxford: Oxford Studies on the Roman Economy, Oxford University Press.

Blue L. & Khalil, E. (eds) 2010. *Proceedings of the International Conference on the Archaeology of the Mareotic Region Held at Alexandria University, Egypt 5th-6th April 2008.* Oxford: University of Southampton Series in Archaeology 2.

Blue, L. & Khalil, E. (eds) 2011. *A Multidisciplinary Approach to Alexandria's Economic Past: The Lake Mareotis Research Project.* Oxford: BAR International Series 2285.

Borghouts, J. F. 1988. Surveying the Delta: some retrospectives and prospects, in E.C.M. van den Brink (ed.) *The Archaeology of the Nile Delta: Problems and Priorities.* Amsterdam, pp. 3-8.

El-Bouhy, G. 2000. Protective solutions to preserve antiquities from environmental factors, in Z. Hawass and A. M. Jones (eds.) *Abstracts of Papers for the Eighth International Congress of Egyptologists.* Cairo, American University in Cairo Press, p. 38.

Brewer, D., Wenke, R. J., Isaacson, J. & Haag, D. 1996. 'Mendes regional archaeological survey and remote sensing analysis', *Sahara* 8: 29-42.

Brink, E.C.M. van den. 1988. The Amsterdam University Survey Expedition to the North-eastern Delta, in E.C.M. van den Brink (ed.) *The Archaeology of the Nile Delta: Problems and Priorities.* Amsterdam: van den Brink, pp. 65-114.

Brink, E.C.M. van den 1993. Settlement patterns in the North-eastern Nile Delta during the fourth - second millennia B.C, in L. Krzyzaniak & M. Kobusiewicz & J. Alexander (eds.) *Environmental change and human culture in the Nile Basin and Northern Africa until the Second Millennium B.C.* Poznan: Poznan Archaeological Museum, pp. 279-304.

Brink, E.C.M. van den & Levy, T. E. 2002. *Egypt and the Levant: interrelations from the 4th through the early 3rd millennium BCE.* London; New York: Leicester University Press.

Brink, E.C.M. van den., Schmidt, K., Boessneck, J., Driesch, A. von den., Roller, G. J. de. 1989. A Transitional Late Predynastic - Early Dynastic settlement site in the Northeastern Nile Delta, Egypt, *MDAIK* 45: 55-108.

Brink, E.C.M. van den.,Wesemael, B. van, & Dirksz, P. 1986. 'A geo-archaeological survey of the North-Eastern Nile Delta, Egypt: the first two seasons, a preliminary report', *MDAIK* 43: 7 -31.

Brissaud, P. 2000. Aerial photography at Tanis, *Egyptian Archaeology* 16: 9-11.

Cattane, V. 2011. Unstable weather in Egypt linked to climate change, *Egypt Independent* - http://www.egyptindependent.com/news/unstable-weather-egypt-linked-climate-change

Chlodnicki, M. 1988. Pottery from the archaeological survey of the eastern Nile Delta, Egypt – Interim report (Italian Archaeological Mission of the Ligabue Study and Research Center, Venice), *BCE* 13: 22-26.

Chlodnicki, M., R. Fattovich & S. Salvatori. 1991. Italian excavations in the Nile Delta: fresh data and new hypotheses on the 4th Millennium cultural development of Egyptian prehistory', *Rivista di Archeologia* 15: 5-33.

Chlodnicki, M., R. Fattovich & S. Salvatori. 1998. The Italian Archaeological Mission of the C.S.R.L.-Venice to the Eastern Nile Delta: A preliminary report of the 1987 -1988 field seasons, in J. Eyre (ed.) *Proceedings of the Seventh International Congress of Egyptologists, Cambridge 1995.* Leuven – Paris - Dudley: Peeters, Orientalia Lovaniensia Analecta 82, pp. 45-62.

Cleere, H. (ed.). 1984. *Approaches to the Archaeological Heritage: A Comparative Study of World Cultural Resource Management Systems.* Cambridge: Cambridge University Press.

Coulson, W. D. E. 1996. *The Survey at Naukratis.* Vol. II, Part 2. Oxford: Oxbow Monograph.

Coulson, W. D. E. 1988. The Naukratis Survey, in E.C.M. van den Brink (ed.) *The Archaeology of the Nile Delta: Problems and Priorities.* Amsterdam: Netherlands Foundation for Archaeological Research in Egypt, Uitgeverij, pp. 259-263.

Coulson, W. D. E. & Leonard, A. Jr., 1982. Investigations at Naukratis and environs, 1980-1981, *AJA* 86: 361-80.

Coulson, W. D. E. & Leonard, A. Jr., 1981. *Cities of the Delta - pt 1: Naukratis. Preliminary Report on the 1978 and 1979 Seasons.* Malibu: Published under the auspices of the American Research Center in Egypt, Undena Publications.

Danforth, R. (ed.) 2010. *Preserving Egypt's Cultural Heritage.* Cairo: AUC Press.

Daressy, M. G. 1912. A travers les koms du delta I, *ASAE* 12: 169-213.

Daressy, M. G. 1914a. A travers les koms du delta II, *ASAE* 13: 1-4.

Daressy, M. G. 1914b. A travers les koms du delta III, *ASAE* 13: 179-186.

Daressy, M. G. 1930. Recherches géographiques, III. — Le nome Hermopolite du Delta IV — Panéphysis V — Le nome Onouphite, *ASAE* 30: 69-94.

Faltings, D. 1998. Recent excavations in Tell el-Fara'in/Buto: New finds and their chronological implications, in C. Eyre (ed.) *Proceedings of the Seventh International Congress of Egyptologists, Cambridge 1995.* Leuven – Paris - Dudley: Peeters, Orientalia Lovaniensia Analecta 82, pp. 365-375.

Flaux, C., El-Assal, M., Marriner, N., Morhange, C., Rouchy, J.-M., Soulié-Märsche, I. and Torab, M. 2012. Environmental changes in the Maryut lagoon (northwestern Nile delta) during the last ~ 2000 years, *Journal of Archaeological Science* 39(12): 3493-3504.

Foucart, G. 1901. Extraits des Rapports adressés pendant une Inspection de la Basse-Égypte en 1893-1984, in *Annales du Service des Antiquités de l'Égypte* 2: 44-83, 258-264.

Fushiya, T. & and De Trafford, A. 2009. From site to society: From a garbage dumping place to a local heritage site, in F. A. Hassan, G. J. Tassie, A De Trafford, L. S. Owens & J. van Wetering (eds.) *Managing Egypt's Cultural Heritage: Proceedings of the First Egyptian Cultural Heritage Organisation Conference on: Egyptian Cultural Heritage Management.* London: Golden House and ECHO Publications, pp. 38-58.

El-Gamili, M. M. 2000. Realization of some archaeological and historical aspects through geoelectrical resistivity investigations in the Nile Delta, in Z. Hawass and A. M. Jones (eds.) *Abstracts of Papers for the Eighth International Congress of Egyptologists.* Cairo, American University in Cairo Press, pp. 68-69.

Gauthier, M. H. 1921. À travers la Basee-Égypte, *ASAE* 21: 17-39 & 197-213.

Gauthier, M. H. 1922. À travers la Basse-Égypte, *ASAE* 22: 81-107 & 199-208.

Gauthier, M. H. 1923. À travers la Basse-Égypte, *ASAE* 23 : 68-72 & 165-182.

Grida, 2011. The Nile Delta study, *Grida Arendal*- http://www.grida.no/publications/vg/africa/page/3117.aspx

Griffith, F. Ll. 1890: *The City of Onias and the Mound of the Jew.* London: Egypt Exploration Fund.

Griffith, F. Ll. 1890. *The Antiquities of Tell El-Yahûdîyeh and Miscellaneous Work in Lower Egypt during the Years 1887-1888.* London: Egypt Exploration Fund Memoir No. 7., Kegan Paul, Trench, Trübner & Co.

Haarlem, W. M. van 2009. *Temple Deposits at Tell Ibrahim Awad.* Amsterdam [Van Haalem].

Habachi, L. 1954. Khata'na-Qantir: Importance, *ASAE* 52: 443-562.

Hartung, U. 2008. Recent investigations at Tell el-Fara'in/Buto, in B. Midant-Reynes & Y. Tristant (eds), J. Rowland S. & Hendrickx (ass.) *Egypt at its Origins 2: Proceedings of the International Conference Origin of the State, Predynastic and Early Dynastic Egypt, Toulouse (France), 5-8 September 2005.* Leuven – Paris - Dudley: Orientalia Lovaniensia Analecta 172, Peeters, pp. 1195-1219.

Hassan, F. A. 1997. The cultural heritage of Egypt: a world legacy, in *African Cultural Heritage and the World Heritage Convention: Second Global Strategy Meeting.* Addis-Ababa: UNESCO, pp. 86-91.

Hassan, F. A. 2000. Kafr Hassan Dawood, *Egyptian Archaeology* 16: 37-9.

Hassan, F. A. 2009. The UNESCO Campaign to rescue Nubian archaeology and monuments, in F. A. Hassan, G. J. Tassie, A De Trafford, L. S. Owens and J. van Wetering (eds.) *Managing Egypt's Cultural Heritage: Proceedings of the First Egyptian Cultural Heritage Organisation Conference on: Egyptian Cultural Heritage Management.* London: Golden House and ECHO Publications, pp. 59-79.

Hassan, F. A. Unpublished. Minshat Ezzat: A Call for Assistance. London.

Hassan, F. A., Tassie, G. J., Tucker, T. L., Rowland, J. M. & van Wetering J. F. L. 2003. Social dynamics at the late Predynastic to Early Dynastic site of Kafr Hassan Dawood, East Delta, Egypt, *Archéo-Nil* 13: 37-45.

Holladay, J. S. (*et al*). 1982. *Cities of the Delta - pt 3: Tell el-Maskhuta, A Preliminary Report on the Wadi Tumilat Project 1978-79.* Malibu: Published under the auspices of the American Research Center in Egypt, Undena Publications.

Holmes, D. L. 1992. Archaeological cultural resources and modern land-use activities: some observations made during a recent survey in the Badari region, *JARCE* 29: 67-80.

Ikram, S. 2013. Cultural heritage in times of crisis: The view from Egypt, *Journal of Eastern Mediterranean Archaeology & Heritage Studies* 1(4): 366-371.

Jucha, M. 2009. The North-eastern part of the Nile Delta - Research perspectives. The Polish archaeological survey in Ash-Sharqiyyah Governorate, in J. Popielska-Grzybowska & J. Iwaszczck (eds) *Proceedings of the Fifth Central European Conference of Egyptologists. Egypt 2009. Perspectives and Research. Pułtusk 22-24 June 2009.* Pułtusk: Institute of Anthropology and Archaeology, pp. 83-94.

Junker, H. 1928. *Bericht über die von der Akademie der Wissenschaften in Wien nach dem Westdelta entsendente Expedition (20. Dezember 1927 bis 25. Februar 1928).* Vienna: Denkschriften der Kaiserlichen Akademie der Wissenschaften in Wien, Philosophisch-historische Klasse.

Junker, H. 1930. Bericht über die vom deutschen Institut für ägyptische altertumskunde nach dem Ost-delta-Rand unternommene enkundungsfahrt, *MDAIK* 1: 1-37.

Kamermans, H., van Leusen, M. & Verhagen, P. 2009. Archaeological prediction and risk management, in H. Kamermans, M. van Leusen & P. Verhagen (eds) *Archaeological Prediction and Risk Management. Alternatives to Current Practice.* Archaeological Studies 17, Leiden: University of Leiden, pp. 9-18.

Kasim, R. A. abu el. 1988. The northwestern Nile Delta: Problems and priorities, in E.C.M. van den Brink (ed.) *The Archaeology of the Nile Delta: Problems and Priorities.* Amsterdam: Netherlands Foundation for Archaeological Research in Egypt, Uitgeverij, pp. 279-80.

Kila, J. D. 2013. Inactive, reactive, or pro-active? Cultural property crimes in the context of contemporary armed conflicts, *Journal of Eastern Mediterranean Archaeology & Heritage Studies* 1(4): 319-342.0

Kirby, C. J., Orel, S. E. & Smith, S. T. 1998. Preliminary report on the survey of Kom El-Hisn, 1996. *Journal of Egyptian Archaeology* 84: 23-43.

Leclère, F. 2008. *Les villes de basse Égypte au Ier millénaire av. J.–C.* Cairo: Bibliothèque d'Étude 144.

Lehner, M. (ed.) 2009. *The Giza Plateau Mapping Project 2009.* Cairo: AREA, Occasional Papers 5.

Malta Treaty: http://conventions.coe.int/Treaty/en/Treaties/Html/143.htm

Marriner, N., Flaux, C., Morhange, C., & Stanley, J. 2013. Tracking Nile Delta vulnerability to Holocene change, *PLoS ONE* 8(7): e69195. doi:10.1371/journal.pone.0069195

McGrath, C. 2014. Nile Delta disappearing beneath the Sea, *Inter Press Agency* - http://www.ipsnews.net/2014/01/nile-delta-disappearing-beneath-sea/

McManamon, F. P., Barnes, J. A. & Stout, A. 2008. Contemporary archaeological resource management and the "liberals' dilemma." in F. P. McManamon, A. Stout, & J. A. Barnes (eds) *Managing Archaeological Resources: Global Context, National Programs, Local Actions.* Walnut Creek, [CA]: One World Archaeology 58, Left Coast Press, pp. 17–34.

Miller-Rosen, A. 1986. *Cities of Clay: The Geoarchaeology of Tells.* Chicago: University of Chicago Press.

Montet, P. 1947. *La nécropole royale de Tanis. Volume 1: Les constructions et le tombeau d'Osorkon II à Tanis.* Paris: Fouilles de Tanis, ser. ed. Jean Pierre Marie Montet.

Montet, P. 1951. *La nécropole royale de Tanis. Volume 2: Les constructions et le tombeau de Psousennès à Tanis.* Paris: Fouilles de Tanis, ser. ed. Jean Pierre Marie Montet.

Montet, P. 1960. *La nécropole royale de Tanis. Volume 3: Les constructions et le tombeau de Chechanq III à Tanis.* Paris: Fouilles de Tanis, ser. ed. Jean Pierre Marie Montet.

Mower, J. P. & Tassie, G. J. 2000. Egyptian Human Remains: Retrieval, Conservation and Analysis: A Conference held at Qantara, Egypt, 25th-27th April 2000, *Papers from the Institute of Archaeology* 11: 116-24.

Mumford, G. D. 2002. Reconstructing the ancient settlement at Tell Tebilla, *Bulletin of the American Research Center in Egypt* 182 (Spring-Summer): 18-23.

Mumford, G. D. 2004. A preliminary reconstruction of the temple and settlement at Tell Tebilla (East Delta), in G. Knoppers and A. Hirsch (eds.) *Egypt, Israel and the Ancient Mediterranean World: Studies in Honor of Donald B. Redford.* Leiden: Brill, pp. 267–86.

Naville, H. E. 1885. *The Store-City of Pithom and the Route of the Exodus.* London: EEF.

Parçak, S. H. 2003. New methods for archaeological site detection via satellite image analysis: case studies from Sinai and the Delta, *Archaeologia Polonia* 41: 243-245.

Parçak, S. H. 2004. Finding new archaeological sites in Egypt using satellite remote sensing: case studies from Middle Egypt and the Delta, in C. Wang (ed.) *International Conference on Remote Sensing Archaeology*, Beijing: Chinese Center for Remote Sensing Archaeology.

Parçak, S. H. 2009. *Satellite Remote sensing for Archaeology.* London: Routledge.

Pavlish, L., Mumford, G. D., & D'Andrea, A. C. 2003. Geotechnical survey at Tell Tabilla, Northeastern Nile Delta, Egypt, in Z. Hawass and L. Pinch Brock (eds.) *Egyptology at the Dawn of the Twenty-first Century: Proceedings of the Eighth International Congress of Egyptologists. Cairo, 2000. Volume 1: Archaeology.* Cairo: The American University in Cairo Press, pp. 361-68.

Petrie, W. M. F. & Duncan, J. G. 1906. *Hyksos and Israelite Cities.* London: Quaritch.

Podzorski, P. 2000. Egyptian Human Remains: Retrieval, Conservation and Analysis, *NARCE* 179: 21-4.

Posner, G. 1962. Histoire et Egypte ancienne, *Annales économices - sociétés - civilisations* 17(4), Julliet-août: 631-646.

Pusch, E. B. 2000. Further Steps towards a map of Pi-Ramesses, in Z. Hawass and A. M. Jones (eds.) *Abstracts of Papers for the Eighth International Congress of Egyptologists.* Cairo, American University in Cairo Press, pp. 145-6.

Razanajao, V. 2006a. *D'Imet à Tell Farâoun : recherches sur la géographie, les cultes et l'histoire d'une localité de Basse-Égypte orientale.* Volume I Volume II. *description archéologique et documentation synthèse.* PhD thesis. Montpellier: Université Paul Valéry.

Razanajao, V. 2006b. Le Delta à la Basse Époque: géographies d'un territoire, *Égypte. Afrique et Orient* 42: 3-9.

Redmount, C. A. 1989. *On the Egyptian/Asiatic frontier: An archaeological history of the Wadi Tumilat.* Unpublished PhD thesis. Chicago: The University of Chicago.

Redmount, C. A. 1995. The Wadi Tumilat and the "canal" of the pharaohs, Journal of Near Eastern Studies 54: 127-135.

Redon, B. 2007. *Le Delta égyptien aux temps des Grecs. La présence grecque en Basse Égypte, de l'époque saïte à la fin de l'époque hellénistique: diffusion, nature, intensité et conséquences.* PhD thesis. Lille: University Lille III.

Romer, J & Romer, E. 1993. *The Rape of Tutankhamun.* London: Michael O'Mara Books.

Rowland, J. M. 2004. *Social Transformations in the Delta from the Terminal Predynastic the Early Dynastic Period: A Comparative Study.* PhD Thesis. London: University College London.

Rowland, J. M. 2007. The Delta Survey: Minufiyeh Province, 2006-2007, *Journal of Egyptian Archaeology* 93: 65-77.

Rowland, J. M., Edinborough, K. & Phillipps, R. 2009. The Delta Survey: Minufiyeh Province, 2008-9, *Journal of Egyptian Archaeology* 95: 35-49.

Rowland, J., Ikram, S., Tassie, G., Jansen-Winkeln, K. & Yeomans, L. 2013. The Sacred Falcon Necropolis of Djedhor (?) at Quesna – Recent investigations from 2006-2012, *Journal of Egyptian Archaeology* 99: 53-84.

Rowland, J. M. & Spencer, A. J. 2011. The EES Delta Survey in spring 2011, *Egyptian Archaeology* 39: 3-5.

Rowland, J. & Tassie, G. J. In Press. Prehistoric sites along the edge of the Western Nile Delta: Report on the results of the Imbaba Prehistoric Survey 2013-14, *Journal of Egyptian Archaeology* 100: 49-65.

Rowland, J. M. & Wilson, P. 2006. The EES Delta Survey – Report for 2004-2005, *Journal of Egyptian Archaeology* 92, pp. 1-13.

Saleh, F. & Grimal, N. 2000. Carte archéologique de l'Egypte, in Z. Hawass and A. M. Jones (eds.) *Abstracts of Papers for the Eighth International Congress of Egyptologists.* Cairo: American University in Cairo Press, p. 160.

Schott, S., Neuffer, E. & Bittel, K. 1932. Bericht uber die zweite vom Deutschen Institut fur Agyptische Altertumskunde nach dem Ost-delta-rand und in das Wadi Tumilat unternommene erkundungsfahrt, *MDAIK* 2: 39-54.

Shenker, J. 2009. Nile Delta: 'We are going underwater. The sea will conquer our lands', The Guardian - http://www.guardian.co.uk/environment/2009/aug/21/climate-change-nile-flooding-farming

Spencer, A. J. & Spencer, P. 2000. The Delta Survey, *Egyptian Archaeology* 16: 25-7.

Spencer, A. J. 2008. New ventures from the EES Delta Survey, *Egyptian Archaeology* 33: 2.

Spencer, N. 2000. The temple of Onuris-Shu at Samanud. *Egyptian Archaeology* 16: 7-9.

Spencer, P. 2013. Nile Delta research, *Egyptian Archaeology* 43: 2.

Stanley, J.-D., Goddio, F., Jorstad, T. F., & Schnepp, G. 2004. Submergence of Ancient Greek Cities Off Egypt's Nile Delta—A Cautionary Tale, *GSA Today* 14(1): 4–10.

Stapp, D. & Longenecker, J. 2009. *Avoiding Archaeological Disasters: A Risk Management Approach.* Walnut Creek: Left Coast Press.

Steinberg, J. M. 1996. Ploughzone sampling in Denmark: isolating and interpreting site signatures from disturbed contexts, *Antiquity* 70 (268):368-90.

Schwartzstein, P. 2014. Egypt's population boom threatens cultural treasures, *National Geographic* - http://news.nationalgeographic.com/news/2014/04/140418-egypt-population-heritage-conservation-threats-world/

Tassie, G. J. 2007. Have we dug ourselves into a hole? Reappraising excavation methodology and approaches in Egyptian archaeology (part two): Kafr Hassan Dawood, a case study, in J-C. Goyon & C. Cardin (eds.) *Proceedings of the Ninth International Congress of Egyptologists.* Leuven/Paris/Dudley: Peeters, Orientalia Lovaniensia Analecta 150, pp. 1769-1782.

Tassie, G. J. & Owens, L. S. 2010. *Standards of Archaeological Excavation; A Fieldguide to the Methodology, Recording Techniques, and Conventions.* London: Golden House Publications.

Tassie, G. J., Rowland, J. M. & de Trafford, A. 2000. The 8th International Congress of Egyptologists, Cairo: 28th March - 3rd April 2000, *Papers from the Institute of Archaeology* 11: 98-109.

Theroux, P. 1997. The imperiled Nile Delta, *National Geographic* January: 8-35.

Torab, M. & Azab, M. 2006. Modern shoreline changes along the Nile Delta coast as an impact of construction of the Aswan High Dam. Paper presented at the *World Congress of Soil Science*, Philadelphia, Pennsylvania, USA, July 9-15, 2006.

Trampier, J. Toonen, W. Simony, A. & Starbird, J. 2013. Missing *koms* and abandoned channels: The potential of regional survey in the Western Nile Delta, *JEA* 99: 217-240.

Trampier, J. 2014. *Landscape Archaeology of the Western Nile Delta.* Atlanta [GA]: Lockwood Press.

Tristant, Y. 2005. Le delta du Nil avant les pharaons. Entre originalités locales et influences étrangères, *Archéo-Nil* 15: 75-102.

Tristant, Y. 2006. *L'occupation humaine dans le Delta du Nil au IVe millénaire.* Ph.D. thesis. Toulouse: Université de Toulouse.

UN World Tourism Organisation: http://media.unwto.org/press-release/2011-05-31/tourism-key-economic-recovery-egypt

Verhagen, P., Kamermans, H., van Leusen M. & Ducke, B. 2010. New developments in archaeological predictive modelling, in T. Bloemers, H. Kars, A. van der Valk & M. Wijnen (eds) *The Cultural Landscape & Heritage Paradox. Protection and Development of the Dutch Archaeological-Historical Landscape and its European Dimension.* Amsterdam; Amsterdam University Press, pp. 431-444.

Verhagen, P. & Whitley, T. G. 2012. Integrating archaeological theory and predictive modelling: A live report from the scene, *Journal of Archaeological Method and Theory* 19-1: 49-100.

Verhagen, P., Nuninger, L., Tourneux, F.-P., Bertoncello, F. & Jeneson, K. 2013. Introducing the human factor in predictive modelling: A work in progress, in G. Earl, T. Sly, A. Chrysanthi, P. Murrieta-Flores, C. Papadopoulos, I. Romanowska & D. Wheatley (eds.) *Archaeology in the Digital Era. Papers from the 40th Annual Conference of Computer Applications and Quantitative Methods in Archaeology (CAA), Southampton, 26-29 March 2012.* Amsterdam: Amsterdam University Press, pp. 379-388.

El Wakil, A. L. 1988. A brief report on the problems met with during excavations at Silvago, Delingat, Behera Governate, in E.C.M. van den Brink (ed.) *The Archaeology of the Nile Delta: Problems and Priorities.* Amsterdam: Netherlands Foundation for Archaeological Research in Egypt, Uitgeverij, pp. 265.

Weeks, K. R. & Hetherington, N. J. 2014. *The Valley of the Kings: A site Management Handbook.* Cairo: AUC Press.

Wendrich, W. 2006. Archaeology and sustainable tourism in Egypt: Protecting community, antiquities, and environment, in N. Agnew & J. Bridgland (eds) *Of the Past, for the Future: Integrating Archaeology and Conservation.* Los Angeles: The Getty Conservation Institute, pp. 184-190.

Wenke, R. J. & Brewer, D. J. 1996. The Archaic-Old Kingdom Delta: the evidence from Mendes and Kom el-Hisn, in M. Bietak (ed.), *House and Palace in Egypt.* Vienna: Austrian Archaeological Institute, pp. 265-285.

Wesemael, B. van. 1988. The relation between natural landscape and distribution of archaeological remains in the northeastern Delta, in E.C.M. van den Brink (ed.) *The Archaeology of the Nile Delta: Problems and Priorities.* Amsterdam: Netherlands Foundation for Archaeological Research in Egypt, Uitgeverij, pp. 125- 134.

Wilson, K. L. 1982. *Cities of the Delta - pt II: Mendes, Preliminary Report on the 1979 and 1980 Seasons.* Malibu: Published under the auspices of the American Research Center in Egypt, Undena Publications.

Wilson, P. 1998. Sais: surveying the royal city, *Egyptian Archaeology* 12:3-6.

Wilson, P. 2003. The Delta Survey 2002, *Journal of Egyptian Archaeology* 89: 1-8.

Wilson, P. 2006a. Prehistoric settlement in the Western Delta: A regional and local view from Saïs (Sa el-Hagar), *Journal of Egyptian Archaeology* 92: 75-126.

Wilson, P. 2006b. *The Survey of Saïs (Sa el-Hagar), 1997-2002.* London: Egypt Exploration Society.

Wilson, P. 2007. The Nile Delta, in T. A. Wilkinson (ed.) *The Egyptian World.* London: Routledge, pp. 15-28.

Wilson, P. 2009. The Egypt Exploration Society: The Delta Survey, *Ancient Egypt* 9(6) Issue 54: 40-45.

Wilson, P. 2010. Recent survey work in the southern Mareotis area, in L. Blue & E. Khalil (eds) *Proceedings of the International Conference on the Archaeology of the Mareotic Region Held at Alexandria University, Egypt 5th-6th April 2008.* Oxford: University of Southampton Series in Archaeology 2, pp. 119-125.

Wilson, P. 2011. Settlement connections in the Canopic region, in D. Robinson & A. Wilson (eds) *Alexandria and the North-Western Delta.* Oxford: Oxford Centre for Maritime Archaeology, pp. 111-126.

Wilson, P. 2012a. The ancient landscape around Lake Burullus, *Egyptian Archaeology* 41: 18-20.

Wilson, P. 2012b. Archaeology in the Delta, in C. Riggs (ed.) *The Oxford Handbook of Roman Egypt.* Oxford: Oxford University Press, pp. 136–51.

Wilson, P. & Grigoropoulos, D. 2009. *The West Nile Delta Regional Survey, Beheira and Kafr el-Sheikh Provinces.* London: Egypt Exploration Society.

Wit, H. de & Stralen, L. van. 1988. Preliminary results of the 1987 palaeo-geological survey, in E.C.M. van den Brink (ed.) *The Archaeology of the Nile Delta: Problems and Priorities.* Amsterdam: Netherlands Foundation for Archaeological Research in Egypt, Uitgeverij, pp. 135-9.

Wit, H. de & M. Pawlikowski. 1992. Comparison of palaeoenvironmental data from Neolithic and Early Dynastic sites of Upper Egypt, the Faiyum and the Nile Delta, in E.C.M. van den Brink (ed.) *The Nile Delta in Transition: 4th - 3rd Millennium B.C.,* Tel Aviv: van den Brink, pp. 289-292.

Wunderlich, J. 1988. Investigations on the development of the western Nile Delta in Holocene times, in E.C.M. van den Brink (ed.) *The Archaeology of the Nile Delta: Problems and Priorities.* Amsterdam: Netherlands Foundation for Archaeological Research in Egypt, Uitgeverij, pp. 251-7.

Yoyotte, Y. 1958. Promenade à travers les sites anciens du Delta, *Bulletin Trimestriel de la Société française d'Egyptologie* 25: 13-24.

Chapter 10

The Great Festival of Luxor: A Brief Study of the Mawlid of Aboul Haggag and its Cultural Significances

Mohamed Hussein Hosny and Mo'men Ghanem

ABSTRACT

The Mawlid (Festival) of Sidi Youssef Aboul Haggag Al Aksori, the Patron Saint of the City of Luxor, has been a major city celebration since he passed away in 1244 A.D. This paper summarises the importance of Aboul Haggag as a Sufi master, and details the evangelical role he played in Luxor in the 12th and 13th centuries A.D. It also tracks the evolution of the festival's ceremonial details, and examines their possible origins in the city's Pharaonic background and also the alleged Tunisian background of Aboul Haggag himself. It supports recent proposals for the protection of the Mawlid of Aboul Haggag as crucial intangible cultural heritage, of paramount importance for the local population of Luxor as well as the Sufi community of Egypt and beyond. The local perception of the event by the inhabitants of Luxor and the cultural significance of the Mawlid of Aboul Haggag are carefully examined. The latter are brought to bear on the recently proposed plan for the city – particularly the area around the shrine of Aboul Haggag – with particular reference to the route taken by Aboul Haggag's Mawlid, known as "Al Dorah". The latter is shown to be deeply rooted in the collective consciousness of the people of Luxor, so much so that it qualifies for listing in the UNESCO World Heritage List.

INTRODUCTION: ABOUL HAGGAG'S BIOGRAPHY, MOSQUE, AND THE MAWLID

Biography

Aboul Haggag real name was Youssef Abdul Rahim ibn Youssef, and was descended from Imam Aly Ibn Abi Taleb, cousin and son-in-law of the Prophet Muhammad (*pbuh*) (Al Haggagy 1968). His exact date of birth is unknown, but has been estimated (Al Haggagy 1968) at around 549 AH (i.e. 1154 AD), given that he died aged 90 in 642 AH (i.e. 1244 AD). No further detail is available for either birth or death. His origin is also questionable. Most references suggest that he was Iraqi, from Baghdad (Legrain 1914; Al Haggagy 1968; CNRS 1981), but Al Haggagy (2009), among others, cite a Tunisian origin from the city of Al-Mahdia, south of Carthage.

He frequented the classes of the famed Nezamiah School of Baghdad and was the disciple of the Shafe'i scholar and Sufi Master Aboul Naguib Al Suhrawardy until the age of forty. He used his personal wealth to travel to other Islamic lands in search of learning, starting with Mecca, where he stayed for a year. Encountering some travellers from Juhayna in Upper Egypt – who informed him that he had ancestors buried in Egypt – he determined to make Egypt his next destination. During his journey through Medina and Mansura, he was beset by visions instructing him to visit Luxor. Upon doing so, he encountered a nun named Tarzah/Theresa, the daughter of a village elder, and who lived in a church situated by the Temple of Luxor. She was also in charge of land allocations, and approved his request for a piece of land the size of his camel's hide, upon which he would build his house. He then braided the camel's wool into a very long rope that he used to encircle a large part of Luxor (Al Aksorein); Tarzah was thus obliged to fulfil her promise, and give him the land. She is then alleged to have converted to Islam, and become his disciple and wife (Wickett 1990; CNRS 1981).[1]

Aboul Haggag settled in Luxor and started to evangelise the local community. He then went to Alexandria in order to become involved with its famous circles of Islamic erudition, making the acquaintance of Sidi Mohamed Abdul Razzak Al Gazouli – disciple of Abou Madyan Shoaib of Telmessan – who predicted that Aboul Haggag would be a key Sufi figure in the southern provinces of Egypt. On his

---

[1] This tale bears a striking resemblance to that of Elissa, daughter of Mattan I, the Phoenician king of Tyre. She requested a piece of land from a local Berber chieftain, stating that it need only be the size of a bull's hide. She then spent all night cutting the largest hide she could find into tiny strips and braiding them into a rope so long that it surrounded the entire building plot of the future city of Carthage, which she began to construct when the Berber chief had begrudgingly agreed to honour the agreement (Bitar 2012; Al Youssoufy 2012).

way back to Luxor, he spent some time with Sheikh Aboul Hassan Al Sabbagh from Qous, and Sidi Abdul Rehim Al Qenawy, the later Patron Saint of Qena and uncontested Pole of Sufism in Egypt.

He remained in Luxor and Qous for the rest of his life, serving the needs of pilgrims to Mecca, conducting moral campaigns in Qous, and combating Shiism. He instructed his sons and followers to build him a shrine and mosque at the same place where Tarzah/Theresa had her church, proclaiming to them his famous words: *"In this place, The One and Only True God Has Always Been Worshiped."*

The fact that this declaration was used to describe the position of Aboul Haggag's Mosque, built on the remains of a church, and surrounded by the vestiges of the Temple of Luxor does underscore the fact that this area should be considered to be a "sacred site and landscape", perhaps the only place in the world where the religious edifices of Islam, Christianity and an earlier faith (the Pharaonic faith in this case) coexist so harmoniously in the same spot.[2]

The Shrine and Mosque of Aboul Haggag

The shrine housing the tomb of Aboul Haggag was built by his son Ahmed El Negm, on the remains of the aforementioned church, on the eastern side of the Temple of Luxor (see Plate 10.1). Buried with him in the same place are his two sons. On the northern side is buried Sheikh Abdel 'Aty Abdel Kerim who accompanied him on his journey from Baghdad. Tarzah/Theresa is also buried on the northern side, in a room by herself. Sometime later, the remains of Sheikh Jibril Ibn Abdul Rahman Al Aksory (Aboul Haggag's cousin) were also moved from his resting place to the mosque of Aboul Haggag (Al Haggagy 1968).

Khedive Abbas Helmy II renovated the mosque and erected the modern minaret in 1914. Further restoration measures have been undertaken at the mosque in recent years, and the anterior plaza has been completely paved and re-landscaped. This redesign will be the subject of our analysis in the second part of this paper.

The Festival (Mawlid) of Aboul Haggag

Shortly after Aboul Haggag's death, the inhabitants of Luxor and its vicinity, started to celebrate his mawlid on the 14th day of the Islamic month of *Sha'ban*; this is the date of his first arrival to Luxor (Al Haggagy 2009; Al Haggagy 1968). The festival originally lasted for three days, ending on the 14th of *Sha'ban*, although there was a time when it was celebrated from the first day of Sha'ban until the middle of the month (CNRS 1981). More recently, the events have been concentrated on the 12th and 13th, culminate in the Grand Finale on the 14th. It is not possible to provide a full chronological sequence of events in the ceremony, given its complexity. However, we shall highlight the main milestones for the first two days, then discuss the Grand Finale.

Events Occurring on the 12th and 13th Days of Sha'ban:

The 12th day of *Sha'ban* commences with large crowds gathering in the Plaza of Aboul Haggag, and appeals for him to intercede on their behalf with Allah. The crowds are fed and watered by numerous street vendors who compete for the optimal strategic spots, selling foul, falafel, tea, coffee, *shishas*, water[3], liquorice juice and other cold drinks. Other items for sale include sugar dolls, horses and cavaliers, and various other children's toys and souvenirs.

In the middle of all this, the following events take place, not necessarily in any particular order:

- The descendants of Aboul Haggag start the official festivities with a ceremonial visit to the shrine, to pray for him and announce the launching of the festivities with the sound of the *sagaat* (small copper cymbals) and traditional chanting by the family elders (Wickett 1990).
- The visitors proceed to line up in front of the shrine of Aboul Haggag to acquire his Barakah (blessing) and ask him for intercession (CNRS 1981).
- The direct descendants sit around a wooden log with twelve lit candles in a closed room and recite verses from Quran starting with the opening section (*Al Fateḥah*), and then move on to catechismal prayers and invocations passed down to them directly by the saint (CNRS 1981).

---

[2] For a more complete story of the life of Aboul Haggag, the reader is referred to Al Haggagy (1968).

[3] Most water *saqquas* do this without expecting any return, as an appeal for Allah's reward both here and in the hereafter.

- The devotees gather in the central part of the mosque and organize a *ḥadrah*: a spiritual circle of invocation of the names and panegyrics of Allah (Wickett 1990; CNRS 1981).
- The visitors gather around the Plaza of Aboul Haggag to perform *Zhikr* (an invocation of one or more of Allah's 99 names) while moving their bodies in an undulating fashion (see Plate 10.2) in order to rid themselves of all earthly instincts and thus become fully absorbed into the spirit of the divine. This is typically accompanied by percussion or similar instruments.
- Male dancing groups are organised outside the mosque, accompanied by percussion and reed instruments and traditional songs extolling the virtues of Aboul Haggag and other saints of his calibre, interspersed with contrapuntal panegyrics of the prophet (*pbuh*) that the audience either repeats after the main performer, or answers with set "refrains" (Wickett 1990).
- Various games and entertainments are made available; weight lifting and target practice for the adults, and swings – of various levels of daring – for the children (CNRS 1981; Wickett 1990).
- *Al Mermah* – an acrobatic form of horse racing – attracts many competitors and large audiences from the entire Luxor area (see Plate 10.3-4).
- *Al Tahteeb* – a traditional stick fencing game somewhat resembling quarterstaff fighting – dates back to the time of the Pharaohs, and is a regular competition fixture (see Plate 10.5).
- Singing troupes called *Al Muzamzameen* march from the town of Qous in order to perform *Al-Gam'*, which resembles troubadour singing, and which concern the panegyrics of the prophet (*pbuh*). The singers stop at every village to collect gifts, sweets and drinks from the inhabitants (Chambliss 2008).
- The arrival of the *Rifa'ïah* – followers of the Sufi master Sidi Ahmed Al Rifa'i – is heralded with great fanfare. Their daring performances with swords and other weapons are a major event in the Mawlid of Aboul Haggag (CNRS 1981).
- Food sharing is a vital part of the ceremonies. *Al Maddate* (elongated table cloths) are spread on the ground in the Plaza of Aboul Haggag, in order to express the local inhabitants' hospitality to the visitors. The most notable food served on the *Maddate* is Kabab Aboul Haggag, which resembles Syrian *Kobebah,* made from meat and crushed wheat. Aboul Haggag is generally believed to have taught the local people the recipe, and to have offered it to all his guests and visitors (Wickett 1990).
- Camels with ornate adornments accompany their owners from all the villages surrounding Luxor, in order to add further colour to the celebration.

Traditionally, the first day of the Mawlid commenced with the raising of a huge pole in the centre of the Plaza of Aboul Haggag, in order to invoke divine favour and thus confer blessings on the festival. This pole serves as a focal point for the Mawlid. It is interesting to note that this tradition was also practiced by the pharaohs, as can be seen in various reliefs at the Temple of Luxor (Wickett 1990). As there is nothing comparable elsewhere in the Islamic world, it seems probable that the practice was directly inherited from Pharaonic tradition.

The Climax of the Mawlid of Aboul Haggag: "Al Dorah" and "Al Maḥmal"

The 14th day of *Sha'ban* marks the grand finale of the Mawlid of Aboul Haggag. It starts off at 7 am with the adornment and preparation of the camels that will lead the procession, while the barques of Aboul Haggag are moved from storage and made ready for the *Al Dorah* and *Al Maḥmal* processions.

Al Dorah is a circumambulation procession that follows a specific path (see Fig. 10.1) that allegedly marks the circle Aboul Haggag traced with the braided wool of his camel. It bears a strong resemblance to the ceremonial path that the ancient Egyptians followed during the Opet Festival of the Nile, in honour of the Theban Trinity: Amun, Mut and Khonsu (Wickett 1990; CNRS 1981; Macpherson 1941).

The camels participating in the event carry simulacra of the coffin of Aboul Haggag in a procession known as *Al Maḥmal.* The second camel carries huge kettle drums (see Plate 10.6) that allegedly date from the time of Aboul Haggag (Wickett 1990); the camel is ridden by a local Haggagi, who recites secret sayings handed down in a direct oral tradition from Aboul Haggag himself. The procession traces the route three times in an anti-clockwise fashion, similar to the Muslims circumambulation around the Ka'bah at the time of the pilgrimage. The camels carrying simulacra of the Saint's coffin are then followed by barques carrying his descendants, pulled by devout individuals who consider the task to be an honour. These are followed by representatives of the various Sufi Tariquahs (Orders), carrying their identifying flags and singing verses from the *Burdah* of Sidi Al–Boussiry, the most famous of Prophet Mohammed's panegyric poems (*pbuh*). Lastly, representatives of the various Luxor craftsman guilds join the procession. Musical accompaniments are provided by marching bands from the Governorate and the Armed Forces.

The cortege stops at specific points on the path, marked by houses of Haggagis who offer their visitors drinks and sweets to express their gratitude at the honour being paid to their ancestor. At the end of the third and last round, the procession ends at the footsteps of Aboul Haggag's mosque, where the camels are unloaded. The Haggagi elders then proceed to his shrine, where they offer their last prayers and supplications before announcing the end of the festivities. Traditionally, this was made apparent to all the visitors in the Plaza by removing the central mast pole, and cutting the ropes that were used to hold the camel loads in place. The small pieces of rope were then distributed to anyone wishing to keep a small memento attesting to their attendance of the Grand Mawlid of Aboul Haggag (Wickett 1990; CNRS 1981).

We would like to highlight one final similarity between ancient and modern festivals, namely Aboul Haggag's barques, which are reminiscent of the vessels used in the Opet Festival, which were used to carry the Theban Trinity from the Karnak Temple to the Temple of Luxor and back (see Plate 10.7, 10.8). This similarity has been dismissed as coincidental by some authors (Jones 2012; Al Haggagy 1968), although we would disagree, and furthermore argue that – regardless of origin – the durability of the tradition means that it now plays an integral part in the collective consciousness of the Luxor people. This makes it intangible heritage as UNESCO defines it, and further makes it worthy of preservation and protection, especially considering that it is also seamlessly woven into the tangible heritage of the city.

INTERPRETATION OF ABOUL HAGGAG'S CULTURAL HERITAGE

In most modern plans involving cultural heritage sites, sustainable socioeconomic development of local communities assumes a leading position among the goals that such plans aim to achieve. However, in most cases, tourism becomes the primary target, and the concerns of local people – and thus their appreciation of the heritage that surrounds them – is neglected (Hassan 2008). This oversight ultimately results in a disassociation of the cultural site from its surrounding population, meaning a lack of positive social values associated with cultural sites, which are a *conditia sine qua non* for the protection and preservation of these sites. In order to bridge the gap between planners and the public, therefore, the authors intends to assess and analyse public perception regarding the Mawlid of Aboul Haggag within its built environment, and examine the factors that influence these perceptions. The data collection methods used are as follows:

- Personal observation in situ
- Personal interviews with Haggagies and random Luxor inhabitants.

We have also opted for a simple technique for the codification and tabulation of the responses of our interviewees, providing a rough indication of the local population's perception of Aboul Haggag's cultural heritage (appendix I). Open-ended questions were used in order to get a true feel of the participant's opinions.

Public Perception of Aboul Haggag's Mawlid

The overall public image of the festivity and the traditions associated with it were may be described as a mosaic of ideas and symbolic meanings – such as uniqueness, particularity, ownership, and belief – invoked by ritualistic practices such as the Dorah, the Zhikr, the spiritual chanting, the visitation of the Saint's shrine, the voluntary prayers, the Maḫmal, the Barques, the flags, the special garb, and so on. Use of the Burra Charter (ICOMOS 1999) led us to realise that the said significances may be subdivided as follows:

- Spiritual
- Social
- Symbolic
- Nostalgic
- Functional.

Spiritual, social and symbolic significances were shown to be the most influential in affecting peoples' perception of Aboul Haggag heritage (see table and chart in Figs. 10.2-3; appendix I).

Spiritual/Religious Significance

Mawlid celebrations in Egypt generally possess a very pronounced spiritual dimension, and it was thus unsurprising to find that all the respondents stated this to be the main factor attracting them to the Mawlid. Most respondents cited the Al Dorah procession and the religious chanting to be the most spiritually loaded practices of the festival (see Plate 10.9). In tangible terms, the mosque itself occupies a central position in the spiritual significance dimension, confirming previous findings as stated above (Wickett 1990; CNRS 1981).

Social Significance

Social significance appears to have been one of the major forces attracting the local population to this event. The social dimension of the Mawlid plays a major role in its appeal to the local inhabitants, who stressed the importance of getting together, strengthening of interpersonal ties, partaking in social and cultural events, eating together, and the communal attendance of festive activities with fellow Luxorians and visitors from elsewhere as being of primary importance in reinforcing their enthusiasm for the Mawlid (see Plate 10.10).

Symbolic Significance

Possibly due to its' multifactorial and culturally diverse nature, Luxor possesses both tangible and intangible cultural uniqueness. Foremost among these is the Mosque-Church-Temple complex, where architectural elements such as the minaret and the obelisk convey profound symbolic overtones from different perspectives (see Fig. 10.3). This symbolic, albeit subtle, significance was detected by some of the respondents and stressed as being the mark of particularity of this special cultural landscape.

Nostalgic Significance

All the interviewees stated that they viewed the area around the Plaza of Aboul Haggag in a nostalgic fashion, evoking a mixture of personal experiences that took place in this Plaza throughout their lives, interwoven with traditional folk stories and local beliefs that may or may not be historically factual, but nevertheless wields an powerful effect on their psyche. The Haggagies, in particular, are deeply proud of their ancestors who lived in this particular locale, and who left behind scores of stories describing their courage, valour, and strong spiritual commitment, notably the Saint himself around whose life story everything seems to revolve. A classic case in point is the story of Aboul Haggag and Tarzah, outlined in section I.

Functional Significance

From the responses of most interviewees, we could discern that the Plaza of Aboul Haggag possessed a functional significance that went beyond the festive events of the Mawlid, to encompass more general occasions such as the regular holding of political forums, singing parties and other similar cultural events (see Plate 10.12).

Contemporary Urban Interpretation of the Site

The importance of its archaeological monuments means that this site has been a focal point for all the management plans to have been proposed over the past 40 years, most recently the "Comprehensive Development Plan for The City of Luxor" (2001). As stated, the respondents were interviewed about their attitudes concerning this built environment, and the results analysed in reference to design principles underlying one of the main projects in the said plan, which concerns the district surrounding Aboul Hagag's mosque.

The strategy of the Luxor Comprehensive Development Plan rests on the amalgamation of two main philosophical premises (Gabriel *et al.* 2001), namely:

- The protection of resources, including culture

- The new urban development plan of the city, aiming at the creation of a new sustainable region where all resources, particularly archaeological sites, are preserved[4].

In cultural/heritage terms, the comprehensive plan has adopted a set of key strategic directions, the most important of which is the delineation of the Luxor Open Museum and heritage district "to protect resources and accommodate additional tourists" (ibid.). The Open Museum region defines the area between the Winter Palace Hotel in the South and the Karnak Temple in the North, including the Souk east of the Avenue of the Sphinxes to the Nile to the West (see Fig. 10.4); this area thus contains the Plaza of Aboul Haggag.

Owing to the ever-increasing number of tourists visiting these sites, this region is generally considered to be overcrowded, with commensurate risk of deterioration and damage. This was the main reason behind the emergence of the idea of an Open Museum, in order to widen the scope of the area requiring restoration and then preservation. This region extends over a three-kilometre strip of land containing "...the most majestic and fascinating cultural landmarks in the world"(Gabriel *et al.* 2001).

The development of the area between Al Mahattah Street (The Train Station Street) and the Plaza of Aboul Haggag is one of the most important components of the Open Museum strategy, and is the core of our research into heritage management and interpretation, and social attitudes thereto. The Aboul Haggag Plaza Upgrading Project (see Appendix II) covers a total area of 70,000 m^2, with a total budget of eight million USD (Aga Khan 2010). This comprises an ideal venue in which to study and analyse governmental attitudes and approaches to cultural heritage sites, particularly given the area's importance to local inhabitants and tourists alike. The consideration is not purely cultural, as the area also contains elements such as the train station, the commercial district, some of Luxor's main hotels (including the Al Mahattah, Al Aksor, and Winter Palace Hotels) in addition to the Luxor Temple, and the Mosque and Plaza of Aboul Haggag. This area may therefore be said to be of fundamental religious and functional importance to local inhabitants (see Fig. 10.5).

The landscape design of Al Mahattah Street and Aboul Haggag Plaza communicates with the surrounding heritage sites in two ways, namely:

- The site boundaries avoid encroachment on the Luxor Temple and instead run into it smoothly, offering easy access from the city centre (Ashour 2007). This also serves to enhance the visual vista from the end of Al Mahattah Street down to Aboul Haggag Plaza, by minimising the number of trees, only planting palm trees (i.e. long trunks and no lower foliage) and thus preserving panoramic views of the site. The high artificial lighting, however – designed to enhance the view of the Luxor Temple – has served to turn the plaza into a very bright space, in defiance of the designer's proclaimed objectives (Plate 10.13).

- Through changing the open space in front of Aboul Haggag Mosque from a public garden into a tiled open space. This, besides enhancing the panoramic view which is sought by eliminating the landscaping obstacles, availed the local population a new space to be potentially used for a wide variety of activities such as public ceremonies, parties and other cultural events (Ashour 2007).

In short, the project's design managed to blend heritage and cityscape by offering what we might call an "Entertainment Open Space", achieving the "unique extensive tourism zone" by enhancing the distinctive architectural character of the temple of Luxor.

Public Perception of the Built Environment Surrounding Aboul Haggag's Mosque

As stated above, public perception of the heritage of Aboul Haggag is inseparable from the public perception of the built environment. Al Dorah and its spatial patterns are key to understanding the local inhabitants' inherited image of the site. We assessed the nature of this public perception by setting questions that also explored the interviewees' opinions of recent urban development that replaced the original plaza gardens with a large open space. They were also asked their opinions concerning the

[4] It also encompasses the agricultural and ecological systems upon which the entire region depends for its survival, a topic beyond the reach of the current paper.

importance of local and foreign tourism throughout the year, and whether they viewed recent increases in touristic activity as being positive or negative.

Responses to questions concerning the new developments can be categorised under two main headings:

- **The adequacy of the place**: referring to physical condition. Most interviewees mentioned the new services that became available to the public after these developments, as well as the visual embellishment and cleaning of the place as a whole. However, the "cultured" among them pointed to one caveat, namely the physical wedge that was created between the general public and this spiritually loaded, traditional environment.

- **The uniqueness of the place:** referring to sensitivity towards potential spiritual impacts. The religious importance of the place would inevitably have prompted fears that changes thereto would prompt the breakdown of spiritual relationships with the site. Indeed, many respondents expressed their concerns that governmental/authority development trends would interfere with the traditional ceremonial aspects of Mawlid Aboul Haggag, particularly the Al Dorah procession.

Tourism is considered to be the primary source of income to most of the inhabitants of Luxor. Accordingly, all economic development endeavours have the increase of touristic activities as their main objective. The responses of the interviewees and our personal observations regarding this particular issue may be tackled under two main headings, namely:

- **Religious Tourism:** all the respondents consider the Mawlid of Aboul Haggag to be a major destination for Egyptian tourists, attracting around one million visitors in 2010 (Salama and Hamed 2012). They also consider it to be a good forum for the sale of indigenous handicrafts such as pottery, wickerwork and weaving products, and that the local Haggagies should be entrusted with trade coordination to ensure its smooth blending with other activities during the Mawlid. It is notable that repeat tourists seem to be aware of the religious importance of Aboul Haggag and his Mawlid.

- **Foreign Tourism:** although all of the respondents confirmed the unquestionable importance of foreign tourism to their local economy, many expressed their concern that Aboul Haggag, his Mosque, and his Mawlid not be commodified. There was a general consensus that foreign tourists are always welcome, as long as they observe appropriate solemnity, and that the adequate respect to his cultural and religious heritage is duly accorded.

CONCLUDING REMARKS

The present paper calls for all future Master Plans involving the Historical District of the City of Luxor to consider the Mawlid of Aboul Haggag Al Aksory to be one of the cornerstones of the city's intangible cultural heritage, worthy of preservation and protection given its crucial role in local people's perception of their city's cultural identity. It is reasonable to assert that the tangible and intangible elements comprise a linking pin between ancient and modern populations, which is, indeed, best exemplified by the similarities between the symbolism of the Mawlid and that of the Opet Festival. Official validation of this underlying cultural continuum could act as a focus for local people's sense of pride, identity and belonging to their city.

In order to appreciate the significance of the Mawlid of Aboul Haggag, it was necessary for us to delve deep into the saint's geographical origin and religious convictions, the folk stories linking him to Tarzah, and the legacy he left the people of Luxor. We have also examined the Mawlid's unique intricacies, notably the Al Dorah and Al Maḫmal, which are deeply rooted in Luxor society in spite of the lack of 'scientific' evidence to support the modern populations' claimed link to ancient (i.e. Pharaonic) groups.

We have assessed the local people's perceptions of their cultural heritage by interviewing them about the Mawlid of Aboul Haggag, and the built environment where it is celebrated. This approach revealed a range of spiritual, social, symbolic, nostalgic and functional significances, of which the spiritual and social significances are the most important. The Al Dorah and Al Maḫmal processions have been singled out as the most important aspects of the festival, and the dominant mental image whenever the Mawlid is brought up in conversation

The convenient grouping of these five elements should not be considered to be finite, as they have all become conflated through a long, shared history, and intertwined in such a way as to render their mutual influences completely opaque to the modern observer. Despite – or perhaps because of – this, the cultural heritage of Aboul Haggag vividly demonstrates how tangible and intangible components may form a homogeneous blend that defies any attempt of demarcation or separability. It also shows that efforts to conserve and ameliorate tangible heritage has been successful in functional terms, but that this has been achieved at the expense of the intangible heritage, which may be seriously affected or even destroyed by such activities. The case of the Plaza of Aboul Haggag is a clear example of this conundrum, for while it was a benevolent attempt to serving the tourist interest by emphasising the panoramic view of the Luxor Temple from Mahattah Street, this was achieved at the expense of the underlying intangible heritage of Aboul Haggag and his Mawlid.

We sincerely hope that any future endeavours to reconceptualise or rethink the urban development fabric of Luxor's Aboul Haggag district will take into serious consideration the intangible heritage dimension of this city's Patron Saint and his Mawlid, particularly its crown jewel: Al Dorah and Al Maḫmal. In this vein, we find no better epilogue to our paper than the following quotation:

> *"The particular heritage and collective memory of each locality or community is irreplaceable and an important foundation for development, both now and in the future".*
>
> (ICOMOS, International Cultural Tourism Charter, 1999).

References

Ashour, M. A. Undated. The concept of Urban Landscaping for the Historical cities. The study of a case for the development of (Mahata and Souq) streets, Down Town Luxor City, *Expériences de réhabilitation urbaine et territorial en Méditerranée.* Cairo.

Al Edfawy, K. A. F. 1914. *Al Talai' Al Said Al Gamei' le Asma' al Fodale' wal Rowah bi A'laal Said.* Cairo: Al Gammaliah Printing House.

Al Haggagy, A. G. A. F. 2009. *Luxor at the Time of Aboul Haggag.* Cairo: A.G.A.F., Al Haggagy Publ..

Al Haggagy, M. A. 1968. *Aboul Haggag al Aksory: The Sufi Seer.* Cairo: El Tadawon Publ. House.

Al Zobaidy, M. 1974. *Tag Al A'rous Min Sharh Gawaher al Quamous.* Cairo: Kuwaity Information Ministry Publications.

Creswell, K. A. C. 1952. *The Muslim Architecture of Egypt.* Oxford: Oxford University Press.

Gabriel, A., Ashraf, B., and Jonathan L. 2001. *The Comprehensive Development of the City of Luxor Project, Egypt – Final Structure Plan, Volume I – Technical Report, Executive Summary.* Cairo: Abt Associates Inc.

Hassan, F. A. 2008. Heritage for development: Concepts and strategic approaches, in F. A. Hassan, A. De Trafford, & M. Youssef (eds) *Cultural Heritage and Development in the Arab World.* Alexandria: Bibliotheca Alexandrina, pp. 13-51.

Ibn' Abbad, A. M. Undated. *Al Mafakher Al A'liah li Ma'ather al Shaziliah.* Cairo: Dar al Kotob al-Masrya, Manuscript no. 430.

ICOMOS. 1999. *The Burra Charter for Places of Cultural Significances.* Burra: ICOMOS.

Legrain, G. 1914. *Louqsor sans les Pharaons.* Paris/Bruxelles: Vromant.

Macpherson, J. W. 1941. *The Mawlids of Egypt.* Cairo: N.M. Press Ltd.

Websites:

Abdel 'Aty, A. 2012. http://Atbara.net/forum/index.php?topic=58190;wap2

(Last consulted, May 5th, 2012, 8pm).

Aga Khan 2010. *Architects Record, Document B, 3681.*EGY. http://archnet.org/library/sites/one-site.jsp?site_id=16725

(Last consulted, April 20th, 2012)

Al Youssoufy, M.A. 2012. http://sawtakonline.com/forum/showthread.php?2985

(Last consulted, May 3rd, 2012, 1pm).

Bitar, E. I. 2012. http://malekat-sharq.blogspot.com

(Last consulted, May 3rd, 2012, 1:35pm).

Salama H., Hamed M. 2012.

http://today.almasryalyoum.com/article2.aspx?ArticleID=29550&IssueID=414

(Last consulted, April 16th, 2012, 5pm).

Documentary Films:

Chambliss, C. 2008. *Annual Moulid of Youssef Aboul Hajj'aj: Ziyarat el Muzamzameen from Qus to El Uqub,* documentary film created by Cassandra Chambliss, original video file: abd_080814_vid.DV_060_061.

CNRS 1981. *Le Mawlid d' Aboul Haggag,* Documentary film created by Alain Bellod, script by Denis Gril and produced by Annick Demeule for SERDDAV, Paris.

Wickett, E. 1990. *For Those Who Sail to Heaven.* Icarus Films, Documentary film created, directed and produced by Elizabeth Wickett.

Persons interviewed:

I- Haggagies or persons related to Aboul Haggag Mosque:

Walid Aboul Haggag, 35 years old, front desk Officer at the Luxor Jolie Ville Hotel, 5-3-2012, 2:30pm, face-to-face.

Mahmoud Ismail Abou Bakr, 45 yrs old, Imam of Aboul Haggag Mosque, 4-3-2012, 7pm, face-to-face.

Haj Mostafa Galal Al Din Mostafa, 62 yrs old, Retired Haggagi, 8-3-2012, 10:30pm, face-to-face.

Hossam Al Dine Aboul Haggag, 31 yrs old, Member of the Haggagy Youth Group, 9-3-2012, 10pm, face-t-face.

Mahmoud Youssef, 45 yrs. old, Luxor International Hospital Employee, 8-3-2012, 9pm, face-to-face.

Mostafa Yousry, 48 yrs. old, Aboul Haggag Mosque Janitor, 4-3-2012, 12 noon, face-to-face.

II- Random Luxor Inhabitants and Artists:

Madd Hamad Nasr Soudany, 32 yrs old, Teaching Assistant at the Luxor School of Fine Arts, 24-4-2012, by phone.

Asem Abd El Hamid Ali, 40 yrs old, Writer and Novelist, 24-4-2012, by phone.

Ammar Abou Bakr Al Saddiq, 32 yrs old, Teaching Assistant at the Luxor School of Fine Arts, 24-4-2012, by phone.

Arafa Salah Al Dine, 18 yrs. old, Soldier holding diploma, 3-3-2012, 8:30pm, face-to-face.

Ashraf, 20 yrs. old, Worker, 3-3-2012, 7:30pm, face-to-face.

III- Expert Egyptologist:

Dr Michael Jones, ARCE, Cairo, 9-4-20012, 12 noon, face-to-face.

Plates

Plate 10.1: Aboul Hagag's Mosque on top of the church, in the middle of Luxor Temple.

Plate 10.2: The Zikr performance.

Plate 10.3: Al Mermah.

Plate 10.4: Al Mermah.

Plate 10.5: Al tahteeb performance.

Plate 10.6: The kettle drums following the simulacra of the tomb of Aboul Haggag.

Plate 10.7-8: The Barques in the Opet (depicted on the wall of the Luxor Temple) and Aboul Haggag Festivals.

Plate 10.9: The Dorah procession, 2009.

Plate 10.10: Women preparing food for the festival.

Plate 10.11: The minaret with the obelisk as the most popular symbolic features of the place.

Plate 10.12: Political events appear to be a new function in the Plaza after Jan 25th revolution in Egypt.

Plate 10.13: Night panoramic view of the Plaza.

Plate 10.14: The entrance to the Mosque of Aboul Haggag.

Plate 10.15: The minaret of Mosque of Aboul Haggag integrated into Luxor Temple.

Plate 10.16: The integration of the Mosque of Aboul Haggag with the Luxor Temple.

Appendix I

The Questionnaires and their Analyses

Essence of the Questions addressed to the Haggagies

1- What does Mawlid Aboul Haggag represent to you?

2- Do you consider Mawlid Aboul Haggag an important part of Luxor's cultural heritage identity?

3- What is the thing that most attracts you to Mawlid Aboul Haggag?

4- What is the thing that bothers you the most in Mawlid Aboul Haggag?

5- What do you think of the upgrading of the square in front of Aboul Haggag's Mosque?

6- What are your suggestions for the amelioration of the area surrounding Aboul Haggag's Mosque?

7- What is your opinion regarding the visitors who come over to visit Aboul Haguag from towns and villages away from Luxor?

8- Would you rather have the Mawlid of Aboul Haguag only limited to the Haggagies?

9- What do you think of the idea of having foreigners attend the Mawlid of Aboul Haggag?

10- Do you agree to having the number of foreigners assisting the Mawlid of Aboul Haggag increase, decrease or stay the same?

11- Do you agree to the increase in marketing campaigns for the Mawlid of Aboul Haggag to encourage more Sufis around the country to attend? And do you agree to the extension of these efforts to cover foreign potential visitors as well?

12- Do you object to having street vendors during the Mawlid of Aboul Haggag, particularly those commercializing typical folk artifacts for which Luxor is famous? And which particular products would you rather see being sold to visitors during the Mawlid?

13- Do you favor the printing of a brochure about Aboul Haggag, his life, teachings, and legacy? And would you rather have it distributed to the visitors for a fee or free of charge?

14- What are your suggestions to raise the number of visitors to Luxor to attend the Mawlid of Aboul Haggag?

15- What, in your opinion, are the services and facilities missing during the Mawlid of Aboul Haggag that should be made available to the visitors to render the Mawlid more successful and attractive to them?

P.S. We are aware of the fact that these questions are more than what we need for the present paper, but they were needed for another paper for one of the authors, as well.

Essence of the Questions Addressed to some of the General Public of Luxor

1- Do you consider the Mawlid of Aboul Haggag a cultural heritage event that is worth preserving?

- Yes - No if No, why?

2- Would you be upset if the government decided to call off the Mawlid of Aboul Haggag?

- Yes - No if No, why?

3- What are the activities whose absence would spoil the Mawlid of Aboul Haggag? In particular:

- Al Zhikr
- The Hadrahs
- Prayers
- Religious chanting and the Prophet's panegyrics
- Al Tahteeb
- Al Mermah
- Al Dorah and Al Mahmal
- The Procession of the Barques
- Al Muzamzameen
- Al Rifaiah entrance to the Mawlid
- The Children's Swings
- Serving Kabab Aboul Haguag
- Rifle-aiming
- …

4- Do you frequently visit the Plaza of Aboul Haggag's Mosque?

- Yes - No if No, why?

5- Do you like the remodeling of the Plaza in front of Aboul Haggag or do you prefer the garden that existed before?

6- Do you agree to turning Mawlid Aboul Haggag into an international festival?

- Yes - No if No, why?

7- In your opinion, is the touristic infrastructure in Luxor adequate and sufficient to support such a festival?

- Yes - No if No, what are the missing things

Samples from the Coding of Participants' Responses Concerning the Significances of Aboul Haggag's Heritage

Waleed Al-Haggagy	- Avails an opportunity for : social gatherings, partaking in Festivities ,exhibiting popular feelings and traditions, joining the Dorah -Mosque and Temple are one
Mahmoud Ismail AbouBakr	Religious significance of Abou lHaggag and the Moslem Saints
Hossam Eldine Mahmoud El Kady El Haggagy	-Luxor's identity -Importance of the Dorah and Festival -Opportunity for socialization and solidarity -Significance of building the Mosque on a church inside the Luxor Temple
Arafa Salah Al-Dine	- Religious significance -Importance of Aboul Haggag and the descendants of the Prophet (pbuh)
Mahmoud Youssef Aboul Haggag	-Historical Heritage -The community activities of the Mawlid - Significance of the Dorah
Madd Hamad Nasr Soudany	- Opportunity for the local inhabitants to deal with Ancient Egyptian temples from a religious belief standpoint - Importance Al Dorah and Al Mahmal - Fascination with the Tarzah folkloric story
Mostafa Youssry	- Cultura lHeritage significance of Abou lHaggag and his plaza

Samples from the Coding of the Participants' Responses Concerning the Significances of Aboul Haggag's Heritage (cont.)

Assem Abdel Hamid Aly	- Linking Egyptian Popular Sufism with Ancient Egyptian Heritage as represented by the Luxor Temple - The Dorah/Opet festivals parallel - The coexistence of the Mosque, Church and Temple in the same sacred site
Ammar Abou Bakr Al Saddiq	- Significance of the Mawlid activities especially the Dorah and Mahmal - Rapel between the minaret and the obelisk - Symbology of the Mawlid's various rituals.

Samples from the Coding of Participants' Responses Concerning the Built Environment Context.

Waleed Al-Haggagy	-The urban development of the plaza helps in providing new services -Aboul Haggag Plaza needs modification to suit the mawlid's events - Both the Mosque and the Plaza receive tourists
Mahmoud Ismail Abou Bakr	-Imperativeness of development -Aesthetic amelioration of the Plaza is a positive point -Absence of services in the Plaza -Suggested plan is not appropriate for the activities of the Sufi Tariquahs -Tourism is an important economic activity in Luxor
Arafa Salah Al-Dine	-Importance of developing the Plaza -Fear from the effect of developing the Plaza on the events of the Mawlid -No objection to tourists attending the Mawlid
Ashraf	-Negative effect of urban development on the spiritual aspects of the Mosque and Mawlid
Madd Hamad Nasr Soudany	-The Garden was more appealing to the people -The new development attracted new categories of visitors with different cultural backgrounds -Aboul Haggag's Heritage should not be comodified or commercialized
Assem Abdul Hamid Aly	-The present development neither engulfs nor is appropriate to the spirit of the Mawlid and the Sufi heritage -Tourists are welcomed as long as they appreciate and respect the spiritual importance of the place - The local authorities do not attribute the adequate importance to the Mawlid as part of Luxor's identity
Ammar Abou Bakr Al-Saddiq	-Restoration of the Mosque was a good thing -Mosque is more important than the temple or plaza -Development of the Plaza unfit to particularity of the place linking the past to the present -Tourism is important but focuses only on the Temple and ignores Aboul Haggag's heritage

Figure 10.1: The Dorah Procession.

	Waled	Mahmoud	Hossam	Arafa	Youssef	Medhamad	Ammar	Assem	Mostafa
Spiritual significance	5	4.8	4.2	4.6	4.3	5	5	5	4.6
Social significance	5	4.4	4.8	4.5	4.7	3.8	4.5	3.2	3.5
Symbolic significance	4.5	3.2	4	3.5	3.2	4.8	4.8	4.5	3.5
Memorial significance	3	3.2	3.2	3	3.1	3.4	3.3	3.2	3.5
Functional significance	3.1	2.1	3	2.1	2.2	2.2	4	2.2	2.2

Figure 10.2: Ordinal values attributed to the participants' responses (from 1 to 5).

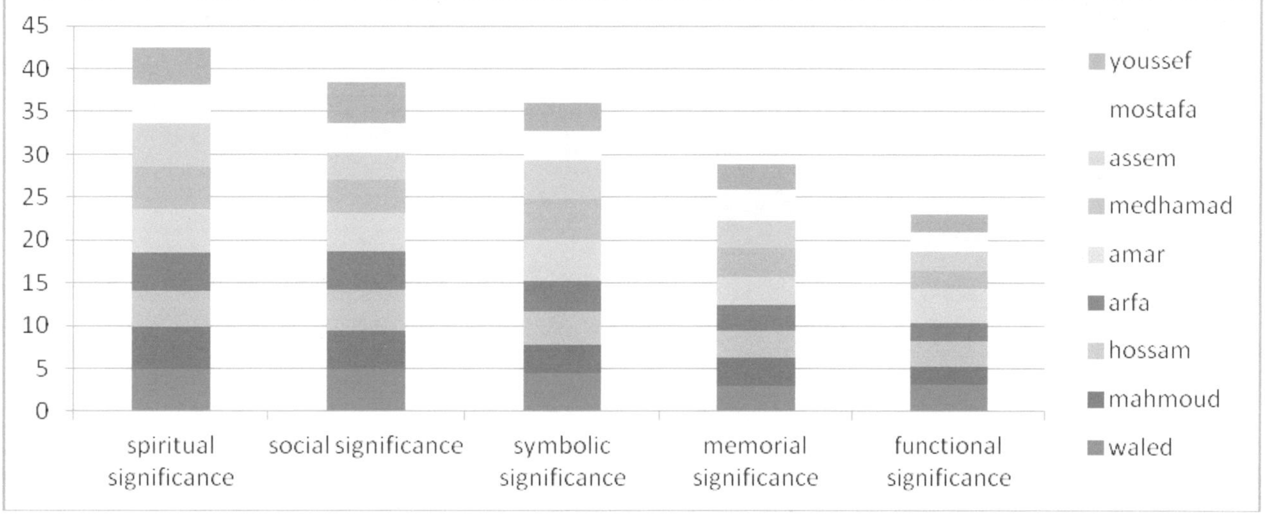

Figure 10.3: Comparison of the different significances among the interviewees.

Appendix II

Aboul Haggag Plaza and Mahattah Street Urban Development Project

Proposed by ArchPlan Office

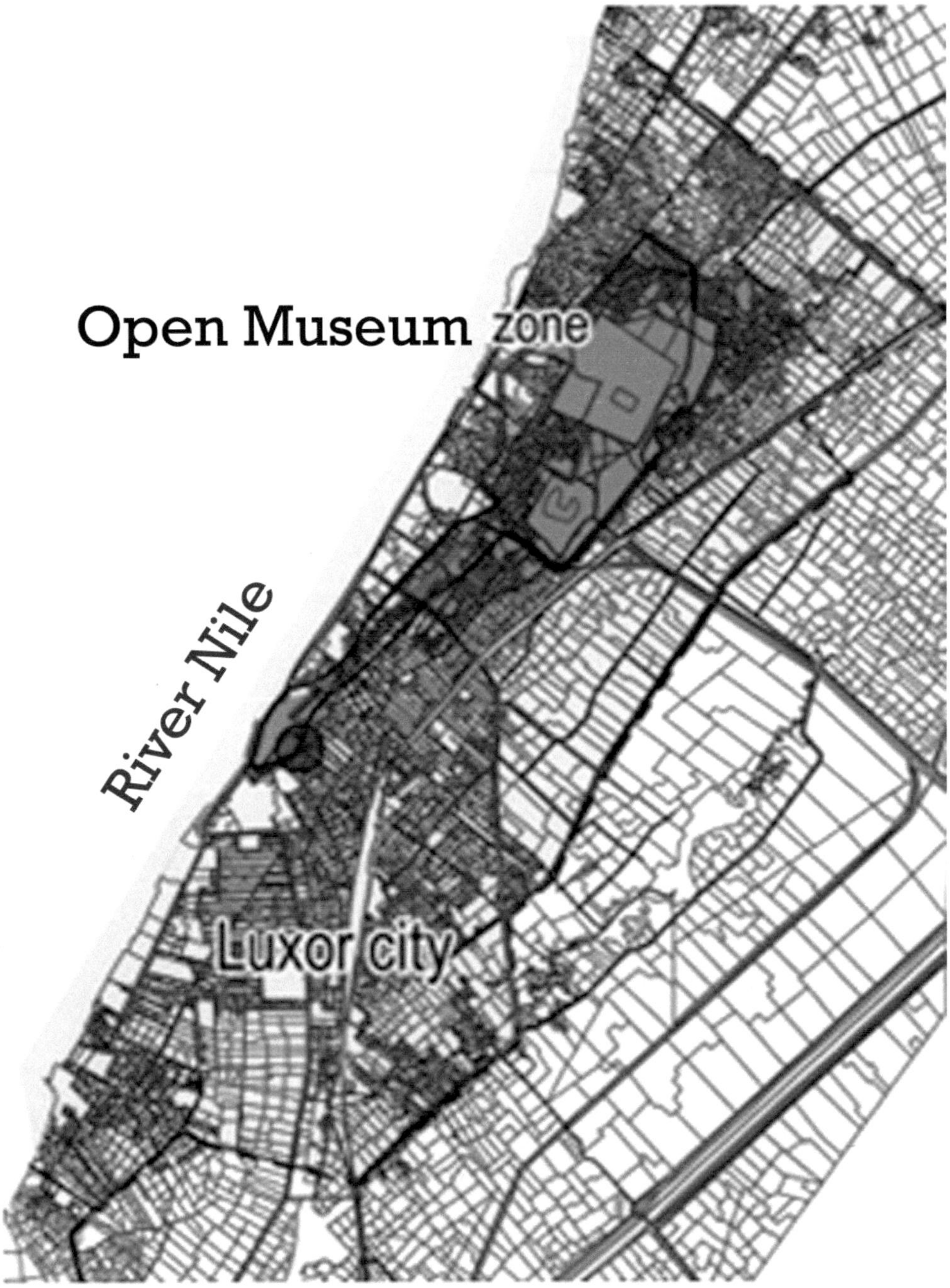

Figure 10.4: The open museum district on the Eastern Bank of Luxor.

Figure 10.5: Aerial view of the project site location.

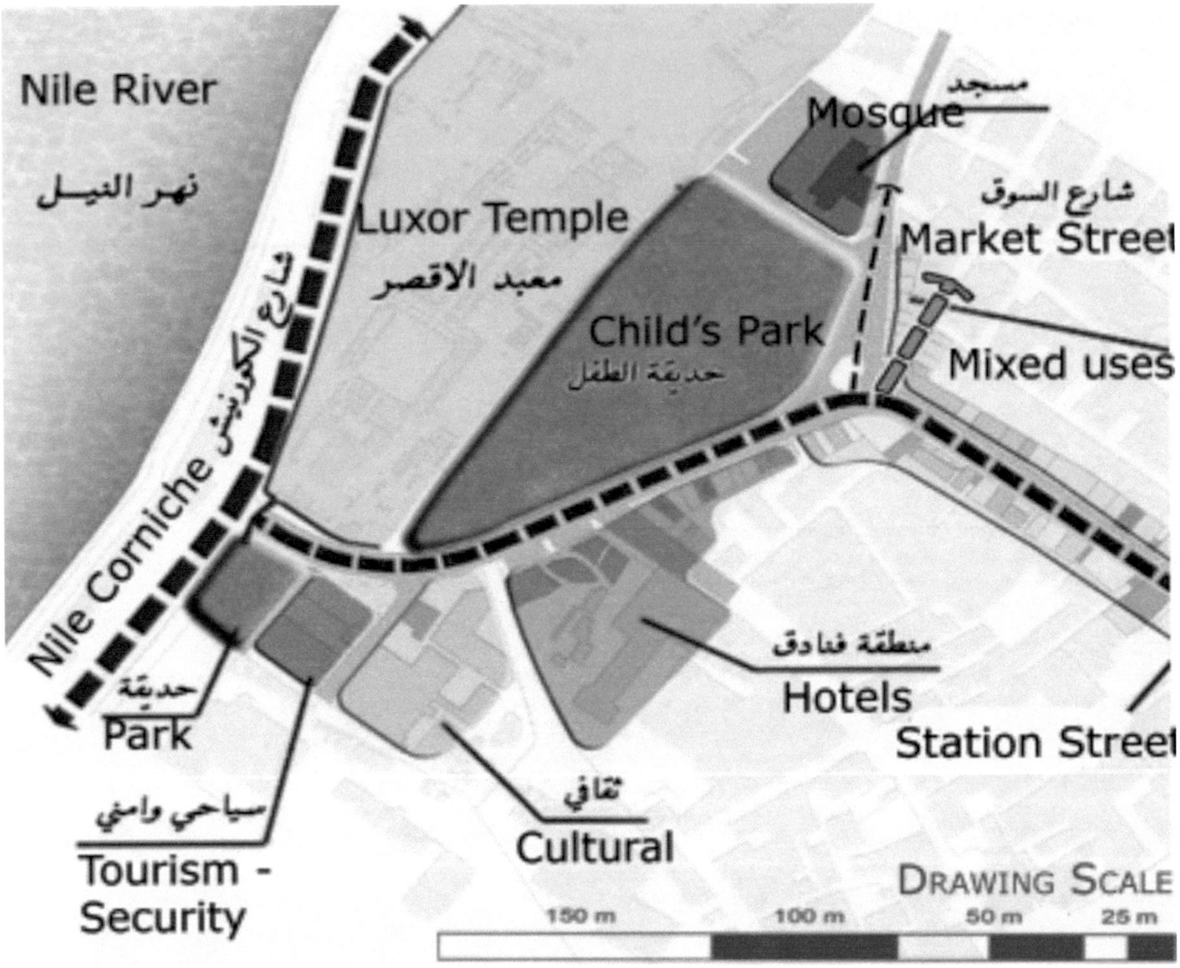

Figure 10.6: Land use analysis of the project.

Figure 10.7: Urban analysis of the project.

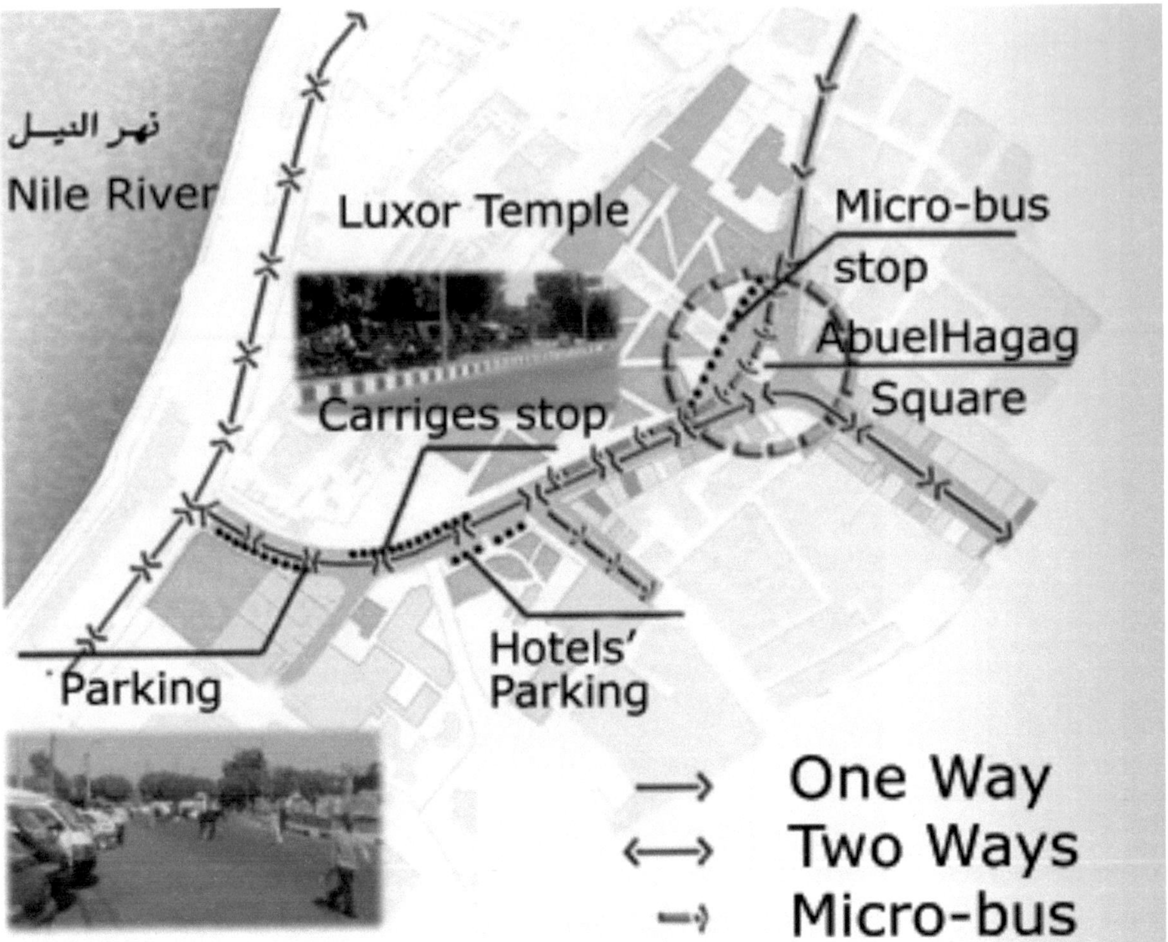

Figure 10.8: Traffic analysis for the project.

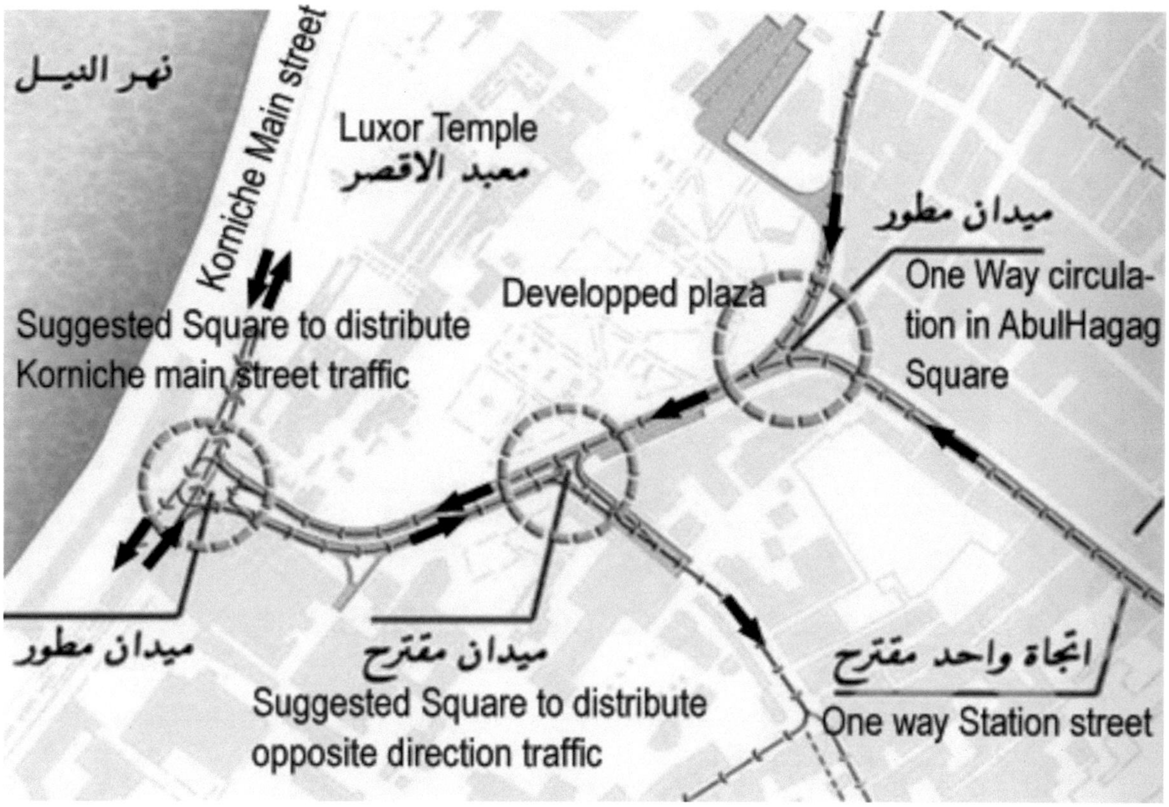

Figure 10.9: Traffic strategy for the project.

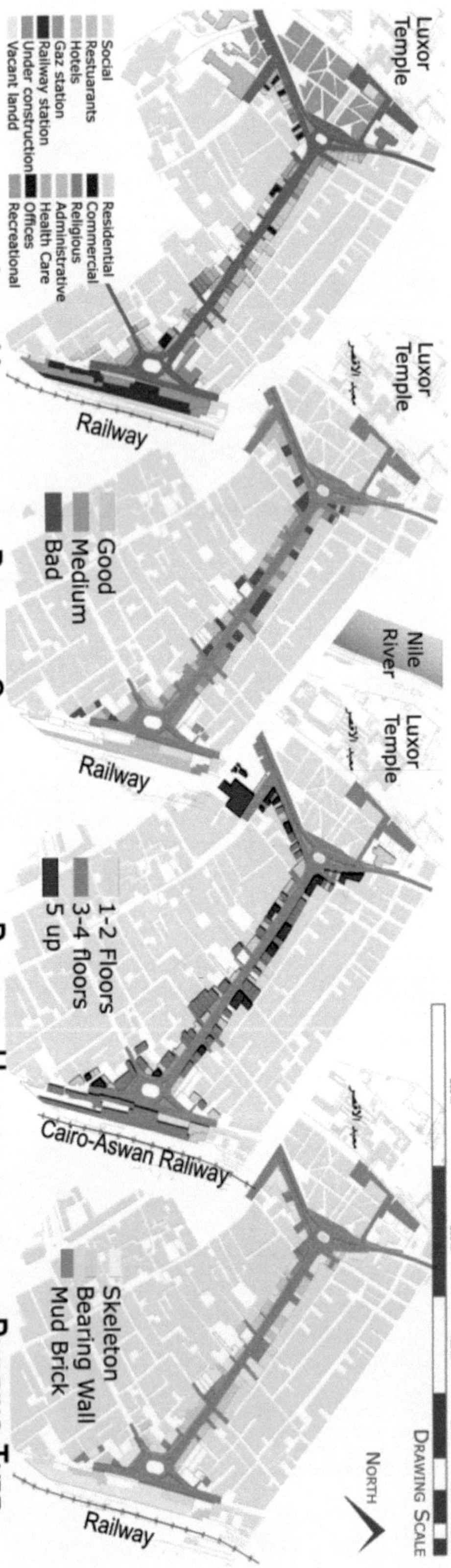

Figure 10.10: Urban analysis of the Mahattah Street.

Chapter 11

Where Did the Nile Harbours Go?

Emad el-Khalil

Abstract

Herodotus described Egypt as the gift of the Nile, as the river not only allowed agriculture to be practiced along its banks, but facilitated ease of movement via boats from one end of the country to the other. As such, the River Nile has also been described as the highway of ancient Egypt. The agricultural produce, along with stone and other goods were transported along the Nile. Each major settlement would have had a harbour or quay so that larger ships could dock and unload their cargoes.

Although several harbours have been located on the Red Sea and Mediterranean coasts, only a handful of Nile harbours are currently known. This flies in the face of historical references to numerous harbours – especially Ptolemaic and Roman examples – although it is probable that the Nile flooding regime has hidden most examples.

The finding of a Late Period to Roman embankment and quays at Karnak due to a site management project is hopefully the first of many such sites that will illuminate Egypt's riverine trade. Moreover, it illustrates the importance of undertaking archaeological impact assessments and conducting research as part of any cultural heritage management projects.

Introduction

Harbours on the Mediterranean Coast (Alexandria) and the Read Sea Coast (*Arsinoë* [Suez], Mersa/Wadi Gawasis, Marsa Nakari, Wadi el-Jarf, *Berenike* [Berenice] and *Myos Hormos* [Quseir al-Qadim]) are well known. These harbours range in date from the 4th Dynasty (Wadi el-Jarf) to the Middle Kingdom (Mersa/Wadi Gawasis) to the Ptolemaic to Late Antique periods (*Arsinoë*, Marsa Nakari, *Berenike* and *Myos Hormos*). The information gained from these harbours has helped to understand not only the evolution of seaborne trade (Blue & Peacock 2006; Bourdon 1925; Facey 2004; Fattovich 2012; Mumford 2012; Seeger & Sidebotham 2005; Tallet 2012; Thomas 2012; Tomber 2012), but also how it connected with the Nile Valley. There are historical and archaeological data indicating that the Red Sea coastal ports were used to launch expeditions to Punt, or to circumnavigate the Arabian Peninsula to reach sites in Iraq, Iran and even India.

However, there have been very few river harbours or quays found, other than those at Karnak (Boraik 2010a; 2010b), Unas' harbour at Saqqara (Šichan 2011), and Birket Habu (Kemp & O'Connor 1974) and the scant remains of a few others (Šichan 2011). Attempts to locate historically-attested harbours have mostly been unsuccessful: the great New Kingdom harbour of Perunefer may be at Tell el Dab'a (Avaris), given that riverfront installations have been located there (Bietak 2005; Herbich & Forstner-Müller 2013; Forstner-Müller 2014). However, this assertion is unsafe, for although there may indeed be a quay there (Jeffreys 2006), there is nothing specific to attest to it's being Perunefer, which could equally be located at Memphis.

The lack of floodplain settlements is generally attributed to the Nile's high rates of sedimentation, and it would be easy to assume that the dearth of harbours is also thus caused. However, settlements are often uncovered, and although the general westward movement of the Nile may account for the disappearance of harbours located at places such as Memphis, this does not account for the almost complete absence of Nile harbours. This may be partially an artefact of research designs, which tend to focus upon sites located in the low desert rather than on the floodplain. Floodplain archaeology is more difficult, not least because pumping equipment may need to be used.

Textual evidence suggests that there were many harbours located along the riverfront, and logic suggests that every major city would have had at least a small quay to service the Nile riverine transport system. Nile harbours were located not only in Upper Egypt, but also in the Delta; it is not infeasible that excavation of large Ptolemaic/Roman tell sites may yet produce evidence of a major Nile harbour.

River Transport in Roman Egypt

The importance of riverine transport to Egypt needs no emphasis. From the earliest times, river transport played a major role in the country's economic integrity and its social and political unity (Hassan 1997: 62-

3), and the Nile remained the spine of the transport system in Egypt until the early 20th century. Under the Roman administration, riverine transport acquired particular significance as the riverboats carried commodities that were considered to be of great value to the empire's capital. The fact that there was no part of the valley more than c.15 km from the Nile – and that the majority of towns were spaced within a half-day's sailing of one another (Bagnall 1993: 18-19) – would have contributed significantly to the abundance of river harbours and the regularity of boats travelling up and down the Nile. The logistics of travel were facilitated by the nature of the river, which runs 1200 km from Aswan to the Mediterranean without any substantial obstacles save for sediment shoals. Moreover, the river continued to be navigable in both directions during high floods, at which point the protruding rocks and shallows were covered with water. The water flowed from south to north, enabling river vessels to drift northwards, while boats sailing upstream were aided by prevailing northerly and north-westerly winds (Said 1993a: 45; Mohamed 2001: 107-118).

Documents from the Roman Period attest that various luxurious commodities were regularly transported by riverboats between towns and villages along the Valley and the Delta. However, the most vital resource carried by the riverboats Egyptian barley and wheat. During the Early Imperial Period, Egypt provided Rome with one third of its annual grain requirements; between 135,000 and 150,000 tons of it travelled annually through the Nile to Alexandria, where it was transhipped by grain-carriers to the Roman harbours of Ostia and Portus, then up the Tiber to Rome (Rickman 1980b: 263; Lewis 1983: 165; Casson 1984: 70-86; 1995: 297-299). The internal transport system was rigged to the processing system: grain was transported from the village threshing floors to local storage facilities, then to the central granaries of the *nomes* where it was taxed. It was then transported to designated river harbours to be loaded onto boats and barges that would carry it to the central granaries of *Neapolis* at Alexandria (Husselman 1952: 70; Rickman 1971: 300, 1980a: 121; Lewis 1983: 115-6). Various types of vessels with capacities that ranged from 70 artab up to 18000 artab (from 2 to 500 tons) were employed in carrying grain to Alexandria (Lewis 1983: 142). The need for large boats was also felt strongly in the Roman mining trade, from the quarries of the Eastern Desert, which produced highly valued grey granodiorite and imperial porphyry (Peacock 1992: 5-7; 2002: 426- 427). The main sources for these stones were the quarries of *Mons Porphyrites*, c.70 km north-west of Hurghada, and *Mons Claudianus*, c.50 km to the south of *Mons Porphyrites* (Peacock 2002: 431- 432). Most of this stone took the form of roughed-out columns, which were transported along a network of routes connecting the quarries and the Nile; the stone was loaded at the harbours of *Coptos* (Qift) and *Kainopolis* (Qena) then transported to Alexandria where it was transferred to seagoing vessels.

The river harbours also served as nodes on the luxury imports transport system, running from Red Sea sites such as *Myos Hormos* (Quseir al-Qadim) and *Berenike* (Berenice) (Blue & Peacock 2006), to across the Delta and India, Arabia and East Africa (Tomber 2012). Spices, incense, silks and gems were routed through the Delta to Rome via Alexandria, while the same nodes were also receiving and distributing Mediterranean and Egyptian goods such as wine, fine pottery and glass destined for trade with the East (Lewis 1983: 140; Casson 1989: 11-14; 94; Peacock 1993: 231, 1999: 5; Young 2001: 45). Internal trade was also catered for, and relied heavily upon the harbour system; transported items include papyri, textiles, foodstuffs, glass, amphorae, timber, clothing, furniture and even beasts of burden such as camels and horses (Lindsay 1968: 110-143, 220-231; Lewis 1974: 101-2; Minnen 1986; Bagnall 1993: 37; Empereur 1993; Nenna *et al.* 2000).

While we know this system was in operation, however, archaeological evidence is rarely forthcoming. Only very limited evidence for Graeco-Roman waterfront installations has been discovered at any town along the Nile Valley, and the only archaeologically known waterfront harbour of this period is at Karnak.

The River's Flood Regime

To fully appreciate the localisation and function of Nile harbours, we must examine them in the light of the Nile annual flood regime. Before 20th century dam construction projects in Lower Nubia, the Nile went through a regular regime of annual flooding. The water level rose and fell, inundating the floodplain along its length and depositing immense quantities of silt and sediments, which continually reshaped the riverbanks and floodplain. The water level would rise in June, following the rainy season in Ethiopia. By the end of September or early October it reached its maximum high level in the Delta, inundating its floodplain and basins to depths of 1-3 metres. The flood would then remain stable for about a month, and then it started falling rapidly, returning to its normal level by December or January, reaching its lowest point by June (Butzer 1976: 18; Said 1993b: 96-7; Hassan 1997).

On the basis of data collected between 1874 and 1899, it has been calculated that the river moved around 110 million tons of suspended matter (measured at Wadi Halfa), only 58 million tons of which reached Cairo; the remaining 52 million tons was deposited over the Upper Egyptian floodplain between those two points (Ball 1939: 120-136). This annual accumulation of Nile sediments resulted in a continuous increase of the thickness of the Nile mud in the valley and the Delta, which varied from time to time and from place to place according to the geomorphic characteristics of the floodplain and the flood regime. Nonetheless, an acceptable average rate of sediment accumulation for the past two millennia is 1.2mm per year (Hamdan 1980: 211; Said 1981: 74-5).

Between Aswan and Cairo, the Nile valley has an average width of about 15 km (Mohamed 2001: 120-2). However, the river tends to occupy the eastern side of its valley; areas such as Minya and Beni Suef have large river plains on the west side of the channel, and the eastern side of the channel abuts the desert. The river therefore tends to deposit its sediments towards the west. The sedimentation process is complicated by differential bank building, high velocity flood rates and uneven attrition, resulting in the river taking different shifts along its course (Said 1993a: 80). The Nile has undergone a general trend towards the east during the past two millennia, by as much as 3 km in some areas. Many of the villages and settlements that were located on the banks of the river in Dynastic, Hellenistic and Roman times are now several kilometres inland; the riverside sites of Al-Qusiyah, Al-Ashmunein (*Hermopolis)* and *Memphis* are now 4 km, 8 km and 2 km west of the Nile channel, respectively (Said 1993b: 61-3). The fact that the Nile deposited most of its sediments on the western side of its plain, and that its course shifted eastward, had significant impact on the construction and eventual decline of ancient Nile harbours.

THE RIVER HARBOURS

Herodotus (2.97) visited Egypt in the fifth century BC, and noted the seminal importance of the Nile: '*When the Nile overflows, the whole country is converted into a sea, and the towns, which alone remain above water, look like the islands in the Aegean*'. His observations were echoed by Strabo (17.1.4), who visited Egypt in 25 AD: '...*but the rising of the Nile, the whole country is under water and becomes a lake, except the settlements, and these are situated on natural hills or artificial mounds and contain cities of considerable size and villages, which when viewed from afar resemble islands*'. Even in historical periods, therefore, towns and villages close to the Nile had to be built on relatively high grounds to avoid being inundated during the flood, while their related harbours were situated on the riverbanks and thus susceptible to the annual depositions of Nile sediments. Therefore, Nile harbours generally consisted of two parts: the towns and the waterfronts. Towns were where the business took place, while the waterfronts handled the movement of people and goods.

Figure 11.1: The harbour before the temple of Amun-Ra at Karnak. One of many representations of T-shaped harbours in Ancient Egypt (after Jones 1995: 81, Fig. 72).

We have no reason to believe that ordinary river harbours in Roman Egypt were substantially different from those of earlier periods. Moreover, there is no evidence that the Roman administration in Egypt had any significant contribution in the building and maintenance of such facilities. Alternatively, local people who were regularly using the ports were probably responsible for building and maintaining them.

There is very little iconographic evidence of river harbours that could be attributed to the Hellenistic or Roman Periods. Examining representations of river harbours from earlier periods, might give us some idea about how the Egyptians conceived such harbours, which could reflect on the way they were built during the Graeco-Roman Period, and probably even later. There are many representations from ancient Egypt of harbours that took the form of rectangular basins excavated inland and joined to the river by canals. They are mostly associated with temples or royal residences (Marcus 1990; Jones 1995: 80-83).

Probably the best-documented artificial harbour of this type is at the palace-city of Amenhotep III (1390-1352) at western Thebes, known as Birket Habu (Kemp & O'Connor 1974). The basin is about 2.5 km by 1.0 km, more than 6.0 m deep, and was connected to the river by a navigable canal (Kemp & O' Connor 1974: 112, 126; Marcus 1990: 20-22). The basin is currently about 2.5 km west of the Nile, although it was presumably once much closer if we consider the sedimentation issues outlined above (Kemp & O' Connor 1974: 123-4). The fact that the original architects felt it justified to excavate an inland basin with a canal system linking it to the river illustrates just how important harbours must have been. In a scene depicted at the Tomb of May (c.1365 BC) at Tell El- Amarna we see a representation of what an ordinary Nile harbour may have looked like. In the foreground of the scene we can see a waterfront with boats moored to riverside posts (Jones 1995: 80), with a sloping pathway connecting the waterfront to a colonnaded building higher up on the levees. The riverbank is bustling with people performing various waterfront activities (Kemp & O'Connor 1974: 104-5; Marcus 1990: 50-51). It would seem that such a workaday harbour would not have had many permanent installations, simply because any waterfront installations would be destroyed each time the river flooded.

The Palestrina mosaic of the late 2nd century BC (Whitehouse 1979; Vörös 2001; Walker 2003) contains a clear representation of a quay and what appears to be part of an artificial harbour. It is generally accepted that the mosaic represents a celebration of the inundation of the Nile taking place in the vicinity of religious and royal buildings (Vörös 2001: 99-111; Walker 2003: 198-9), although there is no consensus about the exact place the mosaic is supposed to represent. The elaborate buildings and the celebration ceremony both tend to suggest that this harbour is not entirely utilitarian, of a special nature. This may explain the rather ambitious constructed quays that project above the water level even during the flood.

Figure 11.2: A river harbour and waterfront activities, depicted in the Tomb of May (c. 1365 BC) at Tell El-Amarna (after Marcus 1990: 52, Fig. 34).

Figure 11.3: A depiction of constructed river port and quays from the Palestrina Mosaic, late second century BC (adapted after from Vörös 2001: 105).

Figure 11.4: An early 20th century riverboat moored at a temporary quay made from Nile clay, while offloading its cargo of carts (after Breccia 1914: 14).

Although ancient iconographic representations of ordinary Nile harbours are scarce in antiquity, inferences about their designs may be obtained from later periods when Egyptian populations were still dealing with the same Nile-based issues. Interestingly, these seem to be characterised by a lack of significant structures: various 18th and 19th century illustrations and photographs show various types of vessels moored at a flat stretch of the riverbank (Breccia 1914: 14; Néret 1997: 584), without any evidence for permanent harbour installations. The boats can easily be loaded and unloaded from their position by the use of simple gangplanks or temporary quays made of the river clay. No matter how much the water level rose during the flood, boats can still be moored at any suitable stretch of the riverbank.

Ordinary river harbours in Hellenistic and Roman Egypt were probably rather similar to their descendants. Regardless to the river's water level, towns and villages situated higher on the levees would have taken advantage of flat stretches of the Nile banks to establish their harbours without the need for permanent waterfront installations. They could have used simple jetties of local wood or piled stones for mooring relatively large vessels, which they could access using wooden gangplanks, while smaller boats could be hauled close to the shore for loading and unloading.

However, we are aware that the scale of trading and import/export under the Romans was extremely significant, and this – coupled with various historical references and some archaeological remains (i.e. *Coptos* and *Schedia* [Kom el-Giza near Alexandria]) – makes it likely that there were large harbour structures, and that we are therefore suffering from taphonomic selectivity rather than a genuine absence. This is probably connected with Nile dynamics and flood regimes, as the silting rate of 1.2mm a year would cover Roman period structures standing 1.0m above the floodplain with at least 1.4m of mud. The fact that the Nile moves eastward and deposits silt towards the west means that west-bank Roman harbours are likely to be land locked, while east-bank harbours (i.e. Coptos), while less vulnerable to silting, are now possibly inundated.

The acts of rebuilding and maintaining the river harbours along the Nile in accordance with the river's flood cycle was probably part of the routine work undertaken by local people in Graeco-Roman Egypt, as did their predecessors and successors. However, the vast majority of Nile harbours were mostly workaday facilities, which are unlikely to have been recognisably preserved in the archaeological record.

The Quaysides at Karnak

In 2006 a site management project for the temples of Karnak was started under the initiative of Luxor City Council in collaboration with the Supreme Council of Antiquities (SCA) and the Centre Franco-Egyptien d'Etude des Temples de Karnak (CFEETK). This project entailed the development of the area between the temples of Karnak and the Nile, which required the demolition of all structures built in this area of the city. This included various houses in the village of Karnak, the French village, the SCA's rest house, the park, the Luxor stadium, numerous shops, the Legrain rest house, the Antiquities offices and the SCA's engineering workshops. The aim of the project was to build a vast esplanade, a visitor centre, a car park, a new complex for the Franco-Egyptian centre and a rest house (Boraik 2010).

Figure 11.5: The esplanade in front of Karnak (photograph: G. J. Tassie).

An archaeological impact assessment (AIA) was undertaken before any construction work went ahead. This involved excavating a series of test pits near to the tribune platform of the first pylon, located at the end of the avenue of sphinxes. These test pits revealed traces of a great embankment and two quays constructed in front of the temple.

Over 250 m of this great embankment was discovered. It is likely to have been built as a defence against site erosion, and also seems to have functioned as a formal quayside. The walls of the embankment were built with large sandstone blocks, some reused from earlier periods, to a height of 14 courses (the façade having a slight batter). The wall was 1.60m thick and currently stands to a height of 4.50 metres, and was connected to – and probably built at the same time as – the tribune. This seems to have been some time after Dynasty XXII, and was later modified by Taharqo of Dynasty XXV; the upper parts of the embankment were repaired during the Graeco-Roman period. A large tripartite ramp was located to the south of the tribune. The maximum width of the ramp is 24.0-22.0m, the south wall is 23.70m long and the north wall 25.5m long: the walls are 4.0m tall. This ramp was modified during the reign of Taharqo, and also during the Graeco-Roman period. To the south of this ramp were two staircases (1.10m wide and 25.50m long) leading down the outer face of the wall from south to north, suggesting that they were part of a quayside, possibly to enable embarkation and disembarkation no matter what stage of flood the river was at (Boraik 2010).

Figure 11.6: The tribune in the foreground and avenue of sphinxes and first pylon in the background (photograph: G. J. Tassie).

The great embankment continued to the north of the tribune; a secondary quayside was built 7.5 m to the north, consisting of two sandstone staircases facing each other and joined by a platform. Both staircases contain twenty steps (to groundwater level): the southern staircase is 6.6 x 1.0m, and the northern is 8.2 x 1.0 m. The tops of the staircases are 3.18m apart, and the height of the wall from the platform between the staircases is 7.0m. Many mooring loops were found in the walls (Boraik 2010).

In the northernmost areas of the embankment (areas 5 and 6) the wall was built with smaller sandstone blocks than elsewhere (from 1.08 x 0.46m to 0.80 x 0.44m), and the wall width narrows to 1.02m. Reused inscribed blocks with the name of Amenirdis of Dynasty XXVI were found, indicating that it was built no earlier than Dynasty XXVII, possibly during the Ptolemaic period (Boraik 2010), which is also represented in the form of industrial habitation (that seems to run through to the 4th century AD) and a Ptolemaic bathhouse. The southern stairways were blocked in during the late Roman era and houses were built on top. These quaysides seem to have gone out of use as the river moved westwards, and this movement of the Nile may explain the later extensions to the north (Boraik *et al.* 2010).

Figure 11.7: The ramp of King Taharqo (photograph: G. J. Tassie).

Figure 11.8: The ramp of King Taharqo (photograph: G. J. Tassie).

The quaysides were probably used not only by worshippers coming to the temples at Karnak, but to bring tribute to the priests and produce from the temples' great estates.

Concluding Remarks

The discovery of an ancient harbour at Karnak underlines the vital necessity of conducting archaeological impact assessments (AIAs) before any construction work starts. The rapid urban expansion in Egypt makes it essential that AIAs should be conducted as part of the legal requirement of any building/construction project (Tassie & Hassan 2009), for the law currently insists upon environmental impact assessments (EIAs) but AIAs are an optional extra (Stapp & Longenecker 2009). Any discovery of archaeological remains should, in principle, be reported to the SCA, but this puts the onus on construction companies, who are unlikely to prioritise heritage rescue over their own profits and deadlines. It is a matter of extreme urgency that the responsibility for identifying and defending archaeological remains be removed from the construction companies and reallocated to the Ministry of Antiquities, and that standardised assessment frameworks be put in place: the first stage is a desk-based assessment, followed by systematic test-pitting, geophysical surveying and drill coring as the situation demands. All construction work must be accompanied by a watching brief, carried out by a fully-trained archaeological inspector (Tassie & Owens 2010).

Figure 11.9: The steps of the northern quay at Karnak (photograph: G. J. Tassie).

Site management projects must set an example to all other types of construction by undertaking full AIAs before any construction work begins. The site management project at Karnak is a stellar example of just such a project, as careful AIAs have resulted in the exposure of a whole new part of the complex, a major addition to Egyptian archaeology, and also the opportunity for infrastructure development by putting it on display to the public. Archaeological investigations must form part of any site management plan.

REFERENCES

Bagnall, R. 1993. *Egypt in Late Antiquity*. Princeton: Princeton University Press.

Ball, 1939. *Contribution to the Geography of Egypt*. Cairo: Government Press

Bietak, M. 2005. The Tuthmoside stronghold of Perunefer, *Egyptian Archaeology* 26: 13-17.

Blue, L. and Peacock, D. (eds) 2006. *Myos Hormos - Quseir al-Quadim: Roman and Islamic Ports on the Red Sea*. Oxford: Oxbow Books.

Boraik, M. 2010. Excavations of the quays and embankment in front of Karnak temples. Preliminary report, *Cahiers du Karnak* 13: 65-78.

Boraik, M., Ghilardi, M., Bakhit, S., Hafez, A., Ali, M. H., el-Masekh, S. and Mahmoud, A. G. 2010. Geomorphological investigations in the western part of the Karnak Temple (quay and ancient harbour). First results, *Cahiers du Karnak* 13: 101-109.

Bourdon, C. 1925. Anciens Canaux, Anciens Sites et Ports de Suez, *Mémoires de la Société Royale de Géographie D'Égypte*. Vol. VII. Cairo: Imprimerie de l'Institut Français D'Archéologie Orientale. Breccia, E. 1914. *Alexandria Ad Aegyptum*. Bergamo: Istituto Italiano d'Arti Grafiche.

Butzer, K. W. 1976. *Early Hydraulic Civilization in Egypt*. Chicago: University of Chicago Press.

Casson, L. 1984. *Ancient Trade and Society*. Detroit: Wayne State University Press.

Casson, L. 1989. *The Periplus Maris Erythraei*. Princeton: Princeton University Press.

Casson, L. 1995. *Ships and Seamanship in the Ancient World*. Baltimore: The Johns Hopkins University Press.

Cooper, J. P. 2009. Egypt's Nile-Red Sea Canals: Chronology, Location, Seasonality and Function, in L. K. Blue, J. P. Cooper, R. Thomas and J. Whitewright (eds) *Connected Hinterlands: Proceedings of Red Sea Project IV held at the University of Southampton September 2008*. Oxford: Archaeopress, pp. 195-210.

Empereur, J.-Y. 1993. La Production Viticole dans L'Égypte Ptolémaïque et Romaine, in M. C. Amouretti and J. P. Brun (eds) *La Production du Vin et de l'Huile en Méediterranée*. Bulletin de Correspondance Hellénique, Supplement 26: 39-47.

Facey, W. 2004. The Red Sea: The wind regime and location of ports, in P. Lunde and A. Porter (eds) *Trade and Travel in the Red Sea Region*. Oxford: British Archaeological Reports, pp 7-17.

Fattovich, R. 2012. Egypt's trade with Punt: New discoveries on the Red Sea coast, *British Museum Studies in Ancient Egypt and Sudan* 18: 1–59.

Forstner-Müller, I. 2014. Avaris, its harbours and the Perunefer problem, *Egyptian Archaeology* 45: 32-35.

Graham, A. and Strutt, K. D. 2012. The Theban harbours and waterscapes survey. Recent fieldwork to investigate the canals and harbours on the west and east banks at ancient Thebes (Luxor), Egypt, *The Newsletter of the International Society for Archaeological Prospection* 31: 6-7.

Graham, A., Strutt, K. D., Hunter, M., Jones, S., Masson, A., Millett, M. and Pennington, B. 2012. Theban Harbours and Waterscapes Survey, 2012, *Journal of Egyptian Archaeology* 98: 27-42.

Hamdan, G. 1980. *Egypt's Identity: A Study of the Genius of the Place*, Vol. 1. Cairo: Alam Al-Kutub.

Hassan, F. A. 1997. The dynamics of riverine civilization: A geoarchaeological perspective on the Nile Valley, Egypt, *World Archaeology* 29.1: 51-74.

Herbich, T. & Forstner-Müller, I. 2013. Small harbours in the Nile Delta: The case of Tell el-Dab'a, *Études et Travaux* 26: 258-272.

Herodotus. *The Histories.* Translated by A. de Sélincourt. Middlesex: Penguin Books, 1971.

Husselman. E. 1952. The Granaries of Karanis. *Transaction and Proceedings of the American Philological Association.* 83: 56-73.

Jeffreys, D. 2006. Perunefer: at Memphis or Avaris? *Egyptian Archaeology* 28: 36-37.

Jones, D. 1995. *Boats.* London: The British Museum Press.

Kemp, B. and O'Connor, D. 1974. An ancient Nile harbour: University Museum Excavation at the 'Birket Habu', *International Journal of Nautical Archaeology* 3(1): 101-136.

Lewis, N. 1974. *Papyrus in Classical Antiquity.* Oxford: Oxford University Press.

Lewis, N. 1983. *Life in Egypt under Roman Rule.* Oxford: Clarendon Press.

Lindsay, J. 1968. *Men and Gods on the Roman Nile.* New York: Barnes & Noble, Inc.

Marcus, E. 1990. *Pictorial Representations of Harbours and Harbourworks in Egypt during the Second Millennium B.C.E.* Unpublished MA Dissertation, Haifa: University of Haifa.

Minnen, P. V. 1986. The volume of the Oxyrhynchite textile trade, *Münstersche Beiträge zur Antiken Handelsgeschichte* 5(2): 88-95.

Mohamed, M. A. 2001. *The River Nile.* Cairo: Hai'a Al Kitab.

Mumford, G. 2012. Ras Budran and the Old Kingdom trade in Red Sea shells and other exotica, *British Museum Studies in Ancient Egypt and Sudan* 18: 107–45.

Nenna, M.-D., Picon, M. and Vichy, M. 2000. Ateliers primaires et secondaires en Égypte à L'Époque Gréco-Romaine, in M.-D. Nenna (ed.) *La Route du Verre: Ateliers Primaires et Secondaires du Second Millénaire av. J.-C. au Moyen Âge.* Travaux de La Maison de L'Orient Méditerranéen 33, pp. 97-112.

Néret, G. 1997. *Description de l'Egypte.* Köln: Taschen.

Peacock, D. 1992. *Rome in the Desert: A Symbol of Power.* An Inaugural Lecture delivered at the University of Southampton.

Peacock, D. 1993. The site of Myos Hormos: A view from space, *Journal of Roman Archaeology* 6: 226-232.

Peacock, D. 1999. Introduction, in D. Peacock et al. (eds) *Myos Hormos- Quseir Al- Qadim: A Roman and Islamic Port Site on the Red Sea Coast of Egypt.* Unpublished Interim Report. University of Southampton, pp. 5-6.

Peacock, D. 2000. The Stone, in D. Peacock *et al.* (eds) *Myos Hormos- Quseir Al- Qadim: A Roman and Islamic Port Site on the Red Sea Coast of Egypt.* Unpublished Interim Report. University of Southampton, pp. 25-26.

Peacock, D. 2002. The Roman Period, in I. Shaw (ed.) *The Oxford History of Ancient Egypt*, Oxford: Oxford University Press, pp. 422-445.

Rickman, G. 1971. *Roman Granaries and Store Buildings.* Cambridge: Cambridge University Press.

Rickman, G. 1980a. *The Corn Supply of Ancient Rome.* Oxford: Clarendon Press.

Rickman, G. 1980b. The grain trade under the Roman Empire, in J. H. D'Arms and E. C. Kopff (eds) *The Seaborne Commerce of Ancient Roma: Studies in Archaeology and History.* Rome: American Academy in Rome XXXVI, pp. 261-275.

Said, R. 1981. *The Geological Evolution of the River Nile.* New York: Springer-Verlag.

Said, R. 1993a. *The River Nile: Its Origin and Utilization in the Past and Future.* Cairo: Dar Al-Helal.

Said, R. 1993b. *The River Nile: Geology, Hydrology and Utilization.* Oxford: Pergamon Press.

Seeger, J. and Sidebotham, S. 2005. Marsa Nakari: an ancient port on the Red Sea, *Egyptian Archaeology* 26: 18-20.

Šichan, D. 2011. *Harbours in Ancient Egypt.* Unpublished Masters Dissertation, Prague: Univerzita Karlova v Praze.

Stapp, D. & Longenecker, J. 2009. *Avoiding Archaeological Disasters: A Risk Management Approach*. Walnut Creek: Left Coast Press.

Strabo. *Geography*. Translation by H. L. Jones. London: The Loeb Classical Library, 2001.

Tallet, P. 2012. Ayn Sukhna and Wadi el-Jarf: Two newly discovered Pharaonic harbours on the Suez Gulf, *British Museum Studies in Ancient Egypt and Sudan* 18: 147–68.

Tassie, G. J. & Hassan, F. A. 2009. Sites and monuments records (SMRs) and cultural heritage management (CHM), in F. A. Hassan, G. J. Tassie, A De Trafford, L. S. Owens & J. van Wetering (eds.) *Managing Egypt's Cultural Heritage: Proceedings of the First Egyptian Cultural Heritage Organisation Conference on: Egyptian Cultural Heritage Management*. London: Golden House and ECHO Publications, pp. 191-205.

Tassie, G. J. & Owens, L. S. 2010. *Standards of Archaeological Excavation; A Fieldguide to the Methodology, Recording Techniques, and Conventions*. London: Golden House Publications.

Thomas, R. I. 2012. Port communities and the Erythraean Sea trade, *British Museum Studies in Ancient Egypt and Sudan* 18: 169–99.

Tomber, R. 2012. From the Roman Red Sea to beyond the Empire: Egyptian ports and their trading partners, *British Museum Studies in Ancient Egypt and Sudan* 18: 201–215.

Vörös, G. 2001. *Taposiris Magna: Port of Isis*. Budapest: Egypt Excavation Society.

Walker, S. 2003. Carry-on at Canopus: The Nilotic mosaic from Palestrina and Roman attitudes to Egypt, in R. Matthews and C. Roemer (eds) *Ancient Perspectives on Egypt*. London: University College of London Press, pp. 191-202.

Whitehouse, H. 1979. *The Dal Pozzo Copies of the Palestrina Mosaic*. Oxford: British Archaeological Reports Supplementary Series 12.

Young, G. 2001. *Rome's Eastern Trade: International Commerce and Imperial Policy, 31 BC- AD 305*. London: Routledge.

Chapter 12

Single-Context Recording in the Context of Archaeological Fieldwork in Egypt: Part One.

G. J. Tassie

ABSTRACT

Although scientific excavation has been conducted in Egypt since Petrie's time, many Western developments in archaeological theory and practice are yet to be adopted by the majority of current fieldworkers. The reasons for this are manifold, but stem from the way Egyptology is taught in universities. Many excavators still use the Wheeler-Kenyon box-grid technique, excavating in spits, and identifying layers and features through the baulk sections. Single context recording (SCR), by contrast, is now starting to be used in Egypt. The effectiveness of this methodology, its advantages over traditional excavation methodologies and a general review of the process are discussed here. This is a part one of a two-part paper; the second part was presented at the Ninth International Congress of Egyptologists, Grenoble, 2004 (Tassie 2007). The use of SCR in an Egyptian context was elaborated upon in the second part of the paper, highlighting both advantages and drawbacks – especially regarding the use of local labourers – and why the International Association of Egyptologists and Ministry of Antiquities should take a more prominent role in promoting good practice in archaeological methodology.

INTRODUCTION AND BACKGROUND

One of the most important aspects of managing Egyptian (or any) cultural heritage is through its careful, precise scientific excavation and recording. If sites are carelessly excavated, then much of the available data is lost and as such cultural heritage is lost or without a proper provenance. However, discussions on excavation methodology within Egyptology have been extremely rare. This point was highlighted by Jones (2003) who observed that papers dedicated to Egyptological methodology or theory are very much in a minority when compared to the amount on interpretation. O'Connor (2003) pointed out that there are hardly any sites in Egypt that are not in some way threatened by imminent destruction, and thus it is apparent that the key does not lie in more excavations, but instead in more cogent site identification, documentation and protection. It is also important that such excavations that are carried out be executed in a timely and professional manner (Myśliwiec 2003). Jones takes pains to point out that of all the papers presented in *ICE 8* there were none that dealt with methodological issues, and that '…with the exception of a handful of exemplary excavations, techniques have not come very far in 40 years' (Jones 2003: 1). Of the three volumes of *ICE 8* proceedings, the only paper that really examines the problem of excavation methodology was Sheehan's study of rescue archaeology in Old Cairo. It is perhaps significant to note that he felt it necessary to state the following as the minimum requirement for excavation of archaeological features: 1) sufficient to date it by record of its stratigraphic position and situation in relation to other features on the site – a task that can only be achieved satisfactorily as soon as the feature is defined and during its removal, 2) enable the identification of the processes involved in the context's creation, and 3) to provide a suitable interpretation within the limits of excavation (Sheehan 2003: 459). This situation did not improve with the publication of the *ICE 9* proceedings, and is not expected to do so either with that of *ICE 10*.

Ucko (2003: v) has posited that Egyptian archaeology's resistance to innovative methodologies reflects Egyptology's insularity, with little awareness of – or perhaps indifference to – developments in archaeologies elsewhere. Much of the problem has arisen in the way the Egyptology grew as an academic discipline and how the public views ancient Egypt. Two introspective papers 'Introduction: Two hundred years of ancient Egypt: Modern history and ancient archaeology' (Jeffreys 2003) and 'The cursed discipline? The Peculiarities of Egyptology at the turn of the twenty-first century' (Moreno García 2014a) examine the way that Egyptology grew and the various influences and forces that were exerted upon it, particularly museum and individual patrons wishing to furnish their collections and national institutions competing with one another. The public interest in spiritual subjects, such as religion, art, and literature (as opposed to socioeconomics, habitat and settlement patterning) is linked to the concept of 'eternal Egypt' that was propagated by the European bourgeoisie at the end of the nineteenth century. This set of people sought beauty, charm and conservative order in the face of the rising power of the masses and their political organisation and regarded ancient Egypt as a repository of arcane wisdom (Moreno García 2014a: 52). Even at the beginning of the twenty-first century the majority of archaeological work is devoted to the discovery of new tombs, temples, and the finding of beautiful objects, 'thus entertaining the popular image of Egyptologists as true embodiments of Indiana Jones. As a consequence, future discoveries will fuel the excitement of the public and of sponsors, attract the attention of the media, and promote emulation among archaeologists, thus paving the way for further research on tombs, temples, and prestigious residential areas' (Moreno García 2014a: 51). Advancement of the discipline is still centred on the finding of a new tomb or stele, rather than advances in excavation methodology or new interpretive approaches (O'Connor 1979). This situation is not being helped by popular culture and the media that consider Egyptology as a provider of escapism from the rather dreary present.

Two further introspective papers titled 'The present state of Egyptian archaeology' (Bietak 1979) and 'The present state of Egyptian archaeology: 1997 update' (Giddy 1999), examined this problem, and also the lack of settlement archaeology. Bietak concluded that the reason for this is that in the majority of universities offering Egyptology concentrate on philology and history, without a specific degree focusing on Egyptian archaeology (Bietak 1979: 156-157) a point further made by Guksch (1991: 38-39) and Tassie *et al.* (2000: 99); although there have been some improvements since that point. Although settlement archaeology is now playing a more important role (Giddy 1999: 110-111), as Moreno García (2014a: 51) observes, social and economic history, urban and landscape archaeology still remain underrepresented in contemporary Egyptological research. This situation is slightly surprising, since the groundbreaking book *Egyptology and the Social Sciences* (Weeks 1979), that sought greater parity with mainstream archaeology was published over 35 years ago. Exemplary practitioners and publications utilising mainstream archaeological practice, theory and interpretation (i.e. Bietak *et al.* 2010; Kemp 2006; Kemp and Stevens 2010; Kemp and Vogelsang-Eastwood 2001; Lustig 1997; Moreno García 2006, 2014b; Rowland 2008; Rowland *et al.* 2013; Wilson 2009) still remain in the minority. However, Midant-Reynes notes mainstream archaeological practice has been conducted in the study of prehistoric and Predynastic Egypt for over half a century although, the study of events before the Pharaonic era still lies outside of mainstream Egyptology (Midant-Reynes 2000: 1), which largely still concentrates on textual material (Sauneron 1968: 41). This situation is due partially to the long history of ancient Egypt, but also for academic convenience, and as such there has been a periodisation of Egyptology into various distinct eras, which has led to the gradual consolidation of historical sub-disciplines linked to these eras that have become progressively isolated, thus making transversal studies difficult with the regrettable effect that specialists of a given period are not necessarily familiar with the sources, current debates, methods, theories and historical problems characteristic of other eras (Moreno García 2014a: 57).

Although archaeology is now considered to be a more legitimate part of Egyptology (Kemp 1989; Davies & Friedman 1998), it is still not recognised as an integral branch of the discipline (Giddy 1999). The teaching of Egyptian archaeology (both fieldwork methodology and theory) at undergraduate level, which is of fundamental importance in forming a new generation of Egyptologists (Bietak 1979), is now a fixture at Liverpool University and UCL's Institute of Archaeology, where a degree can be earned in Egyptian Archaeology, whereas UCLA offers several courses in Egyptian archaeology. However, as Moreno García (2014: 56) observes, most universities offering Egyptology teach the basic rudiments of ancient Egyptian culture (language, writing systems, epigraphy, and papyrology) as well as its more idiosyncratic cultural markers (literature, religion, and art history). Although Giddy (1999: 109) states that one of the reasons for the lack of an archaeological component in general Egyptology degrees is the lack of opportunity for students to participate in fieldwork in Egypt, this is not necessarily the only cause. Giddy goes on to state that many fieldworkers in Egypt have had little or no archaeological training [a degree in ancient history and/or philology does not train a person in excavation techniques and methodology] (1999: 109), which of course has very serious repercussions for the standards of archaeological fieldwork, and also explains why many of the new methods, theories and practices common in mainstream archaeology are not widely practiced by Egyptologists (Giddy, 1999: 110). While it is true that it is by no means easy to walk into an Egyptian field project, those who have a desire to do so can easily find training excavations elsewhere in the world, thus attaining skills that can be turned to Egyptological investigation once their training is complete. The Giza Plateau Mapping Project (GPMP) currently employs many field archaeologists who learnt their skills outside Egypt, and have no training in classical Egyptology. Fieldschools, mainly teaching young Egyptians, have been run by the American Research Centre in Egypt (ARCE), GPMP, EES, and a UNESCO sponsored one at Kafr Hassan

Dawood in the East Delta. No matter where training is received, however, the need for a knowledge of precise recording and various excavation methodologies is paramount.

SINGLE CONTEXT RECORDING IN EGYPT

One of the biggest advances in field archaeology was the development of the Harris Matrix system that diagrammatically portrays units of excavation and can be thus used for stratigraphic analysis (Harris 1974). This system developed by Edward C. Harris was first used in England for the Winchester excavations in 1974. Its use soon spread to Egypt where it was used with modifications on the Tell el-Maskhuta excavations in the Wadi Tumilat (Paice 1992). At Tell el-Maskhuta the site was excavated using the locus system, which led to a few problems in interpreting the stratigraphy using the Harris Matrix, not least because walls that were rebuilt instead of having a separate locus number for the rebuild retained the same number. It is therefore generally recommended that the Harris Matrix system be allied with the Single Context Recording system (SCR), which has been widely used on a variety of UK sites since the 1980s (Barker 1993; Drewett 1999; Westman 1994). First developed by Max Foster in 1972 in order to make sense of complicated multi-phase urban sites, SCR complements the Harris Matrix as each stratigraphic unit is excavated and recorded individually, whether it be a cut or a deposit (Tassie & Owens 2010: 4). The system has spread to a plethora of Egyptian missions, to include those run by UCLA, Groningen University, the EES, SEPE and the SCA. Notable sites excavated using SCR include the Faiyum (Wendrich 2003), the Giza Plateau Mapping Project (Lehner 1994, 1995, 1996), Kafr Hassan Dawood (Hassan & Tassie 2003; Tassie 2007), Tell Tebilla (Mumford 2008), Memphis (Jeffreys 1985), and Quesna (Rowland 2008; Rowland *et al.* 2013). The system can be applied to sites of extraordinary complexity and importance: the multi-period excavations at Kom el-Khilgan in the East Delta (Maadi-Buto; Naqada III; Hyksos Period), carried out by the CNRS and the IFAO under the direction of Béatrix Midant-Reynes (Midant-Reynes *et al.* 2004) are an exemplary example, involving a wide range of specialists, open area excavation, large trenches and full context tagging. The team's close collaboration with the local chief inspector and his SCA team has resulted in a very harmonious excavation and logistical process, sharing knowledge, experience, information and skills with a common end of improving archaeological practice.

While this gradual move to using SCR is welcome, it should be noted that it is being done on an individual basis, without common dialogue within the Egyptological community. The common aim should therefore be for the whole Egyptological community to reassess how sites are excavated, but – as Giddy (1999: 112-113) has stated – there is an unfortunate lack of inter-mission contact, and therefore a shortfall in the exchange and dissemination of ideas and practices. This lack of communication is compounded by the fact that there are no accepted standards that state conventions or best practice for the excavation of Egyptian sites. Perhaps the most suitable tome is the Egyptian Cultural Heritage Organisation's *Standards of Archaeological Excavation* (Tassie & Owens 2010), which is currently only available English, although other archaeologists have chosen to use the Museum of London Archaeology Service (MoLAS, now Museum of London Archaeology - MoLa) Manual, and a similar book on urban archaeology written in Arabic by Sheehan (2003). It is notable that Tassie and Owens and the MoLAS Manual both advocate SCR, the flexibility and near-universal applicability of which is summarised below.

EXCAVATION METHODOLOGY

The choice of excavation methodology should be driven by the research design, which is itself dependent on the type of archaeology that is expected to be encountered. It is no longer acceptable to conduct what Giddy (1999: 109) calls the three Cs – Clearance, Cleaning, and Claiming, as this highly primitive method for emptying tombs is guaranteed to miss the majority of the archaeological data. Another technique of excavation used in Egypt is the Wheeler-Kenyon box-grid technique and the spit excavation methodology. The box-grid technique uses excavation units of (usually) 5 x 5 metres in a trench formation with retaining walls, or baulks of sediment between the units of the grid (Renfrew & Bahn 1991: 92-93). Although the box-grid system was highly innovative and appropriate at the time, its utility is restricted as the baulks are prone to misalignment and can thus obscure the relationships of contexts, preventing the identification of spatial patterning over the site (Drewett 1999: 94). This approach has now largely been replaced by open-area excavation or targeted trench approaches. The use of the arbitrary spit system has also been condemned in recent years (Drewett 1999: 93), owing to the fact that spits may cut several contexts at once, therefore obscuring their relationships and mixing the data. There are some situations in which the spit system may be an acceptable approach, such as when the matrix seems devoid of visible strata (Roskams 2001: 221; Sharer & Ashmore 1987: 262) in environments such as deserts. Rather than excavating entire deposits in one, it is permissible to dig and record in arbitrary spits of 5/10/20 cm until discernable contexts become visible (Sharer & Ashmore 1993: 262).

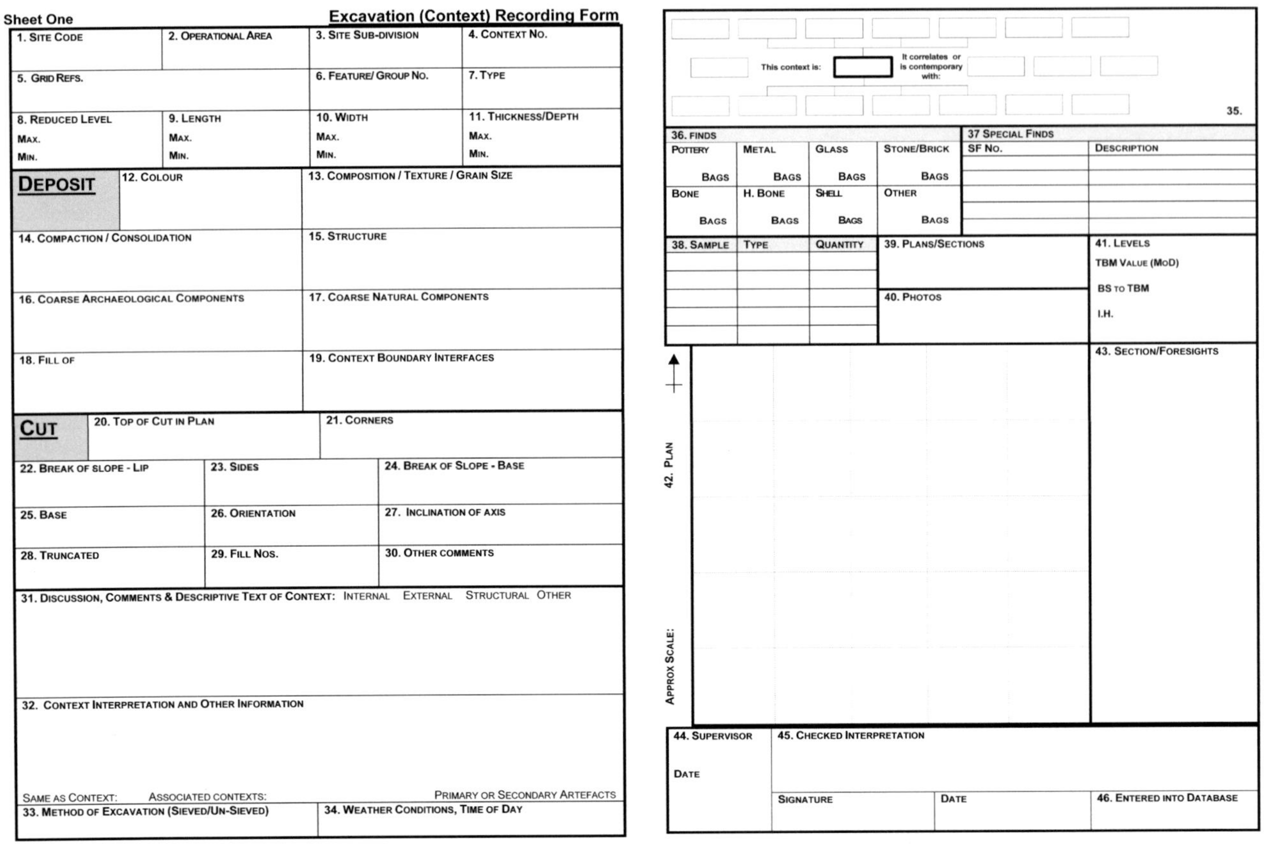
Sheet One
Excavation (Context) Recording Form
1. Site Code | 2. Operational Area | 3. Site Sub-division | 4. Context No.
5. Grid Refs. | 6. Feature/ Group No. | 7. Type
8. Reduced Level Max. Min. | 9. Length Max. Min. | 10. Width Max. Min. | 11. Thickness/Depth Max. Min.
Deposit | 12. Colour | 13. Composition / Texture / Grain Size
14. Compaction / Consolidation | 15. Structure
16. Coarse Archaeological Components | 17. Coarse Natural Components
18. Fill of | 19. Context Boundary Interfaces
Cut | 20. Top of Cut in Plan | 21. Corners
22. Break of slope - Lip | 23. Sides | 24. Break of Slope - Base
25. Base | 26. Orientation | 27. Inclination of axis
28. Truncated | 29. Fill Nos. | 30. Other comments
31. Discussion, Comments & Descriptive Text of Context: Internal External Structural Other
32. Context Interpretation and Other Information
Same as Context: Associated contexts: Primary or Secondary Artefacts
33. Method of Excavation (Sieved/Un-Sieved) | 34. Weather Conditions, Time of Day

This context is: | It correlates or is contemporary with: | 35.
36. Finds: Pottery | Metal | Glass | Stone/Brick — Bags Bags Bags Bags
Bone | H. Bone | Shell | Other — Bags Bags Bags Bags
37 Special Finds: SF No. | Description
38. Sample | Type | Quantity | 39. Plans/Sections | 40. Photos | 41. Levels TBM Value (MoD) BS to TBM I.H.
42. Plan | Approx Scale: | 43. Section/Foresights
44. Supervisor Date | 45. Checked Interpretation Signature Date | 46. Entered into Database

Figure 12.1: Single Context Recording Form, left: obverse and right: reverse (after Tassie & Owens 2010).

A context, as referred to in SCR, is a geologically- or culturally-formed unit of stratigraphic activity, the surfaces of which are defined by its interfaces with other contexts. An action will leave either a positive (deposit) or negative (cut) record on the archaeological site (Westman 1994: 7), and this applies to both geological and cultural processes. For example, the cut of a foundation wall is a negative record, while the wall/rubble fill is a positive record. On a smaller scale, a grave cut is a negative record, and the grave fill, substructure, superstructure, grave goods and body are a positive record. These thus represent two separate, distinguishable activities, which may have occurred in close succession (i.e. the cutting and filling of a grave) or be separated by a significant time lapse (i.e. the ritual burning of a structure years after its construction). Detailed recording of each activity will help place them within their temporal, physical and cultural frameworks across the site (Westman 1994: 7). Every context is treated alike, regardless of size. A group of contexts that constitute a coherent morphological or functional whole may be regarded as a feature, and a context that spreads across a large area may also be a feature, such as a floor (Wass 1992: 114): if it was formed by a distinct phase of activity, it is a context. The medium in which archaeological artefacts, ecofacts, contexts and features are found – and which immediately surrounds archaeological data – is called the matrix (usually some sort of sediment such as gravel, sand, soil, alluvium or clay).

The excavation of sites should be done by removing each natural or cultural context separately, following the discrete stratigraphic layers of the site. This process is usually carried out (where possible) in reverse order of construction/deposition, by removing the most recent material first, then proceeding backwards through the site's history (Drewett 1999: 107; Joukowsky 1980: 159; Wass 1992: 111). Once a context has been identified and fully uncovered, its elevation (asl) must be measured, then it must be planned onto a planning sheet, and described on a single context recording form (Fig. 12.1). Given that the aim is to be able to reconstruct the site after excavation, a running matrix must be kept of all excavated contexts. The associated finds, bags/buckets, samples, photographs and drawings made must all be labelled with a unique sequential context number, identifying this activity in the record and differentiating it from all others.

It is essential that all materials are cross-referenced, so that they can be identified back to their original context. The stratigraphic relationships of the various contexts must also be recorded, both on the recording forms and the single context plans. If multiple contexts are visible in the horizontal plane, they should each be tagged with their context number; contexts can also be tagged in the primary and secondary baulks. After consultation with relevant specialists, the context can then be excavated. Each deposit or cut is excavated separately once it has been identified and defined. As Sheehan (2003: 459) stresses, every context and its collection of finds and samples needs to be recorded by three types of media:

1. A written description
2. Separate plans, sections or elevations
3. Individual photographs

Figure 12.2: Open area excavation at the Giza Plateau Mapping Project's excavations of the workers village Giza (photograph courtesy of Jon Bodsworth, The Egypt Archive).

This system thus results in an array of different context sheets, as a reflection of the increasing complexity required from archaeological data. Ancillary information may be recorded informally in notebooks, but these should not be used for the main data recording process, as they were in Petrie's day. Standardised pre-printed context recording forms MUST be used in order to ensure the recording consistency of data encountered on site, as it is easier to enter into databases, is instantly retrievable and can be compared both within and between sites (Adams 2003). Pavel (2010) conducted a review of various recording systems available, many of which were variations on the MoLas single context recording system, although many others were based on the locus or lot system of recording. However, notebooks should also be used to allow the excavator a freestyle to record the archaeology. Each context is also planned on a single context master-plan, allowing each smaller plan to be superimposed on the site outline (see Westman 1994) thus building the relationships network and site matrices. These are invaluable for multi-period sites, allowing the construction of composite plans showing all the contexts from an array of different periods. The precise recording of artefacts, ecofacts, architectural elements and environmental remains in their sedimentary matrix, along with their association with other elements of archaeology is of the utmost importance in understanding the past. 'Whatever has not been selected by the describer to be a part of a description effectively ceases to characterize the deposits. Indeed, it ceases to exist altogether once the deposit, after recording, is removed' (Pavel 2012: 42). 'Retrieved archaeological remains only become social objects when they are incorporated, by word or image, into strong documents. It is in that moment that they acquire considerable import for society. By producing the record, and on its basis, that second tier of recording which is the publication, archaeology asserts itself socially as a legitimate human science' (Pavel 2012: 40).

One of the central elements of excavation is the recognition and definition of individual contexts, understanding how they come to constitute features, and the recovery of artefacts and environmental data therefrom. This can be easy or difficult, as contexts can be as tangible as walls and as nebulous as colour or consistency changes in sedimentary strata (Drewett 1999: 107; Lapp 1975: 30). It may be necessary to 'feel' contextual changes via the way in which digging implements behave; it takes skill and experience to distinguish faint fill or cut lines, especially in the bleaching light of the midday sun (Drewett 1999: 107; Lapp 1975: 30). It is also necessary to control the excavation area. The size and shape of the area is dictated by the site type, research objectives and threats to the site (as well as the resources available), and the area of excavation is defined by an electronic or string grid. The edges of the excavation areas (or 'trenches', or 'operations') must be kept straight and vertical, unless stepped or slanted for safety reasons. The vertical sections are important for understanding the stratigraphy, and smaller (i.e. non-baulk) cross-sections can be cut through features within the operation area in order to better understand particularly complex stratigraphic relationships.

In practice, open-area excavation involves a group of excavators trowelling back from one side of the area of operation to the other, recording which grid units specific contexts are located in. Some contexts may extend beyond the excavation unit, and it is the job of the area supervisor to decide if the nature of the context justifies extending the area.

Concluding Remarks

For Egyptology to survive in the twenty-first century it has to adapt. It is no longer acceptable to conduct the three Cs type of excavation and class description and source-knowledge as analysis. The writing of Egyptology needs to have sophisticated social and historical narratives, which must incorporate current theoretical approaches and be based on interpretation of the results using advanced analytical techniques developed in archaeology, bioarchaeology, anthropology, ancient history, and the social and earth sciences. However, any interpretation is only as good as the data it is based upon, and the collection of the raw data is dependent on good archaeological excavation methodology (Tassie & Owens 2010). It is vitally important to be flexible in excavation planning, and to adapt both approach and methodology to fit the site while always prioritising cast-iron control over data recording: SCR is the most effective means of achieving this. It also permits the director to be reactive as well as proactive, and to change direction or tempo to accommodate unexpected eventualities in the archaeological record (Roskams 2001: 36) or more mundane issues such as changes in funding, resource availability or time (Drewett 1999: 92). The project should use all the resource at its disposal, and adopt a multidisciplinary approach with on-site (or in-lab) specialists in the social, biological and physical sciences, as well as historians and philologists (Roskams 2001: 36-39), in order to address all possible archaeological eventualities.

As we have seen, arbitrary digging units (spits) can only confuse digging and analytical strategies, whereas the recording and excavation of individual contexts ensures the accurate recording of both data and relationships. Accretionary data accumulation allied with section recording and plan views of an individual context can thus enable neutral database construction, as well as 3-D reconstruction of the site. In other words, SCR provides the greatest amount of vertical and horizontal control, for any site type.

The system has been tested in all climates and parts of the world (Barker 1993; Roskams 2001), and is applicable, appropriate and fundamentally necessary for excavating and better understanding Egyptian sites. Egypt possesses an unrivalled array of spectacular and domestic sites that document key phases in the human story of burgeoning social complexity, state and empire, and these are too important to be left to the whim of antiquated and inadequate excavation and recording systems. SCR has proven to be more than a match for the extraordinarily complex *tell* sites, monumental structures, urban settlements and cemeteries in all of the challenging environments that Egypt has to offer. It is of vital importance that archaeological field techniques and methodology starts to be taught in all universities offering a degree in Egyptology and that more fieldschools be offered for young Egyptian Egyptologists. In this manner best practice in archaeological excavation can be attained by all teams, projects and nations working within the country. However, improvements in methodology will only be possible if the Ministry of Antiquities and other international institutions start to endorse and implement these changes through literature and better training programmes. This is essential if Egyptology is to transcend its historical bounds and develop so that we may obtain a better and clearer understanding of the human story in ancient Egypt.

Most Egyptologists do not find an unrobbed tomb of a Pharaoh, such as Tutankhamun (Carter & Mace 1923) or those of the kings buried at Tanis (Montet 1947). However, if a tomb of a historical figure, such as Alexander the Great were to be found in the near future, it would be essential to use appropriate archaeological methodology to retrieve as much data as possible. The conservation and epigraphic work being conducted at places such as Karnak and the Ramesseum are essential, but only comprise a fraction of the fieldwork being undertaken and needed in Egypt. In the increasingly competitive world of academia and higher education, which in most countries is becoming increasingly enterprise-orientated and dominated by severe financial restrictions, Egyptology has to redefine its place with regard to all the other humanities. Interdisciplinary research financed by international institutions is essential in this respect, and will allow researchers to explore innovative forms of research, including reconstructing the past landscape or hydrology regimes in specific regions (Hassan *et al.* 2006) or undertake an investigation of socioeconomic developments in certain periods of history (Tassie 2014).

ACKNOWLEDGEMENTS

I would like to thank Joanne M. Rowland and Lawrence S. Owens for their editorial skills and comments. I also wish to express my gratitude to my interlocutors Dan Swift and Natalie Cohen from *MoLAS*, Tim Stevens from *AOC* and Maybeline Gormley from *ArchCor* for their comments on the original draft. I bow before their expertise and dedication, and am privileged to share their interest in improving the methodology of Egyptian archaeology. I would also like to take this opportunity to thank all those at the Institute of Archaeology (UCL) who taught me the importance of proper excavation methodology, especially Prof. Fekri A. Hassan, Prof. Harry Smith, Dr. David Jeffreys, Dr. Peter Drewett, Prof. Simon Hillson, Prof. Gordon Hillman and Prof. Sue Hamilton. The opportunities to practice SCR in Egypt, at sites such as Kafr Hassan Dawood (Tassie 2007) have proved invaluable in honing the system, and thanks must be given to all my colleagues. However, any system can always be improved upon, and as such it is an ongoing process.

REFERENCES

Adams, M. J. 2003. The Egypt archaeological database and the birth of computerised inter-site analysis, in A. K. Eyma & C. J. Bennett (eds.), *A Delta-Man in Yebu.* USA: Occasional Volume of the Egyptologists' Electronic Forum, No. 1. Universal Publishers, pp. 169-181.

Ashmore, W. & Sharer, R. J. 2000. *Discovering Our Past: A Brief Introduction to Archaeology,* Third Edition. Mountain View: Mayfield Publishing Co.

Barker, P. 1993. *Techniques of Archaeological Excavation,* 3rd Edition. London: Batsford.

Bietak, M. 1979. The present state of Egyptian archaeology, *Journal of Egyptian Archaeology* 65: 156-160.

Bietak, M., Czerny, E. & Forstner-Müller, I. (eds) 2010. *Cities and Urbanism in Ancient Egypt.* Vienna: Österreichischen Akademie der Wissenschaften.

Carter, H. & Mace, A. C. 1923. *The Tomb of Tut-ankh-Amen. Discovered by the Late Earl of Carnarvon and Howard Carter,* Vol. 1. London: George H. Doran Co.

Davies, V. W. & Friedman, R. 1998. *Egypt.* London: British Museum Press.

Drewett, P. L. 1999. *Field Archaeology: An Introduction.* London: UCL Press.

Giddy, L. 1999. The present state of Egyptian archaeology: 1997 update, in A. Leahy & J. Tait (eds.), *Studies on Ancient Egypt in Honour of H. S. Smith.* London: Egypt Exploration Society, pp. 109-113.

Guksch, C. H. 1991. Ethnological models and processes of state formation – chiefdom survivals in the Old Kingdom, *Göttinger Miszellen* 125: 37-50.

Hassan, F. A. & Tassie, G. J. 2003. Research Methods, *Kafr Hassan Dawood On-Line*, www.e-c-h-o.org/khd

Hassan, F. A., Tassie, G. J., Flower, R., Hughes, M., & Hamden, M. 2006. Modelling environmental and settlement change in the Fayum, *Egyptian Archaeology* 29: 37-40.

Jeffreys, D. G. 1985. *Survey of Memphis* I. London: Egypt Exploration Society.

Jeffreys, D. G. 2003. Introduction: Two hundred years of ancient Egypt: Modern history and ancient archaeology, in D. G. Jeffreys (ed.) *Views of Ancient Egypt Since Napoleon Bonaparte: Imperialism, Colonialism and Modern Appropriations.* London: UCL Press, 1–18.

Jones, A. M. 2003. Egyptology today, in *Books Supplement, Al-Ahram Weekly* 54: 1.

Joukowsky, M. 1980. *A Complete Manual of Field Archaeology: Tools and Techniques of Field Work for Archaeologists.* New Jersey: Prentice-Hall Inc.

Kemp, B. J. 2006. *Ancient Egypt: Anatomy of a Civilization,* 2nd ed. London: Routledge.

Kemp, B. J. & Stevens, A. 2010. *Busy Lives at Amarna: Excavations in the Main City Grid 12 and the House of Ranefer, N49.18,* 2 vols. London: Egypt Exploration Society.

Kemp, B. J. & Vogelsang-Eastwood, G. 2001. *The Ancient Textile Industry at Amarna.* London: Egypt Exploration Society.

Lapp, P. W. 1975. *The Tale of the Tell.* Pittsburgh: The Pickwick Press.

Lehner, M. 1994. Giza, in W. M. Sumner (ed.) *The Oriental Institute 1993-1994 Annual Report.* Chicago: University of Chicago Press, pp. 26-30.

Lehner, M. 1995-1996. Exploring the Giza Plateau, *Explorers Journal* 73(4): 32-7.

Lehner, M. 1996. Giza, in W. M. Sumner (ed.) *The Oriental Institute 1995-1996 Annual Report.* Chicago: University of Chicago Press, pp. 54-61.

Lustig, J. (ed.) 1997. *Anthropology and Egyptology: A Developing Dialogue.* Sheffield: Sheffield University Press.

Midant-Reynes, B. 2000. *The Prehistory of Egypt: From the First Egyptians to the First Pharaohs.* Oxford: Blackwell Publishers Ltd.

Midant-Reynes, B., Briois, F., Buchez, N., De Dapper, M., Duchesne, S., Fabry, B., Hochstrasser-Petit, C., Staniaszek, L., & Tristant, Y. 2004. Kom el-Khilgan. A new site of the Predynastic Period in Lower Egypt. The 2002 campaign, in S. Hendrickx, R. F. Friedman, K. M. Ciałowicz & M. Chlodnicki (eds.) *Egypt at its Origins. Studies in Memory of Barbara Adams. Proceedings of the international Conference 'Origin of the State. Predynastic and Early Dynastic Egypt", Karkow, 28th August – 1st September 2002.* Leuven: Peeters Publishers, Orientalia Lovaniensia Analecta, pp. 465-486.

Montet, J. P. M. 1947. *La nécropole royale de Tanis. Volume 1: Les constructions et le tombeau d'Osorkon II à Tanis.* Paris: Fouilles de Tanis, ser. ed. Jean Pierre Marie Montet.

Moreno García, J. C. 2006. "Introduction: nouvelles recherches sur l'agriculture institutionnelle et domestique en Égypte ancienne dans le contexte des sociétés antiques, in J. C. Moreno García (ed.) *L'agriculture institutionnelle en Égypte ancienne: État de la question et perspectives interdisciplinaires.* Villeneuve d'Ascq: Université Charles-de-Gaulle Lille 3, pp. 11–78.

Moreno García, J. C. 2014a. The cursed discipline? The peculiarities of Egyptology at the turn of the Twenty-First century, in W. Carruthers (ed.) *Histories of Egyptology: Interdisciplinary Measures.* London: Routledge, pp. 50-63.

Moreno García, J. C. 2014b. Penser l'économie pharaonique, *Annales. Histoire, Sciences sociales* 69: 7-38.

Mumford, G. 2008. University of Toronto's SEPE project - http://deltasinai.com/.

Myśliwiec, K. 2003. Response to O'Connor, in Z, Hawass & L. Pinch Brook (eds.) *Egyptology at the Dawn of the Twenty-First Century: Proceedings of the 8th International Congress of Egyptologists, Cairo 2000, Volume 1*

Archaeology. Cairo: Supreme Council of Antiquities / American University in Cairo Press, pp. 10-12.

O'Connor, D. 1997. Ancient Egypt: Egyptological and anthropological perspectives, in J. Lustig (ed.) *Anthropology and Egyptology: A Developing Dialogue*. Sheffield: Sheffield University Press, pp. 13–24.

O'Connor, D. 2003. Egyptian archaeology in the Twentieth Century, in Z, Hawass & L. Pinch Brook (eds.) *Egyptology at the Dawn of the Twenty-First Century: Proceedings of the 8th International Congress of Egyptologists, Cairo 2000, Volume 1 Archaeology*. Cairo Supreme Council of Antiquities / American University in Cairo Press, pp. 1-9.

Paice, P. 1992. Extensions to the Harris Matrix System to illustrate stratigraphic discussion of an archaeological Site, *Journal of Field Archaeology* 18(1): 17-28.

Pavel, C. 2010. *Describing and Interpreting the Past – European and American Approaches to the Written Record of the Excavation*. Bucharest: University of Bucharest Press.

Pavel, C. 2012. Archaeological recording: form and content, theory and practice, AtekNa 2: 33-74.

Renfrew, C. & Bahn, P. 1991. *Archaeology: Theories, Methods and Practice,* 1st Edition. London: Thames & Hudson.

Roskams, S. 2001. *Excavation*. Cambridge: Cambridge University Press.

Rowland, J. M. 2008. The Ptolemaic-Roman cemetery at the Quesna archaeological area, *Journal of Egyptian Archaeology* 94: 69-94.

Rowland, J., Ikram, S., Tassie, G., Jansen-Winkeln, K. and Yeomans, L. 2013. The Sacred Falcon Necropolis of Djedhor (?) at Quesna – Recent investigations from 2006-2012, *Journal of Egyptian Archaeology* 99: 53-84.

Sauneron, S 1968. *L'Egyptologie*. Paris: Que Sais-Je? Series.

Sharer, R. J. & Ashmore, W. 1993. *Archaeology: Discovering Our Past,* 2nd Edition. California: Mayfield Publishing Co.

Sheehan, P. 2003. Brief encounters with the ancient landscape: urban archaeology in modern Cairo, in Z, Hawass & L. Pinch Brook (eds.) *Egyptology at the Dawn of the Twenty-First Century: Proceedings of the 8th International Congress of Egyptologists, Cairo 2000, Volume 1 Archaeology*. Cairo: Supreme Council of Antiquities / American University in Cairo Press, pp. 455-460.

Tassie, G. J. 2007. Have we dug ourselves into a hole? Reappraising excavation methodology and approaches in Egyptian archaeology (part two): Kafr Hassan Dawood, a case study, in J-C. Goyon & C. Cardin (eds.) *Proceedings of the Ninth International Congress of Egyptologists*. Leuven/Paris/Dudley: Peeters, Orientalia Lovaniensia Analecta 150: 1769-1782.

Tassie, G. J. 2014. *Prehistoric Egypt: Socioeconomic Transformations in North-east Africa from the Last Glacial Maximum to the Neolithic, 24,000 to 6,000 Cal BP*. London: Golden House Publications.

Tassie, G. J. & Owens, L. S. 2010. *Standards of Archaeological Excavation: A Fieldguide to the Excavation Methodology, Recording Techniques and Conventions*. London: ECHO Publications and Golden House Publications.

Tassie, G. J., Rowland, J. M. & de Trafford, A. 2000. The 8th international congress of Egyptologists, Cairo, 28th March - 3rd April 2000, *Papers From the Institute of Archaeology* 11: 98-109.

Ucko, P. J. (ed.) 2003. *Encounters with Ancient Egypt*. London: UCL Press.

Wass, S. 1992. *The Amateur Archaeologist*. London: Batsford.

Weeks, K. R. (ed.) 1979. *Egyptology and the Social Sciences: Five Studies*. Cairo: The American University in Cairo Press.

Wendrich, W. 2003. Fayum Fieldschool 2002, week 1 report, *UCLA/RUG Fayum Fieldschool,* www.archbase.com/fayum/reports.html

Westman, C. (ed.) 1994. *Archaeological Site Manual: Museum of London Archaeological Service,* 3rd edition. Over Wallop, Hampshire: Museum of London, BAS Printers ltd.

Wilson, P. (ed.) 2009. *The West Nile Delta Regional Survey: Beheira and Kafr el-Sheik Provinces*. London: Egypt Exploration Society.

Chapter 13

Is the Writing on the Wall for the Writing on the Wall?
Opposition to – and Defence of – Egyptian Graffiti and Street Art

Lawrence S. Owens[1]

ABSTRACT

This study defines the boundaries of modern Egyptian graffiti, and divides it into two main forms: that involved with the aimless destruction of ancient buildings, and the burgeoning street art scene. Current official policy towards graffiti and street art has been indiscriminately negative, which is less a reflection of concern for damage to heritage, and instead seems to be a further attempt to control or eradicate one of the very few remaining means of social communication in the aftermath of the press' voluntary self-censorship. The body of work that has developed is unique, of global quality and importance, and is also heavily under threat from governmental iconoclasm. The potency of wall art as an outlet for everyday Egyptians and – particularly – those who have been marginalised under a succession of governments is discussed in direct reference to specific works and historical events. The problems inherent in its preservation are summarised. Proposals are offered for its recording and collation via computerised open-data platforms, databases and GIS/Google Maps, using recent developments in Hong Kong as a model.

INTRODUCTION

This paper concerns two forms of Egyptian graffiti: one profane, and one sacred. The image of graffiti is almost inevitably negative, and – in the current context – addresses deliberate damage, defacement and destruction of the world's greatest ancient civilisation. While being rightly subject to universal condemnation, it is argued that this regrettable habit may be dealt with in a more constructive manner than has hitherto been the case, and is in part attributable to a lack of socio-historical contextualisation of modern Egyptian populations. The prevalence of destruction and defacement has increased markedly in recent years (since 2011) as a response to the changing social climate, which has led some onlookers to conflate this with the second form of graffiti mentioned herein. While superficially similar, the latter concerns politically inspired and socially aware graffiti that is springing up across the rapidly evolving urbanscapes of Cairo, Alexandria and beyond. The official stance towards this has been extremely hostile, which may be taken as a measure of the fact that it transcends merely destructive aesthetics and puerile 'tagging', a potentiality that can be confirmed when the means, aims and methods of the artists are examined within the social context within which is first appeared. The regular destruction of these works via official sanction is no less than iconoclasm, which is eroding one of the very rare social fora that has become available to Egyptians since the revolution, and the subsequent self-censorship of the national press. There is an urgent need for recording, conservation and preservation of these modern works, just as both national and international communities must bring a halt to the defacement and destruction of ancient sites.

THE ISSUE

The damage sustained by Egypt's architectural and artistic heritage can be considered as an extension of the current epidemic of looting and illegal trade in antiquities (see Gill – this volume). There is evidence to suggest that superficial damage, at least, has a very long history, so much so that it is only in exceptional circumstances that it is reported upon – such as the recent tag reading 'Ding Jinhao was here' written in Mandarin across a wall relief at the Luxor Temple (Coonan 2013) – and then usually only with reference to the unusual fact that the culprit could be traced halfway around the world. Both tourists and local populations seem remarkably casual about archaeological remains, and appear to think little of marking them with their names, excising pieces as souvenirs, or altering them for purposes of censorship or religious/personal conviction. Iconoclasm of all forms has a long history, and while there are few countries that have escaped the attentions of the wantonly destructive, the despoilment of Egypt is

[1] Birkbeck College, University of London.
lawrence_owens@yahoo.co.uk.

particularly visible. Even visionaries and founders of Egyptology such as Belzoni have left their marks on the heritage their academic descendants are sworn to protect (Fildes nd.; ECHO 2001). The central issue, which has been touched upon yet not developed to its full potential, is one of heritage disenfranchisement. In the current volume, for instance, there are at least three papers that deal specifically with the central problem of who Egypt's past actually belongs to. The anxiety of heritage professionals to ensure that Egypt's ancient art, architecture and archaeological sites are protected is rarely accompanied by practical solutions at how protection, consolidation and display systems are going to be sustained once they have been implemented. Surveys of modern populations have invoked a range of disparate responses, unsurprisingly, but the overall impression one receives is that people 1) feel uninvolved, 2) feel involved but fear that too much public exposure may cheapen what they hold dear, or 3) feel involved while believing themselves to have been overlooked by their own nation in favour of attracting tourists (see Hosny/Ghanem, Tull, and Krause – this volume). It is also apparent that there is a lamentable lack of education of both domestic and international populations, and that antiquated sensibilities concerning Egypt's image (and heritage) continue to be remarkably pervasive.

Populations can feel disconnected from their heritage for the reasons stated above, and because they do not feel an attachment to it, they have little reason to take pride in it. This may serve to explain why any given group would feel disinclined to privilege and protect the sites in their vicinity, and would either feel indifferent about maltreating them, or would not feel moved to prevent others from doing so. Luckily this is not universally the case; without the intervention of numerous interested parties, for example, the lootings and damage to museums and sites that took place in the aftermath of the 2011 revolution would have been markedly worse (ECHO[2]).

That said, it is also true that much remains to be done to heighten the perceived importance of Egyptian sites and their contents, in terms of looting (see Gill – this volume) as much as mud-brick digging and – in the context of the current paper – graffiti. In the majority of cases, modern (and indeed, not-so-modern) graffiti that is seen on archaeological sites and heritage monuments tends to be the very barest of signatures, a form of tagging (see below) that holds none of the news casting, gossipy, public announcement qualities that defined so much graffiti in the Roman or Mediaeval worlds (Baird and Taylor 2011; Keegan 2011), and lacking any pictographic qualities that would distance it from a crude expression of territoriality, boredom, ennui, or perhaps a passing romantic gesture. It seems more related to an anxiety to demonstrate presence: 'I am here, I exist' (Reed 1981: 5), which is perhaps a nigh-on universal sentiment given the antiquity and conceptual simplicity of Pleistocene 'tags' such as hand stencils (Bahn 1997: 126; Bahn 2008). This is not to say that such graffiti (or *dipinti*) do not convey social value. Even when excoriating the modern practice of graffitiing archaeological sites, archaeologists can admit the social value of such works as a barometer of social mores through time (Tassie and Owens 2010; ECHO 2001; Fildes nd.; Tassie Pers. Comm.), albeit grudgingly[3]. The challenge, therefore, is to ensure that training and education in Egypt's heritage is universally and freely available, and that people feel personally and socially invested in the survival of their heritage. If central authorities had spent as much time and effort at enforcing extant laws concerning damage to cultural heritage (see Tassie – this volume) as was spent on the constant removal of street art (see below), the threat to ancient cultural heritage would be much diminished. If there is a general cessation of marking ancient monuments, if doing so becomes frowned upon socially rather than just officially, and if ancient remains come to be treated as personally relevant to the people who live among them, then the basic tenets of the 'Broken Windows Theory' (Kelling and Coles 1998) would dictate that the recurrence of such activity would immediately drop and then cease. Minor restoration to superficial damage – which central authorities have stated to be a relatively simple task (Coonan 2013) – twinned with educational policy as to the importance AND the valuable role of ancient heritage as a lynchpin in social identify in Egypt are likely to see a dramatic diminution in such damage.

GRAFFITI VS. STREET ART: DEFINITION AND DISSONANCE

'Graffiti' suffers from lexical and semantic uncertainty, which reflects its uneasy relationship within modern societies. There is little consistency in definitions, although most would probably utilise the terms

[2] http://www.e-c-h-o.org/news/protect.htm.

[3] A notable example is the Cyrillic chalk and soot graffiti inside the Reichstag, left by triumphant Russian troops in the aftermath of WW2, which comprises name 'tags' in addition to triumphal, insulting, celebratory or reflective posts, representing the hopes and fears of Germany under its gleaming new statehood, and the reminders of journeys taken in a foreign land by foreigners wishing for home (Baker 2002: 37; Nash and Chippindale 2002).

'illicit', 'unofficial' and 'unsanctioned'. It may comprise any form of painted, drawn, engraved, spray-painted, stencilled, scratched or – increasingly – installed (if in three dimensions) or even electronically projected writing or drawing, or combinations thereof. What does unite most definitions is the locale – it is typically positioned in places that have not received social or official sanction, and are thus tend beyond the control of authority structures. The term 'graffiti' has bled into other appellations, referring either to the illicit nature of the practice (guerrilla art), the locales where it is most common (street art) or deliberate self-distancing from the negative implications the traditional term now enjoys (post-graffiti, neo-graffiti). There is an ever-widening lexical split between graffiti and street art in that graffiti is increasingly seen as being primarily a short-lived expression of territoriality (see below), or merely an act of boredom or indifference, while street art is a valid form of graphic expression. This, however, is very much a western perspective. Whether or not this is also perceived to be the case in non-western nations – Egypt in particular – is discussed further below.

Western Street Art: Meanings and Purpose

"We recognise that some people consider that street art makes a positive contribution to the urban environment"
Hackney County Council, 2014

The study of graffiti as a means to understanding past groups is evidently not a new one. However, academic AND aesthetic appreciation of graffiti and street art has a more uncertain origin. Perhaps the most lauded efforts were by the late 19th and early 20th century Hungarian photographer Brassaï[4] (more properly Gyula Halász) whose dark monochrome depictions of the Parisian demimonde included extensive documentation of graffiti and how it changed over time. Painted graffiti – which Brassaï referred to as the 'Language of the Wall' in his 1961 work – was particularly eloquent in its endless reworking and changing to reflect social mores and trends, although an aesthetic appreciation of these forms of expression was hardly mainstream. The current western fascination with street art dates primarily to the Bronx art scene of the 1980s with artists such as Keith Haring, Kenny Scharf, Futura 2000 and Jean Michel Basquiat (Thompson 1992), graffiti 'taggers'[5] who became media sensations. Their work echoes political art such as that found along the Berlin Wall (1961-1989), blended with popular culture, Afrocaribbean aesthetics and influences from sources as varied as hip-hop music, rap, sexuality, poetry, the AIDS epidemic, outsider concepts (i.e. social alienation), 'suggestive dichotomies' such as wealth/poverty (Sirmans 2005), race relations, symbolism and contemporary critique (Hoban 2004; Thompson 2007; Marshall 1992). The past twenty years have seen street art's transformation from marginalised guerrilla creativity to mainstream culture, supported by the art market, galleries and national institutions that have all served to make this form of expression very much part of the zeitgeist of modern art. Gallery-based street art (or however one wishes to define it) is now worth tens of millions of pounds, a market that is based primarily in North America and Western Europe (and, increasingly, Eastern Asia). While the Egyptian modern art market is increasingly buoyant – along, regrettably, with the Egyptian antiquities market (Gill – this volume) – this owes nothing to the burgeoning urban street art scene. If it did, such works would be machine-sawed out of walls and their creators feted by bourgeoisie society, in exchange for repainting familiar wall-bound motifs onto canvas for the edification of the gallery scene. The fact that they are not serves to underscore yet further firstly the fact that their primary purpose is political – not aesthetic, and certainly not destructive – and that the powers that be view them as a threat rather than as a potential source of income. Recent work by Grondahl and Manco (2013) is the first major publicity that the genre has received.

Wall Art: Basic Points

Drawing and writing on walls probably has a longer history than is apparent from the archaeological record, given both taphonomic hardships and the seemingly inevitable tendency to rework, obliterate and cover over extant works with new creations. It is not impossible – even likely – that walls were not the primary canvas, as it were, for graphic self-expression, but these are at least the most durable surface and thus the one we are most able to explore. They are apparent in every inhabited continent, and their

---

[4] To see Brassaï work: MetMuseum – online collection.

[5] 'Tagging' – writing one's name or slogan in a memorably graphic fashion rather than as simple script – had existed for some decades prior, but had rarely transcended ornate 'bubble' lettering and a primarily territorial function (Shapiro 2007).

interpretation has been based upon factors that include socioeconomy, ritual, fertility, shamanism, networking, neuropsychology, sexuality, belonging, mythology, story-telling, ownership/territoriality, conceptuality, timekeeping, hunting bestiaries, cognitive mnemonics and many others (Le Quellec 2008, Le Quellec and Huyge 2008, Holl 1989, Lewis-Williams 2013 and references therein). Cities obligingly provided extra walls, and these were generally utilised in the same manner for the communication of news, advertisements, political propaganda and other personal opinions that had a measure of social acceptance, or at least was not a marginalised activity. More and more complex forms of wall decoration emerged, merging with religious dogma for ritualistic ends. Nowhere was this more evident than in the flamboyantly decorated tomb walls of Egypt, although it should be noted that their primary audience was intended to be divinities, rather than humans (i.e. Hill 2007).

Even in the early stages, the literary and pictographic content of walls was endlessly amended according to changing beliefs, social opinions and religious convictions. In Egypt this involved the eradication of gods other than Aten during the reign of Akhenaten, to the excoriation of Akhenaten's name and those of his successors under *damnatio memoriae* at the end of the 18th Dynasty (Reeves 2000), to the defacing of pre-Islamic works throughout Egypt under the reign of Morsi (Tassie – current volume). Overt politicality aside, wall arts seem alien to the post-Renaissance canons of western, elitist art that is the preserve of exclusive 'hidden' spaces (private collections, museums, galleries), in that it tends to be seen in – an even amended by – the wider public in their everyday space. Parallels may include Mexico, where ideology-driven mural art (based upon a fusion of Marxist ideals and Prehispanic wall painting traditions) by artists including Rivera, Orozco and Siqueiros charted the changing relationships between state and the individual, and played a very public role in people's lives (Folgarait 1998)[6]. The power of the wall-bound image in the public eye is demonstrated by Nelson Rockefeller's destruction of 'Man at the Crossroads' by Diego Rivera in 1934 (Gamboni 1997), owing to the fact that the artist had included an image of Lenin within the mural. The lack of official control, therefore, in art that cannot be moved and is not necessarily (or usually) within the confines of a defined space such as a gallery, appear to have the effect of unnerving governmental and authoritative associations, as we shall see below.

Egyptian Graffiti: Cultural Context, Cultural Constructs

"The art of graffiti and writing on walls is one of the great achievements of the Egyptian revolution"
Arab Network for Human Rights Information (ANHRI)
Gulhane 2013

The hinge point for Egyptian graffiti was 2011. Graffiti had, of course, always existed in Egypt, and has distant antecedents in cave art and rock engravings throughout the North African area and beyond (see above), but there is a general consensus that it was "…unimaginable to find anti-regime graffiti in urban spaces prior to 25 January 2011" (Hassan 2013: 626; see also Amin 2014; Armbruster and Taufiq 2014; Haikal 2014; and Van de Bildt 2013). The burgeoning discord with Mubarak's regime resulted in mass demonstrations, confrontations with military unity and attacks – both physical and verbal – on both crowds and symbols of governmental authority alike. Early graffiti art included defacement and emendations to official Mubarak portraits (Van de Bildt 2013) and Bahia Shehab's 'No' campaign (Amin 2014), and it was in this atmosphere that graffiti became a more potent form of protest, to such an extent that military courts began to illegally prosecute civil demonstrators for – in the example of Ali-al-Halaby – spray-painting anti-government sentiments, resulting in imprisonment and a LE 1,800 fine.[7] Nine months after the Mubarak regime had been toppled, graffiti transformed into an agent of change against the military government, ridiculing the state media (via an image of Pinocchio on television [Amin 2014]) then attacking Field Marshal Tantawi (symbolised by underwear decorated with helicopters [Van de Bildt 2013]) and calling for his execution along with his cabinet following the atrocities at Muhammad Mahmoud (Hassan 2013: 470). So-called *Kazeboon* (literally 'liars', a reference to post-Mubarak military leaders) stencilled graffiti became a regular fixture across Egypt and was showcased to the world (ibid. 487-8), carrying political messages powered by Alexandrine rap and hip-hop traditions. The gates of the presidential palace (and the *Mugamma* [Van de Bildt 2013]) became covered in graffiti – not tagging, but much more ambitious works – during mass demonstrations across the capital, which was immediately

[6] Mexico is of course not alone in this – see Garber (2004) for further details.
[7] Around 7% of an average Egyptian annual wage, according to http://www.egyptindependent.com/news/egyptian-family-s-average-annual-income-le25000-agency-reports.

whitewashed by Morsi' supporters (Hassan 2013: 610). It is both ironic and unsurprising that these same supporters immediately took to the walls to declare ideological war on the new military leaders following the ousting of Morsi (Van de Bildt 2013), although it is interesting to note that they have shied away from artistic representations and instead confine themselves to writing slogans directed against the military leader General 'Abd al-Fattah al-Sisi' ('Al-Sisi is a traitor and must be executed') and as a means for advertising future demonstrations (Van de Bildt 2013: 4). El-Sisi's supporters have allegedly attacked graffiti artists – who they consider to be traitors and terrorists – and at least one artist[8] has died under suspicious circumstances, currently under investigation (Amin 2014).

Figure 13.1: Graphic protests to the whitewashing of street art (Photography by the author, 22nd August 2014).

Even when the art is graphic rather than text-based, its very locale can be political, given that it is often executed on politically sensitive places such as the concrete roadblocks built by the SCAF[9] to block the streets against protest marches. Any painting on these military relics have commensurately greater impact upon both artists and onlookers, as laid out in the *ma-fish gudran* ('no walls') and Irsam *fi shawari`* *Masr* ('Draw on Egyptian Streets') projects. The scope of themes is considerable, but none of them could be considered to be 'offensive' in the respects of social provocation of violence or discord (see above). In some respects they are even traditional, representing mid-century film stars, martyrs who have fallen since 2011, and also those who lost eyes during the troubles, leading to Mohamed Mahmoud St being nicknamed *shari' 'uyun al-hurriya*: 'the street of the eyes of freedom'. These have now become memorial spaces, sites for the deposition of flowers and other mementoes (Van de Bildt 2013). The government's recent proposal to ban all graffiti may well be levelled at preventing Morsi supporters' appeals for bloodshed, but the proposed LE 100,000[10] fine (or four years' imprisonment) for graffiti deemed to be any of these could potentially also impact upon wall art created by emergent pressure groups who have

[8] April 6th youth movement member, Hisham Rizk.

[9] Supreme Council of the Armed Forces.

[10] Around $13,981 or £9,279, equivalent to around 4 years' 'average Egyptian' salary (see footnote 6, above). This has been condemned by the Arab Network for Human Rights Information (ANHRI).

socially valid arguments to make and a steadily diminishing number of fora in which to make them (Amin 2014).

Figure 13.2: Detail of El Zeft and Mira Shihadeh's 'Circle of Hell'[11] (Photography by the author, 22nd August 2014).

Reacting to the removal from – or amendment of – female politicians in history books (notably 1950s suffrage heroine, Doria Shafiq) and the sexual assault of female prisoners by the armed forces[12], gender-sensitive art collectives such as Noon el Neswa and the Mona Lisa Brigades have the common aim of making female voices heard (El-Kady 2012; El-Nabawi 2013). Through projects such as Graffiti Haremi (Women's Graffiti), women are attempting to re-enter public spaces from which they have been systematically banished, using demonstrations, marches and immediately-recognisable stencils of Egyptian pop culture icons (i.e. actresses Faten Hamama and Souad Hosni, and songstress Om Kalthoum). Stencils are simple and effective, notably including 'Don't label me', a bare-headed/hijab/niqab triptych by Diaa al-Sayed (similar to Figure 13.3), an eye-patched Mona Lisa with a can of spray paint, and the 'I Want to Be' stencils of children's faces in the Ard al-Lewa neighbourhood in Giza (El-Nabawi 2013[13]).

Barrier art also serves to commemorate the estimated 20,000[14] annual victims of sexual violence, and the fact that official and social lethargy has led to an estimated 96.7% rape-reporting deficit; this culture of sexual abuse has been shown to transcend the three regimes of Egypt's recent past (Moraya 2013). Emblems of the recent graffiti campaigns include the anti-Mubarak activists assaulted in 2005, to the 'blue bra' woman assaulted by SCAF- soldiers, to Samira Ibrahim, Yasmine El Baramawy (see below) and 16-year-old Iman Salama, who was shot dead for confronting her harasser in 2012 (Morayef 2013). Particularly well-known examples of feminist protest art include Mira Shihadeh's 'No to Street

[11] This image has since been extensively reworked: see www.youtube.com/watch?v=pbhm2270czI.

[12] The so-called 'virginity tests'. See Amnesty International 2014; Amin 2014.

[13] For images, see Soraya Morayef (http://suzeeinthecity.wordpress.com/2013/03/11/graffiti-for-a-social-cause-zeft-nazeer-nemo-and-mona-lisa-brigades/).

[14] 2008 figures (Morayef 2013).

Harassment' (a woman blowing away would-be attackers with an aerosol), and a collaboration between this artist and El Zeft, whose perspective on women's social roles is summed up by 'Circle of Hell' – a woman mobbed by a crowd of men, to represent the particularly violent gang rape of Yasmine El Baramawy that took place in Tahrir Square in 2012 (Fig. 13.2). El Zeft is also known for a famous image of Nefertiti wearing a gasmask, labelled 'the voice of the women of the revolution' (Van de Bildt 2013). The fact that women's movements have been able to use street art as a forum for their grievances underscores the social importance of this media. It is also doubly fitting that they do so, given women's social marginalisation, emotional alienation and reduced public role, and appears to be a valid means for legitimising women within the framework of the mainstream revolutionary movement (WomanStats 2013).

Figure 13.3: Stencil of a woman in a hijab (Photography by the author, 22nd August 2014)

DISCUSSION: A PROPOSAL

"...there is a sense in which all graffiti is in danger of being obliterated"

Reed 1981: 5

The foregoing is a brief summation of the social and political context that has been both brought about and railed against by the new wave of Egyptian graffiti. I hope that in so doing I have made explicit the intellectual differences that exist between the aimless scribbling and superficial destruction of historical sites, and the extremely important social functions that are expressed through the manipulation of public spaces in Cairo and other Egyptian cities. The former issue is not one that should be met with Draconian measures; instead, the approach should be one of conciliation, taking care to involve local people and would-be scribblers, and to imbue them with a sense of historical identity, pride and belonging that is expressed through the historical remains among which they live. Once there is widespread social (rather than just official) disapproval of tagging ancient sites, the prevalence will inevitably drop. If even a fraction of the money spent on removal of street art (see below) by current governmental bodies were diverted towards education and low-key maintenance of ancient sites, this problem would disappear in a generation.

Egyptian street art *sensu stricto* is interested not in the tagging of walls, but in challenging social trends, urging regime change and reflecting the current frustrations of a generation. While informed by music and aesthetics that are not necessarily – or even usually – part of the Egyptian mainstream, they have been combined with numerous social influences to produce a vital and eloquent body of work that is seen as a threat to current governmental incumbents. It has not gained formalised social acceptance in that it has not yet entered the western art market – unlike the seemingly rebellious yet 'tamed' graffiti-style art that has characterised the western rags-to-riches gallery scene since the 1980s – but in terms of conceptualisation and skill of execution it far exceeds mere vandalism or political subversion, under which headings it seems to have been reflexively placed by current Egyptian authority structures. There is currently no infrastructure for its preservation within the social context of conservation or governmental policy[15].

It has become a language of the politically powerless, the dispossessed, the under-represented and the alienated, and is one of very few outlets for expression in a country whose media has voluntarily entered a state of self-imposed censorship at the highest level (Kirkpatrick 2014). The strength and importance of graffiti as a means of communication and expression can be measured by the violence with which it is attacked, destroyed, defaced and whitewashed. My own personal experiences in Cairo reflect the fact that most citizens feel proud of their graffiti, and resent its' destruction at the hands of detractors. Whitewashed images along the sides of Tahrir Square were tagged with a single, pointing figure and the phrase: 'I shall kill the man who did this'. Three people interviewed separately along Mohamed Mahmoud Street told me that they had seen the army arriving by night to destroy images: "they have taken away our pictures", said one man, indignantly. It is something of an irony that the army, through barricading and blockading the streets in this area, has provided one of the most fertile canvases for the dispossessed, and graffiti on roadblocks and walls has become perhaps the only form of protest and expression in the aftermath of the press' voluntary self-emasculation. The high prevalence of women's rights and feminist graffiti is a measure of how their world, in particular, has shrunk in recent years (Amin 2013).

> *"Sometimes, residents in the area paint over the images if they oppose our views. I no longer mind when my work disappears. When that happens, I just tell myself it's time to design a new stencil and I head straight back to Mohamed Mahmoud Street."*
>
> Graffiti artist Salma Sami (in Amin 2014)

In heritage terms, the strength of graffiti art can also be its weakness, for as the art is constantly evolving, changing, being destroyed, repainted and amended again, heritage – which by definition aims to maintain things as they are – is in an intellectual quandary at how best to conserve these fleeting, informative and masterful moments of modern Egyptian history. Yet efforts must be made. Tassie *et al.* (this volume) summarises at great length the policies that are in place to protect ancient heritage, and even if these strictures are not necessarily adhered to, there is at least official recognition of the fact that heritage is at base a desirable and necessary part of Egyptian culture. Currently, graffiti is art/communication by the people and for the people, from revolutionaries to art graduates to anyone who happens to walk by and wishes to assist in the creation of something new (Amin 2014).

It is also, ironically, the only cultural resource over which they have some control, and can conceivably benefit from, given that more ancient heritage is controlled by authority structures and presented as a playground for foreign tourists (see Hosny/Ghanem, Tull, and Krause – this volume). In

[15] Changing social attitudes, art market pressure and the financial derivatives thereof have often forced change; Hackney County Council (2014) now acknowledges "that some people consider that street art makes a positive contribution to the urban environment"…and – providing that it is not an incitement to violence, or on a listed building or conservation area – undertake to leave it in place should local residents so desire.

some cases images from the distant past have been subverted and reinvented as symbols of resistance (Fig. 13.4). Yet governmental attitudes view graffiti of all kinds – there is no clearly defined distinction in the legislation – as a criminal activity, subversive by its very nature, and as such are dedicated to controlling it through the imposition of unrealistic fines, or using military resources to destroy it. The fact that graffiti can have such an unsettling effect on a government that successfully requested the national newspapers be muzzled is in itself reason for them to be recorded and conserved, and yet the very fact that they are so threatening means that any such effort is unlikely to meet with governmental approval or sanction.

Figure 13.4: Anubis with a machine gun. Note defacement attempts (Photography by the author 22nd August 2014).

Yet there are precedents, notably the Berlin Wall, which survives in fragmentary form across the world as a potent symbol of revolutionary ideology and unity. However, Egypt differs in being governed by the same authority structures against which the graffiti is targeted, and while there are a few examples of projects to save street art from governmental destruction (such as in Hong Kong: see Wooters Yip 2014: 177), this only tends to occur in the face of overwhelming financial imperatives (notably 'Banksy' artworks in the UK and USA [Sernoffsky 2014; Hackney County Council 2014]).

I recognise that street art rescue and conservation is unlikely to rank highly in the public consciousness when there are such substantial threats to other aspects of Egyptian society, not least to the population itself. The conservation of paintings is an expensive, difficult and time-consuming process that would – in a sense – fly in the face of the art's role as a social barometer, subject to change and emendation in accordance with evolving social mores. When the day come that the press and media are once more free to all sectors of society, politicised street art will become redundant, and it is then that preservation and conservation measures as laid out by Clottes (2002: 133) will become necessary to save whatever social sentiments are adorning the walls and barricades at that particular moment. Until that time, they must remain accessible to an otherwise speech-deprived people. That said, there are means that can be taken to ensure that – if the paintings are to be destroyed, amended or removed (by official agency) – some record should remain of them. While some official/aesthetic recording has already been done (Grondahl & Manco 2013), and also served to promote the causes of street art worldwide, the popularity of such work to tourists and travellers alike means that there are literally thousands of digital images of these pieces on the internet and in private collections.

I would therefore propose the following: a powerful database system into which professional and casual photographs of street art can be uploaded, with electronic date-stamping and GIS data to track the artistic evolution of specific walls, streets or structures. The infrastructure for the project can be borrowed from the UMAP (Umbrella Movement Art Preservation) project, which is dedicated to the preservation of protest art in Hong Kong in the face of its removal by official bodies (Lau 2014). The level of personal involvement in this project has been remarkable, with networks of academics, galleries and private volunteers protecting art *in situ*, creating digital archives (open-data platforms connected to *Google Maps*) for wall art, and physically removing threatened installation pieces to safe locales in the city (Rushfield 2014). The plight of these pieces – which are mainly anti-governmental in stance – has attracted worldwide attention through a concerted online social media campaign, and some have even travelled to the Victoria and Albert's 'Disobedient Objects' show (Duarte 2014).

While there is some social media coverage of Egyptian street art, it is somewhat sporadic, and there is no cohesive platform in the manner of UMAP. Some street artists have *Facebook* pages, although these are very much independent expressions. Online resources are also lacking; for example, there are only six street artists named on 'Egyptian contemporary art' on www.wikipedia.org, and the 'graffiti' section thereof is less than 600 words long. There are some local initiatives, such as New Street Art project in Luxor that record not just street art, but several forms of intangible heritage (https://www.facebook.com/open.art.museum). The great strength of the current proposal is that it utilises resources that are already in existence, and that are constantly being generated by Egyptians, local residents, tourists, photographers and many other casual or dedicated observers who continually record the ever-changing social barometer of Egyptian wall art.

It is probable that the aftermath of Egypt's current socio-political crisis will see the pieces of the barricades and walls lifted from their current positions and placed in hermetic isolation for the edification of future generations – just as happened for the Berlin Wall – but these historical mementos will have far greater impact if they can be situated within the context of Egyptian society's ceaseless evolution. If the walls were merely a reflection of social trends, there would, perhaps, be less need for this programme, as the changes in the works would speak for themselves. However, the fact that Egypt contains an active agent of destruction in the form of governmental censorship and iconoclasm means that if we cannot save the works themselves, then we must preserve the voices of those who risked so much to be heard so that they, at least, are not forgotten.

Acknowledgements

The author would like to acknowledge the commissioning editors for the opportunity to research and write this piece, and would also like to thank the street artists of Egypt to whom this paper, for what it is worth, is respectfully dedicated.

References

Amin, S. 2014. Egypt's nascent street art movement under pressure, *Index on Censorship* 22nd August 2014 - www.indexoncensorship.org/author/shahira-amin/

Amnesty International 2014. *Egypt. Human Rights in Crisis. Systemic Violations and Impunity.* Expanded Amnesty International Submission to the UN Universal Periodic Review, October-November 2014 - www.amnesty.org/en/library/asset/MDE12/034/2014/en/63d8f6f3-2cad-4553-bded-563bcf593170/mde120342014en.pdf

Armbruster, J. & Taufiq, S. 2014. *My Cairo*. Stuttgart: Edition Esefeld & Traub.

Bahn, P. 1997. *The Cambridge Illustrated History of Prehistoric Art*. Cambridge: Cambridge University Press.

Bahn, P. 2008. New developments in Pleistocene Art 200-2004, in P. Bahn, N. Franklin, and M. Strecker (eds) *Rock Art Studies News of the World III*. Oxford: Oxbow. pp. 1-15.

Baird, J.A. and Taylor, C. 2011. Ancient Graffiti in Context: Introduction, in J. A. Baird & C. Taylor, (eds) *Ancient Graffiti in Context*. London: Routledge, pp. 1-19.

Baker, F. 2002. The red army graffiti in the Reichstag, Berlin: Politics of rock art on a contemporary European urban landscape, in G. Nash & G. Chippindale (eds) *European Landscapes of Rock Art*. London: Routledge, pp. 20-38.

Brassaï, H. 1961. *Graffiti de Brassaï*. Paris: Daniel Cordier.

Clottes, J. 2002. *World Rock Art*. Los Angeles: Getty Conservation Institute (JP Getty Trust).

Coonan, C. 2013. Chinese schoolboy, 15, exposed as Egypt's ancient temple graffiti vandal, *Independent* 28 May - http://www.independent.co.uk/arts-entertainment/art/news/chinese-schoolboy-15-exposed-as-egypts-ancient-temple-graffiti-vandal-8633556.html

Duarte, S. 2014. *Updates from the Umbrella Movement* - http://www.vam.ac.uk/blog/disobedient-objects/updates-from-the-umbrella-movement.

ECHO 2001. ~~Belzoni~~ Killjoy woz ere, *ECHO Website* - http://www.e-c-h-o.org/graffiti.php

El-Kady, M. 2012. *A Woman's Place. The Cairo Review of Global Affairs* - www.aucegypt.edu/gapp/cairoreview/pages/articleDetails.aspx?aid=203

El-Nabawi, M. 2013. Graffiti campaigns bring women and children into street art, *Egypt Independent* - www.egyptindependent.com/news/graffiti-campaigns-bring-women-and-children-street-art

Fildes, A. (nd). *Graffiti in the temples of ancient Egypt* - http://www.alanfildes.com/graffiti1.php

Folgarait, L. 1998. *Mural Painting and Social Revolution in Mexico, 1920-1940. Art of the New Order*. Cambridge: Cambridge University Press.

Gamboni, D. 1997. *The Destruction of Art: Iconoclasm and Vandalism since the French Revolution*. London: Reaktion Books.

Garber, E. 2004. Social justice and art education, *Visual Arts Research* 59 **30** (2): 4-22.

Grondahl, M. & Manco, T. 2013. *Revolution Graffiti: Street Art of the New Egypt*. London: Thames and Hudson.

Gulhane, J. 2013. Rights group condemns proposed graffiti law, *Daily News Egypt* Nov 6 - www.dailynewsegypt.com/2013/11/06/rights-group-condemns-proposed-graffiti-law/

Hackney County Council 2014. *Graffiti, street art and murals*. - http://www.hackney.gov.uk/ew-graffiti-584.htm#.VLe5iVrlNG4

Haikal, F. 2014. *Reflections on Turning Points: Egypt between January 25, 2011 and June 30, 2012*. Berlin: Kulturverlag Kadmos Berlin

Hassan, A. F. 2013. *Changing News, Changing Realities: Media censorship's evolution in Egypt*. Oxford: Reuters Institute for the Study of Journalism, University of Oxford - http://reutersinstitute.politics.ox.ac.uk/sites/default/files/Changing%20News_Changing%20Realities_Part%203_Revolution%20and%20Two%20and%20a%20Half%20Years%20On.pdf

Hill, M. 2007. *Gifts for the Gods: Images from Egyptian Temples*. New York: Metropolitan Museum of Art, NYC.

Hoban, P. 2004. *Basquiat: A Quick Killing in Art*. New York: Penguin Books.

Holl, A. 1989. Social issues in Saharan prehistory, *Journal of Anthropological Archaeology* 8: 313-354.

Keegan, P. 2011. Blogging Rome: Graffiti as speech-act and cultural discourse, in J. A. Baird & C. Taylor (eds) *Ancient Graffiti in Context*. London: Routledge, pp 165-190.

Kelling, G. L. & Coles, C.M. 1998. *Fixing Broken Windows: Restoring Order and Reducing Crime in Our Communities*. New York: Simon and Schuster Inc.

Kirkpatrick, D. 2014. Egyptian journalists protest editors' pledge not to criticize state, *New York Times* June 11 - http://www.nytimes.com/2014/11/03/world/middleeast/egyptian-journalists-protest-editors-pledge-not-to-criticize-state.html?_r=0

Lau, J. 2014. Art spawned by Hong Kong protest; How to make it live on, *New York Times* Nov 14 - http://www.nytimes.com/2014/11/15/world/asia/rescuing-protest-artwork-from-hong-kongs-streets.html?_r=0

Le Quellec, J-L. 2008. What's new in the Sahara 2000-2004? in Bahn, P. Franklin, N. & Strecker, M. *Rock Art Studies News of the World III*. Oxbow. pp. 52-88.

Le Quellec, J-L., and Huyge, D. 2008. Rock art research in Egypt 2000-2004, in P. Bahn, N. Franklin & M. Strecker (eds) *Rock Art Studies News of the World III*. Oxford: Oxbow, pp. 89-96.

Lewis-Williams, J.D. 2013. Southern African rock art and beyond: A personal perspective, *Time and Mind* 6(1): 42-43.

Marshall, R. 1992. Repelling ghosts, in R Marshall (ed.) *Jean-Michel Basquiat*. New York: Whitney Museum of American Art/Harry Abrams, NYC. pp. 15-27.

MetMuseum. *The Collection Online (Brassaï)* - http://www.metmuseum.org/collection/the-collection-online/search/262735

Morayef, S. 2013. *Reading Into Rape* - http://tahrirsquared.com/node/2880

Nash, G. & Chippindale, G. 2002 (eds) *European Landscapes of Rock Art*. London and New York: Routledge.

Reed, N. 1981. *The Graffiti File*. London: George Allen and Unwin.

Reeves, N. 2000. *Akhenaten: Egypt's False Prophet*. London: Thames & Hudson.

Rushfield, R. 2014. *Conservation in the news: what happened to the art after the protesters have gone?* (AIC blog update 21/11/2014) - http://www.conservators-converse.org/2014/11/what-happens-to-the-art-after-the-protesters-have-gone/

Sernoffsky, E. 2014. Banksy's SF Legacy: high-priced Graffiti, *San Francisco Chronicle*, Sunday, June 22, 2014 - http://www.fineartconservationlab.com/wp-content/uploads/2014/06/Save-The-Banksy-6.22.2014.pdf

Shapiro, P. 2007. *Rough Guide to Hip Hop*. London: Rough Guides.

Sirmans, F. 2005. In the Cipher: Basquiat and Hip Hop Culture, in M. Mayer (ed.) *Basquiat*. Brooklyn: Merrell Publishers (Brooklyn Museum), pp. 91-105

Tassie, G. J. & Owens, L. S. 2010. *Standards of Archaeological Excavation: A Fieldguide to the Excavation Methodology, Recording Techniques and Conventions*. London: ECHO Publications and Golden House Publications.

Thompson, R.F. 1992. Royalty, heroism and the streets, in R Marshall (ed.) *Jean-Michel Basquiat*. New York: Whitney Museum of American Art/Harry Abrams, NYC, pp. 28-42.

Thompson, G. 2007. *American Culture in the 1980s*. Edinburgh: Edinburgh University Press.

Van de Bildt, J. 2013. Revolutionary Graffiti in Egypt: Resistance and Commemoration, *Tel Aviv Notes* 7: 24. -

Womanstats 2013 ('CB'). *Feminist Street Art in the Egyptian Uprising*. June 10, 2013. - http://womanstats.wordpress.com/2013/06/10/feminist-street-art-in-the-egyptian-uprising/

Wooters Yip, E. 2014. *Conservation of 'Graffiti' in Top Art Markets: Municipal Preservation of Illicitly Created Public Art in Hong Kong, New York City, and London*. Savannah: M.A. Thesis, Savannah College of Art and Design - - https://www.academia.edu/6477619/Conservation_of_Graffiti_in_Top_Art_Markets_Municipal_Preservation_of_Illicitly_Created_Public_Art_in_Hong_Kong_New_York_City_and_London

NB: Hosny/Ghanem, Tull, Gill, Krause and Tassie – papers included within the current volume.

ADDENDUM

ABBREVIATIONS

ARCE – American Research Center in Egypt
ASAE – Annales du Service des Antiquités de L'Egypte, Cairo.
CultNat – The National Centre for Documentation of Cultural and Natural Heritage
DAIK – Deutschen Archäologischen Instituts, Kairo.
EAIS – Egyptian Antiquities Information System
ECHO – The Egyptian Cultural Heritage Organisation
EES – Egypt Exploration Society
GCI – Getty Conservation Institute
GPMP – Giza Plateau Mapping Project
IARC – Illicit Antiquities Research Centre
ICAHM – International Committee on Archaeological Heritage Management
ICCROM – International Centre for the Study of the Preservation and Restoration of Cultural Property
ICOM – International Council of Museums
ICOMOS – International Committee on Monuments and Sites
IFA – Institute of Field Archaeologists
IFAO – l'Institut Français d'Archéologie Orientale, Cairo
IFM – International Fund for Monuments
ISCOTIA – International Standing Committee on the Traffic in Illegal Antiquities
MA – Ministry of Antiquities
MSA – Ministry of State for Antiquities
SCA – Supreme Council of Antiquities
TMP – Theban Mapping Project
UKIC – United Kingdom Institute for Conservation (Archaeology Section)
UNESCO – The United Nations Educational, Scientific and Cultural Organisation
WAC – World Archaeological Congress

GLOSSARY OF TERMS

Height Above Sea Level (a.s.l.) – This is the height in metres or feet Above Ordinance Datum (AOD), which is the average of the sea level at a set place in the country.

Accession – The process of transferring title or ownership from the providing source (fieldwork, purchase, gift, transfer, etc) to a museum or other storage facility.

Conservation – The process of preserving and protecting objects and monuments from loss, damage, decay or other forms of deterioration.

Computerised Tomography (CT) scans – A CT scanner is a special kind of X-ray machine. Instead of sending out a single X-ray through the body as with ordinary X-rays, several beams are sent simultaneously from different angles. The information from the two-dimensional computer images can be reconstructed to produce three-dimensional images by some modern CT scanners. They can be used to produce virtual images that show what a bioarchaeologist would see if the unwrapped and cut open a mummy's body. Therefore, they allow the specialist to inspect the inside the body of a mummy without having to operate or perform destructive examinations.

Deoxyribonucleic acid (DNA) – This is a nucleic acid that contains the genetic instructions used in the development and functioning of all known living organisms and some viruses. The main role of DNA molecules is the long-term storage of information. DNA is often compared to a set of blueprints or a recipe, or a code, since it contains the instructions needed to construct other components of cells, such as proteins and RNA molecules. DNA studies can help in identifying the relationships at the individual level, or long-term genetic history of the wider social group.

Environmental Impact Assessments (EIAs) – As pressure on cultural heritage and the environment increases the need to assess the impact of development on the environment becomes ever more prescient.

The technical term for this assessment procedure is environmental impact assessment. EIAs should be undertaken on relevant aspects of the project, and early in the planning stages. Environmental impact assessments should rely on conclusions derived from data analysis of primary field data and secondary data sources. The EIA process comprises:

- Screening – to decide if and at what level EIA should be applied, Scoping - to identify the important issues and prepare terms of reference
- Baseline Studies – to establish the pre-development condition for each aspect of the environment
- Impact Analysis and Monitoring – to predict the effects of a proposal and evaluate their significance the analysis may need to include a period of monitoring in order to detect the extent and pace of environmental change
- Mitigation – to establish measures to prevent, reduce or compensate for impacts
- Reporting – to prepare the information necessary for decision-making
- Review – to check the quality of the EIA report
- Decision-making – to approve or reject the proposal and set conditions
- Follow-up – to monitor, manage and audit impacts of project implementation
- Public Involvement – to inform and consult with stakeholders.

The five primary environmental components to consider are:

- Physical/Chemical – Covering all physical and chemical aspects of the environment
- Biological/Ecological – Covering all biological aspects of the environment, including renewable natural resources, conservation of biodiversity, species interactions, and pollution of the biosphere
- Palaeo-Ecological/Palaeoenvironmental – A special skill within the group is associated with analysis of sediment and soil cores to generate a broad spectrum of palaeoenvironmental information about geochemistry, mineralogy, and macro- and microfossil assemblages. Such data can be used (with adequate dating methods) to reveal time trends in ecosystem and local landscape changes as a result of pollution, site contamination and disturbance and past water availability and quality.
- Sociological/Cultural – Covering all human aspects of the environment, including social issues affecting individuals and communities; together with cultural aspects, including conservation and management of cultural heritage, and human development
- Economic/Operational – To qualitatively identify the economic consequences of environmental change, both temporary and permanent, as well as the complexities of project management within the context of the project activities.

Gaffir – The guardians of sites around Egypt who are employed by the SCA to protect the sites from looting, vandalism and other threats.

GIS: (Geographical Information System(s)) – A range of techniques using graphic capabilities combined with database facilities of computers for an integrated spatial analysis of maps, images, sites and finds.

Global Positioning System – This is a form of global navigation satellite system, others include COMPASS, GALILEO, and GLONASS. These systems rely on the receiver that the surveyor holds or erects triangulating the position of earth mapping satellites that circle the planet and relating that data to a world grid system such as UTM WS84.

Heritage Environmental Records (HER) – These are a new name for SMRs, albeit with more environmental information stored in the records.

Magnetic Resonance Imaging (MRI) – A scan system that uses a magnetic field and pulses of radio wave energy to make pictures of organs and structures inside the body. In many cases, MRI gives different information about structures in the body than can be seen with an X-ray or CT scan. For an MRI test, the area of the body being studied is placed inside a special machine that contains a strong magnet. Pictures from an MRI scan are digital images that can be saved and stored on a computer for more study. The images also can be reviewed remotely. Mainly used for examining mummies without damaging them.

Protection – Measures taken to guard sites and monuments using a variety of heritage management techniques.

Preservation – The maintenance of sites, monuments and artefacts through various conservation means.

***Quftis* –** These were originally Petrie's workers from the town of Quft in Upper Egypt. Petrie trained these workers in archaeological methods and would use them at many different sites around Egypt. The skills that have been learnt have been passed down from father to son, and these descendents of Petrie's original workers are in demand as labourers around Egypt.

Reconstruction – The rebuilding of artefacts and monuments with the ancient material that is available. For example, the piecing/gluing together of the fragments of a broken pottery vessel from the piece recovered in an archaeological excavation. Although a small amount of filler may be used, to make the vessel stable, new material is generally not added.

Rehabilitation – This is a process used for restoring monuments and is very similar to restoration. The main difference is that the building can then be lived in and become of the living cultural heritage.

Restoration – This is the most intrusive of the methods of conservation, where the artefact or monument is rebuilt to an approximation of its original form. Unlike reconstruction, new elements are added to the object where pieces are missing. The added material is usually as close to the original missing fabric as possible.

Sites and Monuments Record (SMR) – The records of all the sites and monuments in a province of country. At first paper documents were kept, but these records are now usually computerised details of each site or monument, which include cross-references to maps, publications, satellite images and aerial photographs, and also information on the periods of site occupation, size, form, function, condition, location, finds, present status of archaeological protection, history of archaeological investigation, and incident threats.

Stabilisation – This is the most minimal conservation techniques and consists of as little intervention as possible beyond stabilising the object's disintegration/deterioration process.

***Taftish* –** The local archaeological office where the Supreme Council of Antiquities (SCA) Inspectors work.

***Waqfs* –** Charitable religious foundations that make money available for restoration of religious buildings or for people.

ARABIC ABSTRACTS

Egyptian Cultural Heritage at the Dawn of the Arab Spring – a Future for the Past

Kelly Krause

التراث الحضارى المصرى فى فجر الربيع العربى – مستقبل للماضي

كيلي كراوس

نبذة

منذ بداية ثورة مصر يناير 2011 ، عانت بعض المواقع التراثية والأثار والتحف العريقة المعروضة فى متاحف مصر ومخازنها من الإهمال أو ماهو أسوأ. وفى نفس الوقت، لعبت كثير من هذه المواقع والقطع الأثرية دورا هاما كرموز لتطوير الهوية الحضارية المصرية، حيث قامت كثرة من الجماعات والأفراد بالعمل علي حماية التراث الحضارى المصرى خلال فترة الفوضي والعنف وغياب الأمن.

وبالرغم من أن هذا التراث الحضاري بوسعه القيام بتشكيل هوية مصرية جديدة وإيجابية داخل المجتمع المصرى المتغير، إلا أنه يشكل أيضا ميدانا للنزاع والجدل داخل وبين الجهات الإدارية، والمتخصصين فى التراث والمجتمعات المحلية. وتبحث المؤلفة مدى أهمية "المكان" داخل المجتمعات المصرية إضافة إلي الممارسات العملية والنظرية فى إدارة التراث المصرى وما دلالة هذا لمستقبل العمل ومساهمته للشعب المصرى.

Egypt's Heritage in Times of Conflict and Crisis

G. J. Tassie, A. De Trafford and J. van Wetering

التراث المصرى أثناء الصراعات والأزمات

ج. ج. تاسي، ا. دى ترافورد، ج. فان ويتيرنج

نبذة

منحت الثورة المصرية 25 يناير 2011 التي وضعت نهاية لحكم حسني مبارك المتسلط، الأمل فى حرية إجتماعية وسياسية وإقتصادية أكبر لملايين المصريين. غير أن السنوات الثلاث التي تلتها، شهدت غيابا للإستمرارية الإدارية والتمويل الحكومى وإختفاء الشرطة والقوانين والأجراءات الملزمة فى مجال إدارة التراث الحضاري، تركت التراث الحضاري المصرى لقمة سائغة ينهشها أفراد لاضمير لهم. فتعرضت المتاحف والمخازن للسلب، ونهبت مئات المواقع الأثرية علي يد عصابات إجرامية منظمة جيدا ولديها أسلحة أوتوماتيكية. وأدت الهجمات الإرهابية والعنف الطائفى لتدمير متاحف ودور عبادة ومباني تاريخية أخري. كما شهدت هذه الفترة أيضا زيادة فى التعديات على الأراضى الأثرية المحمية وغير المحمية.

وبالرغم من أن كثيرا ممن قاموا بهذه التعديات يزعمون أن السبب هو عدم وجود أراضي للبناء عليها، فإنها عموما مجرد حيلة لإخفاء أنشطتهم الشائنة لنهب التراث. وقد أدى النمو السكاني المتسارع لمصر إلى الحاجة لمزيد من السكن. وبدلا من البناء فى المناطق الصحراوية المستصلحة بعيدا عن المواقع الأثرية، تم هدم كثير من المباني التاريخية التي تعود للزمن الجميل على يد ملاكها الجشعين من أجل بناء عمائر من الخرسانة والصلب لتسكين عائلات بأسعار متزايدة على الدوام. وهو مايدمر ليس فقط جماليات المدن الكبرى مثل الإسكندرية والقاهرة، بل يدمر أيضا جوهر التنوع العرقي الذى يشكل أسس الحضارة المصرية.

كثير من الأفراد وموظفي التراث وعامة الجمهور شاركوا معا فى محاولة حماية تراث مصر الحضاري فى مواجهة هذه الأقلية المجرمة. لقد شكل الناس سلاسل بشرية حول الأثار والمتاحف لحمايتها. كما

ظهرت حملات على وسائل التواصل الإجتماعي للتحذير من التدمير الوشيك للتراث الحضاري والمطالبة بحماية أكبر بالمواقع والآثار. وهذه فرصة لتعاون أوثق بين الأثا ريين المصريين وزملائهم الأجانب ومشاركة أوسع لهؤلاء العاملين فى التراث مع الجمهور العام، وخاصة أولئك الذين يعيشون عند عتبات المواقع والأثار. وهذه فرصة لإنشاء نظم جديدة للإدارة وقوانين لحماية التراث الحضاري، والإستماع لأصوات المصريين المعاصرين فى تشكيل إدارة تراثهم وقيمهم.

Creating Egyptian Archives and the Production of Perfect Paperwork?

Nathalie Cohen

إنشاء أرشيفات مصرىة وإنتاج منتج ورقي مثالي؟

نثالي كوهين

نبذة

تبحث هذه الورقة بعض القضايا المتعلقة بأرشفة المشروعات، والتى تنتج عن الأبحاث الأثرية الممولة من قبل مطورين فى إنجلترا وأيضا مصر. وسيجرى أيضا فحص الأرشيفات الناتجة عن مشاريع بحثية ومعاهد علمية. وسنناقش نوعية الوسائط المستخدمة والطرق التى تم تطويرها لأرشفة المواد. كما سيجرى مناقشة بعض المشاكل المرتبطة بعملية تجميع وتخزين أرشيف، واستعراض مزايا القيام بهذه الوظيفة.

Contemporary Egyptian Dialogues: Collaborative Approaches to Museum Displays of Ancient Egypt

Gemma Tully

حوارات المصريين المعاصرين: وسائل تعاونية لعروض المتحف لمصر القديمة

جيما تولي

نبذة

من المؤكد أن التصورات المعاصرة عن مصر القديمة قد تأثرت بقرنين من التقاليد البحثية الغربية. والتي تأسست على أولوية الأثاروتغليب الموت والنخبة على جوانب الحياة اليومية والتى أدت إلى توصيف المصريين الأحياء بعدم الإستمرارية، "كشرقيين" و "أخرين"، ولاتزال المفهومات الحالية لمصر القديمة تواصل عزل المصريين المعاصرين عن ماضيهم وتعمل على إعادة نسخ الصور النمطية المؤثرة. وهذا التعاطى الحصرى لعلم الأثار المصرية لايتسق مع الأساليب الأثرية فى القرن 21، والتى تهدف إلى التعاون مع مجتمعات متنوعة – تشمل المنبع والزائر والأكاديمى – لتحسين الفهم المتبادل للماضى.

ومن خلال البحث ضمن مشروع تعاوني دام أربع سنوات مع أعضاء من المجتمع المصرى المعاصر، وخبراء فى علم الأثار المصرية، وغيرهم، تسعى هذه الورقة لعرض التصورات المصرية الحالية حول الماضى المصرى العريق. ولأجل تفكيك قرون من الرؤية الغربية "ضيقة الأفق"، تقدم الأصوات المصرية المعروضة هنا إقتراحات لأجل مستقبل البحث العلمى لعلم الأثار المصرية والعرض المتحفي يمكن إدراجها بجانب إحتياجات المشاهدين والأكاديميين الغربيين.إن محاولة العثور علي وسائل للتحاور بين مصر القديمة والحديثة، بين الهوية والأكاديمية، والشرق والغرب، هى التى تجعل هذا البحث جوهريا لأجل تواصل علم الأثار المصرية مع الجدل الحالي ولإستعراض دور قضايا الأخلاق وتعدد التعبير فى نشر المعرفة.

Egyptian Antiquities on the Market

David W. J. Gill

التحف المصرية فى السوق

ديفيد و. ج. جيل

نبذة

تباع تحف أثرية مصرية فى السوق بما قيمته عدة ملايين من الدولارات كل سنة. ويبدو أن أغلبية هذه التحف قد ظهرت للمرة الأولي منذ عام 1973، وهو التاريخ الذى قام فيه معهد الأثار الأمريكي بإتخاذ "قرار حيازة المتاحف للأثار". والظاهر أن بعض المواد المعروضة فى السوق قد جرى نقلها من مخازن أثرية فى مصر. وهناك أيضا دليل واضح على أن نقوشا وقطعا أخرى يتم رفعها من مقابر مسجلة. وهناك قطع أخرى عديدة مثل لوحة أخميم، أتت من مواقع غير معروفة من قبل، وأدى نقلها إلى فقدان المعرفة بسياقها الأصلي. وقد حدث الفضائح التى أحاطت بعودة التحف الأثرية إلى إيطاليا، بمتاحف أمريكا الشمالية إلى تطوير سياسات حيازة أكثر صرامة. والأرجح أن يؤدى هذا إلى خفض الطلب السوقي علي التحف المصرية التى ليس لها تواريخ جمع مسجلة.

"Battered Bulls" Again: Destruction and First Attempts at Conservation of Rock Art in Egypt

Dirk Huyge

"الثيران المضروبة" مرة أخرى: الدمار والمحاولات الأولي لصيانة الفن الصخري فى مصر.

ديرك هوجي

نبذة

انزوي الفن الصخري المصرى غالبا فى ظلال البقايا المذهلة للحضارة الفرعونية، ولم يلق كثيرا من الإهتمام سواء من قبل الجمهور العام أو المجتمع العلمي. ولذا لم يتم سوى عمل قليل لأجل الحفاظ على هذا التراث الضخم المعرض للتلف والمكون من عدة مئات من المواقع تضم الألاف من الصور، تعود أغلبيتها الساحقة إلى عصر ماقبل التاريخ. ومن خلال المسوحات الحديثة، بات من الواضح مدى الدمار الذى لحق بالفن الصخرى فى الماضى، وخاصة كنتيجة لأعمال المحاجر الواسعة النطاق للحصول على مواد بناء على امتداد النيل وفى الصحراء الشرقية. ولايزال هذا التدمير يجرى بكل أسف، غير أن بعض كشوفات الفن الصخرى الرائع مؤخرا قد ساهمت فى ازدياد الوعي داخل سلطات الأثار المصرية بالإمكانات العلمية للفن الصخرى، وقيمته الحضارية الجوهرية ومردود إقتصادياته المحتملة. ولذا جرت بعض المحاولات المبدئية فى الأعوام الأخيرة لحماية مواقع الفن الصخرى بوضع أسوار مع / أو ترتيب خفراء محليين فى الموقع.

Purity, Power and Nudity: Social Dynamics of Hammams in History

Fekri A. Hassan

النقاء، والسلطة والعري: التفاعل الإجتماعي للحمامات فى التاريخ

فكرى حسن
نبذة
تعتبر الحمامات واحدة من مظاهر الإستحمام العامة التي جعلت من هذا العمل حدثا إجتماعيا نشطا وتجربة شخصية فعالة. فمن خلال التحكم فى الجسم وإدارته، يحافظ المجتمع على تركيبه ومبادئه وضوابطه. وفى عديد من الديانات، أصبحت المياه قربي للإيمان وزلفي إلى الرب ومن خلالها يأمل الإنسان أن يذوق رحمته وإحسانه. ولذا فالنظافة لاتقرب الإنسان من قضية الحياة والموت فحسب، بل أيضا تقربه من المقدس. وعلى النقيض من بيوت الحمام الرومانية واليونانية، والتى كانت تتصف بالضخامة والنور والضجيج، فإن الحمامات تتميز بالهدوء. فالحمام يستدعي سكينة الجنة ومكان للإسترخاء، والتواصل الإجتماعي الودود وتجديد الحيوية، حيث تعمل الخطوات الطويلة التى تشمل التعرض لدرجات حرارة وأوضاع وأنشطة مختلفة على إيقاظ الحواس بوتيرة مضبوطة ومطولة لضمان الإنتقال من الضغط اليومى إلى حالة من إعادة الإنتعاش الهادىء والمريح. وفى عهود المماليك والعثمانيين ازدهرت الحمامات فى أنحاء شمال افريقيا وجنوب غرب أسيا، حيث تولي الراعون الأثرياء بناء هذه المؤسسات والتى ألحق بعضها بالمساجد وبعضها شيدت داخل منازلهم ولأجل العامة كمؤسسات خيرية، مؤكدين على مكانتها ووضعها الإجتماعى. أما الأن فأعداد الحمامات، كما فى القاهرة على سبيل المثال، قد تناقصت ولم يعد بوسع مابقى منها مجاراة التكاليف المتزايدة للماء والوقود. وقد هجرها الأكثر رفاهية فى المجتمع ليس فقط بسبب إنتشار الحمامات الخاصة، بل بسبب تغيرات فى مزاج المجتمع وإنتشار ممارسة العائلة الواحدة بأمل المشاركة فى'الحداثة'. وإحدى أهم عناصر الحداثة (والتى تمثلت قبلا فى مراوح كهربائية وثلاجة) هى إمتلاك حمام منزلي.

The Nile Delta in Peril: Cultural Heritage Management in the Delta

G. J. Tassie, J. van Wetering and A. De Trafford

دلتا النيل فى خطر: إدارة التراث الحضاري فى الدلتا

ج. ج. تاسي، ا. دى ترافورد، ج. فان ويتيرنج

نبذة
تعد الدلتا إحدى أكثر المناطق إزدحاما بالسكان فى مصر. وقد تشكلت الدلتا من فروع النيل فى عصور ماقبل التاريخ وشهد سهلها الفيضي إستيطانا بشريا مستمرا حتى الأن. وإستجابة لتذبذب كمية الفيضان النيلي، وتمدد وانحسار ساحل البحر الأبيض المتوسط، إضافة إلى هبوط مستوى الأرض، تعتبر الدلتا حالة نموذجية كيفية تشكيل التغير المناخي والعمليات الجيولوجية للمظهر السطحى (اللاندسكيب). وقد تم فى سياق المظهر السطحى النشط والمتغير والمتحرك إتخاذ الخطوات الأولي فى الحضارة المصرية، حيث شهدت الدلتا تفاعل شعوب من بلاد الشام ومابين النهرين وفارس واليونان وروما واوروبا عبر التاريخ من خلال التجارة والغزوات أو هجرات السكان. وبالتالي، تعتبر الدلتا صورة مصغرة لتراث العالم تغطى زمنيا أولي الخطى لصنع الحضارة والتى تشمل تشكيل أول الدول السياسية وحتى وقتنا الحاضر. ان المحطات التجارية للتجار الشوام وتجار المدن الصناعية اليونانيين، والأديرة والمساجد والمقابر الملكية والقلاع وترسانات السفن، والبساتين ومدن العواصم وغيرها الكثير تقف شاهدة على موكب أحداث العالم. غير أن هذا التراث العالمى النفيس معرض الأن للخطر بسبب التعرية الساحلية، ومزارع السمك، والمستوطنات التوسعية، والأنشطة التنموية العشوائية. وفى الأصل ولزمن طويل، لم يزد سكان الدلتا عن مليون نسمة، بينما تموج الأن بمايزيد عن ثلاثة وأربعين مليونا ويتوقع أن يتضاعف هذا الرقم فى خلال ثلاثين عاما. وتنتشر ألاف القرى والمدن والمزارع فى إعصار بشرى غير مسبوق مهددا مواقع كافة العصور من مدينة رشيد بعمارتها المشهورة التى ترجع للعصور الوسطي إلى مواقع أثرية تكاد تكون غير معروفة والتى كانت يوما ما عواصم مهيبة لمصر القديمة مثل سايس وبوتو. ويصاحب التوسع المادى لسكان الدلتا كثير من الأنشطة التى تهدد وجود المواقع القديمة نفسها: البناء فوق

المواقع، إزالة التربة، والرمال والحصي لأجل البناء، إغراق المواقع بمياه المجارى والمصارف وتحويل المواقع إلى مزارع سمكية. والأكثر خطورة هو الحفر غير المشروع الذى يصعب غالبا مكافحته. أما إرتفاع مستوى البحر إستجابة للتغيرات المناخية فهو مجرد واحد من العوامل الجيولوجية التى تهدد تراث الدلتا. وسيؤثر التغير المناخي على كمية فيضان النيل مما سيؤدى إلى تقلبات جسيمة فى مستوى النيل.

The Great Festival of Luxor: A Brief Study of the Mawlid of Aboul Haggag and its Cultural Significances

Mohamed Hussein Hosny and Mo'men Ghanem

العيد الكبير للأقصر: دراسة موجزة لمولد أبى الحجاج وأهميته الثقافية

محمد حسين حسني ومؤمن غانم

نبذة

ان احتفالات الموالد الصوفية تمثل درجة رفيعة المستوى من النشاطات الانسانية المتكررة التى تحدث فى الفراغ العمرانى لما لها من صدى تاريخى وتأثير روحى ،وبما بها من نسق منظم ومتسق من الحركة، ويمثل مولد أبو الحجاج الاقصرى ، القطب الصوفى الاكثر شهرة فى مدينة الاقصر والمدن المجاورة، نموذجا مثاليا لمثل هذه الاحتفالات، وحدثا ثقافيا بالغ الأهمية فى المنطقة التاريخية بوسط المدينة . تسعى هذه الورقة البحثية الى بيان الجوانب المختلفة المرتبطة بهذا الاحتفال، بدءا من تسليط الضوء على أهمية أبو الحجاج كقطب صوفى ذو تأثير واسع على السكان المحليين من خلال الدور الذى لعبه فى المدينة خلال الفترة الزمنية التى تمتد ما بين نهاية القرن الثانى عشر وبداية القرن الثالث عشر الميلادى. ويركز البحث على أشكال وطقوس الاحتفال المختلفة، ويدرس أصولها المحتملة، سواء بارتباطها بالاصل الفرعونى للمدينة أو الأصل التونسى –المزعوم- لأبى الحجاج.

إن هدف هذه الورقة البحثية هو التأكيد على ضرورة الحفاظ على مولد أبو الحجاج كتقليد ثقافى موروث للسكان المحليين، وفى هذا السياق تم بحث التصور العام للسكان المحليين لهذا التراث والبيئة المبنية المحيطة به، ويتضح لنا أن أهمية هذا المولد تأتى من قيمته الروحية والاجتماعية ، وأن تأثيره يمتد ليشمل التصور العام للتشكيل العمرانى للبيئة المبنية المحيطة ، والذى يؤكد ذلك أن الصورة الذهنية عند السكان المحليين لهذا الجزء من المدينة ونسيجها العمرانى من مبانى وشوارع وساحات يرتبط ارتباطا وثيقا باحتفال (الدورة) فى مولد أبو الحجاج مما يجعل الاخيرة مستحقة للتسجيل على قائمة التراث الثقافى العالمى لمنظمة اليونيسكو.

Where Did the Nile Harbours Go?

Emad el-Khalil

أين ذهبت موانىء النيل؟

عماد الخليل

نبذة

وصف هيرودوت مصر كهبة للنيل. فالنهر لم يسمح فقط بممارسة الزراعة على ضفتيه، بل يسر أيضا التنقل بواسطة القوارب من أدني البلد إلى أقصاها. ولهذا، جرى وصف النيل بالطريق السريع لمصر

القديمة. وكانت المنتجات الزراعية إلى جانب الأحجار وغيرها من البضائع تنقل عبر النيل. فكان لكل مستوطنة رئيسية ميناء أو مرسى كى تتمكن المراكب الأكبر من الرسو وتفريغ حمولتها.
وبالرغم من أننا قد عثرنا على عدد من الموانىء على سواحل البحر الأحمر والبحر الأبيض المتوسط، إلا أنه لم يعثر حتى الأن سوى على عدد قليل للغاية من الموانىء النيلية. ويشير الدليل النصوصي إلى أنه ينبغى وجود عدد كبير من الموانىء التي ترجع للعصرين اليونانى والرومانى. غير أن نظام الفيضان النيلي قد طمس أية بقايا لأغلب هذه الموانىء.
إن العثور على جسر ومراسى من العصر المتأخر حتى العصر الرومانى عند الكرنك بسبب مشروع إدارة الموقع، من المأمول أن يكون أول موقع من مثل هذه المواقع والتى ستلقى الضوء على التجارة النهرية فى مصر. والأكثر اهمية، أنها تبين أهمية القيام بدراسات أثرية لتحديد المؤثرات وإجراء البحوث كجزء من مشاريع إدارة التراث الحضاري.

Single-Context Recording in the Context of Archaeological Fieldwork in Egypt, Part One.

G. J. Tassie

تسجيل السياق الواحد ضمن سياق العمل الميدانى الأثرى فى مصر، الجزء الأول.

ج. ج. تاسي

نبذة
على الرغم من القيم بحفائر علمية فى مصر منذ زمن بيتري، إلا أن كثيرا من التطورات الغربية فى علم الأثار نظرية وممارسة لاتزال تنتظر تبنيها من قبل أغلبية من يقومون بالعمل الميدانى فى مصر الأن. وورغم تعدد الأسباب، إلا أنها ترجع إلى الطريقة التى يدرس بها علم الأثار المصرية فى الجامعات. فكثير ممن يقومون بالحفائر لايزالون يستخدمون تقنية شبكة الصندوق هويلر – كينيون، فيحفرون قطعا أو حفرا لتحديد الطبقات والملامح من خلال أقسام شريطية. وعلى النقيض، بدأ الأن فى مصر إستعمال تسجيل السياق الواحد (SCR). ونناقش هنا مدى فعالية هذا المنهج، ومميزاته مقارنة بطرق الحفر التقليدية ونظرة عامة على هذا الإسلوب. وهذه الورقة من جزئين؛ حيث قدم الجزء الأول فى المؤتمر الدولي التاسع لعلماء الأثار المصرية فى جرينوبل بفرنسا سنة 2004 (تاسي 2007). وفى الجزء الثانى هناك شرح تفصيلي لإستعمال تسجيل السياق الواحد (SCR) فى سياق مصرى، وإلقاء مزيد من الضوء على مزايا وعيوب أخري – وخاصة مايتعلق بإستخدام العمالة المحلية – ولماذا ينبغى للجمعية الدولية لعلماء الأثار المصرية والمجلس الأعلى للأثار أن يلعبا دورا أكثر بروزا لتبني ممارسة جيدة فى المنهج الأثرى.

Is the Writing on the Wall for the Writing on the Wall? Opposition to - and Defence of - Egyptian Graffiti and Street Art

Lawrence S. Owens

هل تمثل الكتابة على الجدار كتابة جدارية؟ المعارضة والمدافعة عن المخربشات المصرية وفن الشارع

لورنس س. أوينز

نبذة
توضح هذه الدراسة حدود المخربشات المصرية الحديثة وتصنفها الى قسمين رئيسين؛ قسم خاص بالتدمير العشوائي للمباني التاريخية وآخر خاص بمشهد فن الشارع المزدهر. وتتصف السياسة الرسمية الحالية تجاه المخربشات وفن المخربشات بالسلبية كما تعكس اهتماما أقل بتخريب التراث حيث تبدو انها

محاولة إضافية للتحكم فى او القضاء على واحدة من الوسائل القليلة المتبقية للتواصل الاجتماعي عقب كارثة الرقابة الذاتية الطوعية الإعلامية. ويتميّز مجمل العمل الذي جري تشكيله بانه فريد وعالمي النزعة والأهمية غير أنه أيضا معرض للتهديد من قبل الجهات الحكومية الكارهة للفنون التجسيدية. ان خطورة الفن الجداري كمتنفس للمصريين العاديين وخاصة أولئك الذين تم تهميشهم تحت الحكومات المتعاقبة سيجري مناقشته هنا بالإشارة المباشرة لأعمال وحوادث تاريخية محددة. كما سنتناول باختصار المشاكل الكامنة فى صيانة الفن الجداري مع تقديم مقترحات لتسجيله وتبويبه من خلال برامج منصات البيانات الحاسوبية المفتوحة وقواعد البيانات ونظم المعلومات الجغرافية / خرائط جوجل باستخدام التطورات الاخيرة فى هونج كونج كنموذج.

INTERNATIONAL AND EGYPTIAN HERITAGE INSTITUTES

Egypt

Centre for Conservation and Preservation of Islamic Architectural Heritage (CIAH)
85, Ramsis Street
Cairo, 11511
Egypt
P.O. Box 764 Cairo
Egypt.
Tel.: +20 (2)5776122/5752495,
Fax.: +20 (2)5748872,
E-Mail: info@ciah.biz
Web site: http://www.ciah.biz
Associated institute: ICOMOS, Associated institute: Organization of Islamic Capitals & Cities.

CultNat
Smart Village
Cairo-Alexandria Desert Road
Giza
Egypt
Tel.: +20 (2)35343222
Fax.: +20 (2)35392929
E-Mail: cultnat@mcit.gov.eg
Website: http://www.cultnat.org

EAIS
6th Floor
3, el-Adel Bakr Street
Zamalek
Cairo
Egypt
Tel.: +20 (2)7350287
Fax.: +20 (2)7350287
E-Mail: eais@eais.org.eg
Website: http://www.eais.org.eg/index.pl/about.eais

International Council of Museum - Conservation Committee (ICOM-CC), Wood, Furniture and Lacquer
8, Sayed Darwish Steet
El-Kousaiareen
Cairo 11291
Egypt.
Tel.: +20 (2)4234474
Fax.: +20 (2)4251411
E-mail: hhnnc@yahoo.com
Website: http://www.icomcc.org/

Ministry of Antiquities/Supreme Council of Antiquities
3, el-Adel Bakr Street
Zamalek
Cairo
Egypt
Tel.: +20 (2)7365645

Fax.: +20 (2)7357239
E-Mail: sca_missions@hotmail.com
Website: http://www.sca.gov.eg
Website: http://www.museumsector.gov.eg

14, Fakhry Abdel Nour Street
Abassyia
Cairo
Egypt
Tel.: +20 (2)6859253
Fax.: +20 (2)6831117

International

The Art Loss Register
The Art Loss Register Ltd
First Floor, 63 – 66 Hatton Garden
London EC1N 8LE
UK
Tel: +44 (0)20 7841 5780
Fax.: +44 (0)20 7841 5781
Email: artloss@artloss.com
Website: http://www.artloss.com/

ECHO
14 Vincent Road,
Kingston-Upon-Thames,
Surrey KT1 3HJ,
UK
Email: echo@e-c-h-o.org, egyptianheritage@yahoo.co.uk
Website: http://www.e-c-h-o.org

Getty Conservation Institute
1200 Getty Center Drive
Suite 700
Los Angeles
CA 90049-1684
Tel: +310 4467325
Fax.: +310 4467702
Email: gciweb@getty.edu
Website: http://www.getty.edu/conservation

INTERPOL
General Secretariat
200, quai Charles de Gaulle
69006 Lyon
France
Fax: +33 (0)472447163
Website: http://www.interpol.com/Public/WorkOfArt/Default.asp

ICCROM
13, via di San Michele
I-00153 Rome RM
Italy
Tel.: +39 (0)6585531
Fax.: +39 (0)658553349
Email: iccrom@iccrom.org

Website: http://www.iccrom.org/

ICOMOS
70, Cowcross Street
London
EC1M 6EJ
UK
Tel.: +44 (0)2075660031
Fax.: +44 (0)2075660045
Email: admin@icomos.uk.org
Website: http://www.unesco.org

Saving Antiquities for Everyone (SAFE)
23 Town Square Place,
#151, Jersey City,
NJ 07310
USA
Email: cho@savingantiquities.org
Website: http://www.savingantiquities.org

UNESCO
7, Place de Fontenoy
75352 Paris 07 – SP
France
Tel.: + 33 (0)145681000
Fax.: +33 (0)145671690
Email: dl.egypte@unesco.org
Website: http://www.unesco.org

World Monuments Fund
95 Madison Avenue, 9th floor
New York, New York 10016
USA
Tel.: +(1) 6464249594
Fax.: +(1) 6464249593
Email: wmf@wmf.org
Website: http://www.wmf.org/

UNESCO Conventions Ratified by the Egyptian Government

Convention	Date of deposit of instrument	Type of instrument
Agreement on the Importation of Educational, Scientific and Cultural Materials, with Annexes A to E and Protocol annexed. Florence, 17 June 1950.	08/02/1952	Ratification
Convention for the Protection of Cultural Property in the Event of Armed Conflict with Regulations for the Execution of the Convention. The Hague, 14 May 1954.	17/08/1955	Ratification
Protocol to the Convention for the Protection of Cultural Property in the Event of Armed Conflict. The Hague, 14 May 1954.	17/08/1955	Ratification
Convention against Discrimination in Education. Paris, 14 December 1960.	28/03/1962	Acceptance
Convention concerning the International Exchange of Publications. Paris, 3 December 1958.	22/10/1962	Acceptance
Convention concerning the Exchange of Official Publications and Government Documents between States. Paris, 3 December 1958.	22/10/1962	Ratification
Convention on the Means of Prohibiting and Preventing the Illicit Import, Export and Transfer of Ownership of Cultural Property. Paris, 14 November 1970.	05/04/1973	Acceptance
Convention concerning the Protection of the World Cultural and Natural Heritage. Paris, 16 November 1972.	07/02/1974	Ratification
Protocol Instituting a Conciliation and Good Offices Commission to be Responsible for Seeking the Settlement of any Disputes which may Arise between States Parties to the Convention against Discrimination in Education. Paris, 10 December 1962.	05/08/1974	Acceptance
Convention for the Protection of Producers of Phonograms against Unauthorized Duplication of their Phonograms. Geneva, 29 October 1971.	15/12/1977	Accession
International Convention on the Recognition of Studies, Diplomas and Degrees in Higher Education in the Arab and European States bordering on the Mediterranean. Nice, 17 December 1976.	17/01/1978	Accession
Protocol to the Agreement on the Importation of Educational, Scientific and Cultural Materials, with Annexes A to H. Nairobi, 26 November 1976.	18/09/1981	Accession
Convention on the Recognition of Studies, Diplomas and Degrees in Higher Education in the Arab States. Paris, 22 December 1978.	23/09/1981	Ratification
Multilateral Convention for the Avoidance of Double Taxation of Copyright Royalties, with model bilateral agreement and additional Protocol. Madrid, 13 December 1979.	11/02/1982	Accession
Regional Convention on the Recognition of Studies, Certificates, Diplomas, Degrees and other Academic Qualifications in Higher Education in the African States. Arusha, 5 December 1981.	26/07/1985	Ratification
Convention on Wetlands of International Importance especially as Waterfowl Habitat. Ramsar, 2 February 1971.	09/09/1988	Ratification
Protocol to amend the Convention on Wetlands of International Importance especially as Waterfowl Habitat. Paris, 3 December 1982.	09/09/1988	Accession
Second Protocol to the Hague Convention of 1954 for the Protection of Cultural Property in the Event of Armed Conflict. The Hague, 26	03/08/2005	Ratification

March 1999.		
Convention for the Safeguarding of the Intangible Cultural Heritage. Paris, 17 October 2003.	03/08/2005	Ratification
International Convention against Doping in Sport. Paris, 19 October 2005	23/05/2007	Ratification
Convention on the Protection and Promotion of the Diversity of Cultural Expressions. Paris, 20 October 2005	23/08/2007	Ratification

REFERENCES

UNESCO WEBSITE –
http://portal.unesco.org/la/conventions_by_country.asp?contr=EG&language=E&typeconv=1

EGYPT AND THE WORLD HERITAGE LIST

The World Heritage List was established under terms of *The Convention Concerning the Protection of the World Cultural and Natural Heritage* adopted in November 1972 at the 17th General Conference of UNESCO.

The Convention states that a World Heritage Committee "will establish, keep up-to-date and publish" a World Heritage List of cultural and natural properties, submitted by the States Parties and considered to be of outstanding universal value.

One of the main responsibilities of this Committee is to provide technical co-operation under the World Heritage Fund for the safeguarding of World Heritage properties to States Parties whose resources are insufficient.

States Parties can request international assistance under the Fund for the preparation of tentative lists and nomination forms, expert missions, training of specialized staff, and supply of equipment when appropriate; they can also apply for long-term loans and, in special cases, non-repayable grants. Requests must concern work necessary for the preservation of cultural or natural sites included in the World Heritage List or assistance to national or regional training centres.

Emergency assistance is also available under the Fund in the case of properties severely damaged by specific natural or man-made disasters or threatened with imminent destruction (UNESCO, World Heritage List, 2003).

Up until 2002 there were only 5 areas of Egypt inscribed on the World Heritage List:

1. Memphis and its Necropolis – the Pyramid Fields from Giza to Dahshur (N29 51 E31 15)
2. Ancient Thebes with its Necropolis (N25 42 E32 35)
3. Nubian Monuments from Abu Simbel to Philae (N22 30 E31 50)
4. Islamic (Old) Cairo (N30 06 E31 26)
5. Abu Mena (Monastery near Alexandria) (N30 51 E29 40)

These areas were inscribed on the List in 1979, however, in 2002 one more area was added to the list:

6. St. Katherine's (Monastery and Area Immediately Surrounding it) (N28 34 E34 00)

In 2001, members of ECHO were involved in site management plans at various archaeological sites in the St. Katherine's Protectorate. Although these sites are not on the World Heritage List they are in the St. Katherine Protectorate and therefore, under the protection of the Egyptian Government.

In 2003, Gebel Barkal and the sites of the Napatan Region in Upper Nubia (Sudan) were inscribed on the World Heritage List. The area comprises of 5 sites:

1. Gebel Barkal (N18 32 E31 49)
2. El Kurru (N18 24 E31 46)
3. Nuri (N18 33 E31 55)
4. Sanam (N18 28 E31 49)
5. Zuma (N18 22 E31 44)

The latest site to be inscribed on the World Heritage List was in 2005:

7. Wadi Al-Hitan (Whale Valley) in the Faiyum Governorate (N30 11 00 E29 20 00)

For more information on these sites and the conservation means being implemented to protect them visit the UNESCO World Heritage List. Although at present only six areas in Egypt are inscribed on the World Heritage List, ECHO hopes that many more important and endangered areas will soon be inscribed on the List. Recent developments within UNESCO have seen a *Tentative List of World Heritage Sites* drawn up by the various member states.

ECHO has drawn up a further list of the most important archaeological sites to supplement the six sites already on UNESCO's World Heritage List. Many of the sites and monuments on ECHO's list concur and complement the Tentative List. The woefully inadequate number of Egyptian sites on the World Heritage List, particularly prehistoric sites, is only the first step to protecting these sites and monuments. However, the list of sites and monuments that fulfil the criteria of the UNESCO Guidelines article 24 should include:

ECHO Proposed List of Sites and Monuments to be Examined

Prehistoric Localities	
1. Bir Tarfawi & Bir Sahara	Acheulian sites and lake beds
2. Kharga Oasis (Tentative W.H.L.)	Acheulian & fossil springs
3. Dendera (Tentative W.H.L.)	Acheulian
4. Wadi Kubbaniya (Tentative W.H.L.)	Middle Palaeolithic and wadi habitat
5. Wadi Feiran (Tentative W.H.L.)	Upper Palaeolithic and oasis habitat
6. Nazlet Khater	Upper Palaeolithic mining
7. Taramsa-Tikh	Early *Homo sapiens*
8. North Faiyum (Tentative W.H.L.)	Terminal Palaeolithic & Lake Moeris shorelines
9. Wadi Mukatab, Sinai (Tentative W.H.L.)	Ancient writing and petroglyphs (Origins of Alphabet)

Origins of Agriculture and the Egyptian State	
10. Bir Kiseiba & Nabta Playa	Earliest domesticated cattle in Africa
11. Farafra Oasis (Tentative W.H.L.)	Rock art & organised communities
12. Merimde Beni Salame	Oldest Delta farming communities
13. Badari	Earliest farming chiefdoms in Upper Egypt
14. Naqada	Predynastic cemeteries, villages and towns
15. Hierakonpolis	Predynastic cemeteries and settlements
16. Tell Ibrahim Awad	Predynastic/Early Dynastic; earliest temple in Egypt
17. Maadi	Late Predynastic site
18. Buto	Early Delta capital
19. Abydos (Tentative W.H.L.)	Tombs of first kings of Egypt
20. Helwan	Early Dynastic tombs (10,000+)

Ports	
21. Quseir al-Qadim	Red Sea port with many Roman remains
22. Berenice	Predynastic - Roman Red Sea Port
23. Fustat and Misr al-Qadima	Old Cairo Nile port
24. Safaga	Red Sea port

Mining

25. Serabit el-Khadim (Tentative W.H.L.)	Mining and temple
26. Wadi Hammamat* (Tentative W.H.L.)	Petroglyphs, ancient mining and historical route
27. Wadi Gimal (Tentative W.H.L.)	Ancient mining
28. Gebel el-Silsila	Chapel of Horemheb, inscriptions and early mines
29. Widen el-Faras (Tentative W.H.L.)	Old Kingdom basalt quarries, north Faiyum
30. Umm el-Sawan (Tentative W.H.L.)	Old Kingdom gypsum quarries, north Faiyum

Historical Routes

31. Wadi Hammamat* (Tentative W.H.L.)	Petroglyphs, ancient mining and historical route
32. Horus Road (Tentative W.H.L.)	Egypt's eastern road
33. Wadi Tumilat	Oldest canal, and Egypt-Near East connection
34. Wadi el-Qash (Tentative W.H.L.)	Koptos to Berenice (Red Sea port) road, Kanays Temple

Religious Sites

35. Tree of Mariam	Sacred tree of the Virgin Mary
36. St. Catherine's Monastery and Gebel Musa (W. H. Listed)	Monastery at the foot of Mount Sinai and the mountain of Moses
37. Abu Mena (W. H. Listed)	Coptic monastery
38. Wadi el-Natrun (Tentative W.H.L.)	Coptic monasteries and Hathor Temple
39. Nag Hammadi	Pachomian monasteries of Tabennesi, Phbow and Sheneset
40. Islamic Cairo (W.H. Listed)	The foundation of the city of Cairo, including Fustat and the Roman fort of Babylon; early Coptic churches
41. Deir el-Abaid (Sohag)	Monastery
42. Monasteries of St. Anthony and St. Paul	Earliest monasteries in the world
43. Medinet Madi (Tentative W.H.L.)	Middle Kingdom temple of Amenemhet III and Ptolemaic temples in the Faiyum

Ancient Dams

44. Balawan Dam (Tentative W.H.L.)	Middle Kingdom dam built across the Hawara Channel, Faiyum
45. Shedmu Dam (Tentative W.H.L.)	Remains of Ptolemaic and historic Islamic dam, built on earlier Pharaonic dam, near Itsa, Faiyum
46. Sadd Al-Kafara	Oldest dam in the world, built in the Old Kingdom, 25 km south of ancient Memphis at Wadi Al-Garawi

Political Sites

47. Al-Azbakia	Mamluk and Napoleon's residence in Egypt
48. Citadel	Site of Mamluk power, and birth of modern Egypt
49. Abdine Palace	Royal residence from Ismail to Farouk
50. Al-Tell El-Kebir	Battle with Ahmed Orabi & British occupation
51. Alexandria (Abu Qir) (Tentative W.H.L.)	Bombardment of Alexandria and navel battles
52. El-Alamein	Site of WWII battle that turned back Nazi invasion into Egypt & war cemetery

Traditional Settlements

53. Old Siwa & Gara (Tentative W.H.L.)	Traditional oasis village
54. Qasr el-Dakhla (Tentative W.H.L.)	Old Kingdom oasis town

Pharaonic Sites

55. Akhmim	Dismantled remains of the 9th nome capital
56. Nubian sites to Aswan (W. H. Listed)	Abu Simbel, Philae
57. Kom Ombo (Tentative W.H.L.)	Ptolemaic temple
58. Edfu Temple	Ptolemaic temple (almost complete)
59. El-Kab	Site of *Nekhbet* & successive temples
60. Esna Temple (Tentative W.H.L.)	Ptolemaic temple and sacred site of *Lates* fish
61. Thebes (W.H. Listed)	Karnak, Valley of the Kings
62. Dendera	Hathor Temple: Early Dynastic - Ptolemaic
63 El-Arabeh Al-Madfuna	Temples of Seti I & Ramesses II
64. Tell el-Amarna (Tentative W.H.L.)	City of Akhenaten
65. Ashmunein (Tentative W.H.L.)	Graeco-Roman necropolis
66. Tuna el-Gebel	Unique tomb of Petosiris
67. Ihnasya	Capital of Egypt in the 9th & 10th Dynasties
68. Beni Hasan (Tentative W.H.L.)	First Intermediate to Middle Kingdom necropolis
69. Al-Lahun (Tentative W.H.L.)	Middle Kingdom pyramid and town of Senusret II
70. el-Lisht	Middle Kingdom pyramids of Senusret I and Amenemhet I
71. Hawara (Tentative W.H.L.)	Middle Kingdom Pyramid of Amenemhet III
72. Dimai, Qasr Sagha (Tentative W.H.L.)	Graeco-Roman city, Middle Kingdom temple Faiyum
73. Byahmu (Tentative W.H.L.)	Bases of colossal statues of Amenemhet III and history of Qarun Lake
74. Maidum	Dynasty IV pyramid of Sneferu and Old kingdom and later cemeteries
75. The pyramid fields from Dahshur to Giza, including Memphis (W. H. Listed)	Pyramids and mortuary complexes with the surrounding tombs of the elite of the Old Kingdom, first and enduring capital of Egypt
76. Sais (Sa el-Hagar)*	Early Capital of Egypt and again in Dynasty XXVI, Neolithic settlement
77. Buto (Tell el-Fara'in)*	Important Pharaonic remains at the ancient Delta Capital
78. Tell el-Maskhuta	Late Period to Graeco-Roman settlement and cemetery remains
79. Bahbeit el-Hagar	Premier temple of Isis
80. Heliopolis (Al-Mataryia)	Ancient Egyptian religious and learning centre
81. Tell el-Basta	The town of Bubastis and the Goddess Bastet
82. San el Hagar (Tanis)	Ramesses II and Late Period city
83. Hibis Temple, El-Kharga	Well-preserved temple of Darius (and others)
84. Aghourmi Temple, Siwa (Tentative W.H.L.)	Site of the Oracle of Amun visited by Alexander the Great
85. Zawiyet Umm el-Rakham	Ramesside fort
86. Tanis	Late Period city

87. Pi-Ramesses	City of Ramesses II
88. Alexandria* (Tentative W.H.L.)	Temples and palaces of Cleopatra and Anthony
89. Kom el-Aushim (Karanis)* (Tentative W.H.L.)	Ptolemaic and Roman city, Faiyum
90. Kom Umm el-Boreigat (Tebtynis)* (Tentative W.H.L.)	Ptolemaic and Roman city, Faiyum
91. Mendes (Tell el-Rub'a and Tell el-Timai)*	Predynastic to Ptolemaic city
92. Tell el-Ratabi*	Predynastic to Late Period settlement, Wadi Tumilat
93. Abu Roash	Dynasty IV pyramid of King Djedefre and Early Dynastic and Old Kingdom Cemeteries

W. H. Listed = World Heritage Listed

* Site that fits two categories or/and is listed twice

This is only a preliminary list, and is by no means comprehensive. The complete list can only be fully compiled after much extensive research. The job of researching the state of preservation of these and other sites to be added to the list; this is the first step in cultural heritage management (CHM).

EGYPT'S TENTATIVE LIST OF WORLD HERITAGE SITES

The World Heritage Committee requested each State Party to submit an inventory of the cultural and natural properties situated within its territory, which it considered suitable for inclusion and it intends to nominate for inscription to the World Heritage List during the following five to ten years. The purpose of these inventories, also known as Tentative Lists, is to enable the Committee to evaluate within the widest possible context the "outstanding universal value" of each property nominated to the List.

In accordance with the recommendations of the 12th General Assembly of States Parties (October 1999) concerning Tentative Lists, the General Assembly invited:

- All States Parties to prepare or re-examine their tentative lists in the light of the methodology developed and regional and thematic definitions by focusing on categories of heritage which are still under-represented on the List;

- The States Parties that already have a substantial number of sites inscribed on the World Heritage List to initiate and encourage bilateral and multilateral co-operation with States Parties whose heritage is still under-represented in the List within the framework of the preparation of tentative lists, nominations and training programmes, and to give priority to the re-examination of their tentative lists within the framework of regional consultations and to the preparation of periodic reports;

- The States Parties whose heritage is still under-represented on the List to give priority to the preparation of tentative lists and nominations;

- The advisory bodies to pursue their programmes of thematic studies and the classification of the themes into sub-themes, on the basis of the tentative lists prepared by States Parties and the recommendations of the regional experts meetings;

- The Secretariat of the *Convention* to support in particular the efforts of States Parties whose heritage is still under-represented on the List in the preparation of their tentative lists and nominations.

At the 28th Session of the UNESCO World Heritage Committee, held in Suzhou, China on 28th June – 7th July 2004 Egypt submitted the following sites for the Tentative Lists of States Parties in conformity with the *Operational Guidelines*:

Number	Site	Cultural Heritage	Natural Heritage
1	Abydos, city of pilgrimage of the Pharaohs	✓	
2	Alexandria, ancient remains and the new library	✓	
3	Bird Migration Routes		✓
4	Dababiya		✓
5	Dahab, Sinai	✓	✓
6	Dahshur Archaeological area	✓	
7	Desert Wadis		✓
8	El Faiyum: Kom Aushim (Karanis), Dimai (Soknopain Neos), Qasr Qarun (Dionysias), Batn Ihrit (Theadelphia), Byahmu to Medinet el Faiyum...	✓	
9	El-Gendi Fortress	✓	
10	Gebel Qatrani Area, Lake Qarun Nature Reserve	✓	✓
11	Great Desert Landscapes		✓
12	Helwan Observatory	✓	
13	Historic Quarters and Monuments of Rosetta/Rachid	✓	
14	Minya (1- Tombs of Beni Hassan 2- Tombs of Tell El-Amarna 3- Hermopolis 4- Tuna El-Gebel sites)	✓	
15	Mountain Chains		✓
16	Necropolises of Middle Egypt, from the Middle Kingdom to the Roman Period	✓	
17	Nuweiba, Fortress of El-Ghuri, Sinai	✓	
18	North Sinai Archaeological Sites Zone	✓	
19	Oasis of Faiyum, hydraulic remains and ancient cultural landscapes	✓	✓
20	Pharaon Island		✓
21	Pharaonic Temples in Upper Egypt from the Ptolemaic and Roman periods	✓	
22	Roda Island Nilometer in Cairo	✓	
23	Ras Mohammed 'National Park'		✓
24	Rutho Monastery	✓	
25	Siwa Archaeological Area	✓	
26	Southern and Smaller Oases, the Western Desert		✓
27	Temple of Hathor built by Ramesses III (#)	✓	
28	Temple of Hathor at Serabit el-Khadim, Sinai (#)	✓	
29	The An-Nakhl Fortress, a stage on the pilgrimage route to Mecca	✓	

30	The Monasteries of the Arabian Desert and Wadi Natrun	✓	
31	Two Citadels in Sinai from the Saladin period (Al-Gundi and Phataoh's island)	✓	
32	Wadi Feiran, Southern Sinai	✓	✓

 # = Also known by another name

EVOLUTION OF NATIONAL LEGISLATION PROTECTING EGYPT'S CULTURAL HERITAGE

The evolution of governmental consciousness concerning archaeological patrimony reflects the evolution of excavation regulations. The successive texts shows a progressive strengthening of the granting of excavating licences, the ever more parsimonious distribution of discovered goods and a stiffening of criminal sentences. Khater (1960) clarifies the measures enclosed in texts prior to 1960.

The first decree of 1835 laid down a fundamental antiquities law, including banning the export of all antiquities without a permit, and stating that all antiquities should be deposited in the newly established Egyptian Museum in the Ezbekiah Gardens. This museum was to be built following European guidelines and was to be under the directorship of Yusuf Ziaeffendi, who was also put in charge of the earliest version of the Antiquities Service. Guards were to be posted at all archaeological sites and the looting of antiquities – and the use of sites as quarries by the local inhabitants – was strictly prohibited. The decree also vowed to protect the integrity of ancient remains and the sense of national pride they brought to Egypt, and was strengthened by further laws in *Antiquities Items* (1869) and *Undiscovered Antiquities* (1874) dealing with ownership of antiquities and their export, even if they had been excavated with a permit. These laws were further strengthened by the Decree of the 19th March 1869, and the Order of the 16th May 1880.

The biggest step was the Egyptian Decree of 17th November 1891, which declared that all objects found during an authorised excavation campaign belonged to the State (article 2), but that the government would donate some of the finds to the excavator in accordance with the expenses they had incurred (article 3). This was a complex procedure involving two lots of equal value that were drawn unless the parties preferred an amicable allocation (article 4). However, article 5 allowed the government the right to repurchase on the basis of an offer that the excavator was allowed to refuse, and to return an offer that – if not accepted by the administration – allowed the excavator to repurchase at the price claimed previously by the administration. The system remained null and void because if the drawing of lots seemed to give the excavator a property law on the plot fallen to him, the following clauses were making it materially precarious, through the measures that allowed the Administration to "ransom" the pieces it liked. Article 6 stated that articles 3, 4, and 5 above are not applicable to: 1. To monuments fixed to the ground, regardless of their state, which in the judgment of the Administration must be conserved in place, as well as the detached fragments which it wants to put back into place; 2. To pieces which are entirely turned over, which in the judgment of the Administration must be set right or conserved in place; and 3. To pieces too heavy which the excavator refuses to transport at his own cost. This decree also forbade searching for antiquities unless a permit had been granted by the General Director of Museums and Excavations and approved by the Permanent Committee of Antiquities. The laws of 1869, 1874, and 1897 all named the Egyptian Government as the sole owner of undiscovered antiquities, setting punishments for illegal excavations, and regulating archaeological excavations in order to prevent smuggling. The law of 12th August 1897 *Concerning the Punishment for Illegal Excavation* laid out further punishments for people excavating without a permit and stipulated that any antiquities thus excavated had to be returned to the Government. These laws passed in the nineteenth century laid the foundations for the idea of a national heritage that belonged to and helped define Egypt.

Law 14 of 1912 on *Antiquities* clarified and unified all previous laws regarding ownership, excavation and selling of antiquities and added to the practice of *partage* an advantage for each side: if a right of levy was provided for the State on the total masses of the findings, the excavator had priority on the choice. It must be noted that the result of the sharing gave no right to the excavator on the objects of his share, only through a decision of the concerned ministerial authority gave the excavator the propriety right (article 6). It reiterated that all antiquities were the property of the State and that they could only leave the country with a legal permit. It also clearly articulated rules for official antiquities shops. This law also provided a list of punishments for any infringement of the law. It also laid out the rules and regulations for excavations in Egypt.

The coming into force of Law 251 on 31st October 1951 on the *Protection of Antiquities* put an end to the system of the sharing of artefacts found on excavations, replacing it by that of the discretionary allocation (article 10 "All antiquities found during the whole length of the works will be handed to the Antiquities Service; except those that the aforementioned Service will decide, at its discretion, to give to the beneficiary, they will be part of the public ownership [...] The scientific principles will that the Service of Antiquities could reserve freely every objects that it does not need for its collections, even those of first importance. The Service, inspired by the aforementioned principles, will neither sell the objects found by the excavators nor put together reserves that could by given to other excavators. On the contrary, the Service is disposed to give to the beneficiary of the authorization every object that it would not be needed for the State collections, both in Cairo and in other cities, whichever important the aforementioned objects. It is however expressly agreed that the Service will build up the aforementioned collections completely freely, and that it will decide with sovereign power of the bestowing and the choice of the objects that will be given to the authorisation beneficiary"). This meant that no antiquity could leave Egypt unless the State owned at least one or more similar pieces. This law also greatly increased the punishments for any infringement of the law. Shops registered with the government were allowed to sell antiquities that had been approved by the Antiquities Service.

CURRENT NATIONAL LEGISLATION PROTECTING EGYPT'S CULTURAL HERITAGE

Egyptian law governing archaeology and the antiquities trade is Law no. 215 (31st October 1951) on the *Protection of Antiquities*, revised by laws no. 529 of 1953, no. 24 of 1965 and no. 117 of 1983. The law 117/1983 further restricts the conditions of the allocation of excavation licences, does not allow the release of objects and other archaeological material found by the scientific teams that have excavated them only along especially restrictive criteria (articles 9, 13, 35 and 36) and strengthens considerably the sanction taken when its clauses are broken (chapter 3, articles 40 to 47) and makes it clearer how to identify sites, monuments and artefacts (antiquities), and what is required to be done in registering them and maintaining a inventory (database) of such property (articles 2, 8, 9, 24, and 26).

Under this law:

1. Antiquities are defined as all movable and immovable objects, which are produced by the arts, sciences, literatures, customs, religions, etc. from prehistoric times to the reign of Ismail. Also included are any movable or immovable objects produced by foreign civilizations that were at one time related to Egypt (i.e. Greek, Ptolemaic, Roman, Libyan, Persian, etc.) that are found within Egypt's borders. Any movable or immovable object declared to be an antiquity including human and animal remains is the property of the State. Article 2, however allows a property of age less than 100 years to be identified as an antiquity provided it is of historical, scientific, religious, artistic or literary value.
2. All antiquities, with the exception of religious endowments (*waqfs*) shall be deemed public property, and the ownership, possession and disposition to them shall be subject to the terms and conditions set out in this Law.
3. All antiquities, either known or concealed, ultimately belong to the State, and are required to be registered on an official inventory. The Organisation (SCA) shall be responsible for inventorying, photographing, making drawings of and registering antiquities and for entering all data pertaining thereto in records established for that purpose. Antiquities shall be registered in accordance with terms and conditions to be set forth in a decision of the Board of Directors of SCA. The Organisation shall make a complete inventory of archaeological sites and lands define their boundaries and features and plot their positions on maps. The Organisation shall make a record of all the environmental and architectural data and other factors affecting every archaeological site, in accordance with their respective importance.
4. Modification, displacement or demolition of classified antiquities is prohibited. However, if repairs need to be made to a cultural property they must make an application to the SCA and the work must be carried out under the organisations supervision. The SCA can instigate under its own initiative conduct necessary conservation work on any cultural property.
5. The SCA, under the auspice of the Ministry of Culture, shall bear the sole responsibility for the preservation of all antiquities and shall carrying out necessary conservation and restoration work, or authorise expert organisations and missions for such work under the supervision of the SCA; while the Ministry of Endowment, the Egyptian *Waqf* Organisation and the Coptic *Waqf* Organisation shall

bear the cost of restoring and conserving their respective registered archaeological and historical properties.

6. The State maintains the right to expropriate any antiquity, or land containing antiquities. Discovery of antiquities should be reported immediately to the nearest administrative official; the State may acquire any such antiquity for national collections, and the displaying of such antiquity and will reasonably compensate the discoverer.
7. A permit is legally required for all field research, the conditions of which are set at the time of granting of the permit. All foreign nationals are required to submit a security declaration form to the Ministry of Culture Security Office, via the SCA.
8. Exportation of cultural property (including environmental and biological samples) is strictly prohibited without a permit, which must be obtained 30 days prior to the intended date of export. Movement of antiquities within the country must be approved 15 days prior to their transportation.
9. Dealers in antiquities must be licensed, and must maintain a daily register of transactions. Antiquities offered for sale must be authorised by the museums in advance.
10. The SCA has sole authorisation on cultural properties as well as near archaeological sites and historic buildings (i.e. the adjacent neighbourhood), forbidding other bodies from their easements, or building, or digging canals, or making roads or farms or planting, or the removal of any soil or sand without written permission from the SCA, in order to safeguard their aesthetic features or general appearance and protecting the environment of the site. However, the SCA has the right to expropriate or cease any cultural property or any of its adjacent land/buildings, with a possible compensation for the affected people/bodies.
11. Any property that has been registered as the property of the Egyptian Government, regardless of when it was discovered, should continue to be regarded as the property of the Government.

Other laws and regulations apply to related issues of the antiquities trade, excavations, zoning of cities and townships the organisation of local governments and the creation of non-governmental organizations (NGOs) and their roles and responsibilities:

1. Ministerial Decree No. 50 of 8th December 1912 *on antiquities trade and authorisation.*
2. Ministerial Decree No. 52 of 8th December 1912 *on the ruling on excavations.*
3. Law No.8 of 13th April 1918 *on the Protection of Arabic Monuments.* Any mobile or immobile object belonging to the Arab conquest period until the death of Mohamed Ali, having an artistic, historic, or archaeological value is considered to be an Arabic monument, comprising also Coptic churches and monasteries.
4. Ministerial Decree of 10th February 1921 *on the Export of antiquities.*
5. Law No. 14 of 29th January 1931 *on the Protection of cultural objects found near and around Al Moallaka.*
6. Rule No. 10613 of 6th March 1952 *on Regulations for the commerce in antiquities.*
7. Law No. 215 of 31st October 1951 *on the Protection of antiquities,* as amended by Rule No. 10614 of 6 March 1952 *on the Export of antiquities.*
8. Law No. 215 of 31st October 1951 *on the Protection of antiquities,* as amended by Rule No. 10614 of 6 March 1952 *on the Protection of antiquities.*
9. Law No. 32 of 1964 on NGOs is now being updated by a new revised law. This law does not provide for any management of sites or buildings and the realisation of regular income and economic assumption of projects due to strong restrictions and direct supervision of the Ministry of Social Affairs.
10. Law No. 106 of 1976, and its amending Law No. 101 of 1996, relating to the organization of erection or demolition of buildings, etc. This law does not touch on cultural heritage.
11. Law No. 43 of 1979 relates to the organisation of local governments, governors, city managers, mayors, and local councils, and sets their roles and responsibilities. Note: while this law provides

regulatory and supervisory responsibilities for the zoning and organization of townships and cities, as well as giving permits for the erection of buildings or sites, the law does not touch on the issue of cultural heritage.

12. Law No. 158 of 1981, modified by Law No. 187 of 1993, relates to taxation for income for individuals, corporations and commercial activities.
13. Rule No. 10827 of 17th August 1952 *on the Ruling regarding excavations.* Law No. 117 of the year 1983 *Concerning the issuance of antiquities' protection law* (11 August 1983).
14. Decree No. 238 of the 14th September 1996 by the Governor of Cairo *on the Prohibition of the demolition of villas and palaces*, including certain buildings of distinctive architectural and artistic style.
15. Article 12 of the Constitution, revised on 25th May 2005.
16. Articles 47, 48, 49 and 50 of the Constitution of 2014.

Law No. 117 of 1983, as Amended by Law No. 3 of 2010 Promulgating the Antiquities' Protection Law

In the Name of the People, the President of the Republic
After having reviewed the Constitution,
The Civil Code,
The Penal Code,
Law No. 529 for 1953 on Organization of Antiquities' Service, amended by Law No. 192 of 1955 and Law No. 27 of 1970,
Law No. 86 for 1956 concerning mines and quarries,
Law on Customs Promulgated by Law No. 66 of 1963,
Law No. 93 of 1973 concerning the General Budget of the State,
Antiquities' Protection Law No. 117 of 1983,
Law No. 10 of 1990 concerning Expropriation of property for the public benefit,
Law of the General Sales Tax Promulgated by Law No. 11 of 1990,
Environmental Law No. 4 of 1994,
Law on the Protection of Intellectual Property Rights Promulgated by Law No. 82 of 2002,
Law of the Demolition of Ramshackle Buildings and Facilities and Preservation of Architectural Heritage No. 144 of 2006,
Law of Unified Building No. 119 of 2008, and
Presidential Decree No. 82 of 1994 to establish the Supreme Council of Antiquities, and after the approval of the Council of Ministers, and based on the view of the Council of State, decreed that the People's Assembly approved the new law.

There are seven main amendments to Law 117. These are as follows:

1. The first was properly and legally to identify three main terms — a) the SCA's permanent committee, b) the inviolable area around every monument, and c) the land found next door to the archaeological site — in an attempt to provide all necessary security measures and a healthy environmental atmosphere.

2. Article 8 states that the trade, sale or commerce in antiquities including all antiquities held as private property shall be prohibited in accordance with the provisions of this law or legal existing possession at the time of implementation of said law or such which originates in accordance with its provisions. The owner or the possessor of any antiquity may not dispose of, allow deterioration of or leave such except after getting a written consent from the Council within 60 (sixty) days at least in accordance with the procedures, terms and conditions, of which a resolution from the Minister is issued, otherwise such act shall be illegal.

The Council in all cases has the priority of having the antiquity from its owner or possessor in return for a fair compensation. Any one who owns any archaeological object in accordance with the provisions of this Law must notify the Council of such object within six months starting from the beginning of March 2010 provided that such persons are required to preserve such objects until the Council registers it.

Moreover, the Council may restitute, from its owners or possessors, antiquities taken of architectural elements whenever the Board of Directors finds a national interest and upon recommendation from the competent Permanent Committee that possessors have in return for a valuable consideration. A new department called the Archaeological Collection Administration (ACA) has been established to address this and to receive registration requests from citizens, in addition to a media campaign to make citizens aware of their responsibility to record and examine what they have.

3. Article 11 states that the SCA is entitled to accept cession of corporations or individuals for their ownership of historic real-estate through donation or sale for a symbolic price or through laying such under the Council's disposal for no less than 50 (fifty) years, whenever the State finds such a national interest.

4. Articles 23, 24 and 25 relate to the treasure trove activities, where individuals find artefacts. Any individual who finds an unregistered real-estate antiquity must notify the Supreme Council of Antiquities of such. This antiquity is considered the ownership of the State and the Council must undertake the necessary procedures to take care of such antiquity. Within a period of 3 (three) months, the Council is entitled either to take stated immovable present in the property of individuals or undertake procedures of expropriation of' the land wherein the same was found or to leave said antiquity at its place together with registering it in accordance with provisions of present law. In estimating the value of the expropriated land, the value of antiquities found at said land is not observed. The Council may grant whoever guided to the antiquity a recompense that is determined by the Competent Permanent Committee.

Whoever accidentally finds a movable antiquity or part or parts of an immovable monument, must give notice of such to the nearest administrative power within 48 (forty-eight) hours as of the time of finding the same. Moreover, he must take good care of such antiquity till handing it over to the competent authority otherwise he is considered as a possessor of antiquity without license, and the authority referred to must immediately notify the Council of such. The antiquity becomes the property of the State and the Council is thereby entitled to grant whoever found the antiquity and notified of such a recompense which is determined by the Competent Permanent Committee.

A committee formed by a decree from the Minister, wherein the Board of Directors is represented, undertakes estimating the compensation stipulated in Articles 4, 5 bis. 8, 13, \5. 16 and 18 of the present law. State Treasury shall pay referred to compensations, and those concerned may raise a complaint to the competent Minister in cultural affairs from the committee's estimation within a period of 60 (sixty) days as of date of notifying them of the compensation estimated by the committee by a registered letter with a receipt otherwise the estimation is considered final. In all cases the action for compensation falls if such is not raised within a three years period as of date of its becoming a final estimation.

5. Article 7 of the old law stipulating that the police were the only department authorised to remove any encroachments on archaeological sites or monuments. This has now been changed and such responsibility for removal of any encroachments is the secretary-general of the SCA, or someone that they entrust. The police agencies are only a safeguarding or enforcement agency executing the secretary-general's decision.

6. Article 30 has been added to the law stipulating that the SCA is the only authority competent to carry out restoration and preservation work for all Egyptian monuments, archaeological sites and historical edifices. The minister of culture will have the authority to assign any scientific authority or mission to execute any such work, but under complete supervision of the SCA's secretary-general.

7. Articles 26 and 27 cover the creation of sites and monuments records: The Council undertakes enumerating, photographing, drawing, and registering immovable and movable antiquities together with gathering information pertaining to said antiquities in registers prepared for such uses. Registration is effected in accordance with terms and conditions of which a decree by the Board of Directors is issued. The registered antiquities are those registered at the date of effecting present law at the registers set for it.

The Council aims at generalising archaeological survey for archaeological sites and lands and defining places and characteristics of the said, and recording them on maps together with sending photocopies of such to both the competent local department and the General Authority for Urban

Planning for the observance of such at the preparation of the general planning. The Council shall prepare a register for environmental and urban data and factors affecting every archaeological site according to its importance.

The Council undertakes preparing the registered archaeological places and sites and historical buildings for visit or study in a way that is not incompatible with their security and preservation. The Council also aims at revealing the aesthetic and historic characteristics and distinguishing features of the same. The Council thereto employs the capabilities of archaeological sites and museums in developing archaeological awareness by all means.

This law outlines more extensive efforts to prevent and criminalise trading in antiquities. The penalties for breaking the various aspects of the law have been doubled or tripled. A smuggler who was sentenced to 15 years and fined LE50,000 under Law 117/1983 will now be sentenced to life imprisonment and fined from LE100,000 to LE500,000. Anyone who steals, hides, or collects authentic artefacts, or owns them without permission, will be imprisoned for 25 years and fined from LE50,000 to LE250,000 instead of three years hard labour and a LE100 fine. According to the new law, stealing or helping in robbing a part of a genuine piece or intent deliberately to disfigure it will land a sentence of 15 years and a fine of from LE50,000 to LE100,000.

The new law does not omit penalties for those who write their names or fix advertising billboards on monument walls. Such actions would be considered a violation of Egyptian heritage, and the penalty ranges from six to 12 months imprisonment or a fine of LE150,000. The law also abolishes the agreement that foreign missions could keep 10% of their discoveries.

The new law allows clemency for anyone who confesses to or divulges information about an antiquities crime on condition that his or her confession leads to the arrest of partners in the theft or smuggling. The SCA will assign experts to check the authenticity of any confiscated objects in an attempt to guarantee an honest and accurate decision.

REFERENCES

Khater, A. 1960. *Le Régime Juridique des Fouilles et des Antiquités en Egypte.* Le Caire: IFAO.

Reid, D. M. 2003. *Whose Pharaohs? Archaeology, Museums, and Egyptian National Identity from Napoleon to World War I.* Berkeley - Los Angeles - London: University of California Press.

Silverman, H. (ed.) *Contested Cultural Heritage: Religion, Nationalism, Erasure and Exclusion in a Global World.* New York: Springer.

UNESCO - http://www.unesco.org/culture/natlaws/media/pdf/egypt/egypt_law3_2010_entof.pdf

A Short History of the Egyptian Antiquities Service

Until the mid-19th century, there were no regulations of the antiquities trade in Egypt. Thousands of artefacts, from jewellery and statuettes to reliefs and even entire monuments, were taken from their ancient contexts and shipped to private and museum collections around the world. The Western demand for Pharaonic artefacts was intensified by the Napoleonic Expedition (1798-1801) and the subsequent publication of the multi-volume *Description de l'Egypte*, which stimulated global interest in Egypt and its ancient monuments.

The first step toward the control of Egyptian antiquities was taken on 15th August 1835, when the ruler of Egypt, Mohamed Ali, issued a decree banning the unauthorised removal of antiquities from the country. This decree also designated a building in the Ezbekiah Gardens, Cairo, to serve as a storehouse for artefacts. However, these antiquities were often given by Egyptian rulers to foreign dignitaries as gifts, and by the mid-1800s, the collection was so small that it could be housed in a single room at the Citadel. In 1855 what remained of the collection was presented by Abbas Pasha as a gift to the Austrian Archduke Maximilian.

In 1858 Said Pasha, then Viceroy of Egypt, approved the creation of the Antiquities Service (officially the Service des Antiquités d'Egypte) to stem the continuing illicit trade in Egyptian artefacts, and appointed French scholar Auguste Mariette as its director. The Antiquities Service was originally attached to the Ministry of Public Works. Later on, it belonged to the ministries of: Information, National Guidance, Education. This new governmental department was responsible for carrying out its own excavations, and also for approving and supervising foreign archaeological missions. Mariette created the first national museum in the Near East, which opened in 1863 in an old City Transit Authority building in the Boulaq section of Cairo. This museum was then transferred to its current location in Tahrir Square in 1902 via a short stay in Giza.

French scholars headed the Antiquities Service for almost a century. In the early 1950s, when British colonial troops finally left Egypt, the Antiquities Service truly became an Egyptian-run organisation. The first Egyptian director, Mostafa Amer, was appointed in 1953 and held the post for three years. For many years, the Antiquities Service was under the direction of the Ministry of Education; in 1960, it was transferred to the Ministry of Culture. In 1971, during the tenure of Gamal Mokhtar, Le service des antiquités was transformed into the Egyptian Antiquities Organization (EAO) by presidential decree 2828/1971, having its own president and belonging to the Ministry of Culture.

In 1994, the name of the department was changed to the Supreme Council of Antiquities (SCA) by Presidential Decree Number 82. The first Secretary General of the SCA was Mohammed Abdel Halim Nur el-Din. In January 2011 the antiquities service became an independent ministry and the name was changed to Ministry of State for Antiquities (MSA). At the beginning of June 2014 the MSA shortened their name to the Ministry of Antiquities (MA), although by the beginning of July 2014 the name was changed to the Ministry of Antiquities and Heritage (MAH), but the heritage was then later dropped. There is now a minister for antiquities and a secretary general of the SCA. The constitution of 2012 created a Supreme Council for Heritage Conservation, which also seems to be under the control of the MA. The MA employs over 44,000 people, about two thirds of whom are security guards. The MA are responsible for the conservation, protection and regulation of all antiquities and archaeological excavations in Egypt. The MA are also responsible for defining the boundaries around archaeological sites and is the only agency permitted to restore or preserve Egyptian monuments. Foreign archaeologists working in Egypt are required to report all discoveries and finds to the MA before publication. The MA also oversees the recovery of antiquities either stolen or illegally exported from Egypt.

Antiquities Service

French Directors

- Auguste Mariette (1858-1881)
- Gaston Maspero (1881-1886)
- Eugène Grébaut (1886-1892)
- Jacques de Morgan (1892-1897)

- Victor Loret (1897-1899)
- Gaston Maspero (1899-1914)
- Pierre Lacau (1914-1936)
- Étienne Drioton (1936-1952)

Egyptian Directors

- Mostafa Amer (1953-1956)
- Abbas Bayoumi (1956-1957)
- Moharram Kamal (1957-1959)
- Abd el-Fattah Hilmy (1959)
- Mohammed Anwar Shoukry (1960-1964)
- Mohammed Mahdi (1964-1966)
- Gamal Mokhtar (1967-1971)

Egyptian Antiquities Organization Directors

- Gamal Mokhtar (1971-1977)
- Mohammed Abd el-Qader Mohammed (1977-1978)
- Shehata Adam (1978-1981)
- Fuad el-Oraby (1981)
- Ahmed Khadry (1982-1988)
- Mohammed Abdel Halim Nur el-Din (1988)
- Sayed Tawfik (1989-1990)
- Mohammed Ibrahim Bakr (1990-1993)

Secretary Generals of the Supreme Council of Antiquities

- Mohammed Abdel Halim Nur el-Din (1993-1996)
- Ali Hassan (1996-1997)
- Gaballa Ali Gaballa (1997-2002)
- Zahi Hawass (2002- July 2011)
- Mohamed Abdel Maksoud (July 2011)
- Mohamed Abdel Fattah (August-September 2011)
- Mustafa Amin (29th September 2011-June 2012)
- Mohsen Sayed Ali (July 2012-May 2013)
- Mustafa Amin (June 2013-present)

Ministers for Antiquities in the Ministry (of State) for Antiquities

- Abdel Fattah al-Banna (Previously nominated)
- Zahi Hawass (Feb-July 2011)
- Mohamed Ibrahim (7th December 2011-4th May 2013)
- Ahmed Eissa (5th May 2013-14th July 2013)
- Mohamed Ibrahim (15th July 2013-16th June 2014)
- Mamdouh el-Damaty (17th June 2014 - present)

References

Reid, D. M. 2002. *Whose Pharaohs? Archaeology, Museums, and Egyptian National Identity from Napoleon to World War I.* Cairo: AUC Press.

SCA Web: http://www.sca.gov.eg/index.html

MINISTRY OF ANTIQUITIES

MA's Regulations for Foreign Archaeological Missions

The Ministry of Antiquities (MA) has a department titled The Department of Foreign Archaeological Missions. This department has standardize the rules and regulations concerning the application and execution of all archaeological work in Egypt. The director or assistant director of a foreign mission will deal solely with this department.

The Application Process:

1. Three months prior to excavation work, the mission's director is required to submit a list of the expedition team, specifying the nationalities and positions of each member. This application must be written in English, clearly stating the time frame of the excavation season. A survey map showing the location of the requested site should be attached to the application form.

2. With the application, the CV's of every team member must be included. The MA expects that all team members will be affiliated with a recognized institution. According to the antiquities protection laws, permission will not be given to anyone who is not a professional in the field.

3. The expedition team will not be permitted to start their work until they have received a security clearance, signed a contract with the MA, and their application has been accepted by the Permanent Committee of Antiquities.

4. An assistant director should be specified for each mission, to act in the absence of the mission director.

5. The MA has the right to request the details of the source of any expedition's funding at any time.

Additional Requirements for Concession Applications Concerning the West and East Desert or Coastal areas:

1. For missions wanting to pursue work at their current site, four survey maps signed by the director of the mission need to be submitted to the MA three months prior to the following excavation season. The map should use the 1 to 50,000 scale or 1 to 25, 000 scale.

2. According to the presidential decree no. 413 of 1998, the following areas are restricted, even for research purposes:

a. The Northern border, from Mersa Wadi Lahmi on the Red Sea Coast to Kom Ombo.

b. The Southern border, Latitude 22 from the Red Sea Coast to Ashkeet.

c. The Western border, from the eastern shore of Lake Nasser, including Kom Ombo Aswan and el-Mafarq, to Ashkeet on latitude 22

d. The Eastern border, the Egyptian Red Sea coast.

Security Regulation:

1. Three months prior to excavation work, personal application for each mission member, including the applicant's full name, date of birth, nationality, two passport photocopies, position, institution of affiliation, religion and six passport photos must be submitted to the MA. For missions working in military areas, the security clearance form must be accompanied by nine personal photographs and four passport photocopies. An additional security from should be filled out and sent it back with the application and a single passport copy via E-mail. The Department of Foreign Archaeological Missions requires personal applications in order to issue security clearance for each team member.

2. A fee of 101 LE for each personal application should be paid to the Department of Security in order to process the security clearance.

3. Sending samples and specimens abroad for analyses is prohibited; samples must be examined in the Research and Maintenance Laboratory of the MA or in approved alternative Egyptian labs. Only if the required facilities are not available in Egypt may a request be submitted to the Permanent Committee to send samples abroad, and these will be accompanied by a member of the MA until they reach their destination laboratory.

4. Adding additional members to the mission's team after application acceptance is prohibited.

5. For missions wanting to work at a location close to their current site in the West or East Deserts or Coastal regions, eleven survey maps signed by the director of the mission need to be submitted to the MA three months prior to the excavation. For missions working in or close to military zones seven survey maps should be sent. The maps should use the 1 to 50,000 scale or the 1 to 25,000 scale.

Rules for the Missions Working on Sites:

1. No new concessions will be given to a current team member wanting to create a new excavation area within the granted site of the mission.

2. The working mission will not be allowed to open new sites anywhere until they publish their current site completely.

3. The mission will be granted only one season per year. The season's start and finish dates must be specified in the application. If the mission needs another season within the year, they should request this at the beginning.

4. The MA prohibits missions to work at more than one site at the same time.

5. In order to renew the contract with the MA the mission is required to reapply and meet the above mentioned conditions.

6 Working on Thursdays can be granted with permission. However, no restoration or excavation is allowed at the site on Fridays.

7 No concessions will be given to graduate students. Graduate students can obtain permission for study or research on archaeological sites through his or her supervisor's proposal.

8. No concession will be granted to any expedition director who does not have good experience in the field.

Responsibilities after Application Approval:

1. After the application has been approved by the Permanent Committee, and security clearance has been

issued, The Department of Foreign Archaeological Missions will then notify, in writing, the Sector of the Egyptian Antiquities of the MA and the mission director.

2. The Department of Excavations of the MA will assign inspectors, who have been trained in recognised fieldschools, to accompany the mission.

3. Before excavation work the head of the mission is required to submit two reports confirming the borders of the excavation area both signed by the director of the mission and the inspector.

4. The inspector must send a monthly report on the work progress.

5. The director of the mission must notify the Minister for Antiquities or the Secretary General of the SCA immediately with any new discoveries. The MA will suspend the mission's concession if formal notification is neglected.

6. The mission is responsible for providing adequate containers for storing and protecting the artefacts.

7. Transportation of the artefacts from the site to magazines or museums will be at the mission's expense.

8. During the excavation season, the security guards working on site will be paid by the mission. However, they should be approved by the MA site director.

9. Employment of recognised expert(s) in conservation and preservation is mandatory.

10. Restoration or site management programs for any archaeological site should be stated in a detailed report and submitted to the Permanent Committee. The conservator may be requested to discuss the methods of restoration or conservation.

11. The inspectorate will oversee all conservation work.

12. A member from the Centre of Research and Maintenance of the MA needs to accompany missions that are working in the field of anthropology and geophysics. The final report of such work should be submitted to the MA.

13. Every precaution should be taken to protect the monuments during epigraphical work. A copy of all epigraphical work should be submitted to the MA.

14. Five copies of the mission's preliminary report, written in English, must be submitted to the MA immediately after the end of the season, prior to the mission's departure.

15. Within three months of the season's completion five copies of a detailed report, written in either: French, German, or English and translated into Arabic, including copies of photographs, charts and plans must be sent to The Department of Foreign Archaeological Missions. A CD and pdf of the report must also be submitted at this time.

16. The MA requests that each mission donates five copies of recently published books, written by the mission regarding the site, to The Department of Foreign Archaeological Missions. They will be distributed to the libraries and the museums of the MA.

17. Every expedition is responsible for the conservation of artefacts and the restoration of tombs and temples discovered by the expedition. Any expedition that fails to conserve the findings of the previous season will not be allowed to return to their concession until the conservation is complete.

Relationship between the MA Inspector and the Mission:

1. The MA will rotate the accompanying Inspectors every season; no mission has the right to request an Inspector for consecutive seasons.

2. The mission is required to pay the MA either:
a. 1500 LE per month for the overtime and transportation of inspectors who do not live with the expedition.

b. 1000 LE per month for Inspectors who do live with the expedition.

3. The Inspectors are prohibited from accepting any cash rewards or getting involved in any money transactions separate from those stated above.

4 Any problems concerning the behaviour of the accompanying Inspector should be reported to the Minister for Antiquities.

New Policies:

1. For the upcoming ten years, new concessions will not be granted from Giza to Abu-Simbel. Concessions will only be granted in this area for restoration, preservation, archaeological survey, documentation and epigraphical work.

2. New applications for excavation concessions will be granted only for the Western Desert, Eastern Desert and the Delta for the next ten years.

3. The MA requires that the mission publishes the site within five years after work has been completed. The Director and Institution backing any mission that does not comply will be denied any future concessions.

4. It is absolutely prohibited for any member of a mission to be involved with dealers of stolen artefacts. Members of foreign missions are expected to yield any, information they have regarding stolen artefacts to the Department of Stolen Artefacts. People who are found by court evidence to be involved with stolen artefacts will be removed from the excavation. If the director is involved, the mission will be terminated.

5. Egypt will not cooperate with any museum or institution that buys stolen artefacts from Egypt.

.

Communications:

Cheques must be written and hand delivered to the Director for the Department of Foreign Archaeological Missions when the contract is signed. Communications with the Department of Foreign Archaeological Missions can be administered via email to: sca_missions2@hotmail.com

SCA Web: http://www.sca.gov.eg/index.html

The Faiyum Declaration

Participants in The International Colloquium "Natural and Cultural heritage landscapes in the Faiyum: Safeguarding and Management of Archaeological Sites and Natural Environments" held in the Faiyum October 31 to November 2, 2010 recognise the potential for mobilizing cultural and natural heritage of the Faiyum for social and economic development. On one hand, these invaluable resources are facing serious threats, and, are on the other hand, under-utilised.
The Participants call upon local, governmental and international authorities and institutions to undertake urgent measures to safeguard and improve the management of the threatened Faiyum heritage, and to participate in efforts to valorise and mobilise heritage resources for development. The Participants recommend the inclusion of the management of cultural and natural heritage in all sectors of governmental authorities.
The Participants recommend a set of principles for safeguarding and managing the archaeological and natural resources of the Faiyum, identify urgent actions needed, and recommend an organizational framework to ensure the completion of the proposed activities.

Principles

- Heritage resources in the Faiyum include geological, environmental, archaeological, historical, rural, and traditional resources. **These resources combined create an outstanding "natural and cultural landscape"** as recognized by UNESCO.
- A regional development plan integrating different types of natural and cultural heritage resources is the most appropriate long-term, strategy to safeguard and manage the Faiyum heritage resources in a sustainable manner.
- Safeguarding and managing natural and cultural heritage include **documentation, risk assessment, prioritising, valuing, zoning, monitoring, protecting, preserving, conserving, raising awareness, enhancement, and capacity building.**
- The Objectives of heritage management include: 1) valorisation of cultural diversity, historical continuities, multiculturalism, and intercultural dialogues; 2) transmission of social values from the past to current and future generations; 3) mobilization of heritage resources for social and economic development to improve living conditions and alleviation of hardships; 4) utilization of heritage resources to cope with current international and global issues, such as climate change, water scarcity, inequities, unsafe migration, and intolerance.

Activities

1. Preparation of an **integrated regional development plan** for managing the whole spectrum of natural and cultural resources in collaboration with local communities of the Faiyum including rural heritage, intangible heritage and vernacular architectural heritage. The plan is to be based on an itinerary that includes key heritage sites, geoparks, museums, visitor centres, eco-stations, facilities, certified outlets for services and goods (including B&B, eco-lodges), and scenic routes provided with signs and information posts.

2. **Protection** of threatened sites beginning with enforcement of the protective measures for designated protected areas, and innovative strategies including civic heritage guards, for example, from university youths, buffer zones, site markers, check-points, and electronic sensors.
3. Promotion of **sustainable agro-, eco- and cultural tourism** based on best practices for the protection of heritage resources, the participation of local communities, and optimisation of social benefits.
4. Provision of necessary **training** to undertake the proposed activities.
5. **Fund raising**, and arrangement with appropriate financial institutions to provide **micro-credit** to promote local crafts, services and other activities, as well as provision of technical assistance, and marketing strategies.
6. Preparation of pamphlets, brochures, and a website and **dissemination** to the public and visitors of relevant information as well as protective regulations, and strengthening contact with the media.

7. Completion of **a comprehensive, authoritative GIS-based database** to serve in decision making and as an encyclopaedic resource on the heritage of the Faiyum; its geology, plants, animals, history, archaeology, manuscripts, crafts, folk traditions, architecture, arts, fishing and agriculture.

8. Recognising that Gebel Qatrani is already on the tentative World Heritage List, the participants recommend preparation of the file for **nomination of the Faiyum cultural and natural landscape on the World Heritage List** and to consider other protection lists such for key areas such as the Biosphere reserves and geoparks.

Organisation

The participants recommend the establishment of a "Faiyum Heritage Consortium (FHC)" of key institutions, authorities and stake-holders with links to international organizations as the most practical organizational framework to achieve the objectives of sound safeguarding and managing of the natural and cultural resources of the Faiyum. Economic Development activities are to be undertaken by entities that will act according to the rules and regulations of the Consortium and in the framework of the principles of this Declaration under the guidance of the Faiyum Heritage Consortium. The Consortium will coordinate the efforts of special task forces entrusted with proposed activities. A steering committee is to be selected to set up the Consortium.

THE CODE OF ETHICS OF THE EGYPTIAN CULTURAL HERITAGE ORGANISATION

The Egyptian Cultural Heritage Organisation (ECHO) is dedicated to the greater understanding, protection and preservation of Egypt's cultural heritage and the dissemination of archaeological knowledge to the academic and wider public audience. ECHO recognises that archaeologists, specialist consultants and cultural heritage managers have a responsibility to practice a moral and professional code of ethics to the cultural material of the past, the public and their colleagues.

I) The Responsibility to the Cultural Heritage:

1. ECHO condemns the looting and destruction of archaeological property and are supporters of: the 1954 UNESCO *Convention for the Protection of Cultural Property in the Event of Armed Conflict*; the 1956 UNESCO *Recommendation on International Principles Applicable to Archaeological Excavations,* the 1964 ICOMOS *International Charter for the Conservation and Restoration of Monuments and Sites*; the 1970 UNESCO *Convention on the Means of Prohibiting and Preventing the Illicit Import, Export and Transfer of Ownership of Cultural Property*; the 1972 UNESCO *Convention Concerning Protection of the World Cultural and Natural Heritage,* the 1990 ICOMOS International Committee on Archaeological Heritage Management (ICAHM) *Charter for the Protection and Management of the Archaeological Heritage*; the 1995 UNIDROIT *Convention on Stolen or Illegally Exported Cultural Objects*; the 2001 UNESCO *Convention on the Protection of the Underwater Cultural Heritage*; the 2001 UNESCO *Universal Declaration on Cultural Diversity*; and the 2003 UNESCO *Convention for the Safeguarding of the Intangible Cultural Heritage.* All members must acquaint themselves with these legislative documents, and comply with their legal requirements. All members should also make themselves familiar with Egyptian law governing archaeology and the antiquities trade, and abide by these laws, especially Law no. 215 (31st October 1951) on the *Protection of Antiquities*, revised by laws no. 529 of 1953, no. 24 of 1965 and no. 117 of 1983.

2. All archaeologists, scientists, art historians or other archaeological specialists, must refrain from giving credence to stolen or looted artefacts, by refusing to study, evaluate or examine them in any manner whatsoever, unless it is to verify that the artefacts in question are indeed stolen or looted, and as such must be reported to the appropriate authorities. These experts must also not consciously contribute any scholarly knowledge to an exhibition that knowingly allows artefacts illegally acquired after 30th December 1970 to be shown in their displays. An artefact may be considered illicit if:

   a) The person in possession of it cannot produce good title to it under the applicable law.
   b) An object has been acquired in - or exported from - its country of origin in violation of that country's laws.
   c) The object was imported or acquired illegally from an official excavation or monument, or originated from an unofficial, illegal or clandestine dig.

3. Archaeologists must undertake to report any dishonest or unethical behaviour, especially that which threatens any cultural materiality, such as breaches of the UNESCO, ICOMOS or UNIDROIT agreements, to the proper legal authorities.

4. Members must not engage in any illegal or unethical conduct involving archaeological material or knowingly permit the use of their name in support of any illegal or unethical activity involving archaeological matters, including, theft, fraud, deceit or misrepresentation.

5. Archaeologists and archaeological specialists should refrain from authentication and testing for any objects not curated in a public institution or where they are not open to scientific study,

interpretation or display, such as those held by private individuals, salesrooms or commercial galleries.

6. The principal investigator or director must ensure that all governmental permits and necessary permissions from landowners and other persons are obtained and that the site and personnel conform to all legal requirements.

7. The principal investigator or director should include adequate plans for conservation, preservation, storage receptacles and materials and archives in their project design, and should secure funds for such purposes from the outset.

8. The principal investigator or director must ensure that experimental design, recording, and sampling procedures are adequate for the project being undertaken.

9. The principal investigator or director of a project must before any archaeological work is undertaken, carefully consider the purpose and consequences of the intended research. The methods and approaches chosen must be the most suitable for not only extracting the maximum amount of information from the archaeological material, but for creating the least amount of damage to the local or regional environment. Less intrusive methods of archaeological investigation - such as survey - should always be sought first before resorting to excavation. The objectives of the research should be adequate justification for the destruction of archaeological evidence which it will entail.

10. The recording and collecting of archaeological material must retain their provenience and identification throughout the whole archaeological process of retrieval, conservation and analysis.

11. The archaeologist shall ensure that resultant records of an investigation, along with the methods and results of any analysis, must be fully described, recorded and archived in an intelligible, readily usable and durable manner, it must be maintained in good condition and the full archive - including any artefacts and specimens - eventually deposited where it can receive adequate curatorial care and storage conditions and be readily available for study and examination.

12. The recovery and study of archaeological material must be conducted only by - or under the guidance - of fully qualified professional personnel.

13. The principal investigator or director must develop a project digest that specifies the project objectives and takes into account all previous work and relevant research.

14. The principal investigator or director must ensure the availability of adequate and qualified personnel and facilities to carry the project through to completion. The archaeologist shall not undertake any work for which he or she is not adequately qualified and shall try to ensure to the best of their ability that all members of the team undertaking archaeological work are adequately qualified. The principal investigator or director should arrange for specialists to be contacted in the event of unforeseen archaeological issues, which they can recommend to their employers, funders or clients.

15. Archaeologists must keep themselves informed about developments in their field of specialisation.

12. When cultural heritage is under a direct threat, such as human induced - war zone or building of a dam or a natural threat such as earthquake or flooding, it is the archaeologist's duty to try and protect/rescue as much of the threatened heritage as possible. Participation in a rescue project in a country where the current regime has low human rights, is corrupt, brutal, illegitimate or has UN sanctions against it, does not imply that the archaeologists working in that country support the regime as long as they do not:

    a) Offer support for the regime, either privately or publicly.

b) Produce literature or other media proclaiming the rights of the regime.
c) Oppress or exploit any of the people in the country or are partisan in anyway.
d) Directly receive money from - or give money to - the regime for the work they are doing in the country. UNESCO money being channelled through the regime is, however, permissible.
e) Participate in any political activities that support the regime.

Therefore, as long as the rescuing (surveying, excavating, conserving) of the cultural heritage and objective report writing of the analysis of the material is the goal of the project it is ethically and morally acceptable to salvage the cultural heritage within that country. The archaeological record is finite, whereas modern political regimes are transient; therefore it is the archaeologist's duty to record as an objective view of history as possible.

13. If the country or regime where a human or naturally induced threat is occurring or about to occur cannot safely and effectively look after the artefacts, monuments and other objects of cultural heritage that are salvaged from an archaeological rescue project and as a consequence offers to share these objects with the agencies participating in the project, then these objects must be:

a) Deposited with a national or local museum or within a teaching collection of a university on a fixed term renewable, and revisable loan. It must be understood and stated that the objects/material (archives) are recognised as belonging to the country of origin and that the intention is to eventually repatriate the objects to that country.

Objects may not be:

b) Sold to any person.
c) Deposited in private collections not accessible by the public and scholarly research.
d) Kept by the archaeologist or funding agency.

II) The Responsibilities to the Public

1. When the principal investigator or director is planning a project, due consideration must be given to the overall impact that the project may have on the local population.

2. All archaeological personnel must respect the cultural norms and dignity of the local population. Archaeologists should take into account legitimate concerns of groups whose material past may be the subject of archaeological investigation.

3. The principal investigator or director should hold consultations with the appropriate representatives of the local community during the planning stage of the project, and invite local participation in the project, giving the local population regular updates of the progress being made.

4. The project personnel should actively engage in outreach programmes through lecturing, popular writing, school education programmes, site tours, and other educational initiatives.

5. Archaeologists must present archaeology and its results in a responsible manner, to avoid and discourage exaggerated, misleading or unwarranted statements about archaeological practice.

6. The principal investigator or director must make adequate provision for continued site management at the planning stage of the project if the site is to be opened to the public.

7. An archaeologist must not offer advice, make a public statement, or give legal testimony about archaeological matters without being as fully informed about such matters as is reasonably possible.

III) The Responsibilities to Colleagues

1. ECHO is an equal opportunities organisation. Members of ECHO must not practice discrimination or harassment based on age, sex, religion, colour, national origin, disability or sexual preference.

2. The principal investigator or director of a project must provide acceptable standards of health, hygiene and safety on site and give due regard to the requirements of employment legislation. Archaeologists must ensure that adequate insurance cover is maintained for all personnel and property that may be affected by archaeological activities.

3. All archaeologists must adhere to the highest standards of ethical and responsible behaviour in the conduct of archaeological affairs, and shall conduct him/herself in a manner that will not bring archaeology or their institution into disrepute.

4. Those in authority on a project must behave with consideration and courtesy to those under their authority, while all team members should reciprocate and strive to promote the success of the project.

5. Archaeologists should strive to make public the record and results of their research in a timely manner providing evidence to others. Yearly interim reports should be submitted to reputable journals to disseminate the latest findings, and a final report must be published.

6. The principal investigator or director is responsible for the analysis and publication of data derived from his or her investigations. If publication is not completed within 5 years of completion of a project then, a waiver of the rights of primacy shall be judged and evidence should be made available to researchers upon request for analysis and publication. Extenuating circumstances shall be considered by interested parties.

7. Archaeologists should communicate and cooperate with colleagues with similar interests, giving due respect to colleagues' interests in - and rights to - information about sites, areas, collections or data where there is a shared field of concern, be it active or potential.

8. Archaeologists must give due regard and appropriate support to the training and development of all personnel to enable them to execute their duties.

9. All personnel must give the appropriate credit for work done by other archaeologists and specialist consultants.

10. All personnel must give reasonable consideration to cumulative service and proven experience of employees, colleagues or helpers when deciding rates of pay and other employment benefits.

11. Requests from colleagues or students for information on the results of research or projects should be honoured by the archaeologist if it is consistent with his or her prior rights to publication and other archaeological responsibilities.

12. Archaeologists must not commit plagiarism in electronic, written (hard copy) or oral communication.

13. An archaeologist shall not reveal confidential information unless required by law, nor use any confidential or privileged information to his or her own advantage or that of a third party.